Men'sHealth GUIDE TO THE
BEST
SEX
IN THE
WORLD

Men'sHealth® GUIDE TO THE BEST SEX IN THE WORLD

WOMEN FROM AROUND THE GLOBE SHARE THEIR HOTTEST SEX SECRETS

Exclusive!
GLOBAL SEX SURVEY
from 42 COUNTRIES

RODALE

Sex and Values at Rodale

We believe that an active and healthy sex life, based on mutual consent and respect between partners, is an important component of physical and mental well-being. We also respect that sex is a private matter and that each person has a different opinion of what sexual practices or levels of discourse are appropriate. Rodale is committed to offering responsible, practical advice about sexual matters, supported by accredited professionals and legitimate scientific research. Our goal—for sex and all other topics—is to publish information that empowers people's lives.

Some portions of this book have appeared previously in *Men's Health* magazine.

© 2008 by Rodale Inc.

Printed in the United States of America
Rodale Inc. makes every effort to use acid-free ∞, recycled paper ♻.

Book design by Tara Long

Library of Congress Cataloging-in-Publication Data

The Men's health guide to the best sex in the world : men, women, and sexperts from around the globe share their hottest sex secrets / by the editors of Men's health magazine.
    p.   cm.
Includes index.
ISBN-13 978–1–59486–726–2 hardcover
ISBN-10 1–59486–726–7 hardcover
    1. Sex instruction for men. 2. Men—Sexual behavior. I. Men's health (Magazine)
HQ36.M46   2008
613.9'52—dc22   2007035971

2 4 6 8 10 9 7 5 3 1 hardcover

RODALE
LIVE YOUR WHOLE LIFE™

We inspire and enable people to improve their lives and the world around them

For more of our products visit **rodalestore.com** or call 800-848-4735

CONTENTS

PART II: YOUR ITINERARY FOR TOURING A BROAD

PART III: THE WORLD'S MOST ADVANCED TECHNIQUES

CHAPTER 15

Have Sex Anywhere in the World

Find Your Bliss in Exotic Locales

CHAPTER 16

Have the Wildest Sex in the World

Make Your Fantasies Come True

INTRODUCTION

From scoring against Brazil in the World Cup to beating the Austrians at the Winter Olympics slalom, there will always be a spirit of competition that compels men to keep up with their counterparts in the rest of the world.

And in no arena is this sense of one-upmanship more exaggerated than when we're talking about sex. Our competitive natures can't stand the idea that some guy across the globe is getting more sex—or better sex!—than we are. Not that throwing down the gauntlet is such a bad thing; after all, the best competitions spur all contestants to fulfill their greatest potential and attain greatness. So it's in that spirit of healthy competition that we offer *Men's Health Guide to the Best Sex in the World*, the first instructional sex book to carry the *Men's Health* brand.

Now, an instructional sex book is nothing new—the oldest ones in the world can be traced to China 5,000 years ago. But this one is different: It's based on an exclusive international *Men's Health* Global Sex Survey that interviewed 40,000 men in 42 countries to figure out who's having the most sex, the hottest sex, the longest sex, and the wildest sex. In all, it was one of the largest sex surveys of men ever undertaken. And just to make sure those polled were being honest, we supplemented their responses with interviews of women and sex experts in more than a dozen countries.

And so the collective sexual wisdom of the world, the "best practices" of men from all over the globe, have been collected here for your perusal. Each chapter addresses one concern that men have about relationships and sex, revealing the world leaders in that area as determined by the survey. Citing input from sex therapists, sociologists, and international research, each chapter starts by exploring why a particular culture has reared such skilled lovers and leads into direct, practical, and surprising tips from international experts, explaining how *you* can have the world's best sex, no matter what country you are in.

Men's Health is the largest men's lifestyle magazine in the world, with 38 local editions in more than 40 countries and a worldwide circulation of 4.5 million. The 42 countries included in our Global Sex Survey are:

1. Argentina
2. Aruba
3. Australia
4. Chile
5. China
6. Colombia
7. Costa Rica
8. Curaçao
9. Czech Republic
10. Dominican Republic
11. Ecuador
12. El Salvador
13. France
14. Germany
15. Greece
16. Guatemala
17. Honduras
18. Hungary
19. India
20. Indonesia
21. Italy
22. Malaysia
23. Mexico
24. Netherlands
25. Nicaragua
26. Panama
27. Peru
28. Philippines
29. Poland
30. Portugal
31. Romania
32. Russia
33. Serbia
34. Singapore
35. Slovenia
36. South Africa
37. South Korea
38. Spain
39. United Kingdom
40. Ukraine
41. United States
42. Venezuela

We noticed a couple of things in the writing of this book, and one of them we'd like to share right up front. One of the most interesting things about looking at erotic art and ancient sex manuals from other cultures is seeing how much *fun* the guys seemed to be having with their partners—and not just when they were getting jiggy with it. For instance, when looking at Chinese and Japanese pillow books, take note of how many props the couples have surrounded themselves with. There are musical instruments for romantic serenades, board games to play, books of poetry to read aloud, erotic pictures to look at—in other words, all the things people used to entertain themselves before Xbox and Tivo.

In fact, there is a strong sense of play in almost all ancient sexual traditions, and certainly in most sacred ones. For instance, according to Jina Bacarr, author of *The Japanese Art of Sex*, geisha—probably the paramount symbol of seduction and sexual knowledge across all cultures—were trained in a variety of traditional arts, including music and conversation. They were also expert game players. Bacarr tells of a variation on strip poker in which a geisha raises the hem of her gown slightly with every turn, opening her legs ever wider until her companion can no longer concentrate on the task at hand.

It would be a shame if that sense of play were lost to the ages. "Lovemaking has been afflicted by one of the worst diseases of modern times—it has been taken too seriously, as if it's a particularly difficult science project," says British expert Graham Masterson, former editor of *Penthouse* and *Penthouse Forum* and author of *The Secrets of Sexual Play*.

How did we get here? Masterson has a theory: While the sexual liberation that made it okay to discuss the most intimate details of our bodies and sex lives on daily talk shows, has represented a quantum leap forward for human sexuality, the information glut on the subject has also increased the amount of pressure that both men and women feel in bed. "If you don't know the ins and outs of deep genital massage or how to achieve extended orgasm or how to 'female ejaculate,' then you are made to feel as if you have flunked sex," he says.

So be warned: If we have any kind of secret agenda with this book, it's to bring that sense of fun, playfulness, and relaxation back into the bedroom.

There is much that we can learn from our counterparts around the world. After months of talking to some of the greatest sexual thinkers—and doers—around the globe, it's clear to us at *Men's Health* that we're all more alike than we are different. As Ava Cadell, PhD, a Hungarian-born, British-raised expert who has traveled and taught widely throughout the world, has said: "Everyone in the world wants to be a good lover; we just have different definitions of what that might be."

So fasten your seatbelts, return your tray tables to the upright position, and prepare to have your sexual passport stamped with tips and tricks that will help you level the international playing field on your way to becoming a sexual superpower: the World's Greatest Lover.

QUICKIE STATS

Demographics of the men who took the *Men's Health* Global Sex Survey:

Age

Under 17	4 percent
18–24	34 percent
25–34	29 percent
35–44	14 percent
45+	9 percent

Marital Status

Married	26 percent
In a relationship	33 percent
Single	28 percent
Divorced	3 percent

Note: Survey statistics throughout the book may not add up to 100 percent. Respondents may not have answered all survey questions.

PART I

LEARN A ROMANCE LANGUAGE

CHAPTER 1

BE THE MOST POPULAR MAN IN THE WORLD
Meet Many Beautiful Women

Brazilian men are having sex with more partners than anyone else in the world, our *Men's Health* Global Sex Survey tells us. After all, Brazil *is* the land that gave the world Gisele and the caipirinha. The secret? "The math is not complicated: the more women you hit on, the more women you'll sleep with," says Felipe from Brazil.

Like many other Latin American countries, Brazil has cultural taboos against promiscuity. But Brazilians also maintain a strict boundary between "real" life and the *fazendo tudo* ("doing everything") culture of private life.

Nowhere is this more in evidence than at Carnaval, the legendary 4-day-long, all-day and all-night celebration of Mardi Gras that features street fairs, samba competitions, fancy dress balls, and a whole lot of sexual chicanery. At Carnaval, what you do as a public person is one thing—and what you do behind the mask and under cover of night and the music's beat is another thing entirely.

Here are some tips on how you,

QUICKIE STATS

The number of sex partners for the average man:

1. Brazil		11.37
2. United States		**8.77**
3. Australia		8.54
4. United Kingdom		8.28
5. Greece		8.25
World average		**7.65**

like our friends in Rio, can meet as many women as possible—since to seduce them, you first have to find them.

Go Where the Girls Are

If we had a dollar for every guy who complained about how hard it was to meet women and then confessed that he'd spent the past 6 weekends holed up in his apartment watching football and playing *Doom* with his buddies, we could retire. And *then* where would you be?

> The absolute first rule of meeting women is to get out of the house.

The absolute first rule of meeting women is to *get out of the house*. The girl of your dreams is not going to crawl out of your laundry hamper or materialize next to you on the couch. This is especially true during prime times, such as weekend evenings.

Bars

"In Brazil, we go to bars and clubs to meet women," says Claudio, an importer who lives in Rio de Janeiro. Hey—we do that too! Everybody's there to have a good time, which lays the foundation. And we hear that this alcohol stuff is a pretty good social lubricant.

If you're anything like us, you'll be relieved to know that dance clubs may be overrated as a way to meet somebody. In a typical scenario, she's dancing with her friends, surrounded by lots of men who are checking her out. How do you differentiate yourself from everyone else in the press of bodies? And when you finally do catch her eye, how do you give a conversation some momentum—let alone volume enough to be heard above a thumping bass line?

On the other hand, dancing is a good way to tell how she's going to be in bed. You can gauge her sense of rhythm, her energy level, and her level of comfort with her body. For advice about approaching women on the dance floor, we turned to Richard La Ruina, also known as Gambler, the CEO and Master Trainer at PUATraining.com (that stands for "Pick-Up Artist Training"), a London-based company that teaches men how to successfully seduce women. His first piece of advice: "Dance. And dance like you mean it, like you're into the music, not just looking to get close to her or grind up against her. Have fun, enjoy the music. This will automatically separate you from the guys who are just standing there."

If you see someone you like, use humor and nonverbal communication to strike up a "conversation." Mirror her dancing in an exaggerated, funny way (be careful with this one). Once you've established eye contact and she's given you some positive feedback, get closer so that you're dancing with her. La Ruina also suggests staging a Michael Jackson–style dance-off, where you do a tricky move, and then point at her expectantly. (You can do this as ironically as you want to.) If she reacts positively, move in closer and dance with her.

> Dancing is a good way to tell how she's going to be in bed.

Alternately, you can concentrate on girls who aren't dancing. Ask them if they like dancing; if they say yes, ask them to join you on the floor. If not, you can agree and establish a bond that way.

Don't try to have a verbal conversation on the dance floor, La Ruina advises. "The goal is to dance with her, escalate physically a little bit, and then lead her to a quieter location—the bar or a booth—where she's away from her friends and you can talk to her."

The Internet

Ten years ago, online dating was for losers and crazies. Now it's pretty much agreed that online dating services like Match.com, Nerve.com, and eHarmony.com are an easy way to get access to a large pool of available people. In fact, in a poll of 1,500 *Men's Health* readers, 64 percent of guys thought they had a real shot at meeting a fantastic woman over the Internet.

If you've spent a whole night in a bar talking to a woman only to be introduced to her boyfriend at closing time, meeting someone online might be for you—this way, at least you know she's available! And meeting online gives you the opportunity to screen her in the privacy of your own home. In fact, some experts argue that far from isolating us from face-to-face interactions, as some people claim, the rise of online dating has brought back many previously lost rites of courtship—you know, like getting to know each other.

"I don't like meeting women in clubs—it's hard to ask real questions about what they're like, hard to hear what they're saying; it's even hard to tell what they really look like some of the time! When I meet someone online, I know what kind of music they like, what they like to read, what they do for a living, and in most cases, what sort of relationship they're looking for," says Friedrich, a sales rep from Mainz, Germany.

WRITE A GREAT PERSONAL AD

Robin Dunbar, a professor of evolutionary psychology and behavioral ecology at Liverpool University in England, studied the evolutionary messages behind personal ads. Most of the adjectives that posters used to describe themselves could be put in one of five categories: attractiveness ("good-looking"), commitment ("seeking serious relationship"), social skills ("great sense of humor"), sexiness ("sultry"), and resources ("professional").

Dunbar then asked 200 college students to rate the appeal of various ads. Men and women were—surprise!—interested in different things. Men cared about attractiveness first, commitment second, then social skills, resources, and sexiness. Women, on the other hand, were looking for someone who prioritized commitment first, then social skills, then resources, with attractiveness and sexiness bringing up the rear.

So when you're writing your ad, try to focus on what *she* will be looking for—not necessarily what you would. Besides describing what you're in the market for, emphasize what you'd bring to the relationship—other than your boyish dimple and cute butt.

Word to the wiseguy: Watch out for scams, especially in the international online dating world. You've been talking to someone for a couple of weeks; suddenly, her beloved mother takes ill, or she loses her job, and would you mind, buddy? Defenses are down when you think there's a pot of gold at the end of the rainbow, so no matter how legitimate she seems, it's a good idea to keep your Internet dating life far away from your checkbook until you're absolutely sure she's bona fide.

Weddings

Maybe that Vince Vaughn guy was on to something. Ask any caterer or disc jockey, and they'll tell you that weddings are a great way to meet women.

Guests tend to be flying one of two flags: super-sentimental (best friend, sister) or bitter (maxed-out bridesmaid, divorcée). To correctly classify your quarry, keep your eye on the audience during the ceremony: your sentimentalist will be drying her eyes, while the cynic rolls hers.

Both are ripe for the plucking. Approach the sentimentalist by complimenting the custom vows; hit on Cynical Girl by reminding her of one of the best reasons we know to stay single: lots of fun, commitment-free sex!

Yoga Class

"A female friend dragged me to a yoga class; I thought she'd be more likely to hook up with me if I went," says Travis, an American who travels often to Brazil. "But once I got there, I forgot all about her! There were fifteen of the hottest women I'd ever seen in my life, wearing next to nothing, and bending themselves into incredibly kinky positions. Afterward, they were all blissed out and mellow; it was easy to strike up a conversation. I felt pretty good myself—even though yoga is harder than it looks!"

Trust us, you won't be the only guy there. And even if you are—where else are you going to find those odds?

The Bookstore

Although probably not in the section where they put the *All Men Are Rats* titles.

At School

We asked 1,800 married *Men's Health* readers where they met their wives. The most popular answer was at school.

Already got a diploma? Not a problem. One of the things that single women do is take continuing education classes. Regret never reading the classics? Never learning French? Never learning to cook a steak? Take a course. Even if you don't meet someone, you'll learn something.

Through Mutual Friends

About 20 percent of respondents to the same survey of married guys said that they'd found their current significant other through a friend.

"When I decided I wanted a relationship, I called or e-mailed all of my friends and asked them to set me up," says Zach, a book designer from Toronto. "But I asked them not to restrict themselves just to the people they thought I'd like. 'I'll have lunch with anyone,' I told them. And it was a smart move, because I ended up hooking up with someone my buddy didn't think was a good match."

The Office

Conventional wisdom has it that pursuing a colleague romantically is more dangerous than bungee jumping without a rope. "You'll be sued for sexual harassment!" in-house counsel warns. "You'll sabotage your career!" managers moan.

None of that seems to deter most men. In another recent *Men's Health* sex survey, 56 percent of respondents said they'd had sex with someone in their company, while almost the same number said it had been a good idea. A 2005 survey by the job-finding Web site Vault.com determined that 58 percent of those who responded had had a workplace romance—and 23 percent of them had even gotten their swerve on in the office!

It's not a surprise that it happens. After all, you spend the majority of your life at work. And it's not a surprise that so many of these hookups turn into relationships, either—you get to know someone much better when you're working with her than you would if you'd chatted her up at a party.

"There are some major benefits to seeing work colleagues," says British writer Judi James, author of *Sex at Work: A Survival Guide.* "You understand what motivates her and all the stresses she goes through. But the biggest benefit is that you get to road-test her before you hook up. You don't get that chance if you meet someone in a bar."

A work fling is trickier than your average romance, but many of the most common pitfalls can be avoided with a little common sense—and putting some of the following suggestions into play.

Choose well. Unlike in a relationship that begins after a quick conversation, you've had the opportunity to see her in a wide variety of situations—not all of them positive. That's very useful information. You've seen how she handles unreasonable requests, annoying co-workers, lazy staff members, and sucking up to the boss. Given what you know, is this someone you really want to start seeing? "Work behavior offers big clues to character," says William Glasser, MD, an internationally recognized psychiatrist based in Chatsworth, California.

What to watch out for: A control freak is a control freak—if it's her way or the highway at work, chances are good it's going to be that way in your relationship as well. And if she's hypercritical and quick to express displeasure, odds are you're going to find yourself on the receiving end eventually.

On the other hand, bear in mind that people are quick to tar a powerful woman with the "bitch" brush even when they wouldn't think twice about similar behavior in a man.

Are you at risk of legal action? Contrary to what you read in the newspapers, the actual risk of a work romance leading to a sexual harassment charge is slim. Dennis Powers, British author of the book *The Office*

Romance: Playing with Fire without Getting Burned, estimates that there are millions of workplace affairs that don't end with a trip to a tribunal.

Still, romance and harassment can become confused if men don't know when to back off. To protect yourself, learn how to take no for an answer. "The bottom line with harassment is that it involves unwanted advances," says Barbara Kate Repa, a San Francisco lawyer and coauthor of *Sexual Harassment on the Job.* Other countries are a little more flexible about what constitutes an advance—in America, it's best to assume that any discussion of sex, outside of a professional context, with someone you know from work has the potential to flare into a problem.

> *The actual risk of a work romance leading to a sexual harassment charge is slim.*

The real risk is with a woman who reports directly to you. If the relationship succeeds, you may find yourself in an awkward position. How will you handle reprimanding her for below-par performance? How will you handle her request for a raise or a promotion? How will you cope with her colleagues' concerns about favoritism? If you break up, you're even more open to an accusation of sexual harassment.

Of course, be sure never to state, or even imply, that going out with you would be a clever career move: That's grounds for dismissal (yours, not hers).

Take the temperature of the room. If your workplace comes complete with snacks and basketball courts and Pajama Day the first Friday of every month, chances are good that it has attracted younger, single people—people who will take your affair in proper stride. But if casual Fridays simply means "no pinstripes" at your office, you can assume that colleagues are relatively conservative, and that the attitude will carry over to sex.

Get on the same page. It's always uncomfortable when she thinks you're planning a wedding while you're planning your escape. If you sense up front that the relationship would be nothing more than a fling, it might be better to keep it on a friendship level. If after a couple of dates you determine that you're not interested in anything more serious, let her know right away. And if there's a serious disconnect between what you want and what she expects, end it immediately.

Tell your boss. He's going to hear about it; make sure he hears about it from you. You don't need to call a meeting—it's your business, after all. A word in the hallway will do.

Bear in mind that he doesn't care whether you're getting laid or not—his only interest in your personal life is in the effect it may have on your performance, and by extension, his bottom line. Take the opportunity to reassure him: "Obviously, neither she nor I planned on this happening, but since it has, we're both dedicated to maintaining the highest levels of professionalism, no matter what happens." Ditto for the breakup: "That thing with Anne didn't work out, but the split was amicable and won't have any effect whatsoever on our professional relationship."

Keep work out of the house! Because you first knew each other as colleagues, you probably won't have a problem maintaining a professional relationship. In fact, work-romance veterans say the bigger concern is work smothering the relationship.

Here's a test: The next time the two of you go out for a postwork beer, note what you're chatting about a half-hour later. If it's work, change the subject. If you're still discussing work another half-hour after that, you're not on a date, you're in a staff meeting. End the relationship, and put your bar bill on your expense account.

It's especially tricky to navigate a relationship when one of you has more power at work. No matter what your professional status, you must be equals in the relationship. "Unless it's 50/50, the relationship has no chance," says Dr. Glasser.

And vice versa: Make sure to keep professional boundaries intact—even if the two of you are pretty much attached at the hip in the rest of your life.

For instance, even if she does talk to you about work at home, don't let on to her colleagues that you've got the inside scoop—and do let them know right away that currying favor with you isn't the way to suck up to her. Don't ever speak on her behalf, act as if you have authority over her staffers, or get overly involved in the decisions made by her department. If they'd wanted you to do her job, they would have hired you for it.

Probably the most important thing to remember is how important it is to restrict home-related conflicts to your personal time. First and foremost, continuing a lovers' quarrel at work is not fair to your colleagues. If unfinished domestic business is causing tension between you at work, there's only one solution: Agree to deal with it later. But don't just hide behind that annual report. Instead, indicate to one another that you know there's an outstanding issue, and agree to tackle it together at a more appropriate (read: non-billable) time.

BREAKING UP IS HARD TO DO

Like any other relationship, a workplace romance can go flat. But you're still going to be together a lot more than most exes have to be.

And while in an ideal world, everyone would behave professionally, the opposite is too often the case. Breaking up over the weekend (a Friday night is ideal) gives both of you the chance to get yourselves together before facing your colleagues. Remember that what happened between the two of you should stay between the two of you. She may not see it that way, but the office isn't a good place to trade blows. And even though you may be tempted to show Stan from Sales that you do not in fact have a squirrel dick, it's best to grin and resist the urge. Like all office rumors, this one will dissipate eventually.

If rumors persist, make the atmosphere unbearably unpleasant for you, or start affecting the way your colleagues treat you, have a conversation with your boss and the human resources department. Don't snipe back. Patience is the key; you'll look better than she does if you stay calm.

Throw a Party

"I don't know why everyone doesn't throw parties. It's such a little fuss for so much return," says Ian, an Englishman living in Bali.

What's Ian so excited about? He knows that throwing a party is a great way to meet women.

Why? First of all, you're in your element, surrounded by people who already like you. As host, you are rock star for the evening and can approach anyone who catches your fancy, instantly talking to them with the natural confidence of someone who knows everyone in the room. You can invite your longtime crush without exposing yourself to the pressure of a first date. And if you score, the bedroom is just a hop, skip, and a jump away.

If you're an entertaining newbie, don't even think about planning a dinner party, unless you have a lot of money and can hire someone to do it for you. The way to practice those particular skills is on your nearest and dearest. But what the British call "a drinks party" is a good thing.

Pretty much the only thing you need to remember: Don't run out of booze. Nothing breaks up a party faster than the realization that there's nothing left in the liquor cabinet except the dregs at the bottom of a bottle of some opaque and obscure liqueur. Don't be stingy with the accoutrements (cups, limes, tonic, soda, juice, ice), either. People will become less fanatical about a perfectly mixed drink as the evening progresses, but they shouldn't have to resort to something unacceptable. Booze keeps, and it will not go to waste; we guarantee it. You should also have a close friend armed with a twenty and prepared to run out to the nearest all-night convenience store, in case of dire emergency. Have plenty of non-alcoholic beverages on hand as well.

And, not to be a buzz-kill or anything, but if you live in a world where people need to drive an automobile to get home, it is your responsibility to make sure that guests leave your home either in condition to drive or by another method of transportation. Period.

If the party is small, pay a lot of attention to the guest list and keep an eye on the social skill level of your invitees. And don't court conflict by inviting two naturally incompatible people. It's a party, not a cockfight, and in this setting, conversational flow is infinitely better than a feisty debate. And people who have slept with each other but are no longer sleeping with each other should be treated like highly unstable explosives, even if they have successfully socialized together at another event.

Here's the most important part: Get each of your friends, single or attached, to bring at least one attractive single woman. That's the price of admission, folks. It's not just selfish on your part. Sherman Billingsley, the founder and owner of New York's infamous speakeasy the Stork Club, presumably knew a thing or two about entertaining. He always advised party-throwers to invite attractive women, and to invite more women than men. This is still true, even now, in the halcyon days of legalized alcohol. Women don't mind meeting and talking to other women, but men just aren't that interested in meeting and talking to each other. There are probably sociological and psychological explanations for this, but we don't know what they are—just that parties with more women are better parties.

If your apartment isn't yet ready for prime-time, there are other options. You can co-host the party with a friend, preferably one with a bigger and better apartment than your own. Double the fun, and the guest list. You must shoulder more than your share of planning, setup, and cleanup by way of compensation, though. Or invite people to meet you at a bar early in the evening. Dinner is a perfect segue into the next portion of your evening with the person you've been chatting up. Or throw a bar-beque or a picnic in a public park. Militantly enforce the repeated application of sunscreen, especially if this is one of those parties thrown exclusively to provide access to your crush. Become sweaty and revel in the stench of grilled meat, then go home to have great sex and weird, melatonin-soaked dreams afterward.

Of course, the best thing you can do to make sure that your guests have a good time is to have a good time yourself. And the best thing about parties is the way they beget invitations to other parties—the universe is generous that way.

‖■‖

So perhaps it's time to take the lead from our Brazilian friends. Give yourself a shave, get a good haircut, and put on your game face. The ladies are out there waiting for you—all you have to do is go find them.

CHAPTER 2

BE THE WORLD'S MOST IRRESISTIBLE MAN
Make a Powerful First Impression

In our global *Men's Health* poll, about a quarter of you said that if you could have any superpower in the world, it would be this one: the ability to seduce any woman—instantly.

Not surprising. Certainly, it's a useful skill—more useful than x-ray vision or the ability to leap the top of giant buildings with a single bound. Because who, after all, can account for attraction? What's to explain the charged current of electricity that sometimes passes between total strangers as their eyes meet from across a crowded room? How do you explain something like the obsessive, out-of-the-blue crush you've suddenly developed on a colleague you've been working with for years? Or the fact that, just as suddenly, she likes you back?

These days, there can be no discussion of the art of seduction without mentioning Neil Strauss's recent bestseller, *The Game*, the book that blew open the underground world of seduction experts who use a variety of tricks to get women into bed. Certainly, many men have used the techniques with good success. But from Felicity, an Australian magazine writer, comes a cautionary tale about relying on a system instead of something a tad more reliable, like your real personality:

> I was having drinks with a friend, and we were approached by this guy wearing this ridiculous necklace. Although he'd started up talking to us, he was also sort of obnoxious, so we basically told him to shove off.

As he was walking away, I was like, "Excuse me, but did you just 'game' us?" He got all embarrassed: "I guess it didn't come off." We ended up talking, and he was a lovely guy. He'd just gotten some terrible advice.

So be careful, gentlemen. Sometimes a game isn't as good as the real thing.

In this chapter, we've collected the very best advice, from stateside and beyond, to help you get what you want. By the end, you'll know everything you need to be completely irresistible. And if you're one of the lucky ones whose little black book is crammed chock full of digits—or who already comes home to that special someone—don't skip ahead. This stuff can help you sustain your mojo.

First Impressions

A crowded bar, a hot summer night, the perfect girl leaning up against the bar. You lock eyes from across the room. Now what?

Your mother always told you that first impressions count—and she was right. One study by Princeton psychologist Alex Todorov, PhD, found that people often decide whether someone is attractive and trustworthy *one-tenth of a second* after laying eyes on them.

> *People decide whether someone is attractive one-tenth of a second after laying eyes on them.*

But don't panic: Even if that hottie doesn't like what she sees, it's not necessarily game over (as it would be with you, you shallow coot). While a man usually will eliminate a woman that he's not initially attracted to, women tend to work differently. "I would never have guessed that I would fall in love with the man who became my husband," says Leonie, a stay-at-home mother in Aix-en-Provence, France. "I did not even think he was attractive until we had talked for a long time."

We've broken down the five stages of a first encounter, from the time your eyes meet to the moment you both decide to take it a step further, with tips to help you maximize your moves during every step of the process. But before we go there, let's get you putting your best foot forward with a quick chat about grooming and what you should wear.

Hey, Good Looking

You're probably very used to judging women by their appearance. Surprise! They're doing the exact same thing to you.

We're guessing you've read all the same studies we have. Women like tall men with big eyes, strong jaws, no baby fat in their faces, long eyelashes, expressive mouths—the list goes on. But don't panic: There are plenty of guys out there who don't look like Orlando Bloom but are still doing all right for themselves. You can't grow taller, but there's lots you can do to make yourself more attractive to the opposite sex.

It's important to remember that what we consider attractive is not just a matter of personal preference, but is in large part determined by fashion and the culture in which we were raised. In ancient Japan, young women dyed their teeth black to indicate that they'd come of age (and perhaps to prevent tooth decay), and young men across Europe practiced swordplay, hoping to receive a scar or two to impress the chicks.

If you had to characterize the looks of the current times in one word, that word would be *health*. When you're in prime form, taking care of yourself, eating right, getting plenty of exercise (as well as plenty of rest), you not only project self-confidence, but you'll be what she wants: On an elemental level, women respond more positively to a healthy, physically strong male.

The *Kama Sutra* (*Aphorisms on Love*) by Vatsyayana is the ancient Indian text that is perhaps best known as a catalog of ultra-athletic sexual positions. But the most notorious sex manual in the world also has a considerable amount to say about how you should look and take care of yourself before you go out and try to get together with someone.

"In fact, the Kama Sutra was intended as an instruction manual for a young bachelor, and much of the first part of it is dedicated to everything he needs to do to make himself a worthwhile catch," says Julianne Balmain, coauthor of *The Kama Sutra Deck: 50 Ways to Love Your Lover*. "Unfortunately, it's the part that most people skip over on their way to the positions." The advice is surprisingly comprehensive; there is, for instance, a chapter entitled "On the Arrangements of a House, and Household Furniture; and about the Daily Life of a Citizen, His Companions, and Amusements." And, despite the fact that the Kama Sutra was penned sometime between the third and fifth centuries C.E., it's extremely relevant.

For instance, Balmain points out that the Kama Sutra takes into account the fact that "sex is intimate, and impeccable grooming is a courtesy that can't be overlooked." The book is specific, down to mandating that you use cologne to smell nice, but don't wear too much—sound familiar? "You need to be clean, well-shaven, otherwise well-groomed, and well-dressed. You did then, and you do now," says Balmain. And a ring on your finger doesn't get you off the hook. Don't you dare complain that she's let herself go unless you're willing to go the extra mile yourself.

We think it's time that American men learned what women have always known: that someone who looks like they'd be good to touch gets touched more often. Perhaps that's why male grooming salons like John Allan's are popping up all over the United States.

> *Someone who looks like they'd be good to touch gets touched more often.*

In Europe, it's been a trend forever. The first men's-only spa and grooming salon in the United States, Nickel, is actually a French transplant. In many cultures, including Russia, Hungary, Japan, and the Netherlands, it's de rigueur to go and get really, really clean at a public bathhouse. Many—from the Japanese *onsen* to the Russian *banyas* to the Finnish saunas to the Hungarian thermal baths to Korean *mogyoktangs* and *jjimjilbang*—offer either grooming services or a place to do it yourself.

But when we think of bespoke tailoring, valets, and the kind of shave that results in a stiff upper lip, we think of the British, so that's where we went for advice—specifically, to Ray Khandpur at London's number one male grooming salon, Jason Shankey Male Grooming, who says, "Girls are getting sick of men looking a mess, but men are afraid of a place that will go too far." Grooming salons specifically targeted to men often have a clubby, masculine feeling to them and specialize in making men look better without making them look perfect.

We asked Khandpur to break down the basics of good grooming for us. Here's what he said.

Hair: Girls care about hair—and nothing can bring out your best features the way a good haircut can. If he asks you which clipper blade to use, it's time to put your childhood barber behind you. Go upscale—at least a little bit—and ask the guy behind the chair for advice on what will make you look best. If you're considering a major change, and you already have a significant other, it might be a good idea to check in with her first. She might already have an idea about a new look that you could try.

Shaving: Not attractive: cuts, scrapes, the tufts of hair you missed. Khandpur recommends that you shave in the shower, or right after, and that you exfoliate your skin a couple of times a week with a gentle scrub. Use a good, moisturizing shaving cream and change your razor blade often. Lose the aftershave: The alcohol in it dries your skin.

Moisturize: Ideally, you'd cleanse, exfoliate, tone, moisturize, and use an eye cream every day. While it sounds like a lot, you can do the whole routine in less than 5 minutes a day—and those 5 minutes will have a dramatic long-term effect.

Moisturizing and cleansing, anyway, are not negotiable. Your moisturizer should have an SPF of 15, and all products should be unscented. You don't have to break the bank on tiny jars of cream (they last forever, anyway), but you probably will want to use something a little better than what you can find in a drugstore. If you're not sure, ask a female, or go to a department store or grooming salon so you can try before you buy.

Eyebrows: Yes, eyebrows. "There's just no reason for any man to have a caterpillar crawling across his face these days," Khandpur says, and among women all over the world, the unibrow rated pretty high on the "yuck" scale. The key to getting rid of it, without looking like you're ready to break out into a number from *La Cage aux Folles*? "Tidy rather than shape." You'll look better, and nobody will be the wiser. Khandpur also recommends that you go to a place that specializes in *men's* brows; you can even get it done at the same time as your haircut. Nose and ear hair is also a deal-breaker; ask the stylist to deal with it for you, or do it at home.

Manicure: You want to put your hands on her body, don't you? Hangnails, bitten cuticles, and calluses all work against you. This is another thing you can get fixed while you're getting your hair cut.

If you don't want to get a manicure—or a handshake improver, which is one of the euphemisms these places use—make sure you take care of business at home. Nails should be short, cut square, and clean at all times, and the skin on your hands should be moisturized.

The extras: The biggest request Khandpur hears from women? "Deal with his back and shoulder hair." The next? "Deal with his feet." If you want to feel her nails running down your back, perhaps it would be a good idea to deforest it first. (Hint for you monogamous guys: This is a very nice anniversary gift.) And if you forgo a pedicure, it's a courtesy to keep everything neatly trimmed and odor-free.

Good grooming doesn't have to take a lot of time. "Within an hour, you can get a haircut, brow grooming, and a manicure and really change the way you look," Khandpur says. And a simple routine is easy to maintain.

Dressing for Success

The clothes may not make the man, but they can help to make his night. "You look at the package to gain an understanding of the product," says Michael Cunningham, PhD, psychology professor at the University of Louisville. "If you're disappointed with the product, you may learn to be more careful about the packaging."

Men's Health asked women what they liked—and didn't like—about the way men dressed. Here's what we learned.

Start at the bottom. An overwhelming majority—63 percent—of the women we polled—say men ruin an outfit with poorly maintained, out-of-style shoes. And 40 percent of women came out against pleated pants. What will it take to get through to you people?

Spend some cash. She doesn't want you to look like a dandy, but "used-car salesman" isn't going to get you where you want to go either. Don't buy cheap ties or shirts—instead, shop discount stores like T.J. Maxx, or affordable, fashion-forward retailers like the Swedish superstore chain H&M.

Throw it out. Replace clothes when necessary—in other words, at the very first signs of stains or frays. Make sure your suits fit properly. The best way to do this on a limited budget is to get to know your neighborhood tailor. Even an inexpensive suit can benefit greatly from a professional nip/tuck.

Lose your PDA. Anything electronic hanging off your belt, even if it's the slickest, slimmest cell phone out there, hurts your chances; 55 percent of women say the gadgets need to go. You're not the only one with the problem, which is why there's such a great selection of messenger bags, laptop bags, and briefcases out there that won't make you feel like you're carrying the proverbial man-purse. Not that there's anything wrong with that.

A little flash isn't bad. Most women prefer men not to wear jewelry, but they *do* look at watches. "Statusy things attract women," says Gilda Carle, PhD, a psychotherapist and the author of *Don't Bet on the Prince! How to Have the Man You Want by Betting on Yourself.* "They suggest that the man can take control of his life and his business situation, and that he can take care of her, too."

Show some skin. "One of the best ways for a man to seduce a woman he's just met is to reveal his vulnerable side," says David Givens, PhD, director of the Center for Nonverbal Studies in Spokane, Washington. "An easy and non-verbal way to do this is to display what's called your 'neck dimple,' that V-shaped area just below your Adam's apple." This area, often hidden by a crew-neck, if not a shirt and tie, could be the key to the castle. Dr. Givens claims that open-collar shirts and V-neck sweaters that show off this area of the skin send the subliminal message that you're open and approachable.

Open collars and V-necks send the subliminal message that you're open and approachable.

Slim down. Women like to eye the merchandise, just like we do, and 55 percent of those we talked to say that the majority of men wear clothes that are too big. It's high time that men learn what most women know: Clothes that are too big make you look like a slob—and like you're carrying extra pounds to boot. That schlumpy sweater/khaki combo isn't hiding your beer belly; it's just making you look like you've got the shoulders and butt to match. You don't have to squeeze yourself into a skintight sweater or skinny jeans; just make sure that your clothes skim your body, instead of enveloping it.

Ask a friend. Every man should have at least one female buddy (or gay guy friend) to field the hard questions. Questions like: Are these jeans lame? Do I wear too much cologne? Should I cut my hair shorter? Do I look better when I've shaved, or when I haven't? Is there anything else about my appearance that you've been dying to tell me since college?

These are hard questions to ask, hard questions to answer, and hard answers to hear. Ask her or him to be completely honest even if it means hurting your feelings. And even if your feelings are hurt, be completely gracious and grateful for the feedback, or they'll never trust you with their honesty again. (You can solicit a second opinion if you feel unsure about the feedback you've received.)

"You're going to feel much better about yourself when you look the part," says Khandpur. That's important, because as you're about to see, confidence is the number one thing a woman notices about a man. So now that you're groomed and dressed, it's time to get out there and show her what you've got.

As promised, we'll be your wingman to walk you through the five stages of a successful pick-up, with lots of advice from both our international experts and women around the world.

Stage I: Across the Room

Experts tell us that what you sound like, how you look at her, and the body language you use may be just as important as a lantern jaw or the way your jeans fit.

Let your body do the talking. The first thing to know is that your body talks even before you've struck up a conversation. Women rank confidence as one of the sexiest qualities in a man. "It's such a cliché, but it's true— the first thing I notice about someone is whether they look confident and in control of themselves," says Barbara, a waitress in England. "But there's nothing more off-putting than a guy who acts like you're lucky just to be in his orbit. It's a fine balance between being sure of yourself and acting like an ass, isn't it?"

The way you hold yourself tells her a great deal about your confidence level, according to Helen Fisher, PhD, research professor in the anthropology department at Rutgers University in New Jersey and author of *Why We Love*. Throw your shoulders back, suck in your gut, and don't be afraid of some eye contact. If you're sitting, keep an open position—legs apart, head up, chest out, back straight. If you're standing, position your shoulders toward her while turning your head toward your conversational partner. "And above all else, smile. A smile goes a long way," says Fisher.

Women rank confidence as one of the sexiest qualities in a man.

Of course we're not all blessed with such self-confidence, but that's not an insurmountable problem, according to Lisa Daily, a Florida-based dating coach and the author of *Stop Getting Dumped*. "It is possible to fake it till you make it," she says.

Have fun. Get into the habit of engaging in fun, sociable interactions with everyone around you, says Richard La Ruina, also known as Gambler, the CEO and Master Trainer at PUATraining.com (that stands for "Pick-Up Artist Training"), a London-based company that teaches men how to successfully seduce women. It makes sense. Who would you rather be: the guy everybody wants to hang out with, or the moody loner holding up the bar? "Any girl would rather be approached by someone who looks like they are fun and having fun," La Ruina says.

So chat with the bartender, or buy a round. You'll gain confidence in your ability to banter easily and hold up your end of a casual exchange and "when the hot girl comes along, it will only be another opportunity to start a conversation."

Take a good look. A Harvard study found that looking at pretty women activates a pleasure center in the brain usually triggered only by food, drugs, and money. You may never progress past the looking stage, so drink her in, and hear the ringing of all the happy bells in your brain.

Bring a wingwoman. Researchers at the University of Louisville found that a man was 50 to 100 percent more desirable to women when other ladies said they liked him. So there might be something to the age-old trick of going to a bar with a female friend—one guaranteed to laugh at all your jokes and then disappear subtly into the shadows when a conversation with someone you like takes off. The courteous thing to do, of course, is to offer to be her wing-man when she needs one.

A wingwoman is a tacit seal of approval, a silent signal to an interested woman that you're not a serial killer or a sexual predator. "It sounds sick, but I pretty much always meet someone when I'm down at the pub with my sister!" admits Harry, an investment banker in London. "Girls get to see me in my most relaxed, confident state—and my sister's bright and attractive, which speaks well for me. I sometimes think I should take her on job interviews."

Simon says . . . While you're still across the room from the woman you're scoping, subtly mirror her movements. When she drinks, you drink. When she changes her body position, do so also. If you begin to see that you and she are moving in tandem, to a beat, it's time to make your move.

SEDUCTION AROUND THE WORLD: A CHEAT SHEET

If there's one thing we've learned from doing this book, it's that women are not all created equal—they all like to be approached differently. Some of these differences are cultural, and so in keeping with our international theme, we asked experts and ordinary women from a host of different countries how best to approach the native female.

So whether you're on vacation or in the corner bar, here's everything you need to know about seducing that hottie from abroad.

Australia: With Australian women, you need both a home and an away strategy, suggests Clint Paddison, CEO of BlinkDating.com in Australia. Australian women on their home turf, especially in the cities, have a stand-offish air. But Australians travel more than almost any other country's residents, and the same rules emphatically do not apply when they're on the road. "I know people who left Australia with a few sexual encounters under their belts, and came home from a month or two in Europe or the States with two dozen more," Paddison says. In other words, an Aussie Sheila is up for a good time, and if you can show her one, you've got a better than fighting chance.

Hitting on a beautiful woman is the same anywhere, Paddison advises. She's heard it all a thousand times before, so don't compliment the most obvious thing about her—which, with an Australian woman, is likely to be her accent.

Brazil: First of all, let's answer one of the great mysteries of the ages: Why are Brazilian women so incredibly hot? Tatiana, a 36-year-old professor from Rio, says that it's because taking care of themselves is such a high priority: "They eat properly, they have the time to go to the gym or to a yoga class, and to the beach to get a tan."

Encouragingly, Tatiana thinks that seducing a Brazilian woman might just be easier than enticing an American. "Brazilian women are perfect for a shy American man. First of all, women outnumber men in Brazil, and there's a lot of interest and curiosity about foreign men as well; it's not a liability. Plus, women in Brazil really like sex, and are more open to it than they are in the colder, more repressed Anglo-Saxon countries. In fact, Brazilian women are likely to be the aggressor, if they see something they like." Maybe all those Carnaval stories are true. . . .

Tatiana's advice for an American man? "Pay attention to the way you look! Brazilian women are spoiled; they'll expect you and your clothes to look good."

Portugal: Men must act carefully to be successful with Portuguese women, warns Mariagrazia Marini, PhD, a clinical psychologist in Lisbon. "Portuguese women are slow to trust. As a result, they seem very reserved, which can sometimes look like arrogance to a foreigner." But don't be fooled; our global sex survey found that the Portuguese led the pack in one-night stands.

Vulgarity, overt sexual come-ons, and drinking too much are obvious no-no's. Your best strategy? Since trust is an issue, it's probably best to wait for an introduction by someone she knows. Dr. Marini also recommends that you be authentic, friendly, receptive to her comments, and sincere—whatever your intentions. Her final piece of advice sounds universal to us: "Do everything with passion!"

Italy: "No real Italian man would ever advise an American man on how to approach our women!" jokes Emmanuele A. Jannini, MD, professor of endocrinology and medical sexology in the department of experimental medicine at the University of L'Aquila. "However, if I have to suggest something, I would say that the best way is to *be American*—as different as possible from the continental model. Of course, it depends on the target, but if an American man wants to seduce a sophisticated Italian girl, he has to dress as a Manhattan artist and must have a big loft facing Soho."

France: We turned to Robert Santo-Paolo, a psychologist and sexologist and the founder of the Web site sexotherapie.com, for advice on approaching the beautiful and impeccable women of France: "American men just have to talk for French women to be practically conquered. . . . American men have always had lots of success with French women. One could say that they're probably the foreigners whom French women most daydream about. The American accent is terrific, and when American men try to speak French, women find them absolutely charming. French is very complicated and so foreigners often make mistakes, like confusing '*le*' and '*la*,' which seem cute because they are like the ones made by children."

He continues: "American men have much more success than English men, so it's clearly not only a question of the language. French women think of American men as very warm and, more than that, exuberant (talking and laughing a lot, expressing their pleasure without holding back). Even while they love the childlike side of American men, French women also perceive American men as big, strong, and very handsome. They see them as sexy and very virile, like so many of the American actors."

It appears that being American is an enormous advantage when you're trying to attract a French woman. Isabelle from Paris adds: "Don't be a braggart. French men are, and we hate it." Santo-Paolo leaves you with one final thought. "If initial contact plays out and leads to sex, a French

(continued)

woman will have the same sexual expectations of an American man as she would for any other: She expects gentleness, tenderness, and for him to bring her lots of pleasure."

United Kingdom: "The most important thing is humor," says British psychologist and sex advisor Dr. Pam Spurr, author of *Naughty Tricks and Sexy Tips*. "When you first meet a British woman, they love a great sense of humor. The British are renowned for their intelligent and quick wit. No good trying some cheesy one-liners. Instead, be interested in her—and make her laugh!"

British expert Emily Dubberley agrees, and gives these do's and don'ts. "Do be polite but cheeky—a glint in the eye goes a long way. Don't force the issue—if a woman isn't interested, chasing her won't help. Do go for a goodnight kiss at the end of a date that's seemed to go well—chances are, she won't make the first move."

Germany: "I think the roles of men and women are much more defined in the United States than they are in Germany," says Inge, a Web site designer from Stuttgart. "You always hear about how the man is supposed to make the first move, how men treat women in a gentlemanly fashion by opening doors and pulling back chairs and such things. You also hear about this rule about the third date: No sex before, but sex then, it seems." We're not sure where she heard that third date thing, but we'll definitely keep listening. . . .

"I would say that making the first move isn't bad in Germany, but it's not necessarily expected," Inge continues. "Women can and will make the first move just as easily, if they are interested, and tabs can be split or traded back and forth—you get this one, she'll get the next."

In fact, Luisa, a German artist living in Switzerland, warns that gentlemanly behavior can even backfire: "A German woman may see what an American man considers to be chivalry as old-fashioned. German women don't see doors opened for them as polite; they're more likely to see it as the man thinking they're incapable of doing it themselves."

We'll let Inge have the last word: "Don't expect sex to happen on the third date—or be astonished if it does happen sooner!"

South Africa: "South African women are generally down-to-earth, fun-

Stage II: The Approach

"The women I talk to are dying for someone to be fun and creative in their approach and initial overture," says Mary Taylor, a former exotic dancer in Toronto and the author of *Bedroom Games*.

Here are some tips that will help.

loving girls who'll see right through a corny chat-up line," says Kim Richter, managing editor at the South Africa edition of *Men's Health*. "There is quite a strong anti-American sentiment here—but nothing that can't be circumvented with a friendly smile and some easy conversation. Use characteristics that break the stereotype of American men as big-spending, brash loudmouths. South African women are good listeners, but ask her what she thinks if she doesn't offer her opinion. She might not be very forthcoming. And always be a gentleman—she'll come back for more."

Japan: Ask her blood type. In Japan, using blood type to predict a person's character is fairly common—so much so that dating services use the system to make matches, and prostitutes will often put the information on the "tart cards" that they post in phone booths. Like astrology in '70s singles bars, it's a way to strike up a conversation and find out something about the other person. And if you get lucky, you can buy condoms to match your blood type as well!

Jina Bacarr, author of *The Japanese Art of Sex,* has a few cautions. "The Japanese are very averse to casual touching. One example of this, of course, is the way they bow to one another, instead of shaking hands like Americans or kissing like Europeans. Even if you hit it off and start seeing each other, expect her to be very uncomfortable with any kind of public display—even very innocent ones." She also advises you to have a plan: "The Japanese take pleasure and comfort from a very orderly life. They don't leave things up to chance. So be on time, be prepared, and be polite."

Russia: "Treat a Russian woman like a lady!" says Anna from Moscow. "Don't do all the talking; listen to what she has to say, too. Compliment her on how she looks, and on her personality. Do show her that you're interested—but don't try to have sex on the first or second date, or you'll be considered vulgar. Try to show her your own personality, and make her laugh. A sense of humor is greatly appreciated."

India: Dr. Mahinder Watsa, a sex therapist in India, says that approaching an Indian woman depends on whether she is modern or traditional. If she's modern, then "woo as you are used to." A traditional woman, however, will be much more conservative, and anxious about maintaining her virginity. Dr. Watsa's advice? "Make haste slowly!"

Stay confident. She wants the confident guy she was flirting with across the room, not someone who's suddenly all thumbs. We know, it can be hard when you're up close and personal and every sentence coming out of your mouth sounds dumber than the one before.

Here's one true thing: Striking out isn't the end of the world. La Ruina recommends approaching lots of girls so that you get experience and become desensitized to rejection. So does Lachan, an Irish sales rep for a software company. "I work in sales and used to spend half an hour preparing for a call. Now I just pick up the phone. I realized a few years ago that approaching women is basically the same as a sales job. The more you approach, the better the chance that you'll hit, and your pitch matters, so make it good. But if you strike out, move on. It's not the end of the world; they just don't want what you're selling."

Get to the point. Don't pretend to bump into her or to recognize her from somewhere else. "Playing games wastes everyone's time," says Nikki Hayia, sex editor at *Men's Health* Greece. "Women want a man who knows what he wants, especially if what he wants is us."

"I know whether I'm attracted to you, so I don't need a pick-up line," says Sara, a 28-year-old bartender in South Africa. "Just introduce yourself." Alternatively, if you're at a party, you can ask a mutual acquaintance to provide an introduction.

A compliment is a good way to break the ice. But there are a couple of landmines to avoid if you choose this approach. First of all, if a girl is really attractive, she's heard it all before. You've probably read about the Neil Strauss "neg" approach, where you deliberately knock a really pretty girl off balance in your opening salvo. "It's a manipulation technique that really works," says Clint Paddison, CEO of BlinkDating.com in Australia. "But another, less manipulative strategy is to 'neg' on someone's terrible fashion moment nearby, easing yourself into a conversation with her." Another approach that Paddison suggests also throws the attention away from you and her and onto a third party: "Focus on a piece of accessory jewelry and ask her where she got it."

Experts are unanimous: For your opening salvo, keep away from anything that might be construed as sexual—in other words, pretty much anything to do with her body or the way she looks. Japanese-German sex educator Midori, author of *Wild Side Sex,* suggests the following ground rule

> *For your opening salvo, keep away from anything that might be construed as sexual.*

(and something tells us this one comes from experience): "Compliment her on something she chose, not something she didn't. For instance, hair style is okay; hair color is not. She chose her necklace; she didn't choose to be born Japanese."

Reach out and touch. Shake her hand as if you mean it. Remember—this is your first touch, and a lot of women use it as a barometer of how you'll touch them elsewhere. In a recent University of Alabama study, guys with weak, clammy handshakes were perceived as shy and neurotic. (If your hands tend to sweat, don't—repeat, don't—wipe them on your pants. Pressing your palm once firmly against your thigh should be enough.)

A real man doesn't need to squeeze until he feels something give; the goal is a firm clasp. There's valuable information here for you as well: That same Alabama study showed that women who give firmer handshakes tend to be more adventurous.

Enjoy the sweet smell of success. Pheromones are bodily secretions that play a role in attraction. Before you get out your wallet, there's actually no evidence that pheromone-loaded colognes and aftershaves actually do anything. But smell does seem to play a part in attraction. In 1995, Claus Wedekind of the University of Bern in Switzerland asked a group of women to smell some unwashed T-shirts worn by different men. What he discovered was that women consistently preferred the smell of men whose immune systems were different from their own. This parallels what happens with rodents, who sniff pheromones to check out how disease-resistant their partners are. So it seems we are also at the mercy of our lover's pheromones, just like rats. How very romantic!

Stage III: The Conversation

What you talk about—and how you do it—can counteract even the most negative first impression.

Hopefully, you'll have a less obvious ice-breaker than Neil, a graphic artist from Sydney: "I met my girlfriend over drinks. Luckily, we had an instant conversation starter: I had lost a wager, and had to wear my Speedo down to the bar. Unfortunately, the conversation starter was the fact that I was wearing a flippin' Speedo. But we got to talking, and hit it off. As she likes to tell people, at least she knew I was interested." Good on ya, mate!

Here are some more deliberate ways you can kick off a conversation.

Employ her master's voice: Breathe deeply and use your lower registers when you speak. According to a recent study by Scottish researchers, the most attractive women prefer deep-voiced men. This probably has something to do with the correlation between high testosterone levels (a

HOW TO TELL IF SHE'S INTO YOU

Is she interested, or just polite? Marianne Legato, MD, New York–based author of *Why Men Never Remember and Women Never Forget*, suggests that the rules of flirtation are ones that supersede geography: "Women who are interested in a man tend to use body language to telegraph their interest. She'll touch her hair and other parts of her body, nod and smile more than usual, and use lots of gestures while she speaks. She'll also lean in toward you, and will often use a light touch on the arm or shoulder to make a point."

There are some other clues, as well. If she's feeling stimulated by you (not just sexually), her pupils will dilate. That's because her body is programmed to want to see more of whatever's exciting her, so her brain tells her irises to let in more light. Bonus: As the inkiness spreads, she'll start looking better to you, too. Research shows that men rate women with larger pupils as more attractive.

When a woman's willing, she'll give you the signal long before the foreplay begins. "If she's interested in sex, then she'll avoid personal stories that are not sexy," say *New York* magazine sex columnists Em and Lo, authors of *Rec Sex*. "And she might be open to talking about some of her more intimate encounters."

---

sign of superior strength and bedroom chops) and a deep voice. Breathe from your diaphragm, the big muscle along the bottom of your rib cage, not from your throat—especially if your voice tends toward the Peewee when you're nervous. And remember that speaking softly can encourage her to move closer to you to hear what you're saying.

Have something to talk about. In the Kama Sutra's section about preparing yourself for love, Vatsyayana also recommends that you be well-educated. He advises, for instance, that young men learn about music and astronomy so that they have something impressive to discuss when they meet a woman.

Good advice, centuries later. The modern equivalent might be keeping up with current events—or just who got kicked off *American Idol* last night—but it's good advice to keep in mind a host of topics that aren't littered with landmines (avoid religion, politics, sex) for your first foray into conversation with her.

Make eye contact. It can be a little nerve-wracking to hold eye contact when you've just met someone. Men especially find it difficult. Why? "Men tend to talk to each other at angles to avoid confrontation," says Dr. Fisher. A direct gaze seems too much like a challenge. "But women face each other head-on and maintain eye contact." Hold her gaze, and listen closely to what she's saying.

If you have to break that contact—when a friend butts in, or to refresh your drinks—acknowledge the break as you would a spoken interruption.

Ditch the class clown impression. Women love a man with a good sense of humor, and in truth, a deft comedic touch is one of the most powerful weapons in your arsenal during this initial contact. But that doesn't mean telling jokes. "Funny is good—funny is great! But I don't like to feel like he's doing a stand-up routine if he's flirting with me. It's too vain and too much like a performance," says Ana from Puerto Rico.

And if you're trying to make the whole room laugh, all the attention is on you. Narrow your focus, so that you're just trying to make *her* laugh. She'll know she's the center of your attention.

Focus on the positive. "On a first date, you should have a selective memory," Paddison says. "Remember only what's great about your personality, your job, your finances, and your family." If there's a lull in conversation, compliment her choice of cocktail or the venue you're in.

And make sure your expressions and the tone of your voice reflect the passion you feel, says La Ruina. "Expressed emotions generate an emotional response."

Don't be goal-oriented. Of course, everything in American society tells us that winners set their eyes on the prize and then do whatever they have to do to obtain it. But that may not be the best route to take during a first encounter. Why? It's hard on her, and it's hard on you.

You know how it feels when you're on a first date and suddenly she starts asking if your parents are together and how many kids you want when you settle down? That's the way it feels to her when you start thinking about how you're going to get her number and what it's going to take to see her outfit fall to your bedroom floor.

La Ruina says women can sense desperation, and they don't like it. And he points out that relaxing is a confidence booster for you, too. If you can stop being so goal-oriented, you'll find that you no longer have to worry about whether she's single or getting out of a bad relationship or the kind of girl who's going to boil your bunny or tell her friends what a joke you are in bed or demand an engagement ring before you're ready to give her one. . . . Suddenly, it's just a conversation again. There—isn't that better?

SEDUCTION DON'TS

At *Men's Health,* we like to keep it positive, so we're mostly about the do's. But every once in a while, we've got to protect you from yourself. Here's what *not* to do if you're hoping to win her heart. In a phrase: Try hard, but not too hard, grasshopper.

Don't douse yourself in cologne. Don't spray it directly on your clothes. And please, please, for the love of God, don't anoint your private parts with it. "Scent should be subtle," says Veronique, who works for a major French perfumer. "Only you and someone very close to you should be able to pick it up."

For most women, the best thing you can smell like is *you*—or the cleanest possible version thereof. If a T-shirt requires a sniff-test, it's a no. And if it requires a second opinion, you shouldn't even wear it to the gym.

Don't check your Blackberry or phone. It doesn't make you look important, it makes you look like a jerk. "In Italy, we are on our phones all the time—but of course not when you are talking to a beautiful woman!" says Gianni, a Venetian doctor.

Don't stare at her boobs. You would think that you wouldn't need to be told again. But anytime *Men's Health* gets a room full of women together, they complain about it, so somebody out there is still doing it. Perhaps it's simply that your supposedly surreptitious glance isn't good enough—she catches you in the act every time. And the ladies' complaints are backed by real, live research: A study done at the University of Mannheim in Germany showed that men look at women's and men's chests more often than women look at either sex's chests.

Engage her. When the conversation is young, yes-or-no questions can sound the death knell. If possible, incorporate a compliment into an open-ended question: "That's such an interesting take on fish—what do you think about all these Brazilian super-foods I've been reading so much about?"

Whenever possible, create a bond: "I don't like sea urchin either. For you, is it the texture or the taste?" For an added bonus, talk at the same pace she does, and she'll consider you intelligent, kind, confident, and ambitious, according to a University of Maryland study.

Don't blab. "When people are nervous, they often overcompensate by running off at the mouth," Paddison notes. "The golden rule is to talk less and listen more. If you're interested, you'll be interesting."

Don't talk yourself up too much—but don't sell yourself short, either. She is listening for clues about you, and you better believe that even though she already clocked the Rolex on your arm, she'll be turned off if you name- or brand-drop. You can communicate your financial or personal successes, as long as the references you make to them are oblique, not obnoxious.

Stage IV: Kicking It Up a Notch

Congratulations. The conversation is going well, and you've engaged her. But you haven't sealed the deal until you've taken it to another level— whether that means securing a phone number, stealing a kiss, or even inviting her back to your place. (For more information on mastering the art of the one-night stand, you'll want to check out Chapter 3.)

As you get more comfortable with her, beware of the dreaded fizzle. You know what we're talking about: Everything seems to be going along swimmingly, and then there's a lull in the conversation, and suddenly all the sexual tension between the two of you dissipates into thin air. Before you know it, her head is swiveling around looking for an excuse to disentangle herself from the conversation.

The key to avoiding this is to keep increasing the sexual tension instead of letting it slacken. Here's some advice for "escalating," as the playahs say. . . .

Don't get too comfortable. La Ruina warns against falling into what he calls "the friend trap." You know, the one where she calls you in the middle of the night to sob about the other guy who did her and then did her wrong.

The easiest way to keep from getting stuck in this trap is to avoid it altogether. "If you try to sneak in with a woman by being friends," says Daily, "you'll project that, and you'll end up as friends." So don't talk to her about her boyfriend problems—you're not her girlfriend. Don't ask her about the weather, or if she's seen the blockbuster movie of the week. She's already had that conversation with her manicurist.

"Sexual tension is created from conversation which challenges her, teases her, or makes her feel emotions. Asking her to prove herself to you frames you as 'the chooser' and gets her trying to win your approval," says

La Ruina. Teasing is a great way to escalate sexually. How will you know you're on the right track, and not just reminding her of her pesky little brother? "Anytime she is playfully hitting you and laughing at the same time is excellent," La Ruina says.

He also suggests making her talk about her passions, things she desires, and times when she has been in love. It's emotional conversation, and you want her to feel emotionally engaged when she's talking to you.

Simon says, redux . . . Remember how we told you to mirror her body language from across the room? Same thing applies when you're up close and personal. Let her set the tone, and follow it.

A gentle touch can be very effective in communicating attraction, and in fact, "successful seducers initiate contact fairly early in a nonthreatening way," says Daily. But again—this is a delicate dance; it's best to let her make the first move. If she's laid her hand on your arm or brushed flirtatiously against your shoulder, then reciprocate in kind. Touch her lower back as you go through a doorway, let your hand brush hers as you pass her a glass. We'd especially like to recommend a gentle touch on the inner forearm, a highly erogenous (and largely overlooked) area that's often right out in the open.

Take touch to the next level. La Ruina says that there are three categories of touching. The first is the way a friend might touch her—a gentle touch on the arm while talking, for instance, or a hug and kiss on the cheek upon meeting. There's nothing wrong with this kind of touch, of

---

NERVOUS?

Traditional Chinese medicine holds that there are points throughout the body that affect your energy flow. The idea that stimulating these points can bring relief for a whole host of problems is the theory behind acupuncture. Acupuncture's little sister, acupressure, is a quicker fix, and convenient for the needle-phobic. We particularly like this "treatment" for nerves:

Apply pressure between the tendons on the underside of the forearm, about two thumb-widths down from the wrist. Hold pressure for 1 minute. Release.

Now breathe from your belly, look deeply into her eyes, and ask for her number.

---

course, but if it's the only kind you're engaged in, you're not likely to break your way out of the "friend" box anytime soon.

The next category of touch, a slight escalation, is playful touching. This category includes things like tickling her, poking her, play-fighting or wrestling, picking her up, and bumping her as you walk. Touching her this way is safe but still allows for some sexual tension between the two of you. It is a good start and can even lead directly to a more sexual type of touch like a kiss.

The next category is explicitly sexual. These are ways of touching her that no one but lovers use with one another. It includes things like holding her hand, putting your arm around her, and touching her hair. You can use the excuse of looking at her rings, bracelets, or nails if you need to. The goal, of course, is to advance to sexual touching as soon as you possibly can without making her uncomfortable, leaving the friend trap behind you in the dust.

You can do the same thing with eye contact as you do with touch. It's a distinction that you may not have made in the past, but the categories are the same. Think about it: There are the ways you look at your friends, the various ways you look at someone you're teasing and flirting with, and then the ways you look at someone you're sleeping with. And while there's some gray area in the first two—you might flirt harmlessly with the lady at the dry cleaner although she hasn't seen her ankles since the '80s—there's none at all in the last. You do not stare searchingly into your buddy's eyes at halftime.

Looking at her more often and more intensely is a way to affect the dynamic between the two of you. "Ultimately, you leave pauses where you're just looking at each other," counsels La Ruina. And if she's on board, she's going to do some escalating of her own, perhaps by breaking your gaze, looking away, and looking right back at you—a way of confirming your interest. Or she may simply look back in a seductive way.

When that kind of excruciating tension exists, it's a good idea to turn the vibe totally sexual so that there's no turning back. "When I've met a girl I think I might like to kiss, I think about kissing her while we're talking. I imagine what her lips will feel like, how she'll smell, what she'll taste like, the feel of her tongue. I look at her lips, then back at her eyes. I look at her lips and lick my own. Sure enough, in a little while, we're kissing! It works every time," brags Sandor, a security expert in Croatia.

Kissing her in the middle of the date is what will deliver a thrill straight to the base of her spine. "Italian boys do not wait for the last minute to kiss a girl," says Emmanuele A. Jannini, MD, professor of endocrinology and medical sexology in the department of experimental medicine at the University of L'Aquila. It's risky, yes, but the payoff is worth it. (See page 30 for ways to guarantee she feels it all the way down to her toes.)

Kissing her in the middle of the date will deliver a thrill straight to the base of her spine.

If you're holding her hand and you're looking silently into one another's eyes, that's a good time to say something like, "I really want to see you again in a quieter place where we can talk. Will you have dinner with me?" Or lean in for a kiss. Or ask her back to your place for a drink. Whatever you do, take action—or risk being left on the curb, another fatality of the dreaded fizzle.

Stage V: Closing the Deal

Don't let her be the one that got away. Before the party breaks up, make sure you get digits.

Ask for her number. Clarify what you'd like: "I'd like to call you for dinner." Avoid noncommittal stuff like "I'd like to hang out sometime." Even though the point of a first date is to figure out whether or not you like someone, it's better to give her the impression that you know already.

Put the number into your phone or borrow a pen, write it down somewhere, and put it somewhere safe. A poll on our Web site showed that a surprising number of guys—15 percent—didn't call after a one-night stand *because they'd actually lost the number.*

Call, don't e-mail. It's tempting, isn't it? You can write and rewrite the message to be sure you're saying exactly what you want to say, and in the right tone, whereas talking on the phone is like walking a tightrope without a net. But certain communications should not take place electronically, and asking someone out for the first time is one of them.

If e-mailing was the reason you exchanged contact info ("I'll send you that article"), then call, ask her out for the date, and *then* e-mail her the *New York Times* feature on Labradoodles.

When do you call? The dreaded question. The jury remains out on this, despite decades of expert opinions piling up on the subject. "I think waiting 2 days to call is so juvenile! We met, there was a connection—why pretend anything else?" says Bella from France. Ana from Brazil disagrees. "I don't like it when a man calls the day after I've met him. It seems desperate and aggressive to me."

Not much help, right? The best advice we can give you is to play it by ear. If there was a genuine connection between you, she seemed interested, and you want to talk to her again right away, go ahead and pick up the phone. If you feel that you need a cooling-off period—either because you think that when you first met you were sweating her a little harder than was entirely necessary, or because you suspect that she's the kind of person who will think you're a desperate loser if you call immediately—then wait.

We don't really advise waiting more than 2 days, unless it's part of a grander strategy: "If you wait for more than 2 days to call, without a good excuse, I'm going to think I was pretty low priority for you," says Zofia from Poland.

Remember the scene in *Swingers* where Jon Favreau goes home and leaves a series of long elaborate messages on the machine of a girl who just gave him her number? Don't do that. Even if you call the next day, wait at least until the afternoon to do it.

Say the right thing when you call. Identify yourself and your purpose fairly quickly: "This is John; we met at Alex's party the other night. I really enjoyed our conversation and would like to see you again."

You must have a plan. Again, do not ask her if she wants to hang out sometime. Instead, ask her if she wants to go to sample the cocktails you were telling her about at the Pegu Club on Thursday evening after work. If not Thursday, then Saturday? If she can't do either one and fails to parry with "Sorry, it's a little crazy with the holidays—what about next Tuesday?" then ask her if she'd like to take your number and call you when her schedule frees up.

Don't sit by the phone waiting; it's pretty much a given that she won't call. But there's always this story, from Tamsin in Wales: "I was in an on-again phase with my ex when I met my husband; I gave him my number but blew him off when he called because I thought it was going to work out with my other guy. When that relationship was finally over for good, I found his number, took a chance, and called. He was single, we met for drinks, and the rest is history!"

If you don't get her, you're going to get her voicemail. And the pitfalls of the voicemail box are legion. If that Jon Favreau example didn't chill your blood, then remember George trying to break into a girl's house to retrieve an answering machine tape on *Seinfeld*. "I can't believe I'm telling you this, but ever since I left a long dumb message on a girl's voicemail and she never called back, I write down what I'm going to say before I call," confesses Tom, an Australian chef.

If you're not smooth on your feet—and even the best of us can trip over our tongues when we're leaving a first message for someone we sort of liked—jot down a few notes so you're working within a framework. "I met this girl and really, really liked her—just head over heels right away. I took her number, called the next day, left a great message, and then—nothing. I was depressed sick about it. We'd had such great chemistry, such a great conversation—what went wrong?" says Aurelio, an advertising executive in Brazil. "Three weeks later, I see her again at the same bar, and as I'm gearing up to be really cold, she runs over and kisses me square on the lips—our first kiss. She hadn't called because *I hadn't left my number on her machine* and she had no way to get in touch." (He married her, by the way.)

Former *Men's Health* relationship editor Lisa Jones reminds you that every voicemail message should contain these crucial words: "Sorry I missed you. Give me a call back. Otherwise, I'll try you again, and we can make plans." This allows you to call back without wondering whether she got your message. And if you call twice and get no call back, it's game over. Further attempts to get in touch—calling, e-mailing, or sending flowers—might work in romantic movies. In real life, that leads to restraining orders.

Call to confirm. "Great. So I'll give you a call on Friday and we can figure out what time is good/where to meet." Jones is adamant about observing what she calls "the 4:00 p.m. deadline." Don't make her sit around all afternoon worrying about whether she's going to get stood up—or worse, eating Chinese food alone in her apartment while her friends all go to a movie she's already seen because they thought she had a date. "Call between noon and four."

Seal the Deal—With a Kiss

Once you know when and where you're going to see her again, give her something that lets her know you'll be looking forward to that next meeting: a good-night kiss. After all, a kiss is a preview of coming attractions. "The way you kiss says a lot about how you make love," says Ava Cadell, PhD, a Hungarian-born, British-raised expert who has traveled and taught widely throughout the world. "I call kissing 'facial intercourse.'"

Paddison agrees. First, he says, "you're finding out whether this person has rhythm. If her kissing is all over the shop, then it's an early sign that you're going to have a problem when there's more involved. That's why women intuitively panic when they discover a guy can't kiss."

But it's not so much a lack of instant kissing compatibility that Paddison warns against as *the lack of the ability to establish it.* "You may have very different kissing styles, but your compatibility should improve dramatically in the first half-dozen times you kiss. If it doesn't, that means you've been unable to create at least a common kissing pattern between the two of you, and that bodes badly indeed for what's to come."

Since many different people like to kiss many different ways, the goal is to find middle ground between you and your kissee. Sarah Hedley, British expert and author of *Sex by Numbers*, recommends that you each take a turn demonstrating your perfect kiss on one another. The rule is that while your partner kisses you, you have to remain completely passive—taking mental notes all the while. "That way you can learn exactly what sort of kiss turns your lover on," Hedley says.

"A good kiss," says Cherie Byrd, who runs the Kissing School in Seattle and is the author of *Kissing School: Seven Lessons of Life, Lips, and Lifeforce*, "is one that you feel all the way through your body. Too often, we concentrate our sexual energy into one tiny spot, where we can control it, and when the energy gets too much for the small space we've allotted, it feels like too much and we stop." But great sex—and therefore great kissing, Byrd believes—is about flow and letting things get a little bit out of control. "You have to be willing to surrender to the other person, and to stay in the moment." See "Five-Minute Kissing School" on the next page for her other tips.

As you'll see, the only hard-and-fast rule of kissing is that there are no rules at all. So here are contradictions from around the world to help you drive her wild with lust.

Ask. "My first kiss with my husband was the best one of my life. He leaned in, took my face in his hands, looked me deeply in the eyes, and

FIVE-MINUTE KISSING SCHOOL

"Most people get—and give—theoretical kisses," says Cherie Byrd, who, at her Kissing School in Seattle, uses Tantric principles to teach couples to connect on a deeper level through kissing. "They get and give a kiss in the abstract. No wonder we don't like kissing and don't want to do it more. It's like showing up for a banquet and being given a sandwich instead."

Byrd's wildly popular kissing workshops take a whole day. But she agreed to give us some highlights, if not specific instructions. "The best kisses are the ones that make you swoon, that curl your toes and have an effect on your soul." But, she says, there's no mechanical advice she can give to get you there. "It's all about the energy behind the kiss."

And this is how becoming a better kisser can help you everywhere in your life, not just in the bedroom. Tantra, after all, isn't about better orgasms, it's about energy mastery, and bringing passion to whatever you do. Kissing is a great way to marshal and share your life force. So pucker up!

Gather your energies. We have to reconnect with our inner selves before we connect with someone else. "You have to recognize your own electricity and desire, and then bring that energy into the kiss."

Byrd's advice is sex-specific: *She* should do something "ecstatic," something that makes her feel a rush of joy—a yoga class, a wonderful bath—while *you* do something, like meditation or a workout, to help focus your scattered or distracted energy.

Byrd points out that "we do this naturally when we get ready for a date. She's dancing around her room to a favorite song, trying out clothes, putting on lipstick. He's making reservations, finding his keys, getting in the car to pick her up."

Relax. The next step is to open up to one another, and the best way to do that is by relaxing with one another. Byrd says you can do this by bringing mindfulness to any activity you do together, whether that's sharing a walk or making a meal. "Let yourself feel what you're feeling!" Byrd says. And then share it: Focus in on something you really like about the other person and tell them about it.

Get tender with it. "We mistake tenderness for wimpiness, when in fact it is a very deep, penetrative way of being with one another," Byrd says.

Engage your entire body. Lean into one another, and make the points of contact between your body alive, not just dead weight. Use your hands to touch her face, her body, her hair—make your whole body part of the connection.

asked if he had my permission to kiss me. I would have said yes to his proposal right then and there!" says Gloria, a dancer from Barcelona.

Or don't ask. "I hate it when a guy asks me if it's okay to kiss me. It totally breaks the mood. We've had dinner and wine and we've flirted all night, and now we're standing in front of my house—you need an invitation too?" says Anna from Ukraine.

Start slow. Brush her lips gently with your own. "I like to be kissed gently at first, perhaps biting my lips and butterfly kissing me lightly, pulling back and looking at me before running his tongue around the entrance and into my mouth," says Lizzie, who works for a London public relations firm.

Start fast. Lots of women describe their best kiss as the time he slammed her up against a wall, mashed his lips against hers, and didn't let her breathe for a full 5 minutes. This might seem to contradict earlier advice (see "Start slow" above), but in fact, these things are not mutually exclusive—*even within a single kiss.* Head spinning? Hey, if it was easy, you wouldn't need a book.

Vary the rhythm. Alternate soft, tender kisses with more powerful ones, says Caroline Hurry, a sex writer in South Africa. "For women, a combination of boldness and tenderness is crucial."

Midori, too, recommends different intensities, from barely there to very much there. She suggests that you avoid what she calls the kissing equivalent of the poke and wiggle, simply moving your tongue in and out of her mouth. "Instead of using your tongue like a dart, try different motions and amounts of pressure," concurs William Cane, American author of *The Art of Kissing.*

Keep it steady. "There is something so beautiful about a long, deep kiss where neither of us moves—the only thing exchanged between us is our breath," says Paula, a social worker in Ireland.

Keep your tongue in your mouth. Kiss her mouth, communicating your lust as passionately as you can—but leave your tongue out of it. Instead, devote all your attention to her lips, and your lips, and the way those lips feel pressed together. Inhale deeply through your nose, drinking in the smell of her. Then kiss her whole face and the surrounding environs with your closed lips, as passionately as you kissed her mouth. Return periodically to her lips en route to her chin, her cheekbones, her eyelids, her hairline, the tip of her nose, behind her ear, and the swell of her throat.

KAMA SUTRA KISSES

There are a total of 40 kisses enumerated in this ancient Indian sex manual, and 17 in the chapter devoted to the subject. Here are some of our favorites.

The Turned Kiss: When you turn her face up to yours, often by gently holding her chin.

The Pressed Kiss: When the lower lips are pressed together forcefully.

The Clasping Kiss: When either partner takes both of their partner's lips between their own. The Kama Sutra recommends that you be clean-shaven. Both of you, we'd guess.

The Fighting of the Tongue: When one partner touches their partner's teeth, tongue, or the top of the mouth during the Clasping Kiss.

Love bites also play a large role in the kissing sections of the Kama Sutra; eight specific types are mentioned. In fact, it's a little surprising to see how rough the recommendations get.

It was considered a sign of real skill to leave a lasting mark without breaking the skin. "It was a time when women wore very little, and it was a trend to suck a pattern of bruises around their breasts, a memento of their lovemaking," says Julianne Balmain, San Francisco–based coauthor of *The Kama Sutra Deck: 50 Ways to Love Your Lover*. The ancient Indians knew that, as a little ache in your groin from too much love the night before can be a very sexy feeling the next day, the bruises left by aggressive kisses can act as a titillating souvenir of the time you've spent together.

And the biting in the Kama Sutra is nothing compared to the Trobriand Islanders of the South Pacific who, according to Don Voorhees in his highly entertaining book of sex trivia, *Quickies*, bite off their partner's eyebrows and eyelashes during sex, as well as scratch and bite, often leaving permanent scars.

Use your tongue. Stiffen your tongue slightly, and trace her lips with it. Stay on her lips, or she'll just feel like you're licking her face. Do this as delicately as you possibly can. Don't forget to spend a little time on the little valley right above her upper lip. Touch the roof of her mouth—but without making her feel like you're trying to get her to swallow your tongue. For best results, stay toward the front of her mouth.

Suck. Slowly (so she doesn't feel like she's got what Midori calls "the face-sucker from *Alien* attached to her head") use suction to *gently* draw her upper lip into your own mouth. Maintaining suction, tease her lip with your tongue.

"The Kama Sutra says that if a man stimulates his partner's upper lip, nibbling and lightly sucking on it, while she nibbles on his lower lip, both partners will be swept away on waves of pleasure," says Mabel Iam, an Argentinian psychotherapist, television host, and author of *Sex and the Perfect Lover*. "The Japanese massage technique known as Shiatsu also suggests that massaging a woman's upper lip, either with the fingertips or the tongue, can unleash her sexual energy and stimulate sexual desire."

It has even been suggested that there is a pathway in the nervous system directly connecting the upper lip to the clitoris. A one-stop shop, if you will.

Call for backup. Kissing may technically be something done with your lips, but it can be very erotic to trace your lover's body with your nose (the Chinese call this sniff-kissing), or to touch her face using only your eyelashes.

Dr. Cadell recommends that you sit in "yab yum" position, facing your lover with her legs over and around your body. "Moisten each other's eyebrows and then lean into each other with brows touching. Feel the energy flow from one to the other, uniting the two of you into a higher level of consciousness."

Lead. "I love it when my boyfriend keeps firm pressure on the back of my head and dominates the kiss. So feral!" says Luisa from Peru.

Follow. Back off periodically to tease her, forcing her to move in aggressively to recapture your lost kiss.

Inhale. Make her feel like you're drinking in the very essence of her.

Exhale. Iam says that if you make your mouth taste sweet, she'll never forget it. "Eat chocolates, a caramel, a mint, or fresh strawberries—whatever flavor you think she'd like—before you kiss her."

Touch her. Run your fingers along her cheek, down her neck. Play with the soft hairs at the nape of her neck. "Try tugging on her hair while you kiss her, exhaling near her ear, or just gently kissing her eyelids," Hurry advises.

Don't touch her. A kiss in which your lips are absolutely the only point of connection between the two of you brings incredible focus and connection to the kiss itself. No hands, no hips grinding into hers, no arms wrapped around one another's necks—just two pairs of lips doing a very sexy dance. Try it; see how long you last.

A KISS BY ANY OTHER NAME

The English language is unusual in that the word *kiss* stands for both the peck you drop on Aunt Matilda on Thanksgiving and the tongue-dueling you engage in with your beloved.

Latin (the language spoken by the ancient Romans in the land we now call Italy, where they still know their way around a kiss) recognized three distinct types of kiss: the affectionate *oscula* (Aunt Matilda), the loving *basia* ("Hi, honey, I'm home"), and the knee-trembling *suavia* ("Take me now!").

In the 17th century, the German scholar Martin von Kempe wrote *Polyhistoricum de Osculis*, a 1,040-page encyclopedia of kissing that outlined more than 20 different kinds of kisses, including the one conferred by one academic on another during a graduation ceremony, as well as the proper way to kiss the Pope's foot. And modern German trumps everybody, with 30 separate words to describe different kinds of kisses, including kisses to make up for ones previously omitted, and a word to describe a kiss that has not yet been named.

We may have only one word for it—but we certainly benefit from the expertise around the world. Here are some of our favorites.

French kiss: A deep kiss that involves the touching of one's tongue to one's lover's lips or tongue. Americans began calling this style of kissing "French" in the 1930s because the French were considered to be hedonistic, sex-obsessed, and depraved, God bless 'em.

The French kiss is also called *maraichinage*, after the Maraichin people of Brittany, who are believed to have invented a kiss that lasted for several hours, as a form of population control. (History is silent on how that worked out.) Ironically, the French now refer to this type of kissing as "Hollywood" kissing, presumably because it's the way they kiss in American movies, which jibes with the French view of Americans as lacking in the subtlety department and unable to differentiate the sexual from the sensual.

Snogging: What the British call French kissing. As in, "Fancy a snog, luv?"

Eskimo kiss: Rubbing noses. In point of fact, Europeans saw the Inuits smelling one another's cheeks. The Maori of New Zealand also greet each other by pressing their noses together.

Australian kiss: Cunnilingus—a French kiss "down under."

Now What?

Even after you've caught her and kissed her, a new romance can fizzle fast if it's not carefully tended. Here's how to make sure the spark lasts past that first passion-packed week.

Keep yourself on her "to do" list. Call within 48 hours of a date to say you had a good time and to ask her out again. There's a big exception to this rule: If you slept together (or even just got close), a next-day call is an absolute must. This is non-negotiable.

Don't let a lost weekend together be followed by a week of radio silence. "There's a momentum to the courtship process, and it will take off at a pretty high velocity," says Ian Kerner, PhD, a sex therapist and the author of *D.S.I.: Date Scene Investigation.* "Even if you don't see each other often at first, stay on her radar."

Rather than swamping her with daily phone calls, strike up e-mail banter or check in with text messages—and let her set the pace. "Doubling up on unreturned calls or e-mails just seems desperate," says Dr. Kerner.

Do what you say you're going to do. In general, tell her when you're going to call, and call her. And don't be late to meet her, or cancel dates (except in the most dire of circumstances). Save the teasing and surprises for the bedroom, where she'll really enjoy them. Outside of bed, reliability counts for a great deal in the relations between the sexes—even if you're not looking for a serious relationship (and be honest about that up front if you're not), it goes toward your dating karma.

Don't dwell. You're going to have to have the much-hated conversation about the ex-girlfriend; keep it short and sweet. Have a 2-minute-long summary of your former relationship at the ready (and no, "we broke up because she's a frigid psychopath" isn't what we're talking about).

Don't get into a heavy-duty analysis of what went wrong or give her more detail than she needs, even if she presses. "Bemoaning a relationship that soured shows you're still fixated on that failure," says Lisa Clampitt, founder of the Matchmaking Institute in New York. "And boasting about a great past relationship can seem like an attempt to pump up your own self-image." It's best to keep both of you squarely focused on the present.

The "what went wrong" conversation can be a good way to telegraph your intentions to your new partner, though. "We wanted different things; I'm pretty focused on getting my career in order right now," sends a very clear signal about what she can expect from you, while "We had a lot of fun together, but I didn't see it working out long-term," says something else entirely. We promise she's listening and reading between the lines.

Take it slow. The temptation to jump into a relationship whole-hog can sometimes be overwhelming, especially if it's going well. But unhealthy codependencies are established early on. "A relationship is about extending our personal boundaries, but it should be a gradual process," Dr. Kerner says.

So let her keep a toothbrush at your house if she wants to. But encourage her to make her own plans and keep her own friends—and do the same yourself. "It's easy to get sucked in at the beginning, with the rush of a fresh start. But the sooner you depend on each other for everything, the faster the relationship can burn out," says Clampitt.

HOW WILL YOU KNOW IT'S THE REAL THING?

One sign is when you stop looking at other women. It's true: Italian researchers looked at the hormone levels of a small group of women in love. The women's testosterone levels were higher than usual, making them more aggressive and increasing their sex drives. The men, on the other hand, had lower levels of testosterone, making them less aggressive and less libidinous. So if you notice that your eye has stopped roving and the desire to collect digits has lessened significantly, it may be a sign that the lady you're with is "the one."

Or you can take her for ice cream. Alan Hirsch, MD, a neurologist and director of the Smell and Taste Treatment and Research Foundation in Chicago, conducted a study of 720 people, ages 24 to 59, in which he correlated personality tests, their favorite ice-cream flavors, their partners' favorite ice creams, and relationship status. Coffee-ice-cream lovers—found to be dramatic, seductive, flirtatious—are most romantically compatible with strawberry fans. Vanilla gals (emotionally expressive and fond of PDA) melt best with rocky-road guys. And mint-chocolate-chip fans are meant for each other, the freaks.

Or you may just start to act crazy. British neurobiologists discovered that when research subjects looked at a picture of someone they had recently fallen in love with, one of the parts of the brain that was activated had a lot of receptors for dopamine—the feel-good hormone. That's why falling in love feels so damn good. It's also why you act like such an idiot when it happens. Dopamine is strongly associated with addiction; in fact, this British study found that the brains of people "on" love looked very much like the brains of people on euphoria-inducing drugs.

CHAPTER 3

SERVE THE WORLD'S BEST NIGHTCAPS

Master the Art of the One-Night Stand—And Make Any First Night Together Memorable

If you've ever been in Lisbon on a Friday or Saturday night, you're probably not surprised by our survey finding that Portuguese men have the most one-night stands. The nightlife in the capital and throughout much of the country is legendary. "In Portugal, any time and place is good for sex," says Mariagrazia Marini, PhD, a clinical psychologist in that country.

"It's much easier to come across a one-night stand if you're going to bars and clubs and staying out all night," adds Marini, "especially in the summer, when people socialize under the moonlight near the sea. All these things, combined with alcohol, can certainly lower people's inhibitions."

But even if you don't live in Portugal, there's a lot you can do to boost your odds of finding a one-night wonder woman. And whether the magic happens the very first

QUICKIE STATS

Percentage of men who've had a one-night stand:

1. Portugal		81 percent
2. Brazil		76 percent
3. Australia		65 percent
4. Russia		64 percent
5. Spain		63 percent
United States		**61 percent**
World average		**58 percent**

Average age at which men had sex for the *very* first time:

1.	Brazil	16.85
2.	Portugal	17.60
3.	United Kingdom	17.64
4.	Tie between Russia and Mexico	17.66
5.	Netherlands	17.86
	United States	**18.11**
	World average	**18.29**

time you meet or later on, you'll find plenty in this chapter to help make your first night together one that neither of you will ever forget.

It Depends on Your Definition of Eternity...

The Brazilian poet Vinicius de Moraes is perhaps most famous for writing the poem that inspired the song "The Girl from Ipanema." But among his countrymen, this famous seducer (married a total of eight times!) is just as famous for summing up his nation's predilection for the one-night stand (Brazil came in second in our survey) with another line of poetry: "May love be eternal—while it lasts."

What's the attraction of disposable love? We asked some of our international friends.

"I can be much more uninhibited with someone I've just met and don't think I'll see again. The things we know about one another don't get in the way." —Alicia in Lisbon

"It's sex without all the emotions. Sometimes that's a good thing— no jealousy, no 'where were you last night,' no 'you were supposed to call.' But it can also feel a little cold, like 'Why did we do this?'— especially the morning after."—Felipe from Brazil

"No fuss, no muss. Just two grown-ups getting together for some fun." —Ian, an Englishman living in Bali

"In my experience, a girl who will go home with you right after meeting you is someone who is comfortable with herself, and who likes sex. My one-night stands have all been awesome in bed!" —Adam from Poland

"Why not? Sex is such a good way to get to know each other!" —Mariebelle in France

Where to Look

We've heard stories about fabulous nights of one-off love blossoming out of the most unlikely venues. Two that stick in our minds? "We had just stayed up all night checking a mutual friend into the hospital after a psychotic break." And this one: "I'd had a crush on him since we were teenagers; we finally got together at the wake for one of our high school teachers."

Not even mental hospitals and funeral homes are unsexy enough to dampen a powerful attraction, apparently—and yet, we feel that other venues lend themselves more organically to the crucial increased libido/decreased inhibition combination you're looking for. The places we mentioned in Chapter 1 as being good spots to meet women are still valid options.

Select a Target

If you're in the market for a one-night stand, who should you go after? The obvious answer is someone you're attracted to who seems to return the interest.

To better your odds:

A German study suggested that women in clubs wearing flimsy clothes were most likely to go home with a guy. And we were proud to vote that study the "dumbest of the year." But now we're not so sure. . . .

DON'T LOOK HERE

Work events can buzz with sexual tension, but few women are willing to taint their professional reputations just for a one-and-done. And that kind of belt-notching doesn't do much for you professionally. If you're going to give the office something to snicker about, at least make sure she's someone you might be interested in seeing again.

Family get-togethers are also generally out of the question. Even when she's not a blood relative, no girl thinks about sex when Uncle Nick's butt cracks a smile every time he reaches for a bocce ball. And you think it's annoying now when the cabal attacks you in the kitchen, demanding to know when you're going to tie the knot and give them a baby to play with? Just wait until they're updating you on the activities of a woman whose face you can no longer even remember.

RED-HOT TO TROT

Blondes have more fun, the saying goes. But when Hamburg sex researcher Dr. Werner Habermehl looked at women's sex lives to see if there was a correlation with their hair color, the conventional wisdom was not borne out. In fact, fiery, passionate *redheads* had sex more often than the average—and with more partners.

He added that women who dyed their hair red from another color were signaling they were looking for a partner: "Even women in a fixed relationship are letting their partners know they are unhappy if they dye their hair red. They are saying that they are looking for something better."

So look for a carrot top. But hurry! A recent study by the Oxford Hair Foundation predicts that redheads will be extinct by 2100; just 4 percent of the population carries the recessive gene for red hair, which means it's becoming less common with every generation.

"A woman who's dressed to thrill is *less* likely to go home with you," says Emily Dubberley, a British expert and author of *Brief Encounters: The Woman's Guide to Casual Sex*. "You don't want to be the third of 25 guys to approach her that evening." Instead, go for the woman in the background. "She's with a friend or two, both of whom are brighter, brasher, and louder than she is," explains Dubberley.

On the other hand, a girl with naked Twister on her mind is usually trying to be noticed. Look for the women who are clearly out to have fun, who are laughing their butts off, who are dancing on the dirty side, and who keep glancing around the room to see who glances back. There's no guarantee that they're out to get laid, but there's no harm in introducing yourself and finding out.

Zeroing In for the Kill

Once you've selected a target, it's time to approach. Dr. Marini says that "the first few minutes are crucial for a successful seduction." Traditionally, the journey from "Hi, we're complete strangers" to "Have you seen my underwear?" takes place over a period of time, in which there are dinners, long walks, witty e-mail exchanges, and innuendo-filled phone conversations. In a one-night-only scenario, you have to go from zero to 60 in no time flat, which means creating a sexual mood right away. Here's how to do that.

Say hello. Stow your witty pickup line; you're better off with something straightforward, like "Hi, I'm Jeff."

Be the quarry. Though women generally like to be pursued, in the land of one-night stands, many like to play seductress—it's a way of turning the stereotypical one-nighter paradigm on its head. Let her have her fun, and show her what it feels like to "take advantage" of the man for a change. Linger in her vicinity, respond when she flirts. But, for the first few stages, let her take the lead.

Get up close and personal. "As you flirt, stand or sit within 6 inches of her. If she seems unruffled, move closer," says the *Men's Health's* Girl Next Door, Nicole Beland. "Eventually you want your thigh to be pressed against hers, whether you're standing or sitting." If she squirms, back off.

Double the entendre. Drop a sexually loaded comment or question and see how she reacts, says Clint Paddison, CEO of BlinkDating.com in Australia. "If it's done in the right

Show her what it feels like to "take advantage" of the man for a change.

way—and the right way is with a huge grin, and without being too intense or creepy—you can get away with almost anything." If she seems comfortable with the innuendo, laughing and joining in, then it's a signal to push it even further. "The more she plays along, the more likely she is to go home with you."

Move to a more intimate location. The game is on when she suggests—or agrees with your suggestion—that you go to another bar (that quieter one down the road). What if she's got a posse she won't separate from? Paddison advises you to take along the baggage. "We're all going back to our place to open up this amazing bottle of wine—come on, and we'll all have a drink." Pay for the cab ride, and continue to act as if everyone's one big happy family. Never ignore the pack, agrees Japanese-German sex educator Midori. "Men don't realize how much power the girlfriend veto has. Be friendly and open and charming to all of them."

Engage in PDA. Once you've reached the new, preferably dark and loungey locale, the first kiss is only a drink away. A make-out session is a prerequisite to a sexual proposition, says Beland. Pay attention to how intensely she's kissing back. You want the "I want to eat you alive, starting with your head" kind of kiss, not the sweet little "I'm not really a dirty girl" kind of kiss.

Showing Her Your Etchings

If all goes well, one of you will ask whether you should go someplace private. Maybe this happens the first time you meet, maybe not until the third date—or the third month. Whenever it happens, tread lightly, since big transitions beg many questions—specifically, "What the hell am I doing going home with you?"

"Coffee at my place?" is too stark a transition because it suggests the fun is ending. The time-honored solution is to have something, anything—a novelty cocktail recipe! a CD she absolutely has to hear! a new puppy!—that you absolutely must show her tonight.

Your approach can be either funny ("So, what do you say we go back to my place for milkshakes and Jenga?"); hesitant and humble ("I don't even know how to ask you this, but I would really love to be alone with you"); or straightforward and sweet ("Please, God, tell me that we can go home together"). Dial back the sleaze factor and, "chances are, if she's been shoving her tongue down your throat, any one of them could probably end up working," says Beland.

British psychologist and sex advisor Dr. Pam Spurr, author of *Naughty Tricks and Sexy Tips,* likes the idea of a drink back at your place: "I've got a great bottle of wine in the fridge at home—could we carry on this conversation back there?" This suggests a continuation of the fun. "It's honest, exciting, and the notion of a man with wine in the fridge is encouraging," says Spurr. "It conjures up an image of someone who might also have fresh towels in the bathroom and clean sheets on his bed."

The ladies do care about this domestic stuff. So much so that we've collected tips on making your nest "bird-ready," as the Brits would say. Check out "Making Your Apartment Nookie-Ready" on page 54.

Or suggest going to her place. She might be more comfortable, and you'll have the option of splitting before dawn.

Once you get there, play it smooth. Small talk is a buzz-kill; compli-

---

WHY SHE MAY BE RELUCTANT

A woman is far less likely to reach orgasm during a one-night stand than with a long-term partner. See Chapter 10 for tips on helping her defy the odds.

---

ments are okay. Tell her that she's beautiful and incredibly sexy, then let the kissing and undressing begin. You're both in this for the sex, so make it adventurous.

How can you make sure you don't get stuck at second base? One sure-fire strategy is to assume it's going to happen—and to communicate that by taking off all your clothes. Getting and being naked is an appealing show of vulnerability, and it's not quite as aggressive as taking all of her clothes off for her. Of course, this has uncomfortable backfire potential, but the payoff is generally worth the risk.

Or get her to do it. "In the middle of making out, whisper, 'Will you take my shirt off?'" say *New York* magazine sex columnists Em and Lo, authors of *Rec Sex*. "If she demurs, chances are she doesn't want you taking hers off yet, either." Green light? Spend at least 10 minutes focused on her upper half before grazing the button of her jeans. Give her the opportunity to move your hand, and even if she accelerates the undressing, keep things even in terms of how much skin is exposed. It should be "I'll show you mine if you show me yours" until you're both down to your skivvies.

And, gentlemen: You really need to know how to remove a bra. If you didn't practice with the one you found in the hamper in high school, buy a cheap one now and practice until you get it right. By "right," we mean one-handed.

The Main Event

Just do it. Use a condom, of course (see Chapter 4 for much more on this non-negotiable element), and no spanking, backdoor entry, kinky toys, or uncomfortable positions (unless she makes a specific request). Go with the standard stuff, plus plenty of enthusiastic squeezing, licking, sucking, stroking, rubbing, and moaning.

Let her be on top. Women who endorse casual sex are more likely to fantasize about dominating a man, reports a study in the *Journal of Sex Research*. Study participants completed a survey on sexual attitudes, then wrote out two fantasies. Researchers then checked the stories for themes of power. "Examples of dominance fantasies included pinning men to the bed, ordering them to perform a specific sex act, and initiating a younger man into sex," says study coauthor Megan Yost, PhD.

But don't break out the handcuffs just yet—you still have to read her

(continued on page 56)

MAKING YOUR APARTMENT NOOKIE-READY

What greets a woman when you open your door may determine whether or not she has sex with you. A report done by the Kinsey Institute found that the two biggest turn-offs for women were poor hygiene and a messy house. (This is true whether you're trying to score with her the first time or the 5,000th, by the way, so even you old married guys should keep reading.)

It's one thing for a buddy to block your game, but your house? It's time to get on top of this situation before you're looking at her retreating back. Don't panic—this isn't *Queer Eye,* and you don't have to ditch the foosball table. But you don't want her worried that there are human body parts in the freezer.

Tidy up. It might feel a little counterintuitive to clean just as you're on your way out, but it's a good habit to get into. You don't have to scrub like your mom is coming over. Take 5 minutes: Put dirty dishes into the sink, laundry into the hamper, magazines into a pile, and trash into the trash. You'll be surprised how much of a difference it makes. And even if you strike out, it'll be much less depressing to come home to a clean apartment.

If you have some disposable income, a housecleaner is a very good investment. You don't even need to hire one on a regular basis; many of the bigger services will do a cleaning one-night-stand every couple of months. Hiring someone who really knows what they're doing not only leads to a much cleaner house (for a week, anyway) but also makes it much easier to stay on top of things in the interim.

Crack the windows. You might not notice the sweatsock funk, but she will. And a little chill in the air when you get back might just drive her into your warm arms.

Make your bed. This whole thing is about your bed, right? So what are you doing with those filthy Snoopy sheets?

Invest in new ones. And we do mean invest. We're talking 100 percent cotton, with a thread count of about 300. Martha Stewart makes nice, tasteful ones (there's a surprise) that are available at Kmart; catalogs like Lands' End and L.L. Bean have simple, inexpensive choices as well. If it's winter and you live in a cold climate, flannel or those jersey ones made out of T-shirt material are cozy. Neutral colors are best.

No satin or anything novelty, although you may want to reserve a special set for playing with food or oil.

This is a situation where there can be absolutely no double-dipping. If you've had sex on your sheets, they need to be changed. *Do this before she comes over.* "If a guy is going out and getting laid a lot, he needs between 5 and 10 sets of sheets," says Japanese-German sex educator Midori.

The same thing goes for towels. We've all wondered how towels get dirty; after all, you only use them when you're clean! But they do, and when they do, they smell bad. Launder them once a week, at a minimum—and always have a fresh set that you can whip out at a moment's notice.

Hide stuff. Hide anything you don't want her to see. Your porn collection, old love letters, your trusty old teddy bear (actually, leave him on the bed). Trust us: She's looking for it, and she'll find it. And when she does, she's not going to believe it belongs to your roommate.

And it's time to accept that it's a fundamental aspect of human nature to investigate other people's medicine cabinets. If you don't want her sending your dog's antifungal cream out to the lab, then stash it somewhere she won't find it. And don't just stop at the disgusting, incriminating, or embarrassing, either. There's nothing wrong with using Rogaine, and your bald spot probably needs no formal introduction. It's just that it's sort of sad to see a can of the stuff in someone's bathroom.

Turn off the phone. It's not just polite, it's prudent. Let's review some possible scenarios.

Your mother leaves a long message about running into Bertie Hermanson (he's a doctor now) in the produce aisle at the grocery store.

Your ex-girlfriend calls in hysterics, wanting you back.

Your current girlfriend calls, furiously demanding to know where you are.

Your wingman calls to find out whether you ended up going home with the bangin' blonde.

Which of these do you want to intrude on your evening? If the answer is none of them, turn off the ringer and turn down the answering machine. For the same reasons, hold off on listening to your messages until she's gone.

Get the lighting right. Nothing dumps cold water on an evening like blinding her with overhead wattage. Dimmers are available at every hardware store, are easy to install (turn off the power at the box, please), and can make a world of difference.

Candles are also a nice touch; the ones contained in glass containers not only look good but are also less likely to set your house on fire while you're getting frisky. For overachievers: The world of scented candles has come a

(continued)

long way from the ones in your grandmother's house. You can now find them in more masculine scents such as hay, leather, tobacco, and wood smoke. Be prepared to drop some cash; the good ones are expensive.

Defluff. Lint rollers are useful for cleaning up pet hair. Speaking of pets, if you have one, let her know before she's having an asthma attack in the back of the ambulance. Seriously, here's Midori's cautionary tale: "I'm allergic to cats, but I can usually cope. One night, I meet a new lover and go home with him. I pet his cat, and then pet my own pussy—which swells to five times its normal size. Needless to say, sex was off."

The story has a happy ending—largely because Midori's lover was a gentleman who bathed her swollen bits and went to the drugstore for an antihistamine. But it's not a good idea to ambush an asthmatic with your Newfoundland.

Cue soundtrack. Keep a seduction-worthy CD in the stereo by your bed, or curate an appropriate playlist on your MP3 player so that you're ready to go when she is (see "Sexy World Music Mix" on page 136 for our suggestions). You don't want to have to search through your Weird Al collection to find the good stuff.

Music can help to make your room moanproof—an important consideration, especially if there's a roommate involved. "There's nothing quite like running into his roommate the morning after to make you feel like a whore,"

---

signals and talk, Yost advises. If a woman takes over the conversation and is willing to share her sexual fantasies with you, chances are you can safely broach the subject, she says. If she whispers something shocking in your ear, ask her if she'd like to take control—at least part of the time. Just sit back and enjoy the show.

Consider your exit strategy. Don't let this be uncomfortable. If you're at her place, ask her straight out whether she wants you to stay the night or make yourself scarce.

If you're at your house, make it very clear that you want her to stay. "Are you staying over?" is not an invite. "Will you spend the night? I can't wait to wake up with you" is.

The Morning After

The way you behave the next morning shouldn't depend on whether you think you've just met Ms. Right or need to flee the state. No matter what, laughs Allie, a bartender in Edinburgh. "It's like, 'Pass the orange juice—and which part in particular did you enjoy? The blowjob or the spanking?'" Allie laughs about it, because that's the kind of gal she is. Other girls will stop doing what they're doing, and that's not at all what you want.

Be the concierge. "I keep a basket of new, sealed products—including a toothbrush, razor, and a small bottle of contact lens solution—in the guest room; I tell the women I bring home to help themselves to the bathrobe and basket of amenities in the spare room. It really gets their attention and makes them feel relaxed," says James, a British banker.

If you've been out with the woman a few times already and seen the inside of her place, Midori suggests that you take note of what types of shampoos/conditioners/lotions she has in her own bathroom, and stock yours with the same. It's a very nice way to tell her that you've noticed—and a good way to make sure she feels comfortable sleeping over as much as you'd like her to.

Throw pillows. You know how you're always making fun of the women in your life for having small pillows on every horizontal surface? Well, we're about to shut you up. Imagine cushioning your one-night-stand's head with one as you start to get busy on the floor. Now imagine placing one under her hips. Time to stop laughing and go shopping? We thought so. Also, they look nice on the couch.

you're going to want to behave like a gentleman, for no other reason than it's good karma. "I was a total man-whore and have no regrets about anything, except that I wish I'd been a little more chivalrous the morning after," says Estevão, a music producer in Portugal.

The best policy? Tell the truth. Tell her you had a great time. If you know you want to see her again, tell her so, ask for her number, and tell her you'll call. "Call within 3 days of shagging someone to arrange to see them again—otherwise she'll think you're not interested," says Dubberley. The lovely Ms. Dubberley may be more low-maintenance than the woman

QUICKIE STATS

Percentage of men who claim to have slept with more women than they can count:

1. Honduras	22 percent
2. Columbia	21 percent
3. El Salvador	21 percent
4. Brazil	19 percent
5. Panama	18 percent
United States	**13 percent**

you've brought home, so to be safe, we recommend calling within 24 hours.

Don't say, "I'll call you," or, "Maybe we can see each other again," if it isn't true. If you harp on the expiration date—"Just so you know, this isn't anything serious"—your message will backfire. "No woman wants to be reminded that you're not in it to win it," says Logan Levkoff, PhD, a sex educator in New York City.

If you want to earn a spot on her booty-call list—or be the type of one-night-only entertainment she might recommend to a friend—send her a single e-mail the next day saying that last night was amazing and that she should feel free to contact you if she ever wants to "do it" again.

CHAPTER 4

BE THE WORLD'S BEST PROTECTED MAN
Fend Off STDs

Well, it might not be the sexiest topic in the world, but there's no getting around it, considering that your hot dog runs the risk of coming into contact with HIV, gonorrhea, chlamydia, syphilis, or genital herpes—and that it could cause unwanted pregnancies. Worldwide, fewer than 40 percent of guys discuss STDs or sexual histories before having sex with a new partner.

And that's just not good enough. AIDS diagnoses in the United States are rising again after declining for a decade. Worse, up to 15 percent of new HIV infections may be drug-resistant strains of the virus.

While you probably know all about the dangers associated with the big sexually transmitted diseases, even your garden-variety STDs can cause a whole world of

QUICKIE STATS

A study by the Centers for Disease Control and Prevention in Atlanta calculated how many years of healthy life Americans lose because of sexual diseases. Here's the annual breakdown, by disease.

Every year, sexual behavior accounts for . . .

Nearly 30,000 deaths (1.3 percent of deaths)
7,666,200 incidences of men contracting STDs
HIV: 557,021 healthy years lost (among US male population)
Hepatitis B: 279,624 years
Genital herpes: 7,014 years
Chlamydia: 2,026 years
Syphilis: 1,598 years
Gonorrhea: 1,352 years

trouble. For instance, did you know that chlamydia, long linked to female infertility, has been shown by a Swedish study to affect male fertility as well? And most men never even realize they have the disease because they have no symptoms, says study author Jan Olofsson, MD, PhD.

And yes, we have quite a bit to learn from much of the world on this count. US rates of premature death and disability attributed to sexual behaviors are *triple* those in other wealthy nations.

It's high time we reversed the trend. As you'll see in this chapter, the best way to protect yourself is to (a) practice safer sex, and (b) get tested frequently.

After all, you don't want to be a *literal* ladykiller. . . .

What Is Safe Sex?

Safe sex means taking precautions so that you and your partner don't expose one another to sexually transmitted diseases (otherwise known as STDs). It can also mean using birth control methods to prevent pregnancy.

Most sexually transmitted diseases are passed from one person to another in one of the following ways: through bodily fluids (saliva, ejaculate, or vaginal fluid) or the exposure of mucous membranes to other mucous membranes (her vagina, your penis) or to a cut or a sore. Safe sex

---

THE ULTIMATE OUCH

One vigorously misplaced thrust is all it takes to rupture the corposa cavernosa, the elongated "erectile chambers" that run the length of your penis. Don't believe us? Try aiming your erect penis at the trunk of a tree—it's roughly the same density as your partner's pubic bone. A complete rupture will require surgery within 24 hours to stanch internal bleeding and reduce the risk of permanent damage. A partial tear isn't as serious, but later on it may cause problems such as Peyronie's disease; as the linings of the corposa heal over with scar tissue, they lose their elasticity—leading to curvature, pain, and, eventually, impotence. By some estimates, more than a third of impotent men have a history of "penile trauma," and one-third of all penile ruptures occur during lovemaking.

To protect yourself, be especially careful when she's on top. That's the position most likely to cause damage.

---

means introducing a barrier so that these kinds of contact are less likely to occur (a condom to catch your ejaculate, for instance).

Safety, of course, is relative; no sex is entirely safe. Is kissing safe? Pretty much—although it does include an exchange of body fluids, and therefore a very small risk of transmission. And when you're talking about sex, although no condom is 100 percent guaranteed (accidents will happen), rubbers are still the best form of protection. Do condoms break? Rarely, but yes (and much less commonly when they're used correctly).

Unless your partner is someone you know and trust, who has tested negative for STDs a minimum of 3 months after her last episode with someone else, you should always take the following precautions.

■ Use a condom for intercourse, vaginal or anal.

■ Use a condom when she gives you oral sex.

■ Use a dental dam or a cut condom when you give her oral sex.

■ Get tested regularly.

A few more things to think about, so you're not ambushed with any unpleasant surprises:

Double up. If you're with a woman who's on the birth control pill, you should know that powerful antibiotics such as rifampin can interfere with hormone levels and make birth control pills less effective, according to Marc Feldstein, MD, an ob/gyn at Northwestern Memorial Hospital in Chicago. Many doctors suspect that more commonly used antibiotics like penicillin and tetracycline can also interfere with birth control pills, though that has never been proved. To be safe, you need to use a condom for a week after she takes her last antibiotic pill. (She shouldn't stop taking her birth control pills when she takes antibiotics.)

Just say no. If your partner has a cold sore on her upper lip, take a rain check on oral sex, or wear a condom. Yes, what you heard in the schoolyard was correct: The herpes virus behind cold sores and the ones behind genital herpes are different. But that won't necessarily stop them from setting up shop elsewhere.

"The herpes simplex 1 virus has a preference for the oral area, while herpes simplex 2 has a preference for the genital area," says Stephen K. Tyring, MD, PhD, professor of dermatology, microbiology, and immunology at the University of Texas Medical School Branch. But it's possible

BIRTH CONTROL:
YOUR GET-OUT-OF-PARENTHOOD-FREE CARD

For protecting yourself against STDs, condoms are your best bet. But if you and your partner are monogamous and have been tested, your big worry is making sure you don't end up with rug rats that you're not ready for. Here's a reminder of your contraceptive options.

Condoms: Good protection against STDs—also very good birth control. Easy, inexpensive, widely available—and one of the only birth control methods where the man's in the driver's seat.

The Pill: Not for nothing did it start the sexual revolution. It's safe, cheap, and effective—as long as she remembers to take it.

Female condom: Effective; slightly more expensive than the male version. Some men who dislike condoms swear by these; others say it's like having sex with a plastic baggie. If you're looking for an alternative to rubbers, it might be worth trying to see which side of the fence you're on.

Diaphragm: A barrier method that's available with a prescription from her doctor or a family planning clinic. Not quite as effective as a condom or the Pill, especially for women who have had a baby. Fit is everything; she may need to be refitted after a pregnancy or a big weight change.

Sponge: Said to be very effective with "perfect use"; anecdotal evidence suggests that perfect use is harder to come by than you might think.

Spermicide: Best used with another form of birth control, such as a diaphragm.

The Patch, the Ring, the Shot, the Implant: These are all hormonal solutions available with a prescription from her doctor or a family plan-

for a cold sore to transmit HSV-1 to your penis, giving you the same painful sores and flulike symptoms that characterize the genital variety. If she gets them a lot, make a condom standard operating procedure when she's down on you.

Getting Tested

Getting tested regularly is important because many STDs present without symptoms in men, which means you may not know about an injection until your girlfriend comes down with a case of crawling cooties—and by then, the damage is done. How often you get tested depends on what ning clinic. Since these have to be replaced infrequently, they're better for the absent-minded than the Pill.

IUD: Although the IUD has had some PR difficulties, it's a very effective, comfortable solution for women who have already had a child. It has to be inserted (and removed) by a medical professional.

Vasectomy, tubal ligation: His-and-hers sterilization options. Although both are reversible in many cases, changing your mind is expensive and nothing's guaranteed; better to be sure before you sign up. Worried about getting snipped? It sounds worse than it is—after the procedure, you'll walk out of the doctor's office under your own power, and you'll be just fine after a weekend's rest.

Some Good Ways to Get Yourself One of Those "World's Best Dad" Mugs

Abstinence: Abstinence works, of course—if you can do it. Which you usually can, right up until the moment where you can't—and then you'll probably want to have something a little more reliable on hand.

Withdrawal: Withdrawal. Doesn't. Work. Pre-ejaculate contains sperm, and sperm makes babies. Any questions?

Continuous breastfeeding: Breastfeeding does have a contraceptive effect, but it's most reliable in the first 6 months postpartum, and then only if she's nursing constantly and a lot. Again, explore alternatives if you're serious about not wanting another child.

you're doing and who you're doing it with. Once a year is standard, and you may want to increase the regularity if you're sleeping with lots of new people or engaging in high-risk behaviors.

Good news: Ask your doctor about the Aptima Combo 2 Assay. Getting tested for chlamydia and gonorrhea used to require a painful swabbing of your urethra. But the Aptima Assay, a urine test recently approved by the FDA, is 100 percent swab-free. "This test is as effective as traditional STD tests," says Harold Wiesenfeld, MD, assistant professor of gynecology at the University of Pittsburgh.

More good news: The OraQuick HIV test takes 20 minutes. Let the tech take a drop of blood, then have a seat in the waiting room. You'll have your answer before you can finish that 1998 *National Geographic* article on "Fascinating Finland."

The old way, it took up to 2 weeks to get results, and roughly one in three who were tested never came back for the verdict. With the new test, very few are expected to bolt. This is good: People who learn they're infected tend to take themselves out of circulation.

Let's Talk about Sex

Before you do the deed with her, you'll have to have a conversation about it. For many people, that conversation goes a little something like this: "Hold on while I get a condom." That's fine.

THE CONDOM, TRANSLATED

Denmark: gummimand ("rubber man")

France: preservatif (literally, "preservative")

Germany: Lummelute ("naughty bags"), Pariser ("Parisian")

Greece: kapota ("overcoat")

Hong Kong: pei dang vi ("bulletproof vest")

Hungary: osver ("safety tool")

India: Nirodh (a government-supported brand), parda (veil)

Indonesia: koteca ("penis gourd")

Mexico: angel custodio ("guardian angel")

Nigeria: okpuamu ("penis hat")

Philippines: kapote ("raincoat")

Portugal: camisa de Venus ("Venus's shirt")

Spain: globo ("balloon")

United Kingdom: raincoat, hazmat suit, French letter

United States: rubber, jimmy hat, love glove, Coney Island blowfish (Okay, nobody calls them that outside of the comics, but someone should start.)

WHAT THEY SAY

"For me, I think it is very easy to be the man. You simply take out the condom and put it on. No conversation necessary," says Andre, from France.

"I simply say, 'I never do it without one.' And then it's not an issue of trusting the person, or judgments, just a personal creed. And it makes it easier for me, too, when she's saying it might be okay and I've had a few. All I have to remember is that I never do it without one," says James, a British banker.

"I hate waiting for the test results—you know, when you're sitting in the waiting room and looking at all the posters, and then they call your name, and even if you're sure everything's all right, there's still that feeling in the pit of your stomach, like 'Oh my God, what if?' That's the moment I think about when I'm tempted to do it without," confides Ian, an Englishman living in Bali.

"It's never been an issue—I've never had a girl complain about me using one," says Friedrich, a sales rep from Mainz, Germany.

If there's pushback, you may actually have to talk some more. It can be uncomfortable, but it's completely necessary, and on this, we agree with the after-school specials: If you're not mature enough to talk about it, you're not mature enough to be doing it.

"In this day and age, you have to overcome your reluctance to talk about sex," says Isadora Alman, a California sexologist who writes a syndicated column called *Ask Isadora*. "It's stupid to jump into bed together and then check to see who's got the condom. Those with severe inhibitions just have to practice until they get over being uncomfortable discussing safe sex."

Remember that using drugs or drinking too much lowers your inhibitions and impairs your judgment—pretty much a handcrafted recipe for agreeing to engage in unsafe sex, or (worse) engaging in it without meaning to because you're too hammered to get the thing on properly.

Condoms: A User's Guide

The best way to protect yourself is by using latex condoms every time you have sex. Actually, the best way to protect yourself is by using condoms *correctly*—otherwise they're not effective for contraception or protection. And a study in the journal *Sexually Transmitted Diseases* reads like a horror show: Half of people visiting a Colorado STD clinic reported condom-use mishaps.

We asked David Fletcher, MD, *Men's Health* advisor and medical director of SafeWorks Illinois in Champaign, to give us a refresher course on safety. Here are the points to remember.

Do use a widely recognized brand. Durex, Lifestyles, Trojans. This is on the list of things (Valentine's Day presents, toilet paper) that you shouldn't buy at the dollar store, okay?

Do use latex condoms and water- or silicone-based lube. No Vaseline, no lotions, no moisturizers, no cooking oil, no mineral oil, no oil-based lube.

Don't carry them around in your wallet. You know how it gets all bent and worn and then your wife gets you a new one for Christmas? All that bending and wearing is really, really bad for condom integrity.

Do check the expiration date. Old condoms are more likely to break.

Don't tear the packet in half, or go at it with your teeth. Rip off the top of the packet, making sure not to damage the condom.

Do get the kind with the reservoir tip. Or make one, by pinching the very end of the condom as you're rolling it on, so that there's a little extra space right at the tip. Otherwise, you run the risk of breakage.

Don't even get us started on people who start having sex, stop, and put on a condom to finish. That's like hollering for defensive help after your man has driven the lane for a layup.

If your bits are anywhere near her bits, let alone *in* them, you should be wearing a condom. You're probably familiar with "pre-ejaculate"

ROOM TO GROW

Trojan's Ultra Pleasure condom is shaped like a light bulb, giving you a little more room at the business end. For once, your penis won't feel like a shrink-wrapped convenience-store snack. In the interest of healthy sex, a few *Men's Health* staffers gave them a whirl and reported that Ultra Pleasure gave us the best condom experience we've ever had.

JUST LIKE THE REAL THING—ALMOST

This is such a great trick, we can't imagine why everyone doesn't use it. Obviously, one of the real sensations that you're missing out on when you're practicing safe sex is that wonderful wetness that tells you you're home. Fake yourself out by adding a tiny drop of lube (a little goes a long way in this instance) inside the rubber before you put it on. It heats delightfully once it's in play, and feels much closer to the real thing.

(that spot on the front of your boxers when you're really turned on). The longer you're hard, the more pre-come you produce. Problem? For the purposes of disease prevention, a body fluid is a body fluid. And if you're worried about pregnancy, pre-come contains sperm. And it just takes one, baby.

Do wait until you're ready for intercourse. You don't want to be doing too much rubbing up against her while you're wearing it—even the silkiest panties can snag and damage latex.

Don't flip it. Start unrolling it on a finger first. If you start putting it on backward, don't flip it over and continue—toss it and grab another. If you put it on wrong, toss it out and grab another. Yes, even if it has spermicide on it.

Do roll it all the way down. All the way down. To the very base of your penis.

Don't hang out too long after the party's over. Pull out right after you come. And when you pull out, hold the bottom.

DEPENDING ON YOUR EQUIPMENT

The technique for putting on condoms does differ for uncircumcised men. In order to avoid the condom "creeping up," the foreskin needs to be retracted before the condom is unrolled onto the penis. When the condom is unrolled about one-third of the way down the shaft, one hand should be used to pull the foreskin with the unrolled part of the condom upward while the other hand continues to unroll the condom to the base of the penis.

ONE MORE REASON NOT TO LEAVE HOME WITHOUT ONE

If you find yourself wading in the Amazon, you'll be glad to have a condom handy. Wearing one will prevent a small fish, known as the candiru (also known as the toothpick fish, or the vampire fish of Brazil), from swimming into your urethra.

Sleep well tonight!

Don't flush! Latex is a notorious drain clogger. Tie it in a knot (trust us on this one) and throw it in the trash instead.

Don't reuse. We're sorry that we have to include this one, but some things, apparently, aren't obvious.

Uh oh: What do you do if the condom breaks?

Get your postorgasmic butts out of bed; the clock is ticking. "Sperm can be in the cervical mucus within minutes," says Katherine Forrest, MD, MPH, a public health physician in northern California. Translation: Your little guys are about to do the hibbity-dibbity with her possibly fertile egg.

First option: Hope she has contraceptive foam with the spermicide nonoxynol-9, so she can spray (while you pray). Or, failing that, a vinegar douche (1 to 2 tablespoons of vinegar to 1 quart of warm water), which is acidic enough to kill sperm. Medicine cabinet empty? Dr. Forrest recommends that your partner take a morning-after pill within 72 hours of intercourse. Have her call (888) NOT-2-LATE for a pharmacy that carries emergency contraception; it's now available over-the-counter for women over 18.

The Condom Shelf, Decoded

There are a wealth of condom choices out there. Here are some pros and cons of the various types, according to experts at the Mayo Clinic (www.mayoclinic.com).

Latex: These provide highly effective barriers against pregnancy and STDs, and they're the most reliable preventive measure against the transmission of HIV.

Plastic: Proven in recent, limited lab studies to be an effective barrier against HIV, but unlike latex condoms, they're prone to slip off.

Animal skin (lambskin): They can stop sperm, but viruses and bacteria can get right through the pores. Lambskin condoms are also more likely to break than latex condoms.

Female condoms: On the plus side, they protect against STDs and pregnancy, and they're her problem, not yours. On the minus side, it's kind of like having sex with a Baggie.

Novelty condoms: Avoid them. You are not a "novelty," and these condoms won't protect you against STDs or pregnancy. In fact, some of these fun condoms are factory rejects that legitimate condom manufacturers have sold to novelty packagers.

If it was given to you by your Secret Santa or comes attached to a penis-shaped pen, or if you have to break a piece of plastic to get it out, it's probably not a real, working-order condom.

Having trouble telling the difference? Real condoms come from legitimate retailers like drugstores (i.e., not the store with the wind-up Jesus toys), and they're sealed in sterile cellophane or foil wrappers. You should see a brand name, an expiration date, and a lot number.

"More sensitive": A euphemism for "thinner," with more risk of tearing.

"Stronger": A euphemism for "thicker," meaning less breakage risk and less sensation.

Size: In condoms, it does matter, so be honest. If it's too tight, it's likely to break. If you buy XXL and you're not, the slippage factor is huge.

Ribbed: Same protection for you, a little more tickle for her. Most women report that the thrill is underwhelming, but it's worth a shot.

Lubricated: May reduce the risk of tearing, but no good for oral sex.

Spermicidal: These offer slightly more protection against pregnancy, thanks to the spermicide nonoxynol-9 (N-9), but they aren't HIV or STD

WHO'S CALLING WHO DEPRAVED NOW?

In the 17th century, Spain boasted that it was free of sexual deviance; when referring to bestiality, the Spanish nicknamed it "the Italian vice." Meanwhile, syphilis was known as "the French disease" in Italy and "the English disease" in France.

---

killers, according to the Centers for Disease Control and Prevention. Watch out for allergies.

Let's Go Shopping

CondomDepot.com features a World's Best Condom Sampler Tin, featuring a selection of condoms from Japan, Britain, the United States, and elsewhere.

Or go in person: The Condomania boutiques in New York, Miami, Las Vegas, Los Angeles, and San Francisco are devoted exclusively to the sale of condoms, with more than 300 styles from six countries in every store. The latex selections include minty, studded, textured, extra-large, extra-small (not many takers for these, say the owners), ultra-thin, lubricated, and the ever-popular "Wrap Your Knight in Shining Armor," a glow-in-the-dark contraceptive. (You can order sized-to-your-penis They-Fit condoms at condomania.com.)

TO THE RESCUE

Swedes in Stockholm, Malmö, and Gothenberg can summon a "condom ambulance"—a white truck featuring a red condom with wings on the side—by phone and get a packet of 10 delivered.

CHAPTER 5

BE THE WORLD'S MOST CHIVALROUS MAN
Woo Your Favorite Woman in the World

Ah, romance. You can't put a price on it, but it costs you dearly.

Thirty-one percent of men worldwide say that money is no object when it comes to wooing a woman, and 38 percent of American guys say they spend a day's pay on a woman before the relationship turns physical. Seventy-seven percent of American *Men's Health* readers say you almost always pay, with half of you typically dropping $150 or more on a big date. Seven percent say it's not unusual to spend $500 if you're really into her. Yowsa!

Researchers at Arizona State University doled out wads of imaginary money to men, then flashed either romantic images or plain old everyday scenes at them. The guys who looked at the romantic photos spent much more of their allowance on luxuries than did those who saw the other photos. What's behind all this generosity? Probably evolution—men want to show potential mates that they can afford to take

QUICKIE STATS

Percentage of men who'd pay anything to please a woman:

1. Indonesia		64 percent
2. Portugal		51 percent
3. Poland		42 percent
4. Netherlands		40 percent
5. Italy		39 percent
United States		**19 percent**
World average		**31 percent**

IF YOU THROW MONEY AT A WOMAN, AIM HIGH

According to a British study, the best gifts in a serious courtship are extravagant but have no takeaway value for her (to deter gold diggers)— for instance, expensive concert tickets or a weekend getaway, not rent money. Costly gestures indicate long-term intentions.

Dates that require considerable planning are also effective. "Anything that takes up a lot of a man's time—as long as the woman knows that—could be a signal of future commitment," says study coauthor Peter Sozou, PhD.

care of them and theirs. And women want men to show that they'll share what they've got.

The motivation behind the big spending? It's expected. "A woman does not pay for her own dinner in Portugal," says Ana, a doctor in Sintra.

Who are the cheapest suitors? The Australians. But they have quite a lot to say in their own defense: "I don't want to be with a woman who cares how much I spend on her," says Dan, an Aussie real estate lawyer. "Women don't care about fancy presents. They want something that shows you've given it some thought," says Neil, a graphic artist in Sydney.

And, to be honest, that's pretty much what we heard from the women we talked to. Yes, a lot of them talked a big game about diamonds being a girl's best friend and how much they wanted a Caribbean vacation. But most of them got all gooey over the little things: the time he ran her a bath or the mix tape her high school boyfriend gave her.

Apparently, it's the thought that counts, not the price. "A gift is a way to show your interest, not your bottom line," says Peter Post, the Vermont-based author of *Essential Manners for Couples*. There should be a compromise between her happiness and your wallet. This chapter focuses on the most cost-effective courtship tactics—the things that are most likely to impress her, regardless of the financial investment.

The Smallest Gesture

Julianne Balmain, San Francisco–based coauthor of *The Kama Sutra Deck: 50 Ways to Love Your Lover*, recommends one very simple instruction adapted from the Kama Sutra: "A man should never visit his lover without a small consideration, a token of his esteem. These gifts were very small, natural things—betel leaves, a carved wooden figurine, a little decorative box or paper cutouts—but they were thoughtful, and often they were something the couple could do together."

Here are some suggestions:

"A bottle of champagne and tiny delicacies—just enough to fuel sex before dinner," says Doug, a restaurant manager in New York.

"There's this great coffee place near my house; I get some ground and bring it when I'm staying at her place to share the next morning," says Matt, a software writer in Seattle.

Our pick: The Lavender Massage Oil Suntouched Candle. This scented candle turns into massage oil. Find it at www.nawtythings.com. As Balmain says, "It's easy to go wrong with a big gesture, and hard to go wrong with a small one."

Dinner Is Served

The point of courtship is spending time together, talking, and having fun. And that doesn't have to cost a lot. In fact, Cupid has no more potent arrow in his quiver than The Romantic Dinner—and it won't cost you more than the price of a bag of groceries and a couple of decent bottles of wine.

Women *love* men who cook. And you've got to love how it moves the ball forward; there's no kind of foreplay that will get you where you need to be faster than a well-seasoned risotto or the perfect chocolate mousse. The whisper of sex and attraction shared between two people can turn any meal—yes, even one you've cooked—into a veritable feast.

And there are plenty of foods out there that can enhance the already-in-the-mood meal both visually and texturally. An indulgent, relaxed state

---

CELEBRATE WHITE DAY

In Japan, women do the giving on Valentine's Day. In fact, there are two categories of chocolate gifts: *giri choco,* small boxes which she gives to her superiors at work, friends, and male co-workers, and *honmei choco,* a more expensive box reserved for the guy she's serious about.

You get your turn on March 14th, which is traditionally known in Japan as White Day. Celebrate by giving your beloved white candy—white chocolate and marshmallows—or anything in a white box.

---

of mind can be heightened by a sweet taste. A glass of wine causes the skin to flush, emulating the glow of sexual arousal.

Cheryl Copeland, a chef who teaches aphrodisiac cooking classes in North Carolina, provided us with some ultra-simple recipes that you can throw together quickly, even if you have very little experience at the stove. (See "Sexy Shopping List" on page 78 for advice on filling your shopping cart with ingredients guaranteed to drive her wild.)

Oysters Marseille

½ cup finely grated Parmesan cheese
½ cup herb-flavored bread crumbs
¼ teaspoon salt
¼ teaspoon pepper
1 dozen shucked oysters, drained
Olive oil

Mix first four ingredients in a bowl. Dredge oysters in mix. Coat frying pan with olive oil. Heat to sizzling over medium high heat. Fry oysters until golden brown on each side. Drain on paper towels.

Serve oysters over a bed of mixed greens (try arugula—it's also an aphrodisiac), lightly dressed with a vinaigrette or blue cheese dressing.

Pasta with Artichokes and Pine Nuts

2 ounces pine nuts
1 pound cheese-filled tortellini
1 large jar marinated artichoke hearts (drained and quartered)
2 ounces crumbled feta cheese
2 ounces ham, minced
2 ounces kalamata olives, pitted
6 cherry tomatoes, halved
2 tablespoons pesto
½ cup vinaigrette dressing

Toast pine nuts in a pie pan in a 375°F oven until light brown, shaking pan several times. Watch carefully—they burn easily. Cook tortellini according to package directions. Combine all ingredients in a large bowl and serve at room temperature.

Scallops Buenos Aires

1 can black beans, rinsed and drained (see Note 1)

1 avocado, peeled, pitted, and cut into $\frac{1}{2}$-inch pieces (see Note 2)

1 tomato, chopped

$\frac{1}{2}$ purple onion, chopped

1 jalapeño pepper, seeded, deveined, and chopped

1 red bell pepper, chopped

1 clove garlic, finely chopped

$\frac{1}{2}$ cup cilantro, finely chopped

Juice of 3 limes

Salt and pepper to taste

1 pound sea scallops

In a bowl, combine all ingredients except the scallops to make the salsa. Refrigerate for 2 hours before serving.

Spray a heavy frying pan with cooking spray. Sear scallops over high heat, approximately 2 to 3 minutes on each side. Scallops should have a slightly blackened appearance. Turn only once. Serve over the chilled salsa.

Note 1: Black beans are an aphrodisiac; the Catholic church forbade nuns to touch or eat them.

Note 2: When you buy avocado, make sure the fruit will dent with some resistance when pressed with a thumb—if it doesn't, it's not ripe yet. You can speed up ripening by putting it in a paper bag on the counter.

This recipe comes courtesy of Mabel Iam, Argentinian author of Sex and the Perfect Lover.

Valencia Orange Ecstasy

6 oranges

2 tablespoons sugar

$^1/_2$ cup Cointreau or other orange liqueur

1 teaspoon ground cinnamon

Peel four of the oranges, and carefully remove all white fibers wherever possible. Divide the fruit into small sections. Juice the remaining two oranges and combine the juice with the sugar and the Cointreau. Place the orange sections in a shallow dish and pour the juice mixture over them. Sprinkle the cinnamon over the oranges and put the dish in the refrigerator to chill for a half-hour before serving.

Chocolate-Dipped Strawberries: A Global Favorite

1 quart large strawberries

1 pound good-quality dark chocolate

8 ounces white chocolate

Wash the strawberries, leaving the stem leaves on. Drain on several layers of paper towels and blot all moisture off with more paper towels. Melt the dark chocolate in a double boiler (one pot with barely boiling water in it and a second, smaller metal bowl or pot on top; the second bowl should be 1" away from the water in the bottom pot). Stir the chocolate pieces until melted. Holding each strawberry by the stem or leaves, dip bottom two-thirds into chocolate and place on a baking sheet lined with wax paper. Place in the refrigerator until the chocolate hardens. Melt the white chocolate the same way (in a different or clean bowl) and spoon into a plastic baggie. Cut a tiny piece off one corner of the bag. Squeeze the white chocolate into this corner, twisting the bag like a mortar bag. Drizzle back and forth over the entire pan of berries.

For best results, drizzle some of what you've prepared across an expanse of bare skin, for a different sort of feast altogether.

What to Get the Woman Who Has Everything

The very best presents have some things in common: "It's something I'd never get myself," says Anja, a holistic health practitioner in Germany. "Something that shows he was paying attention!" says Anzhela, a lab technician in Russia. "I want him to be romantic when he gives me a gift, not practical," says Enes, a wine salesperson in Portugal.

You don't have to look any further than here for great romantic gift ideas.

Suggest starting a tradition. A few weeks before your anniversary, send your wife a card inviting her to meet you at the fanciest restaurant in town. Show up in a suit, order a bottle of champagne, and make a toast to the love of your life. Have the waiter bring out a dessert with a candle in it, then stand up, walk over, and kiss her before she blows it out. If you're an understated, practical guy, that's impressive enough.

If she's used to more creativity, hand her a leather-bound photo album filled with pictures of the two of you from the past year. If you can afford it, upgrade to a weekend at a gorgeous hotel in one of her favorite cities. Now for the tradition part: Tell her you'd like to celebrate your anniversary this way every year. If she agrees, the experience will gather layers of wonderful memories—and you'll never have to wonder what to do again.

This one's a heart-stirrer: For Mother's Day, Kansas woodworker and artist Marc DeCou carved a Welsh lovespoon for his wife out of wood from a walnut tree close to their country home. What's a lovespoon? It's an ornament carved by a young man for the girl of his choice. If she accepted one, it meant the interest was mutual. Spoons were carved with symbols—an anchor, for instance, meant "I want to settle down," while a heart-shaped bowl meant "fulfilled love," and a vine connoted a growing relationship. Marc made one with hearts for his wife, and he'll make one for yours if you want him to. Contact him at www.decoustudio.com.

Slip the corner fiddler a 50-spot to follow you and your date for the evening.

Give her a year of wine. Have the wine store clerk help you put together a mixed 12-pack of good hooch. Pick robust reds for the winter months, lighter whites for the spring and summer. But you're not just giving her a

(continued on page 80)

SEXY SHOPPING LIST

When you're preparing your romantic menu, consider using some of these ingredients, noted throughout history for their aphrodisiac qualities.

Asparagus. It's sweet, it's tender, and its phallic look is so very suggestive. This full-flavored veggie is jam-packed with vitamins and minerals that naturally boost your sex drive! Potassium and vitamin A are a major boon to general health and well-being, but what makes asparagus so sexy is the folate. What's so sexy about that? Folate stimulates the production of histamines, a lack of which has been associated with the inability to have orgasms. So more asparagus = more folate = less risk of having to fake it.

Avocado. The avocado hangs in pairs. Many peoples and cultures across history have taken note of this buttery-fleshed fruit's resemblance to testicles, but it was the ancient Aztecs who actually gave name to the suggestive fruit tree: *ahuacuatl,* which translates to "testicle tree."

The Aztecs, Mayans, and Incans all enacted fertility rituals in which nubile nobles supped on the flesh of the avocado. Thought to enhance sexual desirability, this sensuously curved fruit with its soft, smooth meat and large pit embedded within was so feared that when the conquering Spanish returned to Europe with news of the sexy fruit, the Catholic church forbade its members even a taste.

In the early part of the 1900s, an Aphrodisiac Avocado ad campaign took the United States by storm. The purpose was to convince the public that avocados were an aphrodisiac by denying that they were—a bit of early reverse psychology. The campaign was wildly successful.

Bananas. Bananas may have the highest aphrodisiac pedigree of all. Ancient Islamic myth tells of Adam and Eve in the Garden of Eden, covering their no-longer-innocent parts with banana leaves instead of fig leaves; another tells of the Eve-tempting serpent hiding in a bunch of bananas while he spies his innocent quarry.

Rich in potassium and B vitamins that stimulate sex hormone production, this witness to temptation is also associated with erotic energy in the Tantric tradition. A mid-afternoon snack just may lead to a mid-afternoon romp.

Basil. Sweet, lemony, peppery—basil has many faces, including that of a fertility booster. Said to be a stimulant to the sex drive, basil also increases a general sense of well-being—and being in a good mood might very well translate to being good while *in* the mood. In times past, women would dust their breasts and other parts with dried and powdered basil, since the mere smell of basil perfume was rumored to drive men wild.

Healthwise, the herb promotes a healthy circulatory system, and increased bloodflow is always an aid to a stand-up sex life.

Carrots. It will make them "rut like wild beasts"—or so Roman emperor Caligula once said of feeding the entire Roman Senate a feast made entirely of carrot dishes. The ancient Greeks used carrot as a love potion to "make men more ardent and women more yielding."

Early Middle Eastern royalty included carrots on the menu in hopes that the phallic-shaped veggie would get diners in the mood. They're high in vitamins and beta-carotene, potassium, calcium, magnesium, vitamin A, and folate.

Celery. It's good for the digestion, it cleans your teeth, it's great fiber, *and* its consumption releases female-attracting hormones. Yep, you read right. Celery contains androsterone, the male hormone thought to stimulate sexual arousal in women. The androsterone is released through perspiration, and though her nose may not be able to actually detect the smell of the hormone, her brain will. Lunch may be cozy.

It worked for the ancient Romans—they dedicated celery to the god of sex, Pluto.

Chocolate. Called the "nourishment of the Gods" by the Aztecs, this is certainly the sweetest and, some may argue, most effective aphrodisiac food. Chocolate contains two key ingredients—theobromine and phenylethylamine—that release the most feel-good chemicals the brain has to offer. Phenylethylamine (aka the "love chemical," said to induce feelings of excitement, attraction, and euphoria) sends dopamine coursing through the system, a process that peaks during orgasm. Theobromine packs a double punch: It unleashes serotonin, which relaxes the body and provides a general sense of well-being, and arginine, an amino acid known to enhance the level of arousal and sensation in both men and women. Arginine has been dubbed "nature's Viagra"—it allows increased bloodflow and the relaxation of smooth muscle, especially in the genitalia.

Fennel. The Kama Sutra includes this sweet herb in a recipe for love along with ghee (clarified butter), licorice, milk, cardamom, and honey. Fennel's chemical makeup contains compounds that mimic estrogen, a female hormone. Studies show that the herb increases the libido of both male and female rats. Drizzle olive oil over a combination of fennel, walnut, orange, mint leaves, and pomegranate seeds on a bed of arugula to kickstart your romantic dinner for two.

Figs. The erotic act of eating figs is a centuries-old turn-on. Figs were rumored to be Cleopatra's favorite food. Ancient Greeks associated the fig with love and fertility largely because an open fig strongly resembles the female sex organs. In some Southern European countries, it's traditional to

(continued)

throw figs, instead of rice, at retreating newlyweds as a symbol of a fertile marriage. Breaking open a tender fig and peeling the skin back to reveal the luscious, juicy flesh can be the first and final step to seduction.

Licorice. Practitioners of traditional Chinese medicine say that licorice is particularly stimulating to women. Men aren't exactly immune, though: Studies have found that the smell of black licorice increases bloodflow to the penis by 13 percent. Try chewing bits of licorice root—it's 50 times sweeter than sugar.

Nutmeg. Research shows that nutmeg stimulates mating behavior in mice. Don't go too crazy with it, though. In large quantities, nutmeg can cause hallucinogenic effects. Get high on love instead.

Oysters. Romans first made aphrodisiac claims for these mollusks in the 2nd century A.D., based on their resemblance to female genitals. In 2005, a team of Italian and American researchers found rare amino acids in oysters that trigger greater levels of sex hormones, and the more sex hormones you have, the more you want to get busy. These amino acids can't be found in a bottle at the health food store. As Casanova, the leg-

case of booze. You're going to attach a handwritten list of the dates you want to have with her in the next year: a cozy night curled up by the fire together in January, a crisp fall hike complete with a Thermos of homemade soup. The thought that, in December, you're already planning a late-summer *dejeuner sur l'herbe* (French for "picnic with a naked lady") will make her melt with anticipation.

Serenade her. Actually, pay a street musician to do it. Slip the corner fiddler a 50-spot to follow you and your date for the evening. The background soundtrack will make it feel as if you're in a movie. It's spontaneous, fun, and romantic.

"Quando arriva il treno da Roma?" If she keeps saying she wants to sing, paint, or speak Italian, prepay for some lessons—and then give her the space she needs to do them right. You're showing her you're interested in her soul. "The more you acknowledge who she is, the more you get back," says Lou Paget, a certified sex educator in Los Angeles and the author of *365 Days of Sensational Sex*.

Word to the wiseguy: Think very, very carefully about how she's going to take it before you give her a cooking class or a gift certificate to that new Pilates studio.

endary Italian lover, knew, you have to go straight to the natural source. He was purported to eat several dozen oysters a day.

Pine nuts. Considered an aphrodisiac for their rich store of zinc, a mineral necessary for male potency, pine nuts are also alluring because they play hard to get: The nuts are tucked into the cones of the pine tree. Like a lot of nuts, pine nuts offer good fats, are heart-friendly, and are packed with minerals.

Vanilla. In the 18th and 19th centuries, vanilla tinctures were administered to men as an aphrodisiac. Research shows that a major component of vanilla, helitropin, calms the nerves and relaxes the body. To set a relaxing mood, try natural vanilla scented candles or drop vanilla beans into a flute of bubbly.

Wine. A glass or two will lend a glow to the skin, relax the body, and stimulate the senses. Much more than that and you'll be too drowsy for much more of anything. Hold the glass gently, make a toast, meet her eyes over raised glasses, and drink to romance.

Put stars in her eyes. No matter where in the world she is, she'll be able to see the star you've named after her via the International Star Registry (800-282-3333).

Hopeless? Find a store she likes, and let them do the work. "My wife is impossible to buy presents for, so I go to this amazing Japanese department store in New York City when I'm there and stock up," says Jacques, a wine importer from Paris. "Their buyers are fantastic, and the people who work there will spend a lot of time finding me the perfect thing. Everything I get from there, she loves. They do the work, I get the credit."

Wednesday Night Presents

This concept was suggested to us by Gustavo, an Argentinean-Israeli graphic designer we know who has houses in New York, Buenos Aires, and Miami (we said we know him—we didn't say we didn't hate him). "These are presents that are very sexy and thoughtful, but *only* if they're given for no reason," he cautions. "They completely lose their magic if they show up for her birthday." Here are two random acts of kindness that may lead to random acts of nookie.

"THE MOST ROMANTIC PRESENT I EVER GOT. . . ."

"A picnic by the lake with strawberries and champagne. I was at university and my boyfriend and I at the time were both destitute students. He packed up a bottle of bubbly and strawberries and a little blanket and took me to the lake, where we sat and had a lovely afternoon. Simple but beautiful. It's often who gives you the gift that makes it romantic."—Anja, a holistic health practitioner in Germany

"A CD with all the tracks on it that meant something to me. He made a collage of all the photos of us together for the CD cover and wrote song words on the inside."—Nikki, a jewelry designer in Australia

"I love things that are handmade, as I think they mean so much more. One Christmas, my boy made a card and put a sprig of fresh mistletoe on the front and wrote inside 'You're the only one I ever want to be kissing under the mistletoe.' Perhaps slightly corny and sickening, looking back, but at the time I was a lovelorn 19-year-old and thought it was highly romantic!"—Lizzie, a public relations professional in London

"My husband designed a necklace for me, using emeralds from an incredibly ugly necklace he inherited from his grandmother. It's my favorite piece of jewelry."—Marie-Chantal in Lyons, France

"My husband recreated our first date. He even wore the terrible tie he was wearing, until I begged him to take it off!"—Gloria, a dancer from Barcelona

"I had to fly to China on short notice for work, which meant missing our wedding anniversary, and I was very disappointed. When I opened up my suitcase, I found a gift-wrapped copy of an erotic short story collection—very sexy! But the best was to come: The bookmark, which I didn't discover until I settled in with my book later that night, was a Polaroid of my very aroused husband, all tied up with a bow! And so we had a lovely anniversary evening together—even though we were thousands of miles apart. And I was very happy to celebrate again in person."—Justine from South Africa

"When my computer crashed, my boyfriend made me a CD of every e-mail we'd ever sent to one another, and every picture of the two of us together."—Alexandra in Cairo

"The engagement ring at the bottom of my champagne flute, of course!"—Natalia from Rio

Good-quality bed linens: Few words are sexier to women than "high thread count." Be sure to pay attention to the color scheme in her bedroom, and pick up a new sheet set with a thread count of 300 or more, in Turkish or Egyptian cotton. Then make her bed with the new stuff. Trust us, you'll be spending much more time there now.

Presents that work or make work for her: As a general rule, never buy a woman anything with a plug. But what if it's something she really wants? You know, for instance, that she's got her eye on a fancy bread-maker or some other top-of-the-line kitchen gadget. Sorry, either of those is a terrible Christmas present, no matter how pointedly she brought your attention to it on the Food Network. But you can go ahead and get it—and get brownie points—as long as it's Wednesday night.

Sexy Gifts

"Giving a sexy gift can get a bit tricky," says Michelle Grahame, the managing director of nookii.com, a British company that sells adult games and toys. "There are lots of women where if you turn up with a pair of saucy underpants, she's going to hit you over the head with them." Ditto for the home stripper pole and the French maid outfit.

The trick, Grahame says, is to give her something that's for the two of you. A game called Nookii, for instance—billed as "a gift for someone you love"—keeps her in the picture in a way that other sexy gifts might not. It's also something the two of you are going to do together, something that you'll both participate in and enjoy—not something she does for you. Designed to take about 12 minutes from start to finish, the game doesn't feel like a chore—a lot of work and potential embarrassment, the way a pole-dancing kit does.

In general, it's best to follow her lead. If you know she's harboring a stripper fantasy, a pole-dancing kit is fine. Otherwise, make the sexy gift something the two of you can do together, like a feather tickler, a sexy game, or body paints.

We like:

The Tantalizer feather toy, $10 at www.mypleasure.com

Kama Sutra Lover's Paintbox, $35 at www.mypleasure.com

Chocolate Body Pens, $10 at www.goodvibes.com

GIFTS TO AVOID

We've all been there. The ribbon comes off, the box is opened—and then there's silence. Or weeping. Not, in other words, the gushing gratitude you were all geared up for. "What?" you yell at her retreating back before the door slams. "You don't like it?"

In general, the presents that piss her off are the ones that make her feel like you don't know her. That, it turns out, is what it means when women talk about being thoughtful. It's probably not possible to avoid the bummer gift entirely, but if you can steer clear of these pitfalls, you'll be ahead of the game.

The cliché: For a certain kind of woman, red roses on Valentine's day is a dream come true. But if she throws popcorn during romantic comedies, maybe you're better off bringing a cactus.

The squander: If money is tight for the two of you, maybe spending a ton on a romantic dinner and a bouquet the size of a small island isn't your best move. "My boyfriend gave me a little box with a Monopoly house in it for Christmas when we were thinking about moving in together; the card said 'Let's save up for the real thing.' I still have it," says Maria in Italy.

The sabotage: "I'd just finished losing all the baby weight—and it was really, really hard the second time—and then my husband showed up with a gigantic box of chocolates for my birthday. It was like, 'Where have you been for the last 6 months of carrot sticks?'" recalls Linda from the United Kingdom.

The reproach: If you've never seen her wear anything besides her wedding ring, are those earrings really going to be "just what she's always wanted"—or a sign that you wish she was really someone else?

The Big Gesture

Those diamond commercials? The one where the guy goes down on one knee in some square in Italy and re-proposes in front of the pigeons and her parents and a million strangers? Well, that guy got some, my man. He got some diamond-in-Italy Big Gesture sex.

Every once in a while, the Big Gesture is called for. Put a pair of emerald earrings under her pillow. Surprise her with a trip to the Caribbean. Put a big bow on the sports car she's always wanted.

Nota bene: The Big Gesture is completely invalidated if it is preceded by the Big Screw-Up. No diamond in a square in Italy is going to get you out of the hole you dug when you told her you'd thought about having sex with her sister, even if it was only once. In fact, in these scenarios, the Big Gesture has been known to have exactly the opposite of the intended effect, sometimes resulting in screaming, threats of violence, and extended periods of sleep on the couch.

The Best Gesture

The Italians, who made our top five in the category of guys willing to drop a bundle in the name of love, know a thing or two about love at any cost. So we turned to them for the final word about the best gift in the world. "We do not use 'I love you' just to say ciao, or good-bye, as you do even between friends, or from a parent to a child," says Emmanuele A. Jannini, MD, professor of endocrinology and medical sexology at the University of L'Aquila. "When we say *'ti amo'* with a flower or a diamond, it is not casual—it literally means 'I love you.'"

What, then, is the best gift you can give a woman? Nothing more than this: Take her face in your hands, look deep into her eyes, and tell her *"Ti amo."*

CHAPTER 6

BE THE SEXIEST COUPLE IN THE WORLD
Keep Your Relationship Red-Hot

According to the office of Polish statistics, about 96 percent of the population of Poland belonged to the Roman Catholic Church in 2000, and over 80 percent of them say that they attend mass regularly. Indeed, experts consider it to be one of the most religious countries outside of Latin America. "Poland is a heavily Roman Catholic country, and the Church has an enormous influence on everyday life," says Lech, a political advisor in Poland. Certainly, that religious faith has a great deal to do with why Polish men are so faithful in their relationships—or at least say that they are. Sixty-two percent of them claim to have never cheated.

But our own on-the-ground research tells us that, no matter where you're from, you have the best chance at happy monogamy if you're willing to do a little work. "Athletes have to train to achieve great things on the track, don't they?" asks Christine Webber, a

QUICKIE STATS

Percentage of men who've never cheated (i.e., had sex) with a woman besides their partner:

1. Poland		62 percent
2. Germany		62 percent
3. Australia		60 percent
4. Netherlands		59 percent
5. United Kingdom		57 percent
6. United States		**52 percent**
World average		**50 percent**

psychotherapist and agony aunt (that's sex advice columnist to you) who writes a column on sex and relationships for Netdoctor, the UK's leading independent health Web site—together with her husband, Dr. David Delvin. "It's the same thing with having great sex in a marriage. You have to have a good think about it, and you have to put the effort in."

Stifle your groans. The kind of work we're talking about? Having dinner without the kids. Taking a vacation alone together. And introducing some sizzling sexual innovation into the pleasure palace you call your bedroom. Nice work if you can get it!

Take My Wife—Please!

Marital sex. It's the punchline of a thousand jokes, one of the great oxymorons of all time, like "military intelligence" and "jumbo shrimp." As the Hungarian-born Zsa Zsa Gabor so eloquently put it: "A man in love is incomplete until he marries. Then he's finished."

A relationship is seldom the smooth-flying, first-class affair it's cracked up to be. (As Zsa Zsa surely knows—she's had nine husbands.) Too often, it's more like a long-haul flight in economy class: the exhilaration of take-off, followed by a period of comfortable cruising—until soon you begin to feel cramped in the confined space.

Too much closeness can smother a spark, and without fresh air to feed the glowing cinders, a sexual inferno can be reduced to ashes in just a short period of time. "Love is not only poetry; it also has a strong biological basis," says Enzo Emanuele, MD, of the University of Pavia in Italy. And blood samples have revealed biochemical evidence that intense romantic love fades after just a year in a new relationship.

And while sharing the stresses of everyday life is one of the great pleasures of marriage and can bring tremendous relief to both partners, those same stresses can also be very intrusive on what happens between the two of you in the bedroom.

Not to mention the fact that marriage very often produces children, who are the original wet blankets, after you've gotten over the fun of making them in the first place. Between sleep deprivation, cracked nipples, and Caesarean scars, "children stifle marital libido. Full stop," says Caroline Hurry, a sex columnist in South Africa. It does seem to be borne out by the research: In a 10-year study of the impact of parenthood on couples, researchers found both partners reported a negative change in their sexual relationship after the birth of a baby.

And yet, a good marriage offers real, quantifiable benefits—especially for men. "You earn more money because of it, you live longer, you're in better health all around, your chances of having an active sex life are way better, and your standard of living is higher. If your marriage is happy, you're more productive at work than if your marriage is unhappy," says Steven L. Nock, PhD, a University of Virginia sociologist and the author of *Marriage in Men's Lives*. "If a guy is smart, he's going to realize he's getting a great deal, and he's going to put in a lot of effort to keep his wife happy and keep those benefits flowing."

So it's easy to see why fanning the embers of passion in a long-term relationship has been the subject of so very many bestsellers. As Australian-British expert Tracey Cox so memorably says in her super-hot book *Superhotsex*, "good sex that lasts isn't a gift, it's an achievement." And

Bad sex isn't an automatic condition of matrimony.

an important one. Keeping the spice in a relationship can be a real challenge, but when the sex goes, one partner usually goes with it. Infidelity is an issue that every couple confronts in their marriage—whether as a temptation scorned or pursued.

On the other hand, bad sex isn't an automatic condition of matrimony; in fact, quite the opposite. Many married men find their sex lives richer, more exciting, and more fulfilling after walking down the aisle than before it. And this isn't just us talking: In a poll of *Men's Health* readers, we found that when asked what you enjoyed most about sex, you rate intimacy higher (44 percent) than eroticism (33 percent), orgasm (16 percent), or the thrill of the conquest (7 percent). Sex can really be enriched when you trust someone and know them well. In a comfortable, loving environment, you can often discard the inhibitions and boundaries that might have prevented you from fully exploring your desires. Women, especially, flourish in an atmosphere of trust.

Just ask Richard, 54, and Heather, 52, from South Africa. They have been lovers for 34 years and spouses for 30. "I grew up with the idea that sex started out with a bang and then faded to a whimper. It has been the opposite for us," says Richard. "When we first got together, we were clueless. Somehow we managed to grope our way to mutually fulfilling sex that has grown deeper, more intimate, more erotic, and more satisfying."

For every stand-up comedian, there's a couple who has managed to beat the odds, who has channeled the intimacy that comes with being with someone for a long time into absolutely record-setting sex. We found those happy, horny couples, and the experts who have advised them—all over the world and in our own backyards—and we made them talk. And what they told us is that there's no great sex without a great relationship, so let's start there.

The Most Important Thing: Liking Each Other

Sorry to get all cheeseball on you, but it's true: The first step to a marriage that lasts—and to having great sex for all of it, not just the first 3 years—is liking the person you're with, says British expert Phillip Hodson, author of *How Perfect Is Your Mate?* "The initial honeymoon phase *must* end—there's nothing you can do about it." The most important factor, he says, isn't how attracted you are to one another, but how similar you are and how much you have in common. "To be happily married for a long time, you need the basis for a truly excellent friendship, or chances are that you're not going to survive."

"Your sex life together is a reflection of the rest of your life together," says Dr. Patricia Weerakoon, a popular Australian sexologist and the coordinator of the graduate program in sexual health at the University of Sydney. So developing—and maintaining—intimacy *outside* the bedroom is the first step to making sure that you've got lots of it *in* the bedroom.

The Guy with the Most Points Wins

In case you haven't noticed, women pay attention to all aspects of your performance in the relationship. "There is a certain balance sheet we all keep in our heads, and women attribute certain meanings to behaviors," says Patricia Pasick, PhD, a psychologist in Ann Arbor, Michigan, who counsels couples on the fine art of negotiation.

What do women want? They want a neurotic roommate, a best friend, a charming and thoughtful date, a tender and nurturing boyfriend, and an ardent, innovative lover who provides blisteringly great sex on command. All in one guy. As the lady says, why shouldn't they have it all?

Being a better mate pays dividends. See how you stack up.

Be the World's Best Roommate

The challenge: Living with each other. Not euphemistically, either—we're talking about sharing a bathroom.

Not good enough: Animal house.

The bare minimum: Put the toilet seat down. Put your dirty dishes in the dishwasher.

Good boy: Put gas in the car, take out the garbage, fix the thing that leaks and the other thing that squeaks.

Bonus points: Install a new dishwasher.

What the Experts Say

Keep the door closed. Sharing a home and a bathroom is indeed intimate—and not always in a good way. Remember the "bad naked" *Seinfeld* episode? Seeing the woman of your dreams artfully arrayed against the pillows is good naked—but opening a pickle jar, not so much. The Kama Sutra actually recommends separate facilities for men and women and discusses bathroom etiquette. It's not an appealing subject—but neither is seeing you trim those nose hairs.

"Don't brush your teeth or pick your blemishes at the same time. Close the door when you go to the bathroom. You *can* know too much about someone else, and when you do, it's hard to make the transition back to passionate lovemaking," says Robin Milhausen, PhD, assistant professor at Canada's University of Guelph and the host of *Sex, Toys, and Chocolate,* a no-holds-barred Canadian TV show about sex.

"I work from our home, and it's very easy to get sloppy," says Andreas, an artist from Bern, Germany. "Before my girlfriend gets home, I take 10 minutes to put coffee cups in the sink and move newspapers, to change my T-shirt, or to jump into the shower if need be. I don't ever want her to dread coming home."

Help out. "Tune in to what turns your spouse on," says Hurry. "Sex toys, blue movies, and lingerie might blow your hair back, but she'd probably feel a lot more accommodating if you offered to get up early with the children so she could sleep in." A recent study showed that Italian women have hardly any time to play hide-the-cannoli. Between work, housework, cooking,

FENG SHUI FOR LOVERS

If the Kama Sutra is an advice manual for young men, then the Ananga Ranga, written about 1,000 years ago, is one to help married couples keep passion burning. The book recommends stocking the bedroom with erotic books, scented incense, and snacks and refreshments ("so useful for retaining and restoring vigor"). "In such a place, let the man, ascending the throne of love, enjoy the woman in ease and comfort, gratifying his and her every wish and every whim."

The need to create a space for lovemaking crosses every culture. We talked to Annie Payne, a feng shui consultant and author of *The Dance of Balance—Feng Shui for Body, Mind, and Spirit*, about what the ancient Chinese tradition of feng shui has to say: "Whether you know it or not, your environment displays the internal states of the people who live there. I can walk into a house and know if a couple is happy, and if they're having sex or not."

The good news is that you can change your inner states simply by changing your environment. And you don't have to throw everything out and start over; "even one thing can make a big difference." Traditionally, the bedroom symbolizes the relationship—no surprises there. Keep reading to see how tweaking the space around you can tweak what happens between you.

Power position. Feng shui is, above all, the art of placement. And in the bedroom, that means that the bed needs to be in the "power position," meaning that when you open your eyes, you can see the door.

Equal, equal, equal. If you have a spindly oak table on your side of the bed, with nothing on it but a clock radio, and your wife has a massive marble blanket chest, it speaks to an inequality that's going to reverberate out through the relationship, Payne says. If you have a lamp, she should have a lamp—and while they don't have to be exactly the same, they should be comparable in size, density, and intensity. If there's one chair in the room, there should be two. Getting the picture?

---

exercise, and "grooming," they're left with just 1 hour for sex every 15 days. Not surprisingly, nearly 40 percent say they are unhappy in their marriages.

"I feel guilty because I know my husband works hard all day too," says Dorke, a documentary filmmaker from Germany. "But the work of staying home with our sons is often so repetitive and boring that I think if I have to clean up one more sticky mess, I'm going to scream. And when he complains about not getting enough sex, I feel like putting him on a time-out with the rest of the infants."

Unplug. That 12-year-old treadmill has no place in the bedroom. And neither does that computer. "The bedroom is a place for sex and intimacy and conversation," Payne says. "And sleep."

She's realistic about televisions—"you'll never get people to take the televisions out of their bedrooms in this country"—but she does suggest that they be made as unobtrusive as possible. Throw a blanket over it when it's not in use, or stow it in an armoire.

Eliminate clutter. "Clutter," Payne says, "is drama." Eliminate piles of clothes, books, and old magazines. Reading material is of course okay, as long as it's select and relaxing in nature—not that mountain of annual reports you've been working through.

Go shopping. New linens will also help you to make a fresh start—rearranging the room and slapping a fresh coat of paint on the walls is even better.

Smaller is better. An enormous bedroom needs a lot of sexual energy from the couple to fill it up and make it cozy, says Payne. A small bedroom is best, but if yours isn't, then separate it out into separate "spaces," like a classic boudoir, so that there's a seating area away from the bed—for champagne and chocolate, of course.

Is that a LEGO, or are you happy to see me? In feng shui, it is believed that what surrounds you indicates what you'd like to cultivate. Now your bedroom is supposed to be the site of your romantic life, a private retreat for the two of you. So what does it say when you get a toy truck in the back as you're rolling over to try a new sexual position, or find yourself looking at a picture of your mother-in-law on vacation in Hawaii? If it's not entirely possible to keep the signs of your family life out of the bedroom, at least make them discreet. For instance, if your children enjoy playing in your room, keep a small basket for their toys behind or underneath a chair. Because Elmo shouldn't be the only one getting tickled in your house.

If her energy tank is empty, your sex life is going to stall. One of the best ways you can help to get it back on track is to pick up some of the heavy lifting. "Tiredness, especially for women, is often a barrier," says Steve Biddulph, Australian child psychologist, father of two, and coauthor of *How Love Works: How to Stay In Love as a Couple and Be True to Yourself Even with Kids.* "If a man shares the child care or housework, the couple is more likely to have sex. It's hard to feel loving towards

(continued on page 96)

MAKING THE TIME FOR LOVE

You're thinking about sex—but it's 11:00 a.m., and you're listening to your colleague Stan natter on about market share. It's 6:00 p.m. and you're thinking about it again, and this time your wife's actually in the room—but so are your three kids and the dog, and it's hours before they go to bed. By the time you actually have her alone at 11:00, it's all you can do to peck her on the cheek before you fall asleep.

Sound familiar? It's a very common scenario. "Whether you like it or not, sex is in competition with other parts of your life, social and otherwise. If it's going to happen, you have to make time for it," says Michelle Grahame, the managing director of nookii.com, a British company that sells adult games and toys.

And time, in this instance, means *quality* time and enough of it to have a really satisfying session, with no distractions—including fatigue. Because let's say the gods smile on you, and that aforementioned 11:00 p.m. peck turns into something a little more serious. What kind of sex are you going to have, exhausted after a day of work and domestic responsibilities—and knowing that the alarm clock is going to go off in T minus 6 hours?

Experts are unanimous: Life happens, but the relationship must come first. And in this case, that means sex. "It's very important to give your sexual relationship time, and to protect it from the stresses of workaholism and family obligations," says British expert Phillip Hodson. Here are some thoughts for making sure it doesn't get relegated to the back burner.

Steal a moment. As Tantric experts Stephen and Lokita Carter point out, taking a moment to be together doesn't have to be a massive time commitment. "Begin your day by sharing an embrace with your beloved before getting out of bed, or make time for a special kiss after a long day away from each other. Add more and more of these rituals to your day." A hug and a kiss—that's it. No matter how pressed for time you are, you can unearth the seconds required for these.

Feel her up. The next time you're someplace where lots of teenagers hang out, take a moment to do an anthropological field study. What's the first thing you notice? *They're touching each other all the time.* They find completely ludicrous reasons to make physical contact—backrubs, pushing, tickling, taking a sip of someone else's soda—and those are the unattached! The ones who are already hooked up are putting as much of the other person into their mouths as they possibly can.

You may not be able to match a 16-year-old's natural hormone levels—but all that touching is actually helping them out in that department: The more you fool around, the more you want to fool around. And keeping her at a constant low hum doesn't hurt your cause.

So get out of there before someone calls mall security and put what you've learned into practice at home. Grab a handful as she's getting the groceries out of the car. Let her see and feel how much you like her as you're getting out of the shower. (It's best when she least expects it.) And if that's all the time you have, then put it in the bank and leave it there. You'll collect later. . . .

If the spirit moves you, do it: Let the bills go unpaid and the dishes pile up. If you have a moment for sex, go for it. "Sex is more important than your career and even your kids," says Daniel Stein, MD, medical director of the Foundation for Intimacy in Tampa. "Your career will change, and your children will grow up and leave home, but in the end there will be the two of you."

"They say that to survive the first year, you should sleep when the baby sleeps. My husband and I made a promise to make love when she sleeps!" says Anja, a holistic health practitioner in Germany. "It's fun—we feel like we're teenagers, sneaking around."

Make a date. Childhood experts make much of quality time. But we need it too! And watching *The Wire* with a pizza between you isn't it. Getting out of the house and having a conversation with one another periodically is essential—"you need time to see each other as new," says Ascha Vissel, a Dutch psychologist and sex therapist—and it won't happen unless you make the date, arrange for it, and *keep* it.

"Every time we make a date to go out, I think, 'This is such a hassle!' It's so expensive to get a babysitter, and all I feel like doing at the end of the week is curling up with a movie. But as soon as I'm sitting with my husband and having my first cocktail, I think, 'Why don't we do this all the time?'" says Dorke, a documentary filmmaker from Germany.

No, you don't always feel like doing it. But you will once you're out the door. Yes, it can be expensive, but so is divorce, and if you get *there*, money will be the least of your problems. Think of it as an investment in your relationship. You fix the leak before you need a whole new roof, right? This is the same thing.

If you find that it keeps slipping off the schedule, put it on the calendar: The first Wednesday of every month is date night. If you still have problems, book a babysitter in advance ("We're going to need you the first Wednesday of every month") or make 6 months' worth of reservations.

Make it special for both of you by taking a little extra effort with your plans and your appearance. "Do your best for your partner—be clean and well-groomed, like you would on a date. Wear something you know she

(continued)

likes," advises Vissel. It can be a refreshing change, after a week spent in boring business suits—or a sweatshirt covered in baby puke. "If the basis of the relationship is good, and the attraction is still there, rediscovering one another can be almost like falling in love all over again," says Vissel.

Don't squander date night. It's happened to all of us. You took the trouble to hire a babysitter and get out of the house, and still no sex! What happened? You flirted like teenagers over the appetizers, and she was hot and heavy by dessert—but by the time you got home and the makeup was off and the kids tucked in, there was no loving feeling left.

In *Sex for Busy People*, her brilliant guide to the art of the quickie, British expert Emily Dubberley tells you how to cut this nonsense off at the pass. Talk dirty to one another all the way home, she suggests, and make sure you know exactly what she was thinking about over the tiramisu. Right before you unlock the door, plant a really deep, passionate kiss on her—a promise of things to come very soon. Then pay the sitter as fast as you can and let the cat scratch at the door, because you're not going to let anything get in the way of your best-laid plans.

Schedule it. "Most couples don't spend any time planning for intimacy," says Dr. Stein, "but sex is all about expectation. I call it setting the table for sex."

"I have sex with my wife on Wednesdays. Sometimes on Tuesdays and Sundays too, but always on Wednesday," says Alejandro from Madrid. "It was my wife's idea. We kept waiting for 'the right moment,' and finally she said, 'Forget about it—let's *make* the right moment.' It's not exactly spontaneous, and I thought that would ruin our sex life, but the sex is great. The only difference now is I don't have to wonder about whether it's going to happen or not."

Netdoctor UK sex columnist Christine Webber agrees. "If you're going to wait to have glorious spontaneous sex, you may have to wait a long time! Fixing a date for it doesn't take away from the romance; if anything, it's very romantic—what's more romantic than reserving a special time to use for the two of you alone?"

And Webber reminds you that all that anticipation is on your side—

someone when you are angry with him for not pulling his weight." Dr. Weerakoon agrees: "I tell the groups I speak to that sometimes the kitchen is the sexiest room in the house. There's nothing more arousing to a woman than a husband who has just done all the dishes."

The very labor-intensive years of early childrearing don't last forever—it no-effort foreplay. "When you were dating, you'd rush around all day thinking about your date in the evening, getting yourself into a really ideal state of readiness. This is particularly important for women, for whom anticipation is a form of foreplay."

In fact, many couples find that there are many benefits to scheduling sex, particularly for her. "When we were dating, I would plan for 2 days. I'd work out like crazy, get my legs waxed, moisturize myself head-to-toe. Making a date to have sex means that I can do the same things, even now that we're married," says Assia, a publishing executive in Amsterdam. That's good for you, but it's good for her too; a woman who feels comfortable about her body and presentation is a woman who's relaxed and more likely to try new things.

And for him? "Once a week isn't enough, but it's better than nothing," says Alejandro. "And in our experience, the more sex we have, the more sex we have."

What if you're not in the mood when Wednesday rolls around? Do it anyway. After all, both of you have to depend on the date or the whole conceit falls apart. Don't forget that desire doesn't necessarily precede arousal. It might not be the best-case scenario, but sometimes the horse has to follow the cart. "My clients often say, 'I wasn't in the mood when we started, but once we got into it, I really enjoyed it,'" says Michele Weiner-Davis, author of *The Sex-Starved Marriage*. "Sometimes the hardest part of running is putting on your shoes. So just do it."

And if one of you really doesn't feel like engaging in full-on sex, don't forget that there are lots and lots of very pleasurable and satisfying alternatives to ensure that your partner sleeps the post-orgasmic sleep of the gods.

The best part of waking up . . . Nobody gets up right when the alarm rings. Set your alarm 10 minutes early on purpose—but instead of hitting the snooze button, see if you can't bring some early morning sunshine to the person sleeping beside you. This is especially good for you; there's some evidence that your testosterone is at its highest early in the morning.

just feels that way. In the meantime, see what you can do to help. "Our marriage was saved by a cooking class!" says Steve, an Australian money manager. "For years we fought about chores, and then my mother signed me up for a one-night, introductory cooking class. So, now I cook dinner; I find it a really relaxing way to unwind from my day. Also, the food is better."

Be the World's Best Date

The challenge: She's going to her office Christmas party. You're the arm candy.

Not good enough: Drinking too much, flirting with other women, abandoning her for long periods of time to yell at the Colts with a cluster of other husbands.

Bare minimum: Stay by her side.

Good boy: You procure drinks. You rescue her at least once from her long-talking boring colleague.

Bonus points: You sneak her off to have fantastic, illicit sex in her boss's closet. You participate in after-party gossip forensics on the car ride home.

What the Experts Say

Your number one weapon? The compliment. The way a woman feels about her body correlates with how inhibited she feels in bed. So if you want her freak flag to fly, your best bet is to compliment the areas she feels most insecure about. Every woman has her Achilles heel. That J-Lo butt may seem juicy and delicious to you, but she's spent her whole life trying to cram it into jeans meant for someone smaller. Her breasts may be perfect champagne coupes, but she's not entirely convinced that you wouldn't like your cups to overflow.

Don't save these compliments for the bedroom—in fact, make very sure that you're lavish with them precisely when there's no chance they'll pay dividends. "It's a gift to compliment her outside of the bedroom," says Helen Fisher, PhD, research professor in the anthropology department at Rutgers University in New Jersey and author of *Why We Love.*

> *If you want her freak flag to fly, compliment the areas of her body she feels most insecure about.*

Reinstate one courtesy. Surely there's some social nicety that has slipped through the cracks since the days when you were courting? Opening the car door for her, bringing her flowers, calling the morning after some off-the-charts sex to tell her how smoking she is? Time to bring back some of those oldies but goodies. Get in touch with your inner Cary Grant and see if you don't find yourself in a lip-lock you weren't expecting.

THE BENEFITS OF BEING A KISS-UP

German psychologists conducted a study in which they learned that people who kiss their spouses each morning live 5 years longer than those who don't. Kissers also have fewer car accidents and fewer sick days, and earn 20 to 30 percent more money.

Be the World's Best Boyfriend

The challenge: To be as romantic now as you were the first month you were together.

HOW YOU RATE

Not good enough: Not remembering. Anything.

Bare minimum: You remember her birthday and your wedding anniversary/the day you met at least a week in advance without any dropped hints.

Good boy: You periodically show up with flowers for no reason, a CD or DVD you know she'll like, or reservations for dinner out just because it's Wednesday.

Bonus points: Organizing a weekend away or an elaborate birthday surprise. (See "What to Get the Woman Who Has Everything" on page 77 for more advice.)

What the Experts Say

Spoil her. Everybody needs to feel taken care of, and some women are more romantically oriented than others. And the shortcut to a woman's devotion is the surprise. All the better if you can appeal to her caregiving instinct and turn it back on her in unexpected ways. She'll turn to mush if you treat her to an out-of-the-blue gesture that pampers her. So, produce one of the following out of your magic hat.

- Tell her that she can sleep as late as she wants to on Saturday, and tell her that you will take the kids to karate class and pick up the dry cleaning and do all the other errands that she was going to have to do.

- Agree to do all of the above while she takes advantage of the spa gift certificate in your right hand.

BATHE HER WITH PLEASURE

Bathing before sex is a ritual in many cultures, and a scented, candlelit bath is one of the most-cited romantic gestures. The heat of the water relaxes the muscles and the mind, gives the skin a rosy glow, and, of course, cleanses the body. "It's such a simple thing, but it is a small gesture that will make any woman melt," says Alessandra, who works in real estate in Peru.

In Japan in particular, bathing is a time-honored prelude to lovemaking, says Jina Bacarr in *The Japanese Art of Sex*. Bacarr shows you how you can give your lover the full-on geisha experience: Fill the tub with hot water, and then add 1 to 2 quarts of sake for a *sakeboro*, or "sake bath." Soaking in this mixture for 30 minutes will smooth and soften her skin. Other delightful variations Bacarr suggests include floating edible yellow chrysanthemums in a hot bath, or the petals from the roses you brought her that are now starting to fade.

"My husband will sometimes signal that he wants to make love by asking me if I want a bath," says Ottavia, an illustrator in Milan. "He lights candles and adds oils to the water, and then lies down on our bed. I perfume and moisturize myself at my leisure—I like to have a little time to fantasize! And then we meet up again in the bedroom. It's a very sexy ritual, from our courtship."

If you do decide to join her, there's another trick to be learned from the Japanese. "Soaplands" are Japanese brothels that combine sex with the art of Japanese bathing. "The soaper covers her body with jasmine-scented soap, and then uses her slippery body to lather the man, using her body as a washcloth," Bacarr says. "After he's clean, she often gives him a tongue bath, going over every inch of him." You can take turns "cleaning" one another by keeping the water level low and pouring plenty of bath oil all over one another's skin.

For extra points:

■ Throw in a pair of Rub-a-Dub Dice ($10)—floating foam cubes that, when "rolled," reveal sexy commands like "sponge belly" or "kiss back." They're available at www.mypleasure.com.

■ Throw a towel in the dryer for a few minutes (spritz it with her favorite perfume before you do, or throw in a dryer sheet).

■ When she gets out, all warm and relaxed and delicious smelling, slather her with moisturizer. For best results, warm it in the microwave for 10 seconds. (Test it on the inside of your elbow before applying it to her skin; your finger skin isn't as sensitive to heat.)

- Make and serve her breakfast in bed.

- Run her a bath (see "Bathe Her with Pleasure" on the opposite page).

- Surprise her with reservations at your local bistro tonight.

This is one area where it pays to be accommodating. Too many guys think hearts and flowers and say "That's not my bag." Well, say that often enough, and soon you'll discover that sex isn't *her* bag anymore.

Wax nostalgic. Revisiting that bed-and-breakfast romp of 3 months ago isn't just an exercise in nostalgia. Recalling the relationship's formative moments can stir up the hormone norepinephrine, which helps the brain shine an emotional klieg light on memories. "You'll unlock her passion," says sex therapist Laura Berman, PhD, director of the Berman Center in Chicago, "and intensify the new memories you're making, too." In fact, see if she's up for a challenge: "Remember the time standing up in the basement? I bet we could do even better."

The brain's internal archivist responds best to strong contextual cues—smells, environments, music, textures, even certain foods—so orient her mental rearview mirror by concocting a smorgasbord of evocative sights and sounds.

This trip down memory lane doesn't have to be sexual. Being a man, you can't recall exactly how you behaved before you'd slept with her a thousand times. She, meanwhile, has logged how intensely you gazed into her eyes, how eager you were to tear off her clothes, and all those things you said and did just to make her laugh. What did you do on your first dates? How nervous were you the first time you met her parents? What did you really think the first time you met her best friend (careful!)?

Did you call her in the middle of the day just to say hi? Did you snake a hand up her sweater the second she walked in the door? Did you talk endlessly about all the trips you wanted to take with her? Bring some of that back and you'll have a happy wife.

Be the World's Best Friend

The challenge: To satisfy her emotional needs as well as her best girlfriend. Okay—almost as well.

Not good enough: She's crying. You fall asleep.

Bare minimum: You stop writing e-mail and watching the game when she's talking to you.

Good boy: You listen when she talks—really listen—and ask questions.

Bonus points: You set aside 20 minutes every night just to be with her and give her your full attention, to hear about her day, and to tell her about yours.

What the Experts Say

Listen. One of the biggest trends in marriage studies of the past 30 years is videotaping couples talking and fighting—and then following up 5 years later to see who's divorced. Well, guess what? The couples who got divorced are those who ignored each other or were downright hostile. When the guy actually listened to his wife when she spoke, showed interest and affection, his marriage survived.

A recent major study of 5,010 couples found that women are happiest in their marriages when they get their husbands' attention and feel that they are emotionally engaged. Steven L. Nock, PhD, the study's coauthor, says that successful husbands are good at "showing interest in the routines of their wives' lives—the routine, mundane things that men normally don't talk about."

Granted, it's not most men's style to do this. Dr. Nock wonders how many men find it perfectly natural, after several years of marriage, to sit down every day and say, "Tell me about your day." "It is an effort," he says, but while sympathetic, he's also adamant about its importance.

All it takes, says Michele Weiner-Davis, author of *The Sex-Starved Marriage*, is 15 minutes of daily check-in. It doesn't even matter what you talk about. What's important is that you're talking, touching, and expressing everyday concern and affection. "This sort of daily connection and friendship," she says, "is the foundation for keeping sexuality alive."

Stop the bickering. It's the little stuff that does it, like using her bath towel to wipe off your excess shaving cream. A small infraction, but add that to your fondness for stockpiling dirty plates and farting in bed, and these minor things can add up to something major.

If the bickering is getting on your nerves, Allen Elkin, stress expert at the Stress Management and Counseling Center in New York City, suggests this: In a playful way, ask your partner to make a list of the annoying things you do. Only small stuff: squeezing the toothpaste in the middle, leaving the toilet seat up. "On a scale of 1 to 10, these habits should rate about a 2 or 3," says Elkin. Make your own list and swap. "This is one step towards eliminating the little stresses that can try a relationship," says Elkin. Then, once you've tackled the toilet seat, you can move on to tougher stuff, like her fascination with those Lifetime movies.

Don't let disagreements fester. What happens outside the bedroom doesn't stay outside the bedroom. Unresolved arguments, tension, and disappointments walk right in and wedge themselves between you in bed. "If you're angry with your partner about something else in the relationship, unforgiving about something that has happened, or can't make sacrifices or compromise, it will carry over to what happens between you in the bedroom," says Dr. Weerakoon.

A LITTLE DISTANCE MAKES
THE HEART GROW FONDER

Therapists agree that long-time couples with strong relationships often spend time apart doing different things. Being separate for a while creates an electrical charge between you, and creating space gives your partner a chance to miss you. So it's probably a good idea to develop and nurture friendships—his, hers, and ours. But be careful. It's arguably the ultimate relationship tug-of-war: your buddies pulling in one direction, your wife or girlfriend in the other. And, of course, if either side wins, you lose, which is why it's critical to convince the opponent with the edge—the one who'll withhold sex—to let up a little.

You need to get inside her head. "While men tend to be jealous of potential sexual rivals, women tend to be jealous of time and attention," says Charles Hill, PhD, professor of psychology at Whittier College in California. Therefore, any plans you make to hang out with the guys need to be balanced by corresponding dates with your mate. And no, hitting Home Depot together does not count as memorable couple time. "Give her something to look forward to, since you're going to take something away," says Stan Charnofsky, EdD, head of the marriage and family therapy program at California State University at Northridge. This means dangling the carrot of a matinee play, a museum exhibition, or a wine-tasting event. You get poker night, she gets pinot noir.

This can be especially true after children, when there seems to be even less time for couples to discuss how they feel about things. As a result, "you accumulate misunderstandings," says Biddulph. "When you have children, you can go for 2 years passing in the corridor, living on the memory of when you used to be in love."

"We never talked about anything because neither of us wanted to fight in front of the children," says Laura, a British postal worker. "Finally my husband said, 'We either run the risk of them hearing us, or we really scar them by getting a divorce!' If we do have an argument, we simply explain to them that Mummy and Daddy don't agree about everything, but we love each other very much."

Be the World's Best Lover

The challenge: To deliver torrid, red-hot, sultry affair-worthy sex.

HOW YOU RATE

Not good enough: You do. She doesn't. You fall asleep.

Bare minimum: You do. She does. You fall asleep.

Good boy: You do. She does twice, thanks to your magic fingers and that favorite little trick you'll learn in Chapter 8.

Bonus points: You do. She does, too many times to count—but at least once during the erotic massage, once during the tongue bath, once in each position, and then a couple of times with the vibrator you surprised her with.

What the Experts Say

Keep getting better. "Marriage needs time and innovation," says Dr. Weerakoon. Just because you know how to get her off shouldn't mean that's the end of the line. "If you've learned how to pleasure her, it's too easy to forget about foreplay and all the other things that keep sex fresh," says Debbie Herbenick, PhD, the *Men's Health* "Bedroom Confidential" columnist.

"You can get into a pattern which exercises the law of diminishing returns. Repeating the same stimulus over and over again will eventually achieve a diminished response, and the whole thing feels dull as ditchwater," says Phillip Hodson. "We all have a responsibility to our partners to bring a sense of creativity to how we conduct the relationship. The onus is on all of us to be interesting."

And never more so than in bed. So listen up for tips and tricks that will keep the spark between the two of you as fresh and exciting as it was the day you met.

Play games. We offer to you the universal antidote to boredom, one which has been offered to children on rainy Saturday afternoons around the world since time immemorial: "Quit whining. Go play."

"The common denominator of satisfied couples is that they're very playful," says Ava Cadell, PhD, a Hungarian-born, British-raised expert who has traveled and taught widely throughout the world. "My definition of sex is adult play. It should be fun and recreational. You should laugh and release all those pleasure endorphins. A sense of humor is an essential ingredient in great sex because it takes pressure off performance."

Play allows the two of you to experiment in areas you might not have felt comfortable going before. "As long as you keep the intimacy and the playfulness, you can try different things," says Ascha Vissel, a Dutch psychologist and sex therapist.

Play will also help you to keep up with changing desires as your relationship matures. What she wanted at 20 isn't necessarily what she's going to want at 30, 40, or 50. How are you going to know what's on the new agenda? "People are constantly evolving. Play is a way for you to keep up with the person you're with and the changes they're going through," says

---

GAMES *SEXY* PEOPLE PLAY

British expert Graham Masterson, former editor of *Penthouse* and *Penthouse Forum* and author of the *Secrets of Sexual Play*, gives the following three rules for sexual play:

1. You not only allow each other to act out whatever sexual scenario you desire, but you both enthusiastically participate in it, no matter how wild or extreme it might be.

2. No physical pain or injury is to be inflicted (unless this is part of the game, and negotiated beforehand).

3. If you enjoyed a game, tell each other how much you liked it. If you didn't, agree to put it behind you and move on. You don't have to play a game a second time if you really don't want to.

Julianne Balmain, San Francisco–based coauthor of *The Kama Sutra Deck: 50 Ways to Love Your Lover.*

Innovate. First, a quick lesson in sexual science. There are two common categories of sexual arousal: reflex-based and psychogenic. The former is stimulation through physical touch: Rub here to activate. Psychogenic refers to mental stimulation and other sensory stimuli—from thinking sexy thoughts to seeing a miniskirt to smelling that perfume. Most relationships start out in a psychogenic mode (everything is new!) and gradually become reflex-based. And too often boring.

"Over time, a relationship becomes like an old shoe: There's nothing beautiful or interesting about it, but you don't throw it away because it's comfortable. Often, both partners are hoping for a change, but they're not saying anything or doing anything, so that they end up living in a holding pattern, and the old shoe syndrome keeps getting worse," says Dr. Weerakoon.

"Routine happens when our sexual intercourse takes place always during weekends, at night, or in the bedroom. This routine may affect sexual satisfaction in some couples," warns Miguel Cuetos, a Spanish sexual therapist. Scheduled sex can be a very good thing indeed for busy couples, but it can also represent the worst of reflex-based sex, a kind of forced sexuality. The key is to add psychogenic stimuli. This is where a fantasy and some novelty can help.

"Sexually satisfied couples are sexually adventurous—the two, in fact, feed each other," says Tracey Cox. She goes so far as to suggest that truly satisfied couples "include raunchy, risky things the average couple would gulp at and consider inappropriate."

Before you start funking it up, make sure she's on board: "Both partners have to agree to a change," Cuetos says. And remember that even small changes can make an enormous difference. "Novelty is good for sex, and I don't just mean novel sex. Novelty in your social life," says Dr.

WHY SHE WANTED A RING SO BADLY

In a study, two-thirds of women surveyed claim they had the best sex of their lives with their husbands.

Fisher. It can be as simple as skipping dinner to play miniature golf or listening to a live band instead of the car radio. Anything that makes the start of your date less predictable can change up the ending, as well.

"More than anything, we try to get people to break old behavior patterns," says Dr. Weerakoon. "It's not that he's not satisfying her in bed, but that he kisses her on the left cheek every single time when it's over that makes her want to kill him. It's not that she minds the kiss, but *that she knows it's coming.*"

Create a different atmosphere. One easy way to break predictability is to create a different atmosphere. "Set up a special space, a different environment. Change the lighting. Change the smell," says Dee McDonald, the founder of the Centre for Sexual Wellbeing in London and Sussex.

Eat in. Instead of your standard takeout-and-TV evening, treat her to a bedroom picnic—complete with a blanket on the floor or spread over the bed. Open a bottle of wine (white or champagne is less of a stain hazard than red) and serve up some simple finger foods like sushi, dim sum (extra points if you can feed her with chopsticks), or even homemade English-muffin pizzas.

"Making dinner plays to a woman's heart because it's one less thing she has to deal with when she gets home," says Carolyn Bushong, a psychotherapist and author of *Bring Back the Man You Fell in Love With*. And the proximity to the bed makes it unique and especially sexy.

Be the decider. If you're usually in charge, let her drive. Christine Wheeler, a British psychotherapist and sex columnist for Netdoctor UK, suggests that you tell your lady that you want her to draw up tonight's menu of love—say, half an hour of kissing, followed by an erotic story read aloud, followed by luxurious, slow sex. She can have whatever she wants, and it's your job to execute her commands to the very best of your ability.

If she usually calls the shots, let her know as soon as she walks through the door that you're going to take complete control of the evening—from choosing dinner and wine to drawing her a bath to what position you'll be having sex in. As long as you're prioritizing her pleasure, she's sure to feel relief.

Tough job. . . .

Change *one* thing. "Just make something different. If you have a 10-minute sex routine, change it. Introduce some massage, maybe a nice

GETTING TO KNOW YOU (ALL OVER AGAIN)

Sensate focus is an exercise developed by the pioneering sex therapists Masters and Johnson. But this technique isn't restricted to couples having sexual problems. Pretty much every couple can gain something from it—whether for variety, to catch up with what has changed, or as a way to reconnect after a long absence, a fight, or something else. In short, it helps you to be with each other in a different way than the way you're used to. (It also means no sex for a little bit, and nothing is sexier than not being able to have the thing you most want.)

Most therapists agree on some variation of the following rules:

No sex, please! Sometimes the best way to put your sex life back on track is to take it off the table for a while. So, during these exercises, make it clear from the outset that there will be no intercourse, and (at least for the first couple of sessions) no touching of the breasts, nipples, or genitals.

When sexual arousal and orgasm aren't "the point," then neither one of you will feel pressure to get turned on, or to turn the other person on. No performance anxiety allowed—just concentrate on what feels good! And if the action moves too fast, you can always take a step back and return to a less sexual form of touching.

Shhh. Although the point of this exercise is communication, too much talking during the exercise itself can be distracting. Instead, speak only if something is actively uncomfortable or painful, and review what you liked and disliked afterward.

Stay in the moment. You may feel your mind drift away or race anxiously to think about something else, like the upsetting e-mail you just received or the parent-teacher conference next week. When it happens, gently bring your mind back from where it's gone and concentrate once again on the sensations.

Easier said than done. Concentrate, not on pleasing your partner, but on what is happening to you.

---

book with some pictures, visit a woman-friendly Web site. Get a babysitter, book a hotel room," says Ascha Vissel.

She cautions you not to go straight to the wildest thing you can imagine. "You don't want to go from having sex in the dark with all the lights off to the next second wearing a full rubber suit. Introduce things step by step."

"It doesn't have to mean leather and suspension bondage," says Dee McDonald, "just cutting someone's lacy knickers off them can give a big

Sensate focus traditionally unfolds in three stages—this is a highly simplified version of them, and one that assumes neither of you has a serious problem with sex:

Stage One: The point of the exercise is simply to alternate gentle touching. One person gives, one receives. If you're the toucher, touch the "touchee" everywhere (except where you've agreed that you won't). Vary the types of touch you use. You may want to try using things that aren't your hands—a clean, soft paintbrush, for instance. Or a feather. Or some massage oil.

Stage Two: You progress to some sexual touching—but still no intercourse; you don't want to turn the spotlight on the genitals. Include the breasts, nipples, and sexual organs as just another part to touch and explore and enjoy.

One variation in this stage is called "hand-riding." Without speaking, the touched person puts his or her hand on top of the toucher's hand to indicate what pace, pressure, or spot would feel best. These are suggestions, not orders.

Some couples like to end their sessions with mutual masturbation, which can be educational in its own right.

Stage Three: You can move to mutual touching now. You can also progress to intercourse. (If you're doing sensate focus to address a sexual problem, you may want to take this more slowly. For instance, genital-to-genital touching without penetration.) Many therapists recommend starting with a very minimal penetration (say, 1 inch)—and then stop. Just lie together, and concentrate on the sensations—and emotions—you feel. When you begin to move—and this may be in a different session altogether—concentrate on what you want it to be like, not what you've always done. These may be different, and if they are, this is the time to find out.

enough charge to make the sex great. Wear different textured underwear. Swap one another's clothes. Try lube, or feathers."

Have sex somewhere different (see Chapter 15). Have sex in a different position (Chapter 11). Or take this as an opportunity to try out a fantasy that's been getting you hot since puberty (Chapter 16).

Talk about it. Difficult conversations require preparation. "If you were going to tell her that you'd lost your job, or had cancer, or wanted to spend a great deal of money on something, you'd think a little about how to talk about that with her. A conversation about sex deserves equal respect," says Phillip Hodson.

Find an icebreaker. "Many couples who have been together for a long time have never, ever, ever talked with one another about sex. They

---

THE PERFECT GETAWAY

Men always ask us, "Why do I have such great sex on vacation?" Sun and surf, sure, not to mention the cocktails with the little umbrellas. But the real answer? There's no dishwasher to unload in Aruba.

Life's little complications aren't just exhausting—they're distinctly unsexy. Nothing about changing the light bulb in the den, or spending hours on hold to clear up a billing dispute says, "Take me now." And keeping your sex life on track is particularly bad during stressful life events. Sex life the first year after a new baby? Not so much. The first year after that baby goes off to college? Va va va voom.

You'll also find that going on vacation might make her more sexually adventurous. "My wife had sex with me on the balcony of our hotel; there were people eating dinner just across the way. All I could think was, 'There's no way she'd ever agree to do this at home!'" remembers Angelo, an Italian restaurant supplier.

That's why it's a very smart move, every once in a while—as difficult as it might be to squeeze into the budget, as hard as it might be to find someone to take the kids, as inconvenient as it might be to arrange time off from work—to get the hell out of Dodge.

US couples go on 155 million romantic getaways every year, but our European counterparts have considerably more to work with: While the average amount of vacation time provided by American employers is 10 days, it's significantly higher across Europe—4 weeks in Germany and Spain, 5 in Finland, a stunning 7 in France. One of the reasons that Europeans take such long vacations is because they don't believe you can really relax unless you have some time to do it. Prove them wrong by treating relaxation with the same ultra-efficiency you apply to everything else.

Leave work at home—your vacation starts on the way to the airport. Pack something relaxing to read on the plane. Before you get there, book a massage for your first morning—it's something to look forward to. And put sunscreen, bathing suits, sunglasses, and a paperback in a beach bag, and pack it so it's right at the top of your suitcase—that way, all you'll have to do is grab and go as soon as you hit the hotel. You can unpack later, after you've got a swim, a beer, and a quickie under your belt.

BE HER MYSTERY LOVER

Women are more receptive to scent than men are. So one quick change you can effect without too much difficulty is to change the way you smell. For a subtle effect, use a different soap or deodorant. To make a bolder statement, change colognes, or start wearing some.

need an icebreaker—something fun that breaks open the floodgates to communicating with one another about sex," says Dr. Weerakoon. "I often recommend—even to the church groups I speak to!—that couples go to Sexpo (an Australian sex-industry trade show, featuring everything from lingerie to porn to vibrators to erotic-shaped chocolates) or an adult bookstore together. I tell them, 'You don't have to do anything or buy anything, but it might be interesting for the two of you to know what's out there.' It starts the conversation, and that's the important thing."

Canadian TV host Milhausen agrees. "My hope for our show was that two people would be sitting at home watching another couple talking about sex on television, and they'd turn to each other and say, 'What do you think about that—is that crazy or something we could try?'"

"I saw a vibrating condom in the store the other day," adds Dr. Weerakoon. "You spend a few dollars and take that home, and you have a fun little thing to play with and an icebreaker to talk about other things."

Get creative! One couple we spoke to uses naughty fridge poetry to convey their deepest desires.

Stay positive. Criticisms are counterproductive, no matter how you feel. They will make her feel defensive and angry. Hodson suggests saying something like: "I've never really said this before to you, but what really gets me going these days is this: [insert request here]. Of course I have been enjoying what you've been doing, it's just that if you really want me to go crazy, here's how you'd do it."

Create a safe zone for the two of you to talk about some of your freakier fantasies by agreeing not to freak out when they're shared. "Make a pact never to judge anything your partner suggests," Cox recommends. And remember that you won't get out of that rut by rigidly staying within your comfort zone. Figuratively speaking, get the Pope, your parents, and your exes out of the bedroom. For once, forget about performance and other people's morality. Discover your unique sexual personality. Be open-minded. When the opportunity for novelty presents itself, let yourself enjoy the surprise. Try listening to your body instead of your conscience.

Your Cheating Heart

Cheating happens. In fact, almost every single couple in a long-term relationship will confront temptation at least once, whether they avert their glance or chase that particular rabbit down the hole.

"It's only realistic to acknowledge that infidelity probably will be an issue, so it's essential to manage it. I'm not an apologist for infidelity, but even the most unlikely people are prone to some tremendous wobbles at certain high-stress periods—midlife, of course, is one of the big ones," says Phillip Hodson. "The desire for attachment and family is very strong, but then so is the desire for novelty. A recent survey showed that 94 percent of Britons think that fidelity is essential, but other studies have shown that at least 60 percent of married people are at least occasionally unfaithful. So there is a

QUICKIE STATS

Men's Health asked 5,000 American men to spill their guts about love, sex, women, and dating. Here's what they said about cheating:

I'd cheat on my wife or girlfriend if . . .

A. She were cheating on me   22 percent

B. We were fighting and not getting along   4 percent

C. I knew I could get away with it   12 percent

D. I could sleep with a celebrity   9 percent

E. Never   52 percent

If I cheated on my wife or girlfriend, I'd . . .

A. Feel fine about it and keep mum   8 percent

B. Feel horrible, but keep mum (why hurt her?)   49 percent

C. Feel horrible and confess. I'd need to be honest   43 percent

If my wife or girlfriend cheated on me, I'd want her to . . .

A. Confess. I deserve to know   72 percent

B. Keep it quiet and not let it happen again   28 percent

Your girlfriend's friend makes a pass at you. You . . .

A. Tell her no, then tell your girl-friend   20 percent

B. Tell her no, but remain mum   54 percent

C. Tell her no, but keep the possibility open   22 percent

D. Go for it   4 percent

tremendous disparity between what we believe, and what we want to do, and how we behave."

Different cultures have, at different times, had a different relationship with monogamy. Some still do. In France, for instance, the so-called *cinq à sept* (sometimes translated as "happy hour") is the name for the period of time you spend with your lover after work, before going home to your spouse and children.

Defenders of the practice say that it's not erosive to the marriage but supports it. In some ways, the separation between the business of running a family and the sex/love/romance part of your life makes sense. Why would you expect that you would want to keep sleeping with this person, any more than you like the same clothes you did 10 years ago, or having the same thing for dinner every night?

And yet many of us do hope for the one great love that will see us through to the end of our days. And when those expectations are shattered, the results can be devastating, to say the least. As Ascha Vissel points out, the moral considerations of infidelity are separate from what is, at its heart, a violated agreement. "If you have said that you will not do this, then you need to think very hard before you break that promise."

Vissel suggests taking a strong attraction—something more than the garden-variety head-turning that happens because the world is filled with attractive people to whom you are not married—to someone else as a sign that something is lacking in your primary relationship. And while cheating is certainly not a good way to deliver a wake-up call to your spouse, talking about your inclination in that direction may be a last-resort jolt.

For Phillip Hodson, the fact that so many people do cheat—even when they know it's going to cause a great deal of pain—is a measure of the need behind the act. "Nobody gets married to hurt their partners—nobody cheats to cause maximal pain to the person they love." Neither did any of the experts we spoke to believe that an act of

QUICKIE STATS

Women with whom men most often cheat:

1. A stranger		13.0 percent
2. A co-worker		12.7 percent
3. Ex-girlfriend/wife		10.6 percent
4. A long-time crush		9.3 percent
5. A prostitute		7.8 percent
6. My girlfriend's/ wife's friend		7.1 percent
7. Other		11.9 percent

CHEAT WITH YOUR WIFE

There's no need to feel guilty about infidelity—as long as your mistress is wearing your ring on her finger. How to finesse this magic trick? Pretend to be someone else.

Here's an overview of some classic role-plays to get you started. British expert Graham Masterson suggests that the shy use different names for role play. "With a different name, you feel much less inhibited. After all, it's not actually *you* that's giving that spanking. . . ." And even if there's no bondage or dominance involved, it's a good idea to play with a safe word so that either of you can take a breather if you need to. If you're just starting out or shy about going whole hog, simply incorporating some of the props into ordinary sex can bring all the excitement without the commitment. Have fun!

Prostitute/John

The idea of being paid for sex seems to have a certain magic for women. Most describe the combination of empowerment and debasement to be enthralling. "The power dynamic fascinates me: He's paying, so she does what he wants. But at the same time, he's debased by having to pay for it, and she can be very generous with him, or have utter contempt," says Luisa, a scientific researcher in France.

Obviously, there are many variations on the oldest profession. Perhaps she's a concubine recently arrived into your harem. A geisha-in-training whose virginity has been entrusted to a wealthy patron for 7 nights of initiation into the world of physical love. An international call girl who doesn't get out of bed (or in this case, into it) for less than $20,000 and a designer shopping spree in Dubai. Or maybe she's a streetwalker in thigh-high boots waiting for you under the overpass.

Props: Incense and throw pillows. Or a wad of bills so thick you can't bend it and a diamond tennis bracelet. Or a $20 bill, 40 ounces of malt liquor, and a pack of gum.

infidelity needs to be the end of the relationship. (If you've married someone who is serially unfaithful, you have to look at whether that's something you can live with.) "When you're confronted with it, you have to ask yourself what you want to do about it. I will say that if you can try to turn a blind eye, it will tend to go away again. And there is nothing quite so posthumous as an affair that's over," says Hodson.

Take it further: Buy her some novelty clothes and rent a sleazy hotel room off the interstate. Tip her well.

Doctor/Nurse

Is it time for your annual physical again—already? Whether it's the smell of rubbing alcohol and the feel of cold steel instruments against your bare skin that makes you hot, or just the idea of a sponge bath administered by a very attractive, overly friendly nurse in a not-quite-regulation uniform, this is a very common fantasy, and easy to put into practice.

A nice spin on this one: the "psychologist" asks his "patient" to lie down on the couch, encouraging her to spill all of her deepest, darkest fantasies—things she's never told another living soul.

Props: Latex gloves ("I'll need you to turn your head and cough, sir."), nurse's cap, a man's shirt put on backward to simulate one of those backless hospital gowns. Remember: Rubbing alcohol is a good way to clean toys, but don't let it touch skin.

Prison Guard/Inmate

Cavity search, anyone? There are lots of bondage and domination possibilities in Cell Block A, obviously, but just the suggestion of this kind of out-of-kilter power dynamic can be enough to drive you wild.

"The idea of sex as currency which buys privileges, this makes me crazy," says Camille, a Frenchwoman living in New York. "Not to mention the idea of the other prisoners watching, or being 'forced' into doing one of my fellow prisoners while he watches." Tell her to spread 'em, and then frisk her from behind. Find out what she's willing to do for a pack of cigarettes.

Props: Handcuffs and a flashlight.

But even if it was a one-time thing, you may need some professional help to get over the hump. Certainly, if you both feel that the relationship is a priority and something you wish to salvage, you'll want to figure out why it happened. "You need to talk about it, obviously—a lot, and maybe even get some counseling," says Vissel.

Ultimately, putting it behind you means putting it behind you. "Once

CSI: MATRIMONY

A Japanese woman who suspects her husband is cheating on her can buy a special spray called S-Check that alerts her to the presence of seminal fluid on his underwear by turning green when it comes into contact with the offending stain. Woe to the poor guy who closed his office door at lunch and spent a quiet moment alone with his favorite clown porn site. . . .

you've made the decision to stay in the relationship, it's wise to put it in the past and make a fresh start," says Vissel. "When you've reached the stage where you've accepted it, don't bring it up all the time. Keep it in the past and give the relationship a new chance."

PART II

YOUR ITINERARY FOR TOURING A BROAD

CHAPTER 7

ENJOY THE MOST LEISURELY SEX IN THE WORLD

Use the F-Word: Foreplay

British men take their time, according to our survey results. Maybe it takes longer to penetrate that famous British reserve. Or maybe, as British expert Emily Dubberley suggests, they've been shamed into it. "There was a very popular British television show in the early 1990s that had a woman going around asking men on the street to point to the clitoris on a diagram. It was shocking because practically no one could point it out, and it shamed a whole generation of men into teaching themselves how to touch a woman's body."

British men also have some stiff competition: 50 percent of their women own a sex toy. "British women are told by women's mags that foreplay is something they should expect, and if a bloke doesn't do it, he's a selfish lover and not worth dating, so it could be down to women demanding it. There's a new breed of feisty and sexually confident women in the United Kingdom who are demanding foreplay, so men have no choice," Dubberley adds.

QUICKIE STATS

Average length of foreplay (in minutes):

1. United Kingdom	17.44
2. Australia	17.20
3. Germany	16.92
4. Mexico	16.91
5. Czech Republic	16.43
United States	**16.42**
World average	**15.78**

But if the reactions of our experts are any indication, even men with the most impressive numbers still have some work to do. "There are still lots of British men out there who try to get away with the bare minimum—and lots of women who put up with it," says Dubberley.

Their Australian counterparts, second in the survey's foreplay department, display the same dichotomy. At the same time that they claim to have a slow hand, "Aussie men have a very high sexual ego; they expect women will go crazy over them, even when they have daggy shorts, zinc cream on their nose, and have spent all evening drinking with their buddies," says Jan Hall, PhD, an Australian psychologist who specializes in relationship and sexual issues, and the author of *Sex-Life Solutions*.

Indeed, many of the steamiest and most creative foreplay stories, games, and tricks we heard were from French women—perhaps not surprisingly, given the French devotion to the art of love.

In this chapter, you'll learn everything you need to drive her wild in anticipation of your lovemaking—and some surprising reasons why foreplay is your best bet for more fulfilling sex as well.

"The Secret"

One Englishman who does speak well for the foreplay prowess of his countrymen is Ian, a Brit who now lives and runs a real-estate company in Bali. He provided probably the most knockout piece of sex advice we heard during the research for this book—and he claims that it came from a now-forgotten cheesy sex paperback he read when he was a kid. "I call it The Secret. *I never have sex with a woman unless she is begging me for it.* Literally. Never. Not when I know she's ready, not when she's making noise and grinding my leg. She has to beg me, or grab me with her hands and physically put me inside of her. Even then, I make her wait if I can. And whenever a woman tells me I'm the best she's ever had, I know it's because of The Secret."

Ian says he has received gifts from other men, so grateful were they for this piece of information. (We'll demur from printing his address here—if you're similarly inspired, pay it forward.) But we're not surprised that this technique has worked so well for him and the guys he's shared it with. If there's one single thing, more than any other, that we hear women say about sex, it's that intercourse happens too soon, and too fast. And yet, there's considerable evidence that learning to slow down and enjoy the scenery makes better sex for both parties.

Consider the evidence:

The Argument for Foreplay, Part I (for Her)

"Men are always in too much of a hurry," says Robert Santo-Paolo, a French sexologist and psychologist who runs the Web site www. sexotherapie.com. "It's a habit which they must always fight against. They are in a rush to bring a girl home, in a rush to have sex, in a rush to achieve penetration—and sometimes in a rush to leave!"

Women, on the other hand, *love* foreplay. Certainly, the experts are unanimous: "Don't rush to penetration," says Mabel Iam, the Argentinian psychotherapist, television host, and author of *Sex and the Perfect Lover.* "Women really appreciate a bit of time where they feel caressed and loved, and don't feel rushed into sex," says Christine Wheeler, a British psychotherapist and sex columnist for Netdoctor UK. "Take your time, and really focus on her pleasure," says Mary Taylor, a former exotic dancer in Toronto and the author of *Bedroom Games.* "Make it about pleasing her, and you will reap the rewards."

As it turns out, there are real biological and psychological reasons why all this dinner and dancing is such a necessary ingredient for her in great sex.

1. It's a segue. Real life, tragically, isn't sexy. And yet all too often we expect our partners to make a seamless transition—from harried mom, overworked small-business owner, official worrier-about-the-wasp's-nest-in-the-corner-of-the-garage—to the tantalizing courtesan of our dreams.

But great sex can't happen if she's got one stiletto still firmly planted in the world of snacks for soccer practice. Foreplay allows both of you to make the transition between "real" life and a more magic space.

This is especially important for women. "In my research, I've found that there are literally hundreds of things that can shut down a woman's arousal process, from worrying about work and kids to whether or not their legs are shaven," says Robin Milhausen, PhD, assistant professor at Canada's University of Guelph and the host of the Canadian sex talk show *Sex, Toys, and Chocolate,* a no-holds-barred TV show about sex.

"Obviously, that's a really problematic situation for men. So it's very helpful for them to know what they can do to help their partner to stay actively engaged—excited, enthused, and passionate." And what they can do is make sure that there's lots and lots of time for a woman to get into the groove.

This is a fundamental part of the ancient Tantric sex experience, which always begins with a ritual. Tantric ritual provides an excuse for playfulness and helps to change the atmosphere, say Stephen and Lokita Carter, experts in the ancient Indian tradition of Tantra and the authors of

Foreplay allows both of you to make the transition between "real" life and a more magic space.

Tantric Massage for Lovers. "A ritual can transform being with our mate into a sacred experience that is nourishing and heartwarming."

Before you get all worried, there's no chanting involved; in fact, the ritual can be very simple—as simple as making eye contact. All you need to do is effect that very important break with the outside world, keeping her focus where you want it—on you and what's about to happen between the two of you.

2. Foreplay closes the gap. It's math. Women take longer to become aroused. Without some stimulation before the main event, she'll just be getting warmed up as you're rolling over for some zzzs. Bear in mind that most women can't come from intercourse alone. "Since the number of women who reach the climax just by vaginal penetration is limited," says Spanish sexual therapist Miguel Cuetos, "men need to forget about coitus for a while and concentrate instead on sexual games beforehand, so that she can have one or more orgasms—even without penetration."

The quality of her orgasm will also be better if you take your time. "For me, a little time spent teasing is the difference between a totally toe-curling orgasm and one that's just okay. Not that I'm complaining, either way!" says Enes, a wine salesperson in Portugal. "You don't take your expensive sports car from zero to 60 in the winter, do you?" asks Japanese-German sex educator Midori, author of *Wild Side Sex.* "If you want the best performance, you warm it up first."

3. It syncs her up. Great sex is essentially a battle between two parts of the nervous system, the sympathetic and the parasympathetic. Her sympathetic nervous system is what kicks into high gear when she's confronted by a bear or Brad Pitt in a g-string. Her pupils dilate, her heart rate speeds up, she breaks out into a light sweat, and heavy breathing begins.

But her parasympathetic system is what calms her down enough to enable her to have an orgasm—and it's really important for women. In fact, a Swedish study discovered that it was totally impossible for a woman to have an orgasm if the part of her brain that processes anxiety was activated. In short, great sex is essentially a combination of stimulation and relaxation—a difficult balance to achieve. That's where foreplay comes in.

4. Communication. Her orgasm, while important, is not the sole point of foreplay, or sex in general.

"Foreplay is more than a collection of techniques designed to arouse your partner; it's a negotiation about the level of intimacy and meaning of what comes next," says Caroline Hurry, a sex writer in South Africa.

British sex journalist Megan Roberts points out that foreplay is the hands-down best way to get to know your partner's body—what she likes and doesn't like, what makes her crazy, what leaves her cold. "No matter what you might read in magazines, orgasm isn't the sole objective. Concentrate instead on getting to know her, and her body—and tell her equally what she can do to turn you on."

So that's why foreplay is so important for her. And of course your primary motivation is to make her happy—in sex, and in all things, right? But, as you'll see, foreplay isn't entirely a selfless act: It really does benefit both partners.

The Argument for Foreplay, Part II (for You)

Foreplay is one of those cases where what's good for the goose is indeed good for the gander.

1. What's good for her is good for you. The more foreplay you engage in, the more she's going to enjoy the sex, and the more she enjoys the sex, the more sex she's going to want to have. So you win right off the bat.

And don't forget that the more turned on she is, the more likely she is to agree to more creative positions or fantasy play. "Spend extra time focusing on each other's body and your intercourse will be more action-packed," says San Francisco–based sexologist Carol Queen, PhD, author of *Exhibitionism for the Shy*. The skilled knowledge of her body that

HOLD YOUR FIRE

Worried that too much foreplay is going to make your gun go off as soon as you touch the trigger? It's less of a concern than you think—more relaxed sex actually gives you better control.

Worst-case scenario, you continue the "her pleasure" theme and pull out for a minute to give her a little exclusive attention while you get yourself together. So slow down and enjoy the ride.

comes with good exploratory foreplay will surely come in handy during your next quickie, allowing you to rev her engines more quickly.

2. Better sex for you! You've heard the old saw: "Sex is like pizza; even when it's bad, it's still pretty good." Foreplay is what makes the difference between the tired slice of cardboard you buy at a train station because there's nothing else, and the world's best Brooklyn pie straight out of the brick oven—when you have a hangover. Why settle for "just-okay" sex when you can have "best-ever" sex every night?

If you've ever been teased, you know that the longer you hold off from direct genital contact, the better it feels when it happens. And staying aroused for a long time before ejaculation is the ticket to a mind-blowing orgasm. You'll never settle for what's under the heat lamps again.

3. Sex is fun again! "What are you talking about? Sex is *always* fun," you probably thought after reading that sentence. But is it? If you're being completely honest, you'll readily acknowledge that there's quite a bit of anxiety that goes along with sex in the modern world. Am I big enough? Am I going to stay hard? Am I doing it right? Does she like what I'm doing?

But of course, there's no such thing as "doing it wrong." As Michelle Grahame, the managing director of nookii.com, a British company that sells adult games and toys, says, "Sex isn't about bits and pieces—doing this or that to her g-spot for x number of minutes. It's about intimacy, imagination, and two people having a bit of fun!" Foreplay is a chance to increase the pleasure you get out of your sex life without feeling like sex is "work." By making exploration and discovery the goal—as opposed to how to get one another off in the least amount of time possible—you remove some of the anxiety that's crept into our sex lives—and bring some fun back into it.

4. Who said it had to be all about her? It's worth mentioning that although we sometimes tend to think of foreplay as exclusive attention to her, many women find the idea of pleasuring *you* an exciting way to begin the lovemaking process. "I must be very oral—I get wet in 30 seconds when I'm down on my lover," muses Nikita from Corsica. And that's pretty much all the foreplay *we'll* be needing today. . . .

So think of foreplay as going into extra innings, not a rain delay. And use these tips from around the world to make the preamble to sex as good as it can possibly be—for both of you.

How Long Is Long Enough?

According to a study by the University of New Brunswick in Canada, foreplay lasts an average of 12 minutes, and women would like it to go on for an average of about 18. Emily Dubberley's bare minimum is higher: "Do give her a decent amount of foreplay—at least half an hour—before even thinking about asking for a shag." In actuality, we suspect that some exaggeration is at work, even at the low end of the spectrum. From what we've heard, 12 minutes is a pretty long time, especially for a couple who have been together a long time.

But perhaps a by-the-minute approach is the wrong way to think about it. Dee McDonald, the founder of The Centre for Sexual Wellbeing in London and Sussex, says that she'd really like "people to forget the concept of 'fore' and simply *play* more throughout their sexual activity. If you remove the concept of foreplay, so that both people present are responsible for their own sexual pleasure as well as that of their partner, a greater variety of sexual experience is possible."

Press "Play"

A great deal of the advice in this chapter sounds like we're suggesting that you play games with your partner. Guess what? That's absolutely correct.

You might think games seem contrived, or unnecessary. After all, you're both adults; if you both

Games can greatly enrich your desire for one another.

want to have sex, what's stopping you? But in fact, games can greatly enrich your desire for one another and the gratification you feel when that desire is finally allowed to come to fruition. And that's true whether you've known each other 2 hours or 20 years.

No, you don't have to play naked charades. But you can—or whatever you want that will bring a sense of play back into your sex life. Which delivers us to the most important piece of advice in the whole book, right here, in this sentence: *Have fun with one another.*

Tease her during the cab ride home. Flirt with each other at dinner until your kids roll their eyes. And when you take her to bed tonight, make it as good-humored and lively as you can. Play strip poker. Strip Old Maid. (Strip Snap? Okay, maybe not.) Listen to music. Tell her silly jokes, or dirty ones. Mess around with her body because you're curious, not because you're following the pleasure textbook. Hang out in bed afterward because it's fun, and who knows what the rest of the night will bring?

"Enjoy the thrill of your mutual sexual attraction," says British expert Graham Masterson, former editor of *Penthouse* and *Penthouse Forum* and author of *The Secrets of Sexual Play.* "Find lighthearted ways of arousing each other." In this chapter, you'll find a lot of ways to do so. You certainly don't need to incorporate all of them—or even a small percentage of them—into one session with your partner. Nor do you need to proceed in the way they are presented. Mix and match them; try one tonight, save another for later. Use them as a launching pad for ever-greater explorations, or return with gratitude to the tried-and-true things that make you feel cozy about one another.

The only rules for the following games?

You Can Touch Her Anywhere You Want— Except for Her Genitals

Ah, there's the rub—or not—and it's a big one. And you know what? This is an experiment you're almost certain to fail. But we're pretty sure that by the time you give in and give up, your failure will have made the rest of your evening a rousing success.

Foreplay Starts *LONG* Before the Sex Does

Many men think foreplay starts when the two of you are actually beginning to mess around. (Actually, lots of the women we interviewed think too many men think foreplay means asking "Are you awake?"—but never mind.)

Realize that the more work you do outside of the bedroom, the less you'll have to do when you're in it. "It's really the thoughtful things you do at nonsexual times that make a woman want you," says Paul Joannides, author of *Guide to Getting It On!* And Mabel Iam reminds us that "a caress actually commences before any physical contact takes place, with a smoldering glance, a whispered sweet-nothing. The hands come later."

"There is a very sweet section in the Kama Sutra about all the things that couples can do to 'cultivate your love,' but what Vatsyayana is really talking about is increasing the intimacy that makes sex great," says Julianne Balmain, San Francisco–based coauthor of *The Kama Sutra Deck: 50 Ways to Love Your Lover.* What's surprising is how contemporary these ideas sound, even thousands of years later: admiring the new spring flowers, drinking fermented beverages at your friend's homes, going horseback riding in the country—all pretty good date ideas, aren't they?

One of the most effective forms of foreplay is "just to have a nice time!" points out Christine Webber, a British psychotherapist and sex columnist for Netdoctor UK. "If you surround the sex with things the two of you enjoy together, by the time you get to bed, the intimacy's already going to be there, and the two of you are really going to be in the mood." Whether that's going for a walk or to the movies, having fun together *outside of the bedroom* is one of the best foreplay tips we know.

Women—and you, by extension—really benefit from a long lead time, because they get off on anticipation. In a recent survey, women admitted fantasizing about sex up to twice as often as men do. If you're like most of us, this comes as quite a surprise. The key is understanding that men and women's fantasy lives are different, says Karen Donahey, PhD, director of the sex- and marital-therapy program at Northwestern University. Unlike your wham-bam-thank-you-ma'am numbers, hers are long, interactive scenarios. "The best thing my boyfriend can do to make my shift short at work is to tell me how we're going to do it when I get home," says Kyoto, a Japanese waitress.

Here are some strategies to keep her at a slow simmer all day, making it very easy for you to bring her to a rolling boil when you're finally in the same room.

Not the spreadsheet from marketing after all. First, begin the seduction when she's unattainable—you're both at work, she's stuck in traffic. "It could be a sexy e-mail or a voice-mail," says Birgit Ehrenberg, a sex columnist in Germany.

Sending her a dirty e-mail during the day can indeed be a very effective strategy. First of all, you've got the thrill of the unexpected on your side, especially if you usually use your Blackberries to communicate about the less erotic details of life, like daycare drop-off schedules and who's going to pick up the rotisserie chicken for dinner. This time, when she hears the familiar *bing* to tell her she's got mail, let it be something that will make her cheeks burn and her panties wet.

"I texted the man I'm seeing to tell him that I'd meet him at 7:00 p.m., and he texted back, 'Perfect. I should be deep inside you by 7:30 p.m. then. Can't wait.' The anticipation of what was going to happen later that evening had me throbbing with desire all day," says Emma, a British publicist.

And if you're sending it to her at work, instead of worrying about what that creep in IT is thinking about, use the restrictions to your advantage by speaking in a code that only she'll understand. You spent last night licking every inch of her? "I think I missed a spot." You enjoyed an early-morning quickie before catching the train? "I can still smell you." It's been a while? "There's no escape; you're going to be begging me for mercy tonight."

One couple we know both work at home; they regularly IM each other wicked suggestions from their respective home offices until they can't stand the tension any longer and meet up in the bedroom. Is their electronic lead-up a corner that they could cut? Sure—but where's the fun in that?

Don't be surprised if you find that she's considerably more forward in her e-communications than she is in person. It's easier to say what you really want, and in the naughtiest way possible, when you aren't face to face. In fact, if she's a little self-conscious during face-to-face conversations about sex, then e-mail—and written communications in general—can be a way to talk about fantasies or for her to make a special request that she might not otherwise feel comfortable enough to ask for.

"You're so inappropriate!" And that's what makes it great. Yes, you'll get points for whispering sweet, nasty nothings into her ear as you're taking her clothes off in the privacy of your bedroom—but it's even better if you catch her just before you head off to play golf with her father.

"At my office drinks party, my husband found me alone and began talking dirty to me in a completely conversational tone of voice," says Paula, a social worker in Ireland. "These were some of the filthiest things I'd ever heard come out of his mouth, but his body language and tone were totally normal; you would have thought we were talking about whether it would cost more to have the cooker fixed than to replace it. It took my breath away. I couldn't even wait until we got home."

What do you want her thinking about as she sets off down the aisle at her best friend's wedding: the flowers, or what you're going to do with her later? And truthfully, isn't it just a little hot to know that you're the reason the bridesmaid keeps fidgeting under the huppah?

Delay your gratification. Sometimes the best thing in the world is wanting something you can't have. So get both of you all sexed up—and then leave it there. "Women love to be surprised," says Mabel Iam. "When she's dressed up, ready to leave, hug her from behind, and turn her on." She'll be thinking about you all day.

"I strongly recommend that couples use 'start-stop' techniques—turn each other on, then walk away, picking it up again later," writes the Australian-British expert Tracey Cox in her book *Quickies: Sizzling Spontaneous Sex.* "You could effectively have 10 foreplay 'sessions' in a day, without ever following through."

Drop her off at her door after a wonderful evening, leaving her with a deep, passionate kiss and nothing else. Make out like crazy teenagers right before your guests arrive for brunch. Shower together before you go out for dinner—and no matter how convincing she is, keep your pump primed for later.

A little something to remember you by. Don't get caught thinking short-term on this delayed gratification thing. You may not like the idea of being apart for that business trip, but you can take the sting out of the separation by using it to your advantage. After all, lovemaking delayed a day is delicious—lovemaking delayed a week or two will make her too explosive for carry-on.

Let's say she's leaving for a week. Pack her a snack for the plane, with a sexy note inside. Stick a pair of your boxer shorts into her suitcase, with a card telling her that they're a little something to remember you by.

Is that a pool cue in your pocket? Meeting at the corner bar for a burger and quick game of pool like you do every Wednesday? Fine—but tonight, tell her that the winner gets to come first. Or gets tied to the bed.

Or gets to tie the loser to the bed. Or whatever—the details of the wager are between the two of you, and limited only by your imaginations.

This is, incidentally, a very good way to find out what she really wants. And don't be surprised if you spend the rest of the night a little uncomfortable, especially when she leans over to take aim at the corner pocket.

Give her something to plan. This one is especially good if you're looking for insight into what makes her purr.

Christine Webber recommends that you ask her to set the menu for love. Say: "I'd like to take you to bed later today, and I want you to decide everything we're going to do. If you'd like a half-hour of kissing or oral sex or to be tied up or to tie me up—you tell me what you want, and I'll make it happen."

This is precisely the kind of gentle domination that can work very well in your favor—not to mention that she's going to be fairly well-heated by virtue of the time she's spent thinking about the possible permutations and combinations before settling on her order.

"This show was brought to you by . . ." There's nothing more relaxing than watching television together, but it can be a damper on the sex life. Unless you turn those regularly sponsored commercial breaks into mini-make-out sessions, instead of hitting the fridge for another beer during the commercials.

Here's one of our favorite strategies for getting through one of the shows she loves: Hit mute as soon as the ad starts, and spend 2 minutes on a different part of her body each time, getting progressively naughtier with each one. Start at the back of her neck, move to the small of her back, the inside

Turn those regularly sponsored commercial breaks into mini-make-out sessions.

of her thigh, her breasts. Be scrupulous about sitting up and stopping when the show comes back on, no matter what she offers you to continue. Don't let her touch you at all.

She'll be totally primed to go by the time the credits roll. Note: It's not our fault if you start getting into *Ugly Betty*.

Do something; expect nothing. If there's one thing that's guaranteed to pay dividends in the future, it's doing something really, really nice for her, with absolutely no expectation that you'll get anything in return.

You'll find lots of things in this chapter that she'd really enjoy if they weren't the prelude to more. So, one day, when you know she's in need of a little TLC, take sex off the table. Run her a bath. Give her a foot rub. Give her a whole-body rub with the scented unguent of her choice. Wrap her up in her cuddliest pajamas, kiss her on the cheek, and put her to bed. Then go take the coldest shower of your life.

"It's really important to me that my wife doesn't think that every time I do something nice for her, it's just because I want to have sex," says Jorge, a doctor in Spain. "Yes, of course I want to have sex with her. But I can wait, too." It's delayed gratification to the nth degree—and we guarantee you'll thank us for it tomorrow.

Appeal to *ALL* Her Senses

The Kama Sutra recommends that a lover prepare his room with incense, soft pillows, gentle lighting, and fresh flowers. Sound familiar? Yes, it's true: Soft lighting, mood music, and scented candles are hackneyed old clichés. Except, like most clichés, they're clichés for a reason. "It takes time and lots of ingredients—smells, tastes, sounds—to heat us up," says Marta, a lawyer from Greece.

We're agreed that great foreplay is the art of striking the right balance between relaxation and stimulation. By appealing to each one of her five senses—sight, sound, smell, taste, and touch—you can have a dramatic effect on the state she's in by the time the two of you hit the bedroom.

Here are our suggestions for the five.

Sight

"It's age-old advice, and might seem corny, but you can never underestimate the positive impact of making the room look nice before a date," says Patricia Taylor, PhD, founder of www.expandedlovemaking.com. "When you set up the space, you're putting her in a relaxed state of mind." She particularly recommends tidying the room and making the bed. "It sets the tone and shows that you're sensitive to what she cares about. A pile of laundry in the corner is an unwelcome distraction, and you want her to concentrate."

Once you've removed the eyesores, dim the lights. She doesn't want every crevice and bump illuminated like you were going to perform surgery. She wants to look pretty. If you assure her that she is, and if the lighting is sufficiently gentle, you can have your cake and watch it too.

How to achieve the desired effect? Don't throw a T-shirt over the lamp, like your roommate used to in college. The smell of scorched cotton is not an aphrodisiac, and there are better ways to act out your girlfriend's fireman fantasy. A candle—scented or not, depending on your preference—brings some of the feral heat of the wilderness into the bedroom. "We let the wick get really long so that the flames really flicker—it's like having sex in a cave," says Jessica, a Brit who lives in Cairo.

(By the way, the National Fire Protection Foundation would like to remind you that 40 percent of US home candle fires begin in the bedroom, causing 30 percent of the deaths resulting from these fires. So if you light them, make sure that someone stays awake long enough to blow them out, okay?)

TAKE IT OFF—TAKE IT ALL OFF

Having a woman strip for you was one of the most cited fantasies across the board in our survey. But it might surprise some of you to learn how many women wish (a) that a man would strip for them, (b) that men would understand that undressing is not only an important milestone on the road to getting some, but a very sexy end in itself.

This was certainly true for the geisha, according to Jina Bacarr, author of *The Japanese Art of Sex*. A geisha isn't just wrapped up in mystery and tradition—she's wrapped up in about 27 feet of fabric. And yet, she is the ultimate sex symbol. "The excitement is in the undressing," Bacarr says. "It's what they can't see under a geisha's elegant refinement that fascinates men, like finding a hidden treasure." It can take hours to unwrap all those layers.

So here's everything you need to know about taking off her clothes—and your own.

Leave it on. The first thing to know is that you might do well to keep some of her clothes on—for a while, anyway. As you've probably noticed, a lot of the clothes that women wear are made of fabrics that feel really good: a cashmere sweater, silk panties, a satin blouse. Use that knowledge for good. For instance, remove her bra—but not her sweater. Her nipples and cashmere will soon be getting along famously. Let her grind up against you, using those cotton panties for friction. Run your hands up and down those slippery silk or nylon stockings. You may have to buy her a new pair if you snag them, as you inevitably will. Look on the bright side—how many things can you think to do to her with a pair of ripped stockings?

Pink lightbulbs are widely available at drug- and hardware stores, and the light they cast is much more flattering than the typical flat-white bulb. Consider outfitting a small by-the-bed lamp with a pink lightbulb in a low wattage. When you do, set it on the floor; light from below is more flattering.

Sound

The sounds of sensuality can be as stimulating as touch, as memorable as visual recall. A catch of the breath, a shocking phrase, or a growl is one of the greatest in-the-act aphrodisiacs of all. Here are some of the ways that you can build her arousal with this rich sense.

Slow down. When it's time to take things off, don't be in a big hurry. Stephanie Wadell, MA, who has been a sex surrogate partner for 10 years, says it's important to slow the process. "Undressing is a lost art," she explains. "Most people start making out on the couch, go into the bedroom, undress themselves, and get into bed. But if you do everything slowly and respectfully, even going so far as to ask permission to take things off, it'll increase your passion and desire."

Talk to her. Heighten her anticipation by telling her how much you've been looking forward to it. "You looked so incredibly hot tonight; I can't believe I'm the guy who gets to take you home."

Compliment each part lavishly and specifically as it is revealed, and spend a good amount of time in wordless worship. "My lover and I play a game where he inspects me for a 'perfect part'—some part of my body that looks or feels 'perfect' to him on a given day," says Isabelle from Paris. "He explores my whole body with his fingers or with his mouth, 'rejecting' my hipbone, the inside of my elbow, the part where my breast is heaviest. Of course, he has to feel and lick and kiss all of them for the sake of the evaluation. It's very scientific." Parfait!

Hold steady. When you finally get to disrobing, do it slowly, and maintain eye contact with your partner. The best way to make sure that your expression says, "I am going to show you the best time of your entire life," and not, "I wonder what I won on the Giants tonight"? Think about sex. Not in the abstract, either, but in the very juicy, hard, throbbing particulars.

Erotic Sounds

"Hearing my girlfriend sucking when she's down on me is an incredible turn-on," says Lorenzo, a filmmaker from Italy. "The louder and sloppier the better."

Erotic sounds can be a way to dip your toe into the vast and wonderful pool of dirty talk, says Lynne Stanton, the author of *Dirty Talk*. "Start by ramping up your repertoire of erotic sounds. Try making new noises at different volumes and see how it turns on your partner—and yourself! Your new deep moan or whispered 'mmmmmmm' might just inspire your partner to bring out some new words and sounds, too . . . and may be just the thing to get you talking really dirty next time."

And if you're too shy to even moan and groan, engage in a practice round or two. "If you're feeling shy making new sounds with your partner, try testing them out by yourself first, when you're (you know) 'flying solo.' You can experiment on your own, seeing which sounds get you hot and making them part of your own erotic repertoire—all from the privacy of your own bed. Then, bring them into the action the next time you're with your partner. They'll already be sexy to you!"

> *Almost everyone who makes a lot of noise in bed agrees that making noise makes sex feel better.*

Which raises a good point: Sexy noises are sexy for your partner, but almost everyone who makes a lot of noise in bed agrees that making noise makes sex feel better too. "I've had several men tell me they were embarrassed to make sounds during lovemaking, believing only women make them. But after they've experienced the qualitative and quantitative differences of erotic excitement that the orgasmic sounds can produce, they accept the idea with more enthusiasm," says Carla Tara, a Tantric educator who was raised in Italy and who teaches in New York, California, and Hawaii.

Dirty Talk

Scores of women enjoy some dirty talk—it allows them to get outside themselves and become uninhibited. "When he asks whether I want him inside me, while teasing me there with his fingers, I melt inside," says Mary, an Australian nurse.

"Sketching out a sexually explicit fantasy in tremendous, juicy, explicit detail to my girl is worth about 20 minutes of oral—even on my cellular on the way home!" says Camerino from Mexico. "She's ready to come as soon as I am."

You can also use dirty talk to introduce new concepts into your lovemaking. What as-yet-unexplored erotic areas appeal to you? This is a sexy, unthreatening way to let her know that you want something you haven't done together before, like a threesome or anal sex, and to test whether or not your partner is willing to join you in making those dreams a reality.

Or you can use dirty talk to explore taboo subjects—those things, like sex with a slutty teenager or with someone else watching—that you would not necessarily like to do, but very much like thinking about. The same thing goes for attitudes toward your partner. Your wife may be a distinguished jurist and mother of two by day, but by night she can be a dirty little girl who's left home without her panties again—if you say so.

Remember, the erotic use of words in the bedroom doesn't have to sound like a running list of the words you can't say on network television. With the right intonation, even hearing something as simple as her name can send thrills down your lover's spine. And for some women, just hearing their partner vocalize during lovemaking can be an enormous turn-on. "My husband says 'Oh God, Oh God, Oh God' in our language whenever he's about to come," says Marina from Brazil. "Now when I masturbate, I think about the way he says it, and it pushes me over the edge."

Check out the "Dirty Talk" section in Chapter 16 for lots more information about using your voice to best advantage, as well as "Naughty Berlitz" on page 328, where you'll learn to say all those four-letter words to her and still sound like you're ordering a bottle of the finest champagne.

Love Talk

Neither does all talk in the bedroom have to all be nasty. "Whisper in her ear, whether the words are wild or sweet," says Mabel Iam.

If the spirit moves you, it can greatly increase the level of intimacy and the emotional connection to tell her exactly how you feel about her. Tell her how much you love her, what you like best about her, how happy you are that she is in your life, how proud you are of her accomplishments, how glad you are to be her man.

"I'm not good at love talk, but it's much easier for me to say a lot of the things I feel when we're in bed together," says Miguel, a hotel worker in Puerto Vallarta. "I know she really loves hearing the things I say."

Mood Music

The connection between music and sexual arousal is as old as the hills— and as new as whatever's slamming out of the car speakers passing your house right now. Music integrates your brain's emotional, rational, and movement systems in a way that nothing else does.

And indeed, most of us intuitively know that music can affect our sex lives in a positive way. But all too often, we rely on the same old discs we've been screwing to since high school. "I can literally—literally—time my orgasm to the last song on Al Green's *Let's Stay Together*. I don't ever listen to it, except when I've brought someone home," says Dan, an Australian real estate lawyer.

We asked John Kale, the founder of Blush Records and the author of *Sex between the Beats: The Ultimate Guide to Sex Music*, to explain music's powerful sway over our sexual brains. Kale first understood music's impact when he was working as a DJ at an underground Los Angeles sex club, where couples and single women could find other couples for sex. "What would it take to get *you* extremely sexual with strangers?" he asks. "Music was the only tool I had, and I found that what I played made a tremendous difference on the floor."

What Kale turned into a book: "I came to the realization that intelligently programmed music is the most effective aphrodisiac on the planet, bar none. It's also cheap, harmless, and legal. What more could you ask?" Although the correlation between music and sex seems clear, what is it that makes music so effective as a sex aid?

Kale cites two factors: rhythm and ambiance.

Rhythm: Everyone has, at one time or another, found themselves humming along to the elevator music, or tapping a foot to the repetitive sound of the printer. Kale says that's because when there's a dominant pulse in the environment, every other pulse in the room moves toward matching it. Music, obviously, has a pulse—and so does sex. "When you have a sexual partner who is feeling your natural rhythmic pulse and responding to it, the chances for mind-melting, finger-in-the-socket, exploding orgasmic ecstasy go up a thousandfold. You are literally grooving together."

But men and women have different arousal cycles. How can you make sure you're marching to the same drummer? By giving yourselves a musical pulse that you can *both* tune in to—one that slows you down and speeds her up. "You can absolutely manipulate the pulse and tempo of sexual coupling through music," says Kale. "This is an extraordinarily powerful energy *that you can control.*"

Ambiance: Music also contributes to ambiance, the mood or feeling of the room—something Kale manipulated through music time and time again in his 20 years as a professional DJ. The mood of a piece of music can create a similar mood in you and your partner.

"Music can mask unpleasant feelings or pump great ones up to even higher levels," Kale says. "With a considered choice of musical selections, you can literally orchestrate an erotic experience like a conductor conducts an orchestra." Sounds good to us.

His advice for putting together the sex playlist of all time? "Treat sex as a three-act play, instead of a one-shot deal, and program accordingly." The three acts? Romance and Seduction, Bedroom Play, and Afterglow. You can find playlists for each of the three phases in *Sex between the Beats*. But he's also put together an exclusive playlist of songs for us from all around the world that are guaranteed to get your pulses racing in unison: the "Sexy World Music Mix" on page 138.

Keep it going. When you hit the bedroom, set the CD player to repeat; a sudden silence can be deflating. If everything is going well, you won't mind listening to those songs again—and again, and again.

Hook it up. The iBuzz is a music-activated vibrating sex toy that you can plug into any MP3 player. The louder the music, the stronger the vibrations, and it comes with "his" and "hers" attachments. Gives new meaning to what was going on in those iPod commercials, doesn't it?

Scent

Aromatherapy has been around, in one form or another, for 5,000 years. "The natural nourishing art of aromatherapy can certainly stir passion," says Australian aromatherapist Judith White, author of *Homespa Aromatherapy*.

Modern aromatherapy is largely believed to have developed in

Germany, where the medicinal use of herbs and plants is much more mainstream and widespread than it is in the United States. Aromatherapy is much more widely used in Europe as a result, but we believe that this is a tradition well worth bringing over. "With just a few drops of essential oil and a little imagination, you can give your love life a wonderful new dimension," says White.

After working with essential oils for more than 40 years, Dr. Daniel Denoel, a French researcher and the author of *Natural Home Healthcare Using Essential Oils,* absolutely believes that scent can add a whole different layer to lovemaking. "We have neglected our sense of smell. Using essential oils allows us to regain the lost power of this sense, and its capacity to stimulate all the other senses."

So add scent to your seduction repertoire. It's the kind of detail many women don't expect men to have a handle on, as Rolf, an architect origi-

---

SEXY WORLD MUSIC MIX

John Kale, author of *Sex between the Beats,* put together a *Men's Health Guide to the Best Sex in the World* exclusive: a playlist of music from all over the world, designed to bring a slightly exotic flavor to your lovemaking.

A few words before the list: We are creations of our culture, and music is a big part of our cultural awareness. That can sometimes make it difficult for us to cross out of our musical comfort zone. "Americans happen to groove to a four-beat-to-the-measure pulse; a Greek or Indian person does not," says Kale. "Unfortunately, if music is too culturally different, it can become a distraction instead of an erotic facilitator—not what you want at all!" Of course, you can get used to other beat structures, and they can even become highly eroticized for you if you begin to associate them with fantastic sex. But if having better foreplay and sex *tonight* is your goal, then a musical style wildly different than your own is probably not the best place to start.

This list was put together with that in mind. Courtesy of Kale, here are some songs and entire albums that have the flavors of foreign cultures, but enough familiar elements that you can enjoy them tonight.

Collection of world electronic grooves suitable for sex: *Le Groove Eclectique,* mixed by Mark Gorbulew (Max Music)

African: *Princesses Nubiennes* by Les Nubians (EMI/Virgin)

Enjoy the Most Leisurely Sex in the World

nally from Frankfurt, Germany, points out: "American women go crazy when they find out I know something about scent. In my country, it is not a big deal, and even doctors use oils all the time." And you yourself may be a little surprised at how much changing the smell of a room can change the ambiance—and her mood.

The following are some of the scents most strongly associated with love, sex, and intimacy:

- **Ylang-ylang flowers** are spread on the beds of newlyweds in Indonesia. This scent is a powerful aphrodisiac, used across many cultures.

- **Vanilla** is derived from orchids, and although the name is a synonym for boring, straight sex, it shares a root with the word *vagina*.

- **Jasmine** is the most important flower in Indonesian wedding ceremonies, perhaps because of its deliciously heady scent.

American: *Six Erotic Journeys* by Mystic Ocean (Blush Records); *Objects of Desire/The Best of Blush Records* by various artists

Brazilian: *Wave* by Antonio Carlos Jobim (A&M)

British: *Love Deluxe* by Sade (Sony)

Caribbean: *Wild Orchid* soundtrack (Sire/London/Rhino)

Chinese: "Energy Awakens" from the album *Prayers of the Flesh* by Mystic Ocean (Blush Records); *Oriental Sunrise* by Riley Lee (Narada)

French: *French Kiss* by various artists (Intent City)

Indian: *Kamasutra: Shah Featuring Al Gromer Khan* (Eversongs)

Latin: *Sensual Sensual* by B-Tribe (Atlantic/Wea)

Middle Eastern: "Sensuous Rendezvous" from the album *Under a Lover's Moon* (Blush Records); *The Best of Natacha Atlas* (Beggars UK–Ada)

Spanish: *Nouveau Flamenco* by Ottmar Liebert (Higher Octave)

Blush titles are available at www.blushrecords.com.

- **Sandalwood** is considered to be a sexual stimulant in Nepal and China, and in the Ayurvedic tradition of India.

- **Roses** are what you show up for a first date holding a bouquet of. For centuries, the essences of this flower and its wood have been the perfumes worn by goddesses, literal and figurative.

Taste

As with music, there is a strong connection between sex and food that crosses time and cultures. In fact, food and sex are appetites so intrinsically linked that we often use the same words to describe both: "tantalizing," "juicy," "sizzling," *"caliente,"* and "hot, hot, hot." Even the stereotypes we have about certain cultures are connected to their foods—a Latin lover is as dangerous as a habanero, while the sophisticated French lover draws out foreplay like one of the classical sauces it takes him 3 days to prepare.

Food can be sexy, but there may be a simpler, more biological explanation for the mental connection we make between the two things: We need calories and nutrients to energize us for what can be quite an athletic expenditure!

Feed her. Eating is a fundamentally sensual act, and done properly, it can be a very sensuous one: anything bite-size will do for feeding one another—just make sure your fingers are clean, and that they linger long enough in her mouth to give you an idea of how she'll put that tongue to good use later.

Americans have a great deal to learn from the Europeans on this count, according to Ava Cadell, PhD, a Hungarian-born, British-raised expert who has traveled and taught widely throughout the world: "Bonding with food means taking your time and savoring each bite of a meal. Turn it into a sensual ritual. Enjoy the aroma and the taste of the wine as part of the whole experience." See Chapter 5 for our thoughts on a romantic dinner.

> *The European men we talked to made explicit the connection between the way a woman enjoys food and the way she'll be in bed.*

Preview her appetites. Tune in to the right signals during a dinner date and you'll satisfy more than just your palate. Certainly many of the

European men we talked to made explicit the connection between the way a woman enjoys food and the way she'll be in bed. "A woman who enjoys food and good wine, who has a discerning palate, who is experimental in her tastes? This is a good lover," says Alejandro from Madrid. "When she took a bite of my dessert, stopped, and closed her eyes for a minute, I knew she was going to be a tiger in bed," says Lorenzo, an Italian filmmaker.

Candida Royalle, a producer of femme-friendly adult films and a veteran adult-film star, agrees that her appetite at the dinner table can be a barometer of her appetites elsewhere. "Watch how she uses her fork. Does she enjoy things? Is she sensuous? Is she poky and grabby?" she says. "If someone eats slowly, it's likely that they like to make love for a long time. I'm one of the slowest eaters I know."

Dessert is the big tell. Does she snack stoically on her chocolate mousse, or does she close her eyes and moan softly, savoring the velvety texture? "This means she appreciates the sensual, hedonistic side of life," says Sandor Gardos, PhD, a sex therapist and the founder of mypleasure.com. "She's just had an orgasm on her tongue," agrees Laura Corn, author of *101 Nights of Grrreat Sex*. "Piggyback off that."

Be moderate. Just don't eat too much, as British expert Sarah Hedley sensibly warns in her book *Sex by the Numbers*. Order wisely—foods that are overly rich or decadent will leave you feeling bloated and listless. And bear in mind Shakespeare's wise counsel that alcohol dramatically provokes desire—and just as dramatically reduces performance. You probably already know what it does to you, but did you know that it has similar results on your lady friend? Women who have been drinking report less sensation, less lubrication, and (unsurprisingly, with all that) fewer orgasms. So quaff moderately. And if you need a libation for the side of the bed, try mixing a small amount of juice with an effervescent soda water—you'll get all the bubbles of champagne, with none of the disappointment.

Kiss her. Pass an ice cube back and forth until it melts away to nothing at all. Try this same trick with a piece of candy, a strawberry or almost-overripe mango, or expensive chocolate. The Israeli company Max Brenner Chocolate by the Bald Man (www.maxbrenner.com) features a chocolate egg called Magnet, designed specifically for this purpose—as you pass it back and forth between your lips, it slowly melts, revealing a secret filling. Or pass wine, sake, or champagne from mouth to mouth until you have to lick the insides of her cheeks for the last drop.

Try the fruit of her loins. Strawberries and raspberries have been known as "fruit nipples" for centuries—use a few to show what you're going to do to hers. Make a decorative line of blueberries down into the cleft of her bottom and use your tongue to retrieve them. Freeze a bunch of grapes, and run them lightly down her back, over her tender inner thighs, or dangle them so they touch just the very tips of her nipples.

Serve breakfast in bed. There's nothing more decadent than morning lovemaking—but it can sometimes be difficult to stoke the fires of passion. The Argentinian sex expert Mabel Iam suggests breakfast in bed. "The aphrodisiac that is perfect for both sexes is bananas or plantains," says Dr. Iam. "Since ancient times, the banana has been lauded as an important fruit for a healthy body and mind, and has even been believed to stimulate erotic energy. German studies have highlighted their high levels of protein, calcium, phosphate, vitamins, zinc, magnesium, potassium, and glucose, which are essential to regulate brain functioning, and they have a positive effect on serotonin levels like no other fruit or vegetable." Treat her to warmed banana-nut bread, which has an aroma that, according to one study, increases bloodflow to the vagina. Instead of coffee, serve her hot chocolate (a sexual stimulant). And bring a bowl of raspberries and strawberries for yourself, to replenish the zinc you lose when you ejaculate—5 milligrams, or a third of your daily requirement.

Touch

Settle in—we're going to spend some time here. After all, this is what it's all about, isn't it? Everyone is affected by touch, especially when the body interprets the sensation as being sexual in nature. And, strangely enough, erotic touch not only stimulates the desire to be touched again but makes you view the person who's touching you in a more pleasurable light.

It's all due to a hormone called oxytocin that researchers sometimes refer to as "the love hormone." Oxytocin is released when the body is touched. Its effects are significantly enhanced by estrogen, a hormone that women have in greater quantities than men; this heightened sensitivity may be why women seem to be so much more sensitive to touch than men are, says Marianne Legato, MD, New York–based author of *Why Men Never Remember and Women Never Forget*.

As foreplay progresses, oxytocin levels continue to rise, making nipples, genitals, and all the other erogenous zones more sensitive. By the time orgasm approaches, the amount of the hormone in the blood is three to five times the normal level. And afterward—guess what? It's oxytocin that's responsible for the feel-good afterglow you bask in after orgasm.

So oxytocin, the greatest aphrodisiac of all, can't be bottled—only unleashed. Touching—and lots of it—inspires the desire for more of the same.

Whatever the reason, it certainly seems to be true that touch is the way to her heart. This opens up a whole world of sexual play, because there are as many different ways to touch as there are people to touch. We'll "touch" on some of them here.

Hold steady. "Women are soothed and relaxed by a constant, smooth continuous touch," says Patricia Taylor, PhD. And that's true no matter how you're touching her—whether you're stroking her body, performing cunnilingus, stimulating her manually, or anything else. "If touch is jerky or discontinuous, a woman has a hard time dropping in to the experience," Dr. Taylor says. "Continuous touch puts her into a relaxed, open, receptive frame of mind and allows her to surrender to the sensations she's feeling."

Master the foreplay of the periphery. Imagine a dartboard. Now imagine that your partner's genitals are the bull's-eye at the very center of the dartboard. That's a male point of view. You probably wouldn't mind if a woman walked up to you and grabbed your crotch; in fact, you'd probably find it quite exciting. But you're a guy. Perhaps the biggest difference between the sexes is in the way they wish to be approached.

"Women want to be touched in ever-smaller circles," says Taoist sex expert Rachel Carlton Abrams, coauthor of the *Multi-Orgasmic Couple*. French sexologist Robert Santo-Paolo agrees: "Most women hate it when a man starts out by caressing their breasts or their sex."

Midori coined the phrase "the foreplay of the periphery" for the best way to approach the physical seduction of a woman, and we think it's perfect. "Start around the edges, and work your way in," she says. "I teach a workshop in sensual foot massage, and men invariably have one of two reactions. They're either like 'What does this have to do with sex?' or they really get that it's the scenic route of the path to seduction. Those are the ones that are having great sex, and having it all the time."

The key, then, is to focus on the erogenous zones: the non-genital areas of her body that experience heightened sensitivity and result in sexual arousal when stimulated. Her ears. The small of her back. The backs of her knees. Her ankle bones. Her arms. Her armpits. A man should know at least 10 hot spots that drive her wild, says Dr. Ava Cadell—think of these as the colors that you'll blend together to create your sexual masterpiece.

Here's the thing: These erogenous spots are different for every woman. For one woman, the feeling of her toes in her lover's mouth is enough to make her come—even with no genital stimulation at all. Another recoils in horror, and it leaves yet another completely cold. So you're going to have to do a little trial-and-error experimentation on your own model. Simple exploratory techniques—a kiss around the earlobe, a stroke between her toes—will help you find them. To give you a head start, here are some of the more common erogenous zones.

■ **Her ears:** Some women can take or leave this—others will do anything you want if you do it right. Try this: Stiffen your tongue and run it very lightly around the rim of her ear. Then suck her earlobes, alternating a firm pressure with a feathery-light one. If the firmer pressure is working for her, try a nibble or two. Remember to take the occasional detour over to that incredibly sensitive area behind her ear where her neck turns into her head. Brushing your nose over this area is a great way to drink in what the French call her *cassolette*, her unique odor, released particularly when she is aroused. One of the things that makes this so sexy is the feeling of your breath on her neck and the sound of your heavy breathing in her ear. Please note: Women in general prefer not to receive a wet willy.

■ **Her neck:** The neck is home to some very important blood vessels, so it's in our best interest for it to respond quickly when touched. This, of course, is an undeniable asset in the bedroom. Start with a feather-light touch, so gentle you're barely making contact. Brush your lips all over it. See if you can locate her pulse, then gently hold your lips against it. As she gets more excited, your kisses can become more aggressive, even progressing to gentle nibbles and bites if she seems enthusiastic. But the love-bite, or hickey, is something probably best left in high school. Don't forget the nape of her neck: The area between her shoulders and where her hairline begins is one of the most deliciously erotic spots on her body, for both of you. Try brushing your lips a quarter of an inch away from the surface of her skin, so that you're only touching the fine hairs at the back of her neck. Do this while reaching around to gently fondle her nipples, and we guarantee you'll drive her wild.

■ **Her hair:** There's nothing like long, flowing hair to get your motor revved—and women love to have theirs played with. You can tell, because *they're* always playing with it. "My boyfriend will sometimes lean across the table and gently brush my hair out of my eyes. I would never make him self-conscious by telling him, but I think it is so sensual!" says Marie-Chantal in Lyons, France. Brushing a woman's hair for her can be a very erotic experience for both of you: "I grew up brushing my hair 100 strokes every single night. I have no idea whether it does anything for my hair, but it feels spectacular—especially when my husband is working the brush!" says Anja, a holistic health practitioner in Germany. "Needless to say, sometimes we don't get all hundred strokes in. . . . "

It's worth noting that in a menshealth.com poll of 3,200 men, 76 percent said they have shampooed their woman's hair. And damned if they're not on to

> *In a poll of 3,200 men, 76 percent said they have shampooed their woman's hair.*

something. "Choose a fragrant shampoo and swirl your fingertips around her scalp with the warm, sudsy water," says British psychologist and sex advisor Dr. Pam Spurr, author of *Naughty Tricks and Sexy Tips*. "The massage and smells will help her relax, unleashing oxytocin." Rake your hands through her hair using the very tips of your fingers (a truly insane amount of conditioner will facilitate this; do make sure long hair doesn't become entangled), increasing the pressure every time. It might feel like you're scalping her, but her groans of pleasure will surely convince you otherwise. Make large and small circles on either side of her head. You can even pull the hair slightly—and very gently—right at the root to intensify the sensation.

So go ahead, do what you want to do anyway: Pet her. Smooth her hair while you're driving, run your hands through it while you're kissing her, or grab a hank of it and wrap it around your wrist while you're having sex, so she feels like she's really yours.

■ *Her tummy:* In Taoist sexuality, the line between her pubis and her belly button is rife will all kinds of sexual power spots. Many women are self-conscious about this area, so you can win major points simply by paying some fond erotic attention to it.

■ *Her perineum:* Guiche. Grundle. Landing strip. Taint. You probably spent a good amount of time on the playground blowing chocolate milk through your nose about this one, but it's time to grow up. That little patch of skin between the things "it ain't" is a virtual wonderland of sensation, for both of you. Don't leave it out of a massage, whether with your hands or tongue, and experiment with different types of pressure to see what she likes. If she's uncomfortable about the idea of anal play in general, leave this until after a shower, when she'll be less self-conscious about hygiene. And reassure her ahead of time that you're not going to do anything penetrative without a discussion first. That gives her the luxury of relaxing into the sensations instead of wondering every second if you're going to roger her, as our British friends say. Speaking of British friends, Sarah Hedley, author of *Sex by the Numbers,* advises that "men and women who find their rears are responsive to stimulation but don't like the idea of anal penetration will find this is the next best thing, as pressure applied here can be felt within the anus."

■ *Her lips:* Is there a more suggestive or erotic part of the body? There is a high concentration of nerve endings in the lips, and the skin there is exquisitely thin—the result is one of the most sensitive body parts. Perhaps because of their similarity to her other lips, which are not usually quite so accessible, they are also one of the most alluring, and are often decorated as such; in ancient Babylon, semiprecious jewels were smashed and used as lipstick; Cleopatra covered her lips with carmine made from crushed beetles. (According to Don Voorhees, author of *Quickies: Fascinating Facts about the Facts of Life*, it is believed that lipstick was first worn by Egyptian prostitutes who specialized in fellatio and wanted to "advertise" their talents.)

The Art of Erotic Massage

Massage has been used therapeutically for centuries to relieve tense muscles, to alleviate stress, to speed the elimination of waste products, to

---

HOW YOU CAN TELL IF IT'S WORKING

Sex flush, a pinkish look to the skin of her chest, occurs during foreplay. It stems from changes in blood pressure and circulation, along with pulse and respiration rates. Think of it as her coy way of telling you that if you keep doing what you're doing, you just might get lucky.

Another sign that things are working: A woman's breasts grow by as much as 25 percent as things turn hot and heavy. And Mabel Iam, Argentinian author of *Sex and the Perfect Lover,* suggests that you pay close attention to her breathing. "If the pace increases, you're on the right track. Otherwise, keep trying."

---

improve bloodflow, and—yes, simply because it feels good. Every culture in the world has a rich tradition of massage: Anma and Shiatsu in Japan, Tui Na in China, Lomilomi in Hawaii, Shantala in India, bodywork in Thailand, and Swedish massage from Sweden (although it may have been a Dutch masseur who popularized the techniques). Ancient Greek and Roman doctors prescribed massage; Egyptian tomb paintings show people receiving them.

With your partner, massage can be an astonishingly intimate and sensual experience. It's certainly one of the best forms of foreplay out there, for the following reasons. The best foreplay combines a *deep state of relaxation* with a *high level of stimulation*—not an easy balance to discover and maintain, but one that can be very precisely achieved through erotic massage.

"You need to know only three things to give a great massage," says Barbara Carellas, sex educator and author of *Urban Tantra: Sacred Sex for the Twenty-First Century.* "How to breathe, how to touch, and how to ask for feedback." But a little knowledge (and a little practice) can elevate your game. Before we begin with a discussion of technique, we'd like to share two pieces of slightly counterintuitive advice that came to us courtesy of our experts.

> *The best foreplay combines a deep state of relaxation with a high level of stimulation.*

1. Don't try to do two things at once. "The messiest, least satisfying sexual situations for me have been when I was trying to give to my partner who was simultaneously trying to give to me," says Carellas. "When I was trying really hard to give, I felt that I wasn't a very good lover if I couldn't get my partner to lie back and enjoy what I was offering. Then when I was trying really hard to receive, I felt guilty—guilty about taking too long to come, guilty about receiving more than I was giving, guilty about receiving too much pleasure." After facilitating more Erotic Awakening workshops than she can count, Carellas has come to an interesting conclusion: "I can safely and surely say that most people find it much easier to give than to receive." Ironically, most people love giving to a receptive, willing partner who's truly enjoying herself or himself—something we unwittingly cheat them out of in our haste to give them pleasure as well. Her advice? "When you're receiving, go totally into receiving. Receive it all. When giving, go totally into giving.

Give everything." She makes the important distinction that neither is an entirely passive position. "As the receiver, you are participating; it is not something someone is doing to you. When it is your turn to receive, it is the giver's job to ask what you would like and how you'd like it, but it is your responsibility to say, 'A little harder,' or 'A little softer,' or 'I would like something completely different. . . .'"

2. Focus on your own pleasure. "Concentrate not on how what you're doing feels to her but on your *own* sensations," says Charla, a Tantric practitioner who specializes in the art of erotic massage and the author of *Erotic Massage: Sensual Touch for Deep Pleasure and Extended Arousal.* "Focus on the way her skin feels under your fingers, the way her body looks when you touch it. Touch for your own pleasure, not for hers. In this way, you'll really get something from the experience—besides a very hot partner, of course. And by being 'selfish' in this way, you let her off the hook, so she can concentrate on her own erotic sensations." French sexologist Robert Santo-Paolo agrees: "Think of your own pleasure, since if you are not turned on, a woman will sense this and you risk lessening her excitement."

Like everything important, giving a good massage requires a little preparation on your part. Here's what you need to know.

Keep it warm. Heat means sweat-soaked bayou sex (neon sign and saxophone music optional), while deep winter equals—well, the dreaded cuddle. It's impossible to relax if you feel even the slightest bit cold. So keep the room warm—around 77°F, warmer than you think is comfortable when you're fully dressed. You'll just have to find another way to get her nipples perky.

If you live in a chilly climate and have an electric blanket, this is the perfect time to use it: Set it on "low," and cover it with a towel so she can lie down on it.

And watch those hands! If you have a warm heart but chilly extremities, blow on them or rub them together before touching her.

Get naked. Most people feel that there's a disruption in the power balance if one of you is clothed and one of you is naked. If you're naked, you won't get oil on your clothes. And you won't hesitate to use other parts of your body—your chest, your whole arm, your legs—to help out your hands. If you sense that she's not comfortable—because she's either cold or insecure about her body, do as a professional would: Move a towel or folded sheet to cover the places you're not focusing on.

Blindfold her. Eliminating one of her senses heightens the rest even further. Humans focus on the information they have. So if you remove the visual information she has, she's going to be forced to concentrate much more closely on the stimulation her other senses are receiving. A blindfold might sound kinky, but it doesn't need to be—in fact, Japanese-German sex educator Midori says that the best starter blindfold is in the seat pocket in front of you: an airline sleep mask. (She swears by the black one you get if you fly Virgin First-Class. Just so you know.)

If you don't have a sleep mask, use anything soft—a silk scarf or a rag ripped from a soft old T-shirt. Make sure she's not lying on the knot, and don't tie it too tightly—her comfort, the suggestion of sightlessness, and the feeling of the fabric against her skin are all considerably more important than a total black-out effect.

This is important: Being blindfolded can be disorienting. Don't leave her alone for any period of time. (In fact, many erotic massage experts suggest that you maintain contact with her by touching at least one part of her body at all times.) Don't do anything to surprise or alarm her while she is blindfolded—for instance, although a variety of sensation is the point, dripping ice-cold water if she's not expecting it can be more than she bargained for. And no tickling!

Tell her to be selfish. Many women find it difficult to fully relax and take their time; let her know that this is her time to embrace selfishness with both hands. Tell her that you will get the most pleasure from seeing her relaxed and aroused under your hands, and that you expect nothing in return—not even her orgasm. Charla suggests making this explicit by saying something like: "Your job is to drink in every good feeling I give you. I'll check in with you; don't worry about a thing. Just lap it up shamelessly and we'll switch turns later."

Additionally, let her know that you welcome her feedback and want to know if there's anything you can do to make the experience more pleasurable for her. "This new guy I was seeing gave me this amazingly sexy massage, but I had to pee the whole time!" says Lola from Berlin. "It completely ruined it for me; instead of relaxing, I spent the whole time trying not to wet the bed. He had this whole thing set up, and I just couldn't bring myself to interrupt him."

Reassure her that it's okay for her to talk about what she likes and doesn't like—and to tell you if she needs a bathroom break! But in general, keep talking to a minimum: Speaking brings the pedestrian into what should be a very special experience. Try to rely on nonverbal cues instead.

Grease her up. A small bottle of real massage oil is a good investment. If you're caught short, raid the kitchen: The oil you use for cooking is a good substitute. Warm it either by microwaving it for a couple of seconds or by holding it in a warm water bath. Shake the bottle and pour the oil into your own hands before putting it on her body. Bear in mind that oil can be messy. Many couples who regularly give one another erotic massages reserve a sheet and a set of towels for precisely this purpose. "Just seeing them in the laundry basket makes me juicy," says Marta, a professor in Guatemala.

Warm your hands. Tantic experts believe that the warmth you create when you rub your hands together is actually energy that you will then transfer to your lover's skin when you touch her. Rub your hands together vigorously until you create heat.

Keep her awake. "Keep her focused on the erotic nature of the massage, not the relaxing, sleep-inducing side of it," says Dr. Queen. One way to do that: Straddle her so that she can feel that you're hard. Have her open her legs so that she's spread-eagled—the position itself can be very erotic, especially if you take a break from that fantastic backrub to nuzzle gently between her legs.

Hit the hot spots. You don't really need us to bring your attention to these special spots—but she'll be glad you know where they are.

■ *Rear end:* Professional masseurs know that while tense back and shoulders get all the press, the gluteal muscles (otherwise known as her ass) store just as much tension, and they're a little more fun to rub. Get lots of oil, and start with long, slow strokes. Although it will be tempting to stay right on her ass, it will feel better if you follow through to her lower back and down to her upper thighs. Glide your hands up and down her back, moving your thumbs closer toward the center of her back. Rub your hands up and down the cheeks of her butt, making big circles that go out to the large muscles that run down the sides of her hips. Repeat these strokes—she's enjoying them! Because the butt is covered by a layer of muscle and fat (you'll want to omit this detail when you're explaining this technique to her), this area responds to a much firmer touch. In other words, this might be the time for a playful, gentle slap or two as well, if that's something you both feel comfortable with—the blood rushing to the surface will heighten her sensitivity to touch. If you've experimented with anal play before, glide your thumbs down between her cheeks. Using lots of oil, massage the outside of her anus very gently. If she's enjoying these ministrations, you may want to insert the tip of your finger—again, very, very gently. After a little while, return to rubbing the large muscles of her ass, hips, and thighs.

■ *Feet:* "Some women can have orgasms just from having their feet rubbed," says Bob Schwartz, PhD, author of *The One-Hour Orgasm*. "When my lover rubs my feet, it makes me feel like he's my slave," says Maria from Argentina. Midori thinks this is such an important technique for relaxing a lover that she teaches a whole workshop on the subject.

Obviously, the art of a great foot rub is one worth learning. There are 26 bones in the foot, and they are protected by very little in the way of fat or muscle, so a touch that is too aggressive can be very painful. At the same time, the feet are intensely ticklish if the touch is too light (a sign of how rich in nerve endings this area is). So, it's essential to strike the right balance. The most important

In some people the middle toe has a direct nerve connection to the genitals.

thing to remember is to gradually build pressure. No grinding allowed—especially on the arch or any other bony area, probably the most common mistake. But you do want to keep the pressure firm. Cover the whole foot and ankle with oil or lotion, massaging fairly gently. Don't hesitate to go up her leg a little farther, toward the calf.

When one foot is thoroughly greased up, do the other. *Go slowly.* Return to the first foot. You're going to increase the pressure slightly now. Put both hands around the foot, fingers on the sole and thumbs along the top. Starting at the ankle, squeeze your hands, drawing them down in long strokes toward the toes. Keep your thumbs between the tendons (the ribs at the top of her feet); too much pressure directly on them can be painful. Repeat this action a number of times, moving your hands so that your thumbs and fingers are touching a different area on her foot with each stroke. Now use your thumbs to make small, firm circles on the bottom of her foot. You can use more pressure on the heel than on the ball. Again, be very careful about the arch. If she's lying on her front, bend her knee

Use the F-Word: Foreplay **151**

TIPTOE THROUGH THE TWO LIPS

Many women dearly love the sensation of having their toes sucked. It's called "shrimping," and it's not just for foot fetishists; toes, by virtue of their size, shape, and general prettiness practically beg to be put in your mouth.

Obviously, you can do whatever moves you, but here are some things that we've heard the ladies like: Kiss her feet gently. Then start to use your tongue, tracing small circles underneath the toes, and moving into the areas between them before putting each individual toe into your mouth and sucking on it gently. Because the skin on the toes is relatively tough, you can even use your teeth a little, nibbling gently.

---

gently (don't wiggle it side to side). Using lots of oil, weave your fingers in between her toes so that the heel of her foot rests in your palm and your fingers reach through her toes. Close your hand, giving the area right between her toes a thorough massage. Grasp each toe individually within your closed fist, and squeeze as your hand moves the whole length of the toe. Pay special attention to the middle toe—in some people this digit has a direct nerve connection to the genitals. Return your fingers to the earlier position, where they were between her toes. Then—gently!—straighten your fingers and squeeze her toes, and giving them a soft pull away from her body, stretch the individual toes. Done properly, this feels amazing. Then use your fingers between her toes to rotate the whole foot at the ankle. Go a few times in one direction, then in another. Finish the foot by repeating the slow, gentle massage you gave the whole foot at the very beginning.

■ *Hands:* Massaging the hands is very similar to massaging the feet. It feels wonderful, and makes for a great "quickie" if you want to show her a little affection but don't have time for the whole shebang. If it's winter and her hands seem dry, using a thick moisturizing cream, such as cocoa or shea butter, can be a welcome gesture. Start by facing her and sandwiching one of her hands between yours, gliding back and forth over the skin. Then, with your thumbs on top of her hand and your fingers on the palm, begin a kneading-type massage stroke, with your thumbs moving outward and your fingers pressing in to the palm of her hand. Continue this motion all the way up her wrist to her forearm—heaven if she's a heavy computer user! Holding her hand in one of yours, use the nonsupporting hand to run your fingers down her arm and hand, in between the tendons you can see on the back of her hand, running off the ends of her fingers. For a final move, you can interlace your own fingers with hers and squeeze, finally running your fingers through hers.

■ *Breasts:* Not only one of the most erogenous zones for her, but one of the most erotic for you too. However, there's an art to touching them so that both of you derive the maximal amount of pleasure possible. Dr. Ava Cadell suggests that when you roll her over after massaging her back, you place your hands lightly over the top of her belly button. Then slowly slide them up the center of her stomach and around her breasts, then back to the belly button. This is a highly effective way of moving the energy around the body—and it feels really good! Do this at least five times. When you get to her breasts, let your hands move around them in ever-smaller circles, letting your palms cover more of her breasts with every revolution. Gently brush the tops, bottoms, and sides of her breasts; these areas are actually more sensitive than an unaroused areola and nipple. Austrian researchers have found that an oft-neglected region of the breast, the northern part from roughly 10 o'clock to 2 o'clock, is the most sensitive. Stimulate the outer sides of her breasts, just below the armpits, with your tongue or fingertips. Investigate with light kissing and a gentle massage using the heel of your hand, not the fingers. The palm gives even sensation without causing pain. The areola—the dark-colored circle that surrounds the nipple—is actually more sensitive than the nipple itself. Spend lots of luxurious time here, and don't be shy: Her nipples and areolas may not be as sensitive as you think. In fact, they're two to three times less sensitive than her index finger, say researchers at the Boston University School of Medicine. When you finally do get to the nipple, use a light touch at first, so that you graze over it a few times, says sex therapist Laura Berman, PhD, director of the Berman Center in Chicago.

BUT THEY'RE SO PRETTY!

In a study conducted at the University of Vienna, researchers found that large breasts were about 24 percent less sensitive than small ones. "This is probably because the nerve that transmits sensation from the nipple is stretched," says Alan Matarasso, MD, a plastic surgeon in New York City.

Dr. Ava Cadell suggests that you use your thumb and index finger to gently massage the nipple in a rotating motion, moving clockwise and then counterclockwise. Ask for feedback so that you get the pressure just right. Then place your hand gently over the nipple and roll it in the palm of your hand. Finally, using your thumb and third finger, gently pull up on the nipple so that you are elongating it. Do one nipple at a time in slow motion.

Those are the hands-down best touchy-feely techniques we could find. Keep in mind that you should never stop using your hands, even once you're inside her. Think of it as the really deep type of massage that's not available at her friendly neighborhood spa.

That Extra Special Touch

Skin-to-skin massage is just one of the ways you can engage this most erotic of the five senses. Here are some others.

Look, Ma, no hands! British expert Kesta Desmond, author of *Pure Kama Sutra* and *Pure Erotic Massage,* suggests banning your hands. "Explore each other's bodies with your nose, tongue, lips, hair, knees, toes," she says. "You'll be amazed at how sensational it feels." For an added bump, tell her to tie your hands loosely behind your back. Talk about making something difficult just to make it fun! It might be hard to get her to roll over using only your tongue, but we have faith that you're the right man for the job.

Look, Ma, mittens! Gloves that fit over the hand are a nice addition to a massage, especially for someone who likes additional stimulation. We've seen them in rabbit fur, raw silk, a jelly-type plastic with hundreds of little bumps, a microwaveable pair—even a pair with vibrators built into the fingers. Not to mention the standard terry cloth variety—or the medical-grade latex ones easily found in drugstores.

"My husband had a bad cut on his hand a few years ago, which led us to discover the wonders of massage with latex gloves," says Alessandra, a real estate broker from Peru. "His hands glide over me; it's a completely different sensation than with the calluses on his bare hands. I love the feeling, and he does too."

Keep her guessing. Collect a variety of household objects that you think will result in pleasant sensations on her skin. Some ideas: steal a pair of her softest silk panties, one of her tiny, round-headed makeup brushes, a feather, a piece of soft, fragrant suede or leather or velvet, even a blunt-tined fork. Then blindfold her, lay her down, and touch her softly with each of the implements. Go slowly, zig-zagging across her body unpredictably. Pay close attention to those ultra-sensitive spots: the inside of her thighs, the undersides of her breasts, the base of her throat, the inside of the hollow of her hipbone. Make her guess what's causing each sensation. Pay special attention to which ones she particularly likes—and enjoy the sight of her arching up to meet your next touch.

Float like a butterfly. Cover her naked body with tiny, light, feathery kisses. The pattern should be completely unpredictable—except that they land where she least expects them!

Give her a tongue bath. Plant the most erotic, soulful tongue kisses you can muster—everywhere but her mouth and the place she most wants you, between her legs. Perform the best cunnilingus she's ever gotten—on the bone on the inside of her ankle. Drive her wild with your tongue, but only behind her knee. Suck, lick, nibble—savor every single inch of her with your tongue and lips and mouth and teeth. And don't give in, no matter what she bribes or threatens you with!

Be a greased pig. Bring back the '70s-era Mazola parties, where everyone got greased up and slid up against one another. The French call this frottage. We call it good, greasy fun. If you think she'll stress about the mess, split open a couple of trash bags first, or purchase a special pair of rubber sheets for the occasion. The Hustler Slippery Sex Sheets & Black Light Paint are $48 at www.erosboutique.org.

Use a vibrator. After all, massage is what it's supposed to be for—or didn't you read the package? Experiment with different spots on her body—especially those that will indirectly stimulate her g-spot or clit. "I love to lie on my front while my lover works the vibrator between my inner thighs and the cheeks of my ass. If he leaves it there, I can come just from the vibrations and the feel of the towel underneath me," says Lizzie from London. Use all the attachments as well!

▪

Remember, this is foreplay, so even though your plan is to eventually give her some all-in loving—whether with your hands, your mouth, or your penis—take your time getting there. If you want to progress to genital massage, whether with your hands (wash them first!) or your mouth, you'll find a wealth of information on those topics in the next two chapters.

Hopefully, by this point, you're sufficiently convinced that foreplay that arouses all her senses is a subject worth tackling, if not mastering. Our best advice? Slow down. Take your time. Hang out. Get to know her body—and your own. Try something you haven't tried before, and see if you can't take one another to places you've never been before. And hey—send us a postcard, will ya?

CHAPTER 8

BE THE HANDIEST GUY IN THE WORLD
Follow Our Manual on the Art of Manual

Women are like British racing cars. Each one requires a little work to make her "go"—and what works for one won't necessarily work for the next. Some like it rough, some like only the most gentle of touches.

"I was with my first girlfriend for 9 years. Then we broke up, and I was a real dog for a couple of years, sleeping with a different girl every night. I liked to ask girls to masturbate so I knew how they liked to be touched—and was it ever an eye-opener!" says James, a British banker. "I never saw two girls come the same way. Some have to have their legs closed, some have to have them straight. Some need something inside them, some get off by rubbing up against something, some like to be on their stomachs. They use their fingers, their whole hands, the quilt on the bed! There isn't the same variety amongst blokes—we just pull!"

Helen Fisher, PhD, research professor in the anthropology department at Rutgers University in New Jersey and author of *Why We Love*, agrees. "Human tastes in bed are just as varied as tastes in food. A person may like Japanese food but hate pizza. Some women want their nipples chewed on; others need you to be more delicate."

In our survey, 27 percent of men worldwide said that if they could have one sexual superpower, they'd want the ability to make any woman orgasm by touch. It would be a useful superpower: Only 30 percent of women can climax through intercourse alone. Most also need direct clitoral stimulation, as evidenced by the fact that it takes women an average of just 4 to 6 minutes to climax when they masturbate—versus 10 to 20 minutes during intercourse.

Your hands are one of the best tools to give her what she wants. Gather round for everything you need to know to be her favorite handyman.

The Lay of the Land

Before we get into specific techniques, here's a quick tour of the landscape through which you'll let your fingers do the walking.

Vulva: This is everything on the outside.

Labia majora: The outer lips of the vagina.

Labia minora: The inner lips of the vagina. As you've probably noticed by now, the way these look and feel can vary widely among women.

Clitoris: The bump hiding at the top of the labia. The visible tip of the clitoris has two parts. The *hood* is a protective fold of skin that keeps the ultra-sensitive *glans* hidden away. Many women find that direct stimulation of the glans creates too much sensitivity to feel good. Certainly, playing directly with it is something that should be reserved for when she's already very juicy and aroused.

And this is just the part of the clitoris that you can see—the tip of the iceberg, if you will. Australian researcher Helen E. O'Connell, MD, has reported that there's a whole lot more than meets the eye. The glans is connected to the shaft (which is the hard bit you can feel underneath her skin), and the shaft is split into two arms, like a wishbone, that extend down around the vaginal opening. This explains why some of the indirect moves we'll show you are so effective—they not only stimulate the clitoris without directly stimulating the glans but also put pressure on her hidden pleasure points.

> *The clitoris is an organ with no purpose other than providing sexual pleasure.*

The clitoris is interesting in that it's an organ with no purpose other than providing sexual pleasure. That's a job it does very well, comprised as it is of some—wait for it—8,000 nerve endings, the greatest concentration in the human body—and considerably more than in your penis. It can be a fickle mistress, though, in that it changes with arousal. It fills with blood, becoming larger in size and more sensitive to the touch, just as your penis does. And as it becomes aroused, her sweet spots may move.

U-spot: This is a small hot spot right around the urethral opening, just above the vaginal opening and an inch below the clitoris. When it's touched very gently, it can feel very good. To stimulate it, make very small circles around it with your finger. Or when you're going down on her, focus on her clitoris but use your lower lip (brace it against your teeth) to apply strong, constant pressure to her u-spot. Don't probe the opening with your finger or tongue, though. There's a small chance that this could lead to a urinary-tract infection, says sex therapist Barbara Keesling, PhD, author of *Sexual Healing.*

Vagina: The outer third of the vagina—the first 2 inches or so—are where the majority of nerve endings are. That's why short, shallow strokes feel so good to her. But there are two spots on the inside of the vagina— the g-spot and the a-spot—that respond very nicely to the pressure of your fingers, penis, or toys. So let's take a closer look at them—but before we do, bear in mind that every woman is different and has different internal "yes!" spots.

G-spot: The g-spot was discovered—or named, anyway—in 1950 by the German gynecologist Ernst Grafenberg. It's a rough (some say "spongy") patch of tissue on the front wall of the vagina (the part closest to her belly), about 2 or 3 inches above her vaginal opening. "If you divide the vagina into three parts, it's at the intersection

Every woman is different and has different internal "yes!" spots.

between the second and third," says Emmanuele A. Jannini, MD, professor of endocrinology and medical sexology at the University of L'Aquila in Italy. Like the clitoris, it will swell when she is aroused.

The g-spot is the subject of some controversy. For instance, not every woman can find hers, which raises the question of whether every woman has one. According to Dr. Jannini's research, not every woman does, apparently. If your partner doesn't, no amount of spelunking will bring her to an earth-shattering G-force orgasm. But if she does, it's worth exploring to see what positions and movements make this sweet spot sing.

G-spot stimulation can lead to the buildup of a clear fluid in the paraurethral glands (Skene's glands). This fluid—anywhere from a teaspoonful

Next time she claims a headache, you can just chuckle and say (in your worst Barry White voice), "I've got just the thing, baby." Stimulation of the g-spot has been shown to be an erotic Advil, according to Beverly Whipple, PhD, professor at the college of nursing at Rutgers University. "The pressure and stimulation make [women] feel pain much less intensely," says Dr. Whipple. Technically, orgasm isn't even necessary for a woman to benefit. (The sound of male cheers fills the auditorium.)

Don't worry if you can't find the exact spot; stimulation anywhere along the front wall of the vagina is generally appreciated.

---

to more like a cupful—is sometimes expelled through her urethra when she comes. The first time this female ejaculation happens, many women think they've lost control of their bladders. "We both thought I had peed, and neither of us said anything," says Camille, a Frenchwoman living in New York. "I thought for sure I would die of embarrassment. But as soon as he was asleep, I snuck out onto the balcony to call a friend, and she told me it happens to her all the time."

Camille's friend was right; the fluid is not pee—that's been scientifically confirmed. But the question of what it is remains slightly mysterious. It appears to have some similarity to the prostate fluid released during the male orgasm.

A-spot (AKA the anterior fornix erogenous zone, or AFE zone): This sensitive spot right above the cervix was first reported by a Malaysian doctor. Here's the long and short of it: Don't worry about it. If you're the right shape, and she's the right shape, stimulating this zone will happen naturally through intercourse. The two of you may find that deep-penetration positions work particularly well for stimulating this spot. If this is a treasure chest for her, you'll know about it.

How to Know What She Wants

By now we've established that every woman wants something different. So how's a man supposed to know what to do?

Unless you're psychic, there's only one way: *Ask.* And watch, and listen, and ask again. "It's not a man's responsibility—or not his alone, anyway—to determine what a woman wants or needs in bed," says Achsa Vissel, a Dutch psychologist and sex therapist. "If she knows what she likes, she can show him."

Of course, this can be easier said than done. "Even intimate partners often have difficulty opening up," says Shirley Zussman, a sex and marital therapist in New York City. "They're afraid they'll become too vulnerable; they're afraid of what their partner might think. Often, you'll hear men and women make the excuse, 'My ideal lover doesn't need to be told what I like.'" This can be particularly hard in a long-term relationship, although you'd think the opposite would be true.

Asking gives her permission to speak up, which many women want. "When I was first dating my husband, he told me that I could always tell him to slow down," says Marta, a professor in Guatemala. "He said it in a sexy way—of course he was always going to be in too much of a hurry because I drove him crazy—but I could tell that he meant for me to get as much as he was getting out of it. And for the first time, I felt comfortable asking a guy to slow down. I had no idea what I'd been missing with everyone else! It really has made the difference for us."

As with everything, talking about sex gets easier every time you do it. The first conversation might be awkward, the second less so, the third not at all. The key is to stay relaxed and to remember that you're both working toward the same goal: more fun in bed. Here are some tips from the experts to help you have an open dialogue about what she needs, when, and how.

BE CAREFUL WHAT YOU WISH FOR

A small percentage of women are afflicted with a condition called PSAS, or persistent sexual arousal syndrome. (In Japan, this is known as *iku iku byo*—or "come come disease.") This state of excruciating sexual sensitivity means that women with the syndrome have many—up to 300—orgasms throughout the day, whether or not they're aroused. Fun the first couple of times, debilitating by the afternoon; not only can it be painful, but it makes living an ordinary life virtually impossible. Apparently, it's most common amongst postmenopausal women who have done hormone treatment, but it's not exclusive to that group.

Model communicative behavior. "I'm very communicative with women, and I think it helps them to be more communicative with me," says James, the British banker. "I always say something positive to make it easier, like 'God, that feels incredible; suck me harder, sweetheart.' And then, when it's my turn, I ask them to tell me. But I always make it part of the thing: 'Watching you is making me so hot. Do you want me to rub you faster, you gorgeous minx?'"

Yes—or no? "When you're in a sexual situation and trying to learn what he or she likes, ask only questions with a yes or no answer," says Patricia Pearlman, a former sex surrogate who worked with a variety of men, from the severely disabled to sex offenders, during her 9-year career. "'Do you want me to do this harder, touch you here, nibble there?' Never ask 'What do you want me to do?' Most people won't know how far you want to go or whether you'll think it's strange or gross, and they'll be reluctant to answer."

PLAY DOCTOR

Regardless of the reams of advice we're giving you in this book, the fact remains that ultimately, your partner is your best sex teacher. Patricia Taylor, PhD, founder of www.expandedlovemaking.com, recommends that you set up time on an ongoing basis to play doctor. Start by asking your partner to show you how she touches herself and the different strokes she uses, and pay close attention to the places she concentrates her attention. Then ask her if you can put your hand over hers while she touches herself. Finally, ask if you can put your hand underneath hers so that you can feel exactly what kind of pressure she prefers.

"The first time I ever saw my wife get herself off, I couldn't believe my eyes," says Steve, an Australian money manager. "First of all, I practically came without touching myself. But I also realized that she touched herself very differently—much slower and more gently—than I tended to touch her, even when she was right about to come."

Of course, while the primary objective might be learning and exploration, many of the couples that Dr. Taylor sees tell her that it's often the lead-up to some of the most mind-blowing sex of their relationships. "It's a huge turn-on when someone turns their full attention on your pleasure," says Dr. Taylor. "It's intensely intimate and erotic when someone says 'I really care about this; I really want to know what you like,' and you let yourself be vulnerable enough to show them."

Ask her to show you. Unless you're a gynecologist, it can be difficult—not to mention distinctly unsexy—to talk about specific spots or techniques outside of the bedroom. Ask her instead to tell you in a nonverbal way—by moaning or raising her hips to meet you when you've landed somewhere good. "I like to make noise and move around a lot—it gets me even more turned on," says Perla, a Filipino nurse.

And let her know that you won't be hurt if she moves your hands or her body to make something better for her. Encourage her to be honest—and don't feel hurt when she is!

Keep the focus on her. It can be tempting to fish for compliments or reassurance during these conversations. The good thing about sex is that it's intimate. The scary thing about sex is that intimacy brings out everyone's insecurities. Avoid the impulse to ask if it was good, and how good, and was it the best?

Reverse roles. "I like to encourage people to play games in the bedroom; I find it helps with communication," says Robin Milhausen, PhD, associate professor at Canada's University of Guelph and the host of *Sex, Toys, and Chocolate*, a no-holds-barred Canadian TV show about sex. One of Dr. Milhausen's favorites: For 20 minutes, your partner touches you exactly the way she'd like to be touched, and then you touch her exactly the way *you'd* like to be touched. This game gives you a very sexy, nonverbal way to show each other how and where you'd like to be touched.

Be Very Hands-On

Among the things your partner may tell you when you ask her what she likes is that the clitoris is not a bull's-eye, power switch, or launch button. "You can't just go for the gold," says Rebecca Chalker, author of *The Clitoral Truth*. "You might short-circuit her body's elaborate arousal process." Here some tips that will have her wrapped around your finger.

Tease her. Indirect contact can be even more pleasurable than skin-on-skin. So don't take off her panties right away; instead, take advantage of this gentle barrier and the friction it allows. "The longer it takes him to touch me, the better," says Lavina from St. Lucia.

When you feel that it's time to move on, start with her labia. These aren't as rich in nerve endings as other areas down there (the inner ones

WHEN IT PAYS TO HAVE BUTTERFINGERS

As you well know, a hand job is much improved by a lube job. That being the case, allow us to introduce you to Megan Roberts, the UK representative for ID Lube, the number one lube in a test done by *Men's Confidential* magazine and published in *Men's Health*. Megan (Megs to you) even writes a column on the subject for Britain's sexy *Scarlet* magazine. So we gave her the run of the place (trust us, this was not a hardship) and let her tell us what she thinks we need to know about the different kinds of lubricants and how they might be used.

Megs sez: All lubes are pretty much one of three types.

Oil-based: Oil-based lubes tend to stain fabrics but are very long lasting and never become sticky. They are *not* compatible with latex and not recommended for vaginal use. They are great for anal sex and male masturbation—specially formulated for men to enhance pleasure. Megan calls them the hand-job helper. (Seriously—you'll never go back to your girlfriend's moisturizer once you've tried this stuff.) Oil-based lube wipes clean with a paper towel or whatever you have handy.

Water-based: These are the most "natural-feeling" lubes. Try a dab between your finger and thumb; you'll be surprised at how similar it feels to the body's own natural lubrication. Water-based lubes do not stain, are safe for use with latex, and rarely cause irritation. While the lubes can dry out during extended sex, they're quickly revived with a spritz of water or a little saliva. Because of their versatility and effectiveness, water-based lubes are the form recommended most often by experienced couples. They can be used both for vaginal and for anal sex.

Silicone-based: This has a totally different feel than water-based lube. Place a drop on the back of your hand and stroke it over your skin's surface. Notice how it glides across your skin—unlike water molecules, the silicone molecules are too big to be absorbed, so they stay on the top. This means that silicone-based lubes retain their lubricating properties better and longer than water-based lubricants. They're also highly concentrated, so a little goes a long way. The best thing is that they are oil-free, so no stains.

---

are more sensitive than the outer ones), but it can be very pleasurable to have them massaged. Part her outer lips "with both of your thumbs and caress in a circular motion," says Ava Cadell, PhD, a Hungarian-born, British-raised expert who has traveled and taught widely throughout the world. "Next, slide your thumbs up and down her outer lips until they are

Silicone lubes are *great* for massage. You can have sex after and still be "lubed up" from a sexy massage. Megan says she often uses this lube as a moisturizer! (Regretfully, we have no photos of this.) Many of the most expensive anti-aging/moisturizing products on the market use silicone as a main ingredient; it is very long lasting and leaves your skin feeling amazing. Guys and girls can both use it as a shaving oil—no prickly rash on her thighs after you've gone down on her with cheeks as smooth as a baby's bum, and perfect pins for her too.

Silicone lubes are completely waterproof, making them ideal for use in showers and hot tubs. Silicone will not harm latex and is perfectly safe for internal use. Just remember not to use silicone lube with silicone toys. Over a period of time, silicone on silicone will loosen the molecules of the sex toy, causing possible disintegration.

Silicone lubes are great for anal sex as they are very lubricating and very long lasting.

But wait, there's more!

Some lubricants have added ingredients—red clover, in the case of ID Pleasure, for instance—that send blood rushing to the genital areas. Others are "warming liquids," designed to literally heat things up.

Still others are flavored—strawberry-kiwi, banana, raspberry, chocolate, piña colada . . . you name it. One suggestion: "Hide" a drop of flavored lube, blindfold your lady, and tell her to find it with her tongue.

Many couples like to keep a selection of lubes on hand and delight in discovering "off-label" applications for the stuff. "My girlfriend can't take the warming one on her clit—it makes her too sensitive. But she loves it on her nipples!" says Adam from Poland. "We keep a bottle of silicone lube in the shower, next to the shampoo," says Camille, a Frenchwoman living in New York.

It goes without saying that the amount of lube you use dramatically affects the amount of friction you can achieve. Sometimes it's great to get really slippery—it will certainly slow you down. But if you're touching her, you'll probably want to start with just a little and add as you need to.

spread apart, and then do the same with her inner lips. Watch for her body language and for the swelling of her vaginal lips, which is a natural progression when a woman gets sexually aroused," she says.

Knead her. Pressure or vibrations on the so-called mound of Venus, the pad right over her pubic bone (where her pubic hair grows), is an

Women use their fingertips, the pads of their fingers, their knuckles, the palms of their hands. They use a single finger, two, three, four, or their whole hand. Experiment to see what she likes.

oft-overlooked way to stimulate her clit. Pet the hair, if there is any (even if not, petting still feels pretty good!). Place the palm of your hand over her mound—you'll find it's the proverbial perfect handful. Experiment with different types of touch, knowing that you're stimulating the clitoris below. See how she likes it when you knead her mound gently—and maybe not so gently. Try vibrating your hand, or giving the area a few light taps if she's been naughty.

Warm her up. You'll soon notice that she's breathing more heavily, and her heart is beating faster than it usually does. That's to get more blood to her extremities—a change you can actually notice if you've kept the lights on. Take a look at her nipples and labia: The additional blood there will actually make them appear darker. Her clit will also be heavily engorged, and very, very sensitive. As we've said before, more isn't always better— some women can't handle direct stimulation when they're in this ultra-sensitive stage. Your best bet here is slow, steady, rhythmic stimulation. Unlike you, she can go right back to ground zero, even at this advanced stage, if stimulation stops or changes. So stimulate the inner shaft of her clit: Push down on her lower abdomen with your outstretched fingers, massaging the skin on either side of her vagina in a scissors motion, causing the skin of her inner labia to caress the shaft.

Why You Have Two Hands

While you're stimulating her clit, you can use your other hand to:

Put your fingers inside her. Many women enjoy having the sensation of something inside their vaginas when they come. Continue to stimulate her clit. Using lots of lube (she may be providing all you need by this point), run the fingers of your other hand around the lips of her vagina, and then insert a finger inside. Stay there without moving for a moment— if she pushes against your hand, it's an invitation to continue.

You can then stroke the walls. Use your thumb to press on her g-spot, as if you were making a thumbprint on her vaginal wall, says Ian Kerner, PhD, a sex therapist and the author of *She Comes First*. "The g-spot responds to firmer pressure than the clitoris does," says Dr. Kerner. An alternate g-trick: Insert your index finger in a "come-hither" curl position inside her vagina while applying pressure on her pubic bone with your other hand.

Or you can move your finger inside and out, simulating penetration. If she's game, insert another finger. Use the same motions with your fingers that your legs would make if you were doing the breaststroke, suggests Lou Paget, a certified sex educator in Los Angeles and the author of *365 Days of Sensational Sex*.

Don't neglect her perineum and anus. These spots have lots of nerve endings, so simply touching the skin feels good; gentle pressure on the perineum can also be very enjoyable for her. Dr. Cadell recommends gently rubbing massage oil or lube around her vaginal lips, all the way down to her anus. Then, using the pad of your thumb, trace the outline of her anus and then slowly slide your thumb up her perineum, from her anus to her vaginal opening.

Or stand behind her and reach around, putting your thumb on her clit and your forefinger (and middle, if she's asking for more) in her vagina. Your pinky finger is now available for exploration.

"I love the way it feels when he touches my anus, but I can't relax because I really don't like anal except under very certain circumstances. So my boyfriend and I made a deal," Anissa from Morocco tells us. "He can do anything he wants on the outside of my bum as long as he doesn't ever try to penetrate without telling me first. This way, I can relax completely when he's using his hands or his tongue, without worrying that I'm about to get rogered."

Getting closer: Gradually tease inward with your fingers, occasionally brushing against the clitoral hood and the length of her inner lips in a light up-and-down motion. Some women like to have four fingers held together over the hood of the clitoris rather than over the glans, says Sarah Hedley, British expert and author of *Sex by Numbers*. Others like it when you fork your index and middle finger down either side of the labia, pinching the clitoris between your fingers while stroking from side to side. And some like you to press your palm over their mound, moving it from side to side.

Another favorite is the *circular stroke*. "I like him to make circles with

RULE OF THUMB

The more turned on she is, the more intense you can allow your touch to become. For instance, if you used a light touch around her nipples during foreplay, perhaps a gentle bite might now be appropriate. Ditto for her more sensitive bits.

his fingers—but not right on the spot. Above and below is better," says Agata, a 26-year-old Brazilian who works in television. Hedley recommends experimenting until you hit on the type of pressure she prefers: Some women like this to be done with the whole palm; others prefer just a single finger.

You can also hold the clitoris gently between your thumb and forefinger, and roll it gently. "Start slow, until you hit on a rhythm she enjoys, then gradually pick up the pace," Hedley says.

Or tap: "Men tap their penises to bring blood to the erectile tissue, making them hard and more responsive. Some women like to tap their clitoris in a similar way," Hedley advises. Pull back the labia to expose her clitoris, then tap it gently and repetitively with your index finger to build arousal.

Vary the pressure and the direction of the strokes to see what feels best. Once you find her favorites, keep both the speed and pressure of your touch consistent. Hedley reminds you that your fingers can travel back to the vaginal opening, penetrating her with each stroke—picking up lots of delicious lubrication and transferring it to her clit as a bonus. "I love it when he alternates his fingers inside me with touching my clit—it's better than anything in the world," says Barbara, a waitress in England.

Be direct. On the brink of orgasm, a symphony of muscles and ligaments pulls the clitoral tip back under its hood. "It's a good sign," says Debby Herbenick, PhD, the *Men's Health* "Bedroom Confidential" columnist. "Just before orgasm, look for contractions around her vagina and lower abdomen." If she's comfortable with direct stimulation, replace your palm with two fingers on the tip of her clitoris. Start light and increase pressure until you find her sweet spot. And, for God's sake, once you find it, do not let up; maintain the same rhythm and intensity of stimulation until she climaxes. She'll pay you back for this later, with interest.

Blast-off! A woman's orgasm can feel like a whole-body affair, and in fact, she will experience muscular contractions in her vagina, uterus, and anus. The whole shebang usually lasts between 10 seconds and a full minute. "I like more direct, intense touch when I am coming," says Marta from Guatemala, and many women agree. Don't stop until she tells you to.

Game over. When she's done, her vital signs will return to normal: Her heart rate will slow, her breathing will regulate. Her clitoris will probably be very sensitive, so direct touch is too much, but you can stimulate it indirectly until she's ready to go again. Some women like you to cup the whole area with your hand, maintaining contact without overstimulation. (See page 258 for advice on how you might help her to have multiple orgasms.)

Now Give Yourselves a Hand

To our minds, there's nothing more intimate than getting off together. It's educational, incredibly sexy to watch, and let's face it—it's easier. And if you have exhibitionistic or voyeuristic tendencies, it can scratch those itches as well.

"One of my favorite ways to come is lying in my boyfriend's arms," says Nadja from Croatia. "He's so big and I feel so loved and safe. He kisses my neck and holds me tight, and I have an amazing orgasm."

"After many years together, we discovered something we both enjoy: I tie her up and masturbate over her," says Jorge, a doctor in Spain. "She never knows when—or where on her body—I'm going to come, and the anticipation drives her wild. We also enjoy the reverse, where she teases me by tying me up and making me watch her touch herself without being allowed to participate or touch myself. I've come without being touched at all."

IT'S NO AIR-SEX CONTEST, BUT WE'LL TAKE IT

Try a circle jerk, grown-up style, by betting your partner a sexual favor that you can hit the finish line before she does. "I used to do this with my friends when we were kids—now I do it with my wife! We'll face each other and race to the finish," says Gustavo, an Argentinian-Israeli graphic designer. "We're pretty evenly matched, actually."

"My wife will sometimes be ready right away for another orgasm after we have come together, and she does it very fast herself," says Angelo, an Italian restaurant supplier. "I used to mind—hey, that's my job—but now I think it's fine."

We agree, Angelo—*molto bene.*

CHAPTER 9

BE THE MOST CONFIDENT MAN IN THE WORLD
Impress Her with Your Native Tongue

Thirty-five percent of the men in the world rate themselves as above average lovers—and 6 percent consider themselves sexual Supermen. The guys with the biggest, um, egos are Ecuadoreans: 63 percent of them place themselves in one of those two categories.

We asked women around the world what men should base their sexual confidence on, and the answer was pretty much unanimous. The thing that's most likely to make you a superhero in the sack to her is mastering the fine art of making love with your tongue. For lots of women, this is the most direct route to ecstasy, and it might be what's behind all the Ecuadorian swagger. "In Ecuador, men know how to take their time," says Dora, a lawyer from Guayaquil. "They don't stop until it's a job well done."

Dining Out

According to Australian-British expert Tracey Cox, when researchers asked a group of college kids which they'd pick if forced to choose between intercourse and oral sex, "both sexes gave penetration the 'heave-ho.'"

There seems to be a consensus amongst Cox's colleagues: "Making love with one's penis is like trying to write calligraphy with a thick Magic

Marker," says Ian Kerner, PhD, a sex therapist and the author of *She Comes First*. "The tongue is mightier than the sword."

"Making love with one's penis is like trying to write calligraphy with a thick Magic Marker."

It's certainly your ticket to being considered a great lover. "For many women, oral sex is more intimate than penetration," says Patti Britton, PhD, a sex therapist and the author of *The Art of Sex Coaching*. It can be a very tender, intimate way to tell someone you love her—or just part of a total package of toe-curling "best orgasm of her life" sex.

The importance of paying lip service is not a new development restricted to modern, postfeminist societies. According to Don Voorhees, the author of *Quickies: Fascinating Facts about the Facts of Life*, a Chinese empress named Wu Hu who reigned during the T'ang Dynasty (700–900 C.E.) compelled all visiting male dignitaries and government officials to kneel before her and lick her clitoris in homage. It's good to be queen!

Best Table in the House

Our bodies fit together so nicely for sex. They do for oral sex too—it just requires a little more maneuvering.

The classic: The classic position for oral sex is where she lies flat on her back, legs apart, with you between her legs. The popularity of this position is sort of mysterious—although you do have lots of access to pretty much everything, it's very uncomfortable to sustain for a long period of time. To make it more comfy, ask her to lie at the edge of the bed or sit in a chair, so that you can kneel in front of her, thereby keeping your spine straight, just like the chiropractor told you to, says Japanese-German sex educator Midori, author of *Wild Side Sex*. Midori also suggests propping your friend's bottom up with some pillows so that her clitoris is nicely presented. She can lean back—and when things get interesting, she can either hold the backs of her thighs and pull her knees back or place her feet or calves on your shoulders.

Classic 69: In this position, of course, she lies as described above, while you turn around to face her feet, supporting yourself on your elbows. This puts your genitals right above her face, which has its benefits. If you and your partner like to use a dildo or a vibrator, this is a good position in which to do it—and to watch. "Having his fingers inside me, or having him use the vibrator while he's eating me and I'm sucking him, is the best way for me to come," says Nikki, a jewelry designer in Australia. "It's overwhelming in a good way, and I feel very full."

This position also has its drawbacks; many people report that they find 69 unsatisfying because there's too much going on: "I can't concentrate on what I'm feeling, so I just end up sore," says Bree, a German nurse. "No way—she gets close and forgets to watch her teeth," says Jorge, a doctor from Spain. Of course, you can always start with 69 and have one of you take a break to concentrate on the business at hand when things get serious. See the 68, below, for one possible option.

The "68": If you're someone who finds the 69 position more distracting than pleasurable, Midori recommends the "68," a variant in which you're above her but your body is angled slightly to the side of her, with both of your legs at one side of her head, "so that she knows that her job at that moment is to focus on your masterful tongue technique." You'll get yours later!

Side-by-side: "I like to lie beside her, with my head on her thigh and my body away from hers in a T-shape," says Lorenzo, an Italian filmmaker. "This started as a way to keep my penis away from her so I wouldn't make a mess, but we discovered that she can come really fast from the position my tongue is in when I lie this way."

On top: Some couples enjoy having her on top for oral sex: "I can come in seconds if I grind myself into his face," says Nikki the Aussie. You lie on your back, and she straddles your face. Or have her straddle you at the top of the bed, arching her back against the wall. You can give her oral sex and stimulate her breasts at the same time.

Standing: Her standing, you kneeling in front of her. It's a little difficult to access everything you need to get to, but many women enjoy the dominant feeling this gives them (it's great if she's wearing stilettos). And many couples enjoy the fantasy elements of reversing the traditional blowjob position.

"I can come in seconds if I grind myself into his face."

On top, reversed: A variation on the 69 is also possible—she slides her torso along the length of yours, holding or kissing and sucking your penis while your tongue stimulates her clit. If you keep your tongue firm and stiff, she can move back and forth. A little massage oil makes the journey even nicer.

From behind: "She's got to be fairly confident for this one," says Midori. "But the unusual angle of approach makes it more stimulating, as you'll touch and arouse different parts of her vulva. Have her bend forward, using a tall table or kitchen top to support herself. Position yourself behind her, sitting on a chair if necessary, and eat her as though she were a ripe peach."

The Appetizers

Midori teaches a workshop on cunnilingus, often at London's premiere upscale sex emporium, Coco de Mer. In that class, she literally demonstrates the techniques she's teaching by performing oral sex on her female assistant. Sound interesting? She travels all over the world doing this class: You can find the schedule at www.planetmidori.com. And while this book doesn't provide visual aids, we can tell you what Midori has to say, nonetheless.

Draw her a bath. A shower or bath is a good way to kick-start the proceedings. Not only is this relaxing for her (an essential for women before they can start to feel sexual arousal), but it's a pre-emptive strike against any feelings of self-consciousness she might have.

Try it last. For some women, cunnilingus is a good way to get warmed up. But for many more, there's no point in starting there. "I always think, 'Already?'" says Sarah, an Australian student. "It just doesn't feel all that good before I'm really turned on. I'd rather he start with his hands—or even just with kissing—so I can get all hot and creamy first." For many women, clitoral stimulation before the area is already engorged with blood is at best useless and at worst, irritating.

Let her be your guide. "Go down her body gently and in increments, first with your hands, pausing to see how she responds," recommends Dr. Britton. If she's enjoying herself, there will be no ambiguity when your mouth starts its downward trend.

Midori also recommends starting with an ample amount of foreplay. "I'd go so far as to say that the time you take *before* going down on her is inversely proportional to the time you'll have to spend down there." Tease

TONGUE FU

Pound for pound, the tongue is the strongest muscle in the body, but that doesn't mean that you don't have to train. Your partner might suggest that you "work out" by giving her a tongue lashing every night. Barring that, you'll find that doing some of the following exercises a couple of times a week will get you in fighting shape and reduce the fatigue you feel.

"Place a Lifesaver between the front of your teeth and your lips," says Japanese-German sex educator Midori. "The hole is her clitoris. Use your tongue tip to trace a circular pattern in one direction and then the other. Then poke the hole with your tongue. Sweep the hole from bottom to top and side to side, circle again and then poke. Repeat often until the Lifesaver breaks or your tongue gives out."

Also courtesy of Midori: Put a Tic-Tac inside a small clear plastic sandwich bag and pull the bag taut. Kiss and suck it until you can trap the Tic-Tac—standing in here for her clit—using your lips and suction power alone. Don't—we repeat, *don't*—grip with your teeth or bite down. Then try a more advanced step: When you suck the Tic-Tac inside your lips, drive at it with the tip of your tongue the way you went after the Lifesaver. "This is truly advanced clitoris sucking and licking—it gives her the equivalent feeling you get when she sucks strongly on the head of your penis," says Midori.

Stick your tongue out as far as possible. Once it's out, waggle it—up and down, around and around. Then reverse direction on the circles. Don't do this on the subway.

Keeping your jaw loose and relaxed, point your tongue and dart it out of your mouth repeatedly. Or stick your tongue out of your mouth and try to curl the tip up. Hold for a couple of seconds, relax, and repeat.

You can also use a plum. Make a split in the center and press your tongue against the slit. "Use the thick, middle part of your tongue on the base of the split and slowly sweep up," says Midori. "Try pressing and striking with different pressures and speeds. When it comes to the real thing, her moans will be a sure indication of what sends her crazy." Use your tongue to access the stone and then to remove it (no freestone cheating!). "This exercise works your tongue muscles, increasing your power and stamina while performing cunnilingus—you don't want your tongue to whimper and die at the crucial orgasmic moment, do you?" Midori asks. No, ma'am, we don't.

But there's one more thing to bear in mind: Cunnilingus need not include orgasm for it to be very pleasurable and satisfying.

her through her clothing, give her a thigh to grind up against while you're making out, lick the spot where her thigh joins her body. The inner thighs, particularly the area directly leading up to her bits, are agonizingly sensitive. Blowing, licking, even light bites can be very effective. At these early stages, Midori suggests that you concentrate on what she calls "the washing-machine-on-spin-cycle principle—the overall vibration has a greater arousing effect than just using a finger or two."

"Ripping back the covers and diving straight for it isn't a turn-on," agrees Tracey Cox in her book *Supersex*. "Anticipation is everything. Work your way down her body—kissing, nibbling, licking nipples, tummy, thighs—and make her wait." Once you get to her panties, breathe heavily like a prank caller, lick her through them, and then pull them aside. "This will transport her straight back to her first oral experiences (when she was young trying hard to be good—and failing spectacularly)," says Cox.

And when you get down there, leave her clit for last. By the time you finally touch it, expect "an explosive reaction," predicts Midori.

READ HER LIPS

As always, a woman's body language will tell you a lot about how she likes the way you're touching her. If your touch is not firm enough, she'll press against you; too rough and she'll withdraw.

Australian-British expert Tracey Cox has some advice for facilitating communication between the two of you during these most delicate of moments.

Show: Let her demonstrate which tongue technique she prefers by asking her to lick your palm with the pressure and rhythm she'd like you to use. You can also get her to do this to your earlobe. Or other protruding bits.

Tell: Ask her to keep her verbal instructions to single-word commands, like "faster," "slower," "harder," and (okay, two words) "don't stop."

Point: "If you're having trouble hitting her hot spot, ask her to guide you to the right place by forming a V with her fingers, positioning them where she wants you to focus. You lick between them," says Cox.

Experimenting is half the fun—and something you shouldn't abandon, even if you've already found her sweet spots. "As long as he's not hurting me, it's all good when he's down there," says Veronica, a secretary in Ecuador. "Even if I can't finish, it feels great."

The Main Course

There's no hard-and-fast rule about what she's going to like. Some women love a very gentle, almost ghostlike sensation; others, particularly when they're close to coming, want a much more aggressive stroke. The more turned on she is, the more pressure she can take. "As arousal increases, you must also increase the strength and/or speed of your caresses," says Mabel Iam, an Argentinian psychotherapist, television host, and author of *Sex and the Perfect Lover.*

Best bet: Experiment with different parts of your tongue. If you stiffen it and use the tip, she will feel a very different sensation than if you relax it and use the whole thing. That doesn't, however, necessarily mean a pointed tongue, just more pressure. In general, unless you have a master plan, a relaxed tongue should be your go-to move. Lick her as if she were an ice-cream cone. With sprinkles. And hot fudge.

Here are some specific moves you can try.

Start with the lips. Kiss her labia as if you were kissing the lips on her face. Nuzzle your face in there. Lick her mound. Separate the outer lips, and then the inner ones. Run your tongue around her labia.

Go in circles. With a relaxed tongue, lick up and around the clitoris—not on top of it. Do this gently and slowly. "Make slow circles around the circumference and combine this with an up-and-down lapping motion," Cox recommends. Remember, what you can see and feel is just the tip of the iceberg, so covering the surrounding areas is not a waste of time.

"According to some experts, one side of the clitoris is often more pleasure-prone than the other," says Cox. At any rate, you can have fun testing the hypothesis: Cox recommends asking her to keep one leg bent at the knee and angled outward—then switch sides.

Be her friend flicka. After a few long strokes that gently massage her whole vulva, add a tongue-tip flick at her clit. "The combination of stimulation on her inner lips and the erotic tickle of your tongue tip sends her into an extreme pleasure spin," says Midori.

Midori also advises you to forget about the advice your camp counselor gave you: Don't lick the alphabet on her clit. "For the majority of women, this will simply prove frustrating, and it's highly unlikely to bring her to orgasm."

Make the sound of one tongue lapping. Again, consistency is key with this basic stroke. Keep your tongue broad and relaxed.

Hold your tongue. "A flat, still tongue is one of the most underestimated oral-sex techniques," says Kerner. "It's great for inducing orgasm, but it's also a nice breather between strokes." Gently push your tongue into her vulva and let her do the work, setting the pace, pressure, and rhythm.

| *Lick her as if she were an ice-cream cone. With sprinkles. And hot fudge.*

Roll your tongue. If you're one of the genetically able (some people can do this, some can't—and no amount of practice will get you there if you can't), roll your tongue into a tube around her clit and then slide it back and forth.

Suck. Take her clit into your mouth and suck it—ever so gently. "Sucking on her clitoris and labia creates a unique feeling, and when contrasted with the usual friction can lead to more and better orgasms," says Bob Schwartz, PhD, author of *The One-Hour Orgasm*. We repeat, do it gently—no hardcore hoovering—and release it quickly. This is a very intense sensation.

Insert your tongue. You can, of course, insert your tongue into her vagina. A little of this goes a long way—the greatest concentration of nerve endings in this area is right at the opening, so spending your time and energy there makes the most sense. You probably will want to penetrate her when she's getting ready to come; using your hands makes the best sense.

Use your lips. Your tongue will get tired if you don't change it up. Purse your lips and nuzzle, or give passionate, deep French-style "kisses" to her clit. Another stamina tip: The farther your tongue is extended, the more tired it's going to get. Instead, get up close and personal.

Use your hands. You probably already use them to caress the rest of her body while you're busy down there, and that's fine, but you shouldn't hesitate to involve them in the main event. Use them on her clitoris when your tongue needs a break. Use them to stimulate her g-spot, or to adjust her position for the most favorable possible access to the clitoris. You can give a woman an orgasm without your hands, but with them, you can give her a much, much better one.

"When my partner goes down on me, I love him to do a 'come here' signal very slowly with two fingers inside me, especially if he's gently licking my clit at the same time," says Emma, a British publicist.

Ava Cadell, PhD, a Hungarian-born, British-raised expert who has traveled and taught widely throughout the world, suggests full-on multitasking: Lick her clitoris, stimulate her g-spot with one hand, and brush your other hand all through the intimate terrain of her butt. "If you can do that," Dr. Cadell says, "she's never going to let you go."

Use your—nose? Your nose, believe it or not, makes an excellent clitoral stimulator. "Why not? It's right there!" says Neil, a graphic artist in Sydney. "It also allows me to have my tongue inside her when she comes, which is my favorite thing."

Use a toy. A dildo or vibrator can be an excellent addition to oral sex. If it buzzes—or even if it doesn't—it can give your tongue and hands a welcome break, or hold the line while you shift position. And many women enjoy the sensation of having something inside when they come.

But *not* your teeth. Be "very careful about teeth," warns Mabel Iam. "Use them ever so softly." 'Nuff said.

Hum. Vibrations of any kind can be very pleasurable. "I sometimes put my mouth over the whole area and then hum—buzzing her. It's like using a vibrator," says Alessio, an Italian museum curator.

Blow bubbles. Take a swig of champagne before going down, then use your tongue to swirl the bubbles around her clitoris. Nerve endings react to bubbles. In a very good way.

Curiouser and curiouser. A mint can give her a curiously strong orgasm. Stick to the wintergreen flavor; peppermint oil can sting her. (One of our staffers found this out the hard way. About which he can only say, "Sorry, honey.")

The Single Most Important Piece of Advice in This Whole Chapter

"Women orgasm through consistent rhythmical stimulation, so once she's enjoying a particular move, *don't change what you're doing*," says Midori.

Many women do enjoy a variety of sensations, particularly at the beginning. Don't continue for too long with the same stroke unless she asks you to. But once you've hit something she likes, keep a constant repetitive motion going.

Midori advises you to pay attention to how she moves her hips when you're going down on her. "If she's grinding or moving about, don't follow that motion with your mouth or change your rhythm to suit. Stay as you are, and allow her to find the right spot or movement to get her to orgasm. She's just adjusting the positioning, so if you move with her, you're spoiling her efforts."

And then don't stop—for the love of God, don't stop. "If she suddenly freezes in a position, holding her hips up while tensing her abs to stay as she is, it means only one thing: you're getting it spot on," says Midori. "If you continue as you were, keeping the pace and pressure steady, she'll begin to feel fantastic waves of pleasure."

Don't stop until you're sure it's over—and until you get to know her very, very well, that might mean wait until she moves away. Many women want to be stimulated all the way through, and misjudging this can severely upset her applecart at a most sensitive moment. "Don't stop until the shuddering of her body slows and her body becomes limp," warns Midori.

If You Encounter Resistance

"I love eating pussy—I dream about it! But it makes my current girlfriend uncomfortable," says Jonas, a journalist in Portugal. "If she lets me go down at all, it's just for a few minutes, and she's stiff as a board; I can tell she's counting the seconds until it's over."

We asked women why they turned down oral sex, and we used their objections to come up with a series of recommendations to help even the most resistant woman to come around, so to speak.

She's worried it's going to take too long. Despite the advances women have made in the last century, "most women are conditioned to nurture and give to others and to put themselves last—so much so that many women actually get more pleasure out of giving than receiving," says Barbara Carrellas, sex educator and author of *Urban Tantra: Sacred Sex for the Twenty-First Century.* "When they make love with someone else,

PHILIPPINES

INDONESIA

UKRAINE

MONACO

VENEZUELA

POLAND

HUNGARY

SLOVENIA

BULGARIA

CZECH REPUBLIC

SPAIN

CURAÇAO

DOMINICAN REPUBLIC

JAPAN

TURKEY

FRANCE

S E N E G A L

THAILAND

I
T
A
L
Y

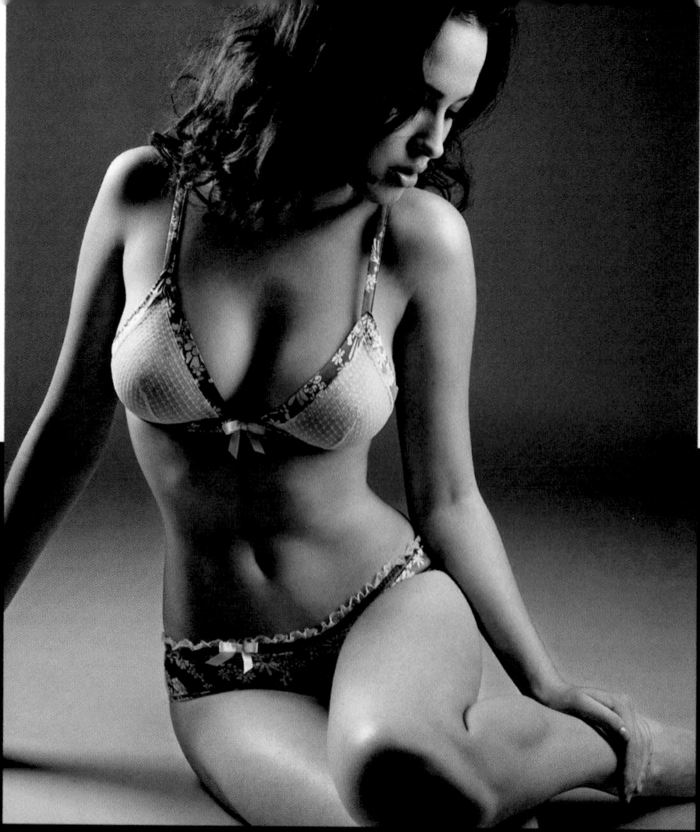

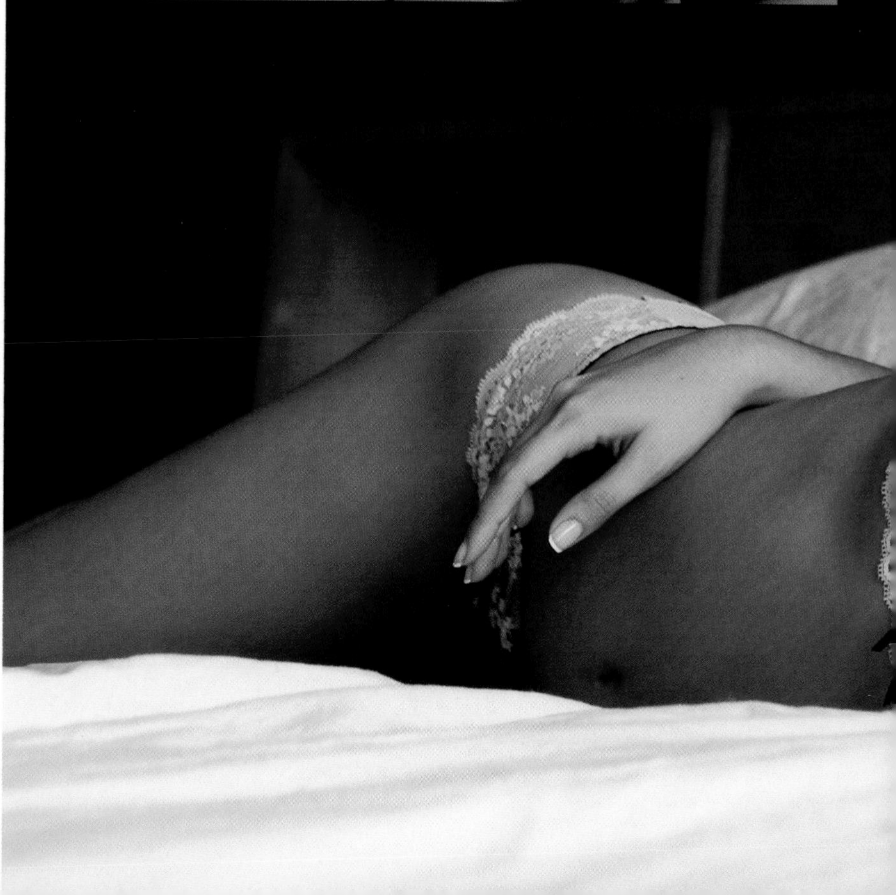

ECUADOR

INDIA

ENOUGH ABOUT HER—WHAT ABOUT YOU?

This chapter is supposed to be about making you the most confident man in the world. Well, there's nothing like the ministrations of a good woman to make a man feel invincible. So we asked women around the world for their best (and most beloved) fellatio tricks. Here are some you're not going to want to miss.

"Lots and lots and lots of saliva. And if he's big, it helps to use my hands at the bottom."—Devon, a pharmaceutical sales rep in London

"I call it the corkscrew. It sounds more complicated than it is, but it's basically a swirling motion, with my hands and mouth going in the opposite direction. Never fails."—Anonymous

"I like to alternate hot and cold. I always have a tisane before bed; a sip of warm tea makes for a very surprising sensation. So does cold water—or champagne!"—Yvonne, a cosmetics executive in Paris

"A well-lubricated and well-placed finger is a special treat in our house. When he's in my mouth, I can really feel the difference in how he comes." —Mika, a model from Ukraine

"Eye contact. My boyfriend likes to watch, and it always made me self-conscious. But it gives both of us an incredible charge to watch the other."—Belinda, a pediatric nurse from Surrey, England

"One hand on him, one hand on me! The more into it I get, the more uninhibited—he loves to feel (and hear!) how excited I'm making myself." —Anonymous

So let her know how much you appreciate what she does for you, and don't forget to compliment her technique—the women we talked to were surprisingly insecure.

A note: Pretty much every woman we talked to complained about having your hands on her head. While that might be a turn-on for you, cupping her face or playing with her hair (maybe clearing it out of her face so that you can watch) is a much better strategy.

Now all you have to do is lie back and enjoy. . . .

they often deny their own pleasure by thinking they are taking too long to orgasm and that their partner must be getting bored."

This is one of the arguments Midori gives for ample foreplay—and for making sure that she's all revved up before you go down: "She'll feel self-conscious if she's taking ages to come and will be inclined to fake it to save your ego."

Give her the greatest gift of all—all the time in the world. Make it very clear to her that there's no timetable, that you'll rest when you're tired, and that you really, really like what you're doing. And if you're just learning the lay of the land, take her orgasm off the table—for both of you. It can be a lot of pressure, on both of you. Tell her that you just want to experiment with what feels good.

Bathe her. "When I was growing up, the boys down the block used to make jokes about prawn and mayonnaise whenever the girls were around," says Elizabeth, a 33-year-old nanny from Leeds, England. "The shame of it still makes my face red. Even when I'm sure that I'm completely clean, I still feel self-conscious about having someone down there."

Although the majority of men find the smell of their lovers very sexy, a lot of women hold on to this insecurity, most often the result of a playground joke. It's a tragedy, but it can be overcome.

First, make sure that you approach for oral sex only when you know she's had the chance to take a shower or bath first—perhaps because you ran the water and scattered the rose petals? "I love oral, anywhere, anyhow. No self-consciousness for me! But sure, even I wonder if everything's copasetic after a long day's walking about in the heat. Better wait till I've had a shower, mate!" says Mac, a doctor from Perth, Australia.

You'll also want to make it clear that her personal smell not only doesn't offend you, but in fact has strongly the opposite effect on you. "I finally got over this because my boyfriend would always bury his face in my crotch while we were watching television and breathe in deeply, telling me how much he loved the way I smelled," says nanny Elizabeth. "I finally gave in and believed him!"

KNOCK YOURSELF OUT

The thing we heard over and over from the women we talked to was that enthusiasm is everything. "The thing that turns me on most is how enthusiastic my boyfriend is about oral sex," says Liat, a retail store manager from Israel. "He buries his face, and just goes crazy! It makes me feel so sexy when I see how excited he gets—better, even, than the feeling itself."

WHO WEARS SHORT SHORTS?

To depilate, or not to depilate—for many women, that is the question. Some men are turned on when she goes totally bare; others prefer a thicket they can run their fingers through. Or you can have the best of both worlds—former Playmate Deborah Driggs and Karen Risch, coauthors of *Hot Pink: The Girl's Guide to Primping, Passion, and Pubic Fashion*, say they've been hearing about a new trend: natural up top, bare below.

There's historical precedence for all kinds of artistry down there. Explicit images from ancient Chinese and Indian art show proudly revealed vulvas. In medieval Europe, total hairlessness was practiced also— probably to contain lice epidemics. And of course, we have Brazil to thank for the eponymous Brazilian wax, which leaves just about everything down there completely bare.

Whatever your preference, oral sex will be easier if the hairs directly above the clitoris are kept short. This is, of course, something that you can do together. In fact, you can try pubic grooming as a starter kit for kink: More than 67 percent of women we surveyed said they'd be up for a trim, if asked (and 55 percent have gone completely bare at least once). "It helps pave the way for more playful experimentation," says Candida Royalle, a producer of femme-friendly adult films and a veteran adult-film star, who suggests offering to let her trim you first. (Ninety-five percent of men said they'd be up for a trim. It does, incidentally, make your junk look bigger.)

If she's nervous, remind her that in ancient Greece, plucking to achieve the desired shape was the norm—ouch! And while you're down there, have fun with it. If she goes completely bare, you can experiment with stencils, stick-on jewels, and patterns.

Hot Pink: The Girl's Guide to Primping, Passion, and Pubic Fashion is an eBook, available at www.hotpinkbook.com. If you're in the mood to send a sexy e-mail, a link to this site will do the trick—tell her to pick out something she likes, and you'll happily help her implement it tonight. And don't forget to let her reciprocate.

Some other products we think you may appreciate as you embark on this project:

The Schick Protector Safety Razor: Uses ultra-fine safety wires to give you a close shave without fear. $10.99

Coochy Shave: Extra-gentle, rashproof shaving lotion for your most private of parts. $9.99

Both are available at www.shopinprivate.com.

And, if you don't like the way she tastes, that doesn't have to mean that you can't dine in style. Use a flavored lube—the ID brand, for instance, has 12 flavors ranging from passionfruit to strawberry kiwi. Just make sure that it's dye- and sugar-free—anything that isn't can cause her uncomfortable yeast infections.

"He's too rough!" "My boyfriend has magic fingers and is a very gentle lover, but the second his mouth is between my legs, he's a jackhammer!" says Anna from Ukraine. "When I try to move away, he grabs my ass and pulls me even closer. I finally had to tell him: 'I'm not being coy—you're hurting me!'"

According to the ladies we interviewed, this is probably the worst technical mistake men make during oral sex. But don't despair—it's very easy to correct course! "Guys think they need to thrust and flick," says Dr. Kerner. "But often what she wants is a firm, still tongue—a point of pressure—so she can set the rhythm and pace."

Compliment her. Women who worry about the way they look down there are less likely to orgasm easily during oral sex, according to Debbie Herbenick, PhD, the *Men's Health* "Bedroom Confidential" columnist. And a recent study published in the *Journal of Sex Research* suggests that women who feel embarrassed or ashamed about their bodies have less sexual experience and are less sexually assertive.

"Seduce her with soft words all the time to raise her self-esteem," says Mabel Iam. Clearly, you have everything to gain with flattery. If you love the way she looks naked—and you do, right?—share the news with her.

CHAPTER 10

MAKE HER THE HAPPIEST WOMAN IN THE WORLD
Treat Her to the Consummate Consummation

In our survey, the men of Italy—guys not generally known for their modesty anyway—report making their partners orgasm more often than anyone else. "Italian men have always considered giving pleasure a test of their manhood," says Laura Rivolta, a psychologist and sexology specialist at the University of Milan. "Whether it's a fine Armani suit, an amazing opera, or a great-looking woman, we are a culture that appreciates and treasures beauty."

What's the Italian secret? Well, perhaps there's something in the words of Paolo Mantegazza, a prominent Italian neurologist, physiologist, and anthropologist who in 1885 published the book *The Sexual Relations of Mankind*: "There is more and better love in Italy than in all the rest of the world because ours is the country of beauty and art."

Or perhaps it's because they

QUICKIE STATS

Percentage of men who report making their partners climax every single time:

1. Italy	60 percent
2. Hungary	58 percent
3. Philippines	54 percent
4. Indonesia	53 percent
5. Netherlands	50 percent
United States	**43 percent**
World average	**43 percent**

make it a priority. "Italian men like the idea of satisfying every woman they sleep with," says Chiara Simonelli, PhD, a professor at the University of Rome. "They spend a lot of time thinking and talking (and boasting) about sex." She concedes that they do "have a nice attitude about sex—playful, and with a good sense of humor."

They're also die-hard romantics—and that translates to giving their women a lot of attention in bed. "Italian men need to seduce their women each day," says Emmanuele A. Jannini, MD, professor of endocrinology and medical sexology in the department of experimental medicine at the University of L'Aquila. Attitude, he says, is everything: "Italian men understand that life is the time for pleasure. The Italian way is to take pleasure from her pleasure."

But there's juice to back up all these hearts and flowers—Dr. Jannini, for instance, is a world-renowned expert on the g-spot. Which brings us to the topic at hand. We've talked about digital and oral stimulation. What's left? Oh, yes—intercourse. (Don't forget to cross-reference what you find here with the catalog of positions in Chapter 11!) So let's talk about sex, baby, and we'll see what tips and tricks the Italians and their international counterparts have to share. And while we're at it, we'll give you a shopping guide to some sex toys that'll make it easier for the two of you to come together when you come together.

The Ins and Outs of Intercourse

Let her take the lead. A study from Illinois State University found that sexual satisfaction was greater in relationships in which the female regularly initiated sex. Check out Chapter 12 for more information on how to get that particular miracle to take place.

Breathe. "They say that sex is all in your head—I say that's bad sex!" says Charla, a Tantric practitioner who specializes in the art of erotic massage and the author of *Erotic Massage: Sensual Touch for Deep Pleasure and Extended Arousal*. "We need to get out of our heads and drop into our bodies. . . . That's why the breath is the first fundament of good sex. You can't have 'high sex' if you're using what I call computer breathing: short, shallow, autonomic breaths. You can't sustain it. You have to open it up, breathe big and slow, to silence the chatter in your head." She recommends keeping your belly soft and your breath audible. Also known as hissing breath (or, somewhat less traditionally, "Darth Vader breath"),

THE MOTION OF THE OCEAN

British expert Kesta Desmond, author of *Pure Kama Sutra,* says that the way in which you move your penis inside your lover is an important sex skill, according to the Kama Sutra. There are nine different ways! She says that three of the best are:

Churning. When you're both really aroused, hold your penis in your hand and use the glans to massage her clitoris in a circular churning motion. A sure route to orgasm for many women—and men!

Piercing. Penetrate her vagina at a high angle—so that the shaft of your penis is parallel to her vulva rather than at right angles to it. Now thrust. This provides lots of fantastic clitoral friction.

Giving a blow. After entering her, withdraw your penis completely, wait for a fraction of a second, and then plunge into her again. Great for vigorous sex with an element of surprise!

---

this is a loud-sounding breath made through the nose, with a closed mouth and a slightly constricted throat. Imagine that you're trying to fog up your glasses in order to clean them, but with your mouth closed. If you're doing it correctly, it should be audible to the person standing next to you.

Ask permission. Before you enter her, ask if it's okay. "Some women find it incredibly endearing," says Barnaby Barratt, PhD, president of the American Association of Sex Educators, Counselors, and Therapists. "It gives them a sense of respect. It gives them the security to become more sexually relaxed." And when you're first entering her, kiss her lips or caress her face.

Increase the intimacy. Want to drive her wild with desire? Look her straight in the eye during sex instead of burying your head in the goose down. Add in a little play-by-play of the action and solicit her opinion, too. The combination of eye contact and dialogue—that direct connection during sex—is an incredible turn-on for women.

"Making electrifying eye contact whilst having sex with someone is one of the most amazing experiences ever," says Maria in Italy. "Looking deep into his eyes while he is inside you is intensely erotic. His eyes say a lot about him too, when he's happy or sad, or turned on as his pupils dilate with wanton lust. . . . For me, being sexually intimate with someone is about connection on a much higher level, and looking at someone and having them look at you really turns me on."

BE ANAL ABOUT IT

Experimenting with anal sex is something that more and more couples are trying. After all, why not? The anus, the closest neighbor to the genitals, is rich in very sensitive nerve endings, and interconnected to the very same muscles and nerves that make everything else down there feel so damn good.

This may be virgin territory for some of you, so we talked to Em and Lo, authors of *Rec Sex*, for the basics.

Rule #1: Use lube.

Rule #2: Just in case you skipped the first rule, it's really a good idea to use lube, and lots of it. "Spit just doesn't cut it," says Em.

Rule #3: Really. Even more lube than you think. Don't be stingy with it, man; you can't take it with you.

Get it? Got it? Good. Here are some other suggestions to help you on your way.

Start in the shower. This eliminates any hygiene issues that either one of you might have. And if any present themselves, you can deal with them right away.

Ease into it. Em strongly warns you away from the "oops" manueuver. "Start slowly and small," agrees Lo. What does that mean? Rubbing the outside, use lots and lots of lube, and introduce a (small) finger. Gradually.

If you do decide to take it to the next step, as in intercourse, Em begs you to remember that "the anus is much less forgiving than a vagina. It's not self-lubricating, it doesn't grow with arousal, and the tissue is much more delicate." Even if she loves it when you go gangbusters during vaginal intercourse, you're going to want to take a different approach when you're knocking at her back door.

Slow down. Have regular sex—but at a snail's pace. Instead of spending 30 seconds licking her nipples, spend 3 minutes. Stretch foreplay out for as long as you possibly can. Once you're actually inside of her, make every single thrust as languorous and slow as you possibly can. When you feel like you're going to come, pull out and take your time with another part of her body. Only speed up when she won't take "slow" for an answer.

Go partway. As we've mentioned before, most of the vagina's nerves are

Be safe. Remember that anal sex is the *ne plus ultra* of high-risk activity as far as STD and HIV transmission go.

No double-dips. Don't do it. Period. If you're using a condom, use one for back there, another for everything else. If you're going skin-to-skin, carefully wash your hands—and anything else that came in contact. This isn't just an aesthetic consideration. Fecal bacteria in her mouth can make her sick, and in her vagina, it can give her a serious urinary tract infection. Which, we don't need to tell you, substantially reduces the chance of a reprise. (If she's prone to UTIs, suggest that you shower together afterward as well; lube tends to move around and can cause problems even if you were scrupulous.)

Use your other hand. If you make sure you're doing something you know she really likes with your other hand, you're creating a positive association.

Give and ye shall receive. "In our own unscientific poll, the number one thing guys wished women did more often was to put a pinky up there," says Lo. Of course! Prostate massage isn't just good for you (and it is)—it feels great for a lot of men. Let's face it, it's not like someone having sex with your ear or another unrelated area. As Lo points out, the nerve endings in the pelvic floor are all interconnected, and the prostate is responsible for the manufacture of ejaculate; you might even think of it as the root of the penis.

And yet, the taboo against enjoying this activity prevails. The experts suggest that you put all that behind you and think of it as just another move in your playbook, like another position or tongue trick. "There are no gay sex acts," says Em. "There's no such thing as a gay nerve ending. If it feels good, why on Earth wouldn't you do it?"

Want to try it? Shower first, and then we'll refer you right back to rules one, two, and three above: Use lube, and lots of it. Ask her to start with a pinky. Relax. And then just enjoy all the fantastic sensations.

---

located in its outer third, the area most of us are best equipped to deal with. "The man who learns how to tease a woman at the outset—by putting it partway in and taking it out—will be perceived as a better lover than the man who uses his full length to drill for oil," says Mark Elliott, director of the Institute for Psychological and Sexual Health in Columbus, Ohio.

An average-size man can better target this sensitive outer third by entering from on top while the woman lies with her legs flat on the bed.

This reduces the depth of penetration by preventing your pelvises from coming all the way together. In addition, when her legs are extended, it puts more tension on her vaginal lips, which improves stimulation for the both of you.

Change it up. Resist the urge to thrust fast, hard, and deep in a repetitive one-two pattern. Instead, try being more creative: mixing slow, deep thrusts with quick, shallow ones. "My husband will tease me by not going in all the way," says Judit, an accountant in Hungary. "It feels wonderful when he finally does."

Start with mostly shallow thrusts that target the first third of the vagina but don't create too much stimulation on the head of your penis. As her arousal builds, add a higher ratio of deep thrusts. Go in slowly and come out quickly; the fast withdrawals will generate even more sensation for her clitoris.

Or try the fast-slow-fast technique: Thrust quickly, slow down for a full minute, and then give her one deep, surprise thrust. Her muscles will relax during the gentle thrusting, and the final thrust will penetrate the deepest area of her vagina, causing spasms and inviting an orgasm.

Use your hands. Use your palms to cup and gently bounce her breasts during sex. Use them to touch her clit or to gently stimulate her anus. Run them all up and down her body. Put your fingers in her mouth. Caress her hair.

The final touch. Kiss her right as she's beginning to come.

Faking It

According to Al Cooper, PhD, the clinical director of the San Jose Marital and Sexuality Center, two-thirds of women in a study admitted to occasional "orgasmo-fibbing." Why do so many women fake us out? It seems that when we ask, "Was it good for you?" what she hears is, "Tell me how great I was." Women lie either to nurture our egos or because they feel like they were taking too long, or to avoid analyzing why they didn't climax. If you suspect that your partner is regularly faking for your benefit, then you need to remove the pressure she's evidently feeling to validate you.

Unfortunately, there's no easy way to know whether your partner is being truthful about her pleasure level. Some men believe they can tell if their partner has an orgasm by being aware of her contractions; however, if you want to feel them, you're more likely to do so with a finger, since the penis is not as sensitive to variations in pressure as you might expect. But even an inserted digit isn't foolproof. If she's sexually astute and really intent on fooling you, she can always fake the contractions.

On the other hand, don't accuse her of faking just because it doesn't "look" like an orgasm to you. For instance, while some women sing *Carmen*, others are totally silent. And while wetness, muscular contractions, and toe curling are common signs of women's orgasms, they're not incontrovertible evidence.

Researchers at the University of Groningen in the Netherlands have used scans to show that certain areas of the brain are stimulated during an orgasm but are not activated when a woman fakes it. If you don't have a brain scanner, the best alternative to playing Sherlock Holmes is to ask the direct, but always welcome, question: "Did you come?" And if you have your doubts, you can follow up with a perfectly timed comment like " . . . because if you haven't yet, there's nothing I'd love more than to keep going."

"If this is someone you care about, don't let her get away with it," says Logan Levkoff, PhD, a sex educator in New York City. "Say, 'I have a feeling you're not enjoying this as much as you could be. Tell me what I can do to make it better.'" By finding out what she wants, you'll help her get there.

Staci Keith, in her book *Drive Your Woman Wild in Bed*, recommends a technique she calls delayed orgasm, in which you ask your partner to resist climaxing as long as she can while you perform oral sex. By removing the pressure to perform and please you, you remove her reason to put on an act. The result is usually a genuine, resounding climax. Oh, and studies show that it takes 15 to 40 minutes for the average woman to reach orgasm. Going somewhere?

One important point to remember is that you shouldn't overestimate the importance of an orgasm. Since orgasm is the end-all for us, we assume it must be for women. And we unwittingly pressure them toward that conclusion. But women don't necessarily need to climax for them to feel that the sex is terrific.

Top five countries where men are sure
she "never" fakes:

1. Netherlands	58 percent
2. Portugal	56 percent
3. Slovenia	54 percent
4. Italy	48 percent
5. Indonesia	45 percent
United States	**34 percent**

"I don't have to come every time for the sex to be great," confirms Perla, a Filipino nurse. "Sometimes, I feel like I'm going to die if I don't have one. Other times, I feel very satisfied, even though I haven't had an orgasm. My boyfriend sometimes has hurt feelings if I don't let him keep going, but I mean it when I tell him that I'm perfectly happy to go to sleep."

"Sometimes sex is over, and I'm perfectly contented—almost post-orgasmic, even if I haven't had an orgasm," agrees Leonie, a stay-at-home mother in Aix-en-Provence, France. "Other times, he'll stop, and I'll think: 'What the hell? You're not going to leave me high and dry, are you?' But even I can see that it's unreasonable to expect him to know the difference. So now I tell him—usually nonverbally, by kissing his neck or moving my hips—that I'm not done."

No Sex, Please, We're British

Or so says the title of the longest-running show in London's West End. In point of fact, while the Italians claim to hold the record for keeping house-wives happy, the Brits turn out to be much more playful and fun-loving than anyone might ever have imagined. And nowhere is that more apparent than in their open-minded embrace of sex toys. Don't believe us? Let us present two exhibits in our defense.

Exhibit A: *Good Housekeeping* magazine—you know, the one in the supermarket with the creative Christmas craft articles? The organization behind the Good Housekeeping Seal of Approval, which can be found on Metamucil and reliable irons? In Britain, *they review vibrators*. That's correct: Right alongside their consumer opinions on patio heaters and juicers, *Good Housekeeping* Britain reviews sex toys. Categories include Best for Clitoral Stimulation, Best for Vaginal Stimulation, and Best All-Rounder (the much-beloved Rabbit, if you must know).

Still not convinced? Okay, let us unveil Exhibit B: Let's say you're out shopping in a mall with your sweetie in Britain. She drops into The Body Shop to buy some cruelty-free eye cream and body butter, the store next door for some shoes, and then into a cheerful, brightly lit Ann Summers store—one of 134—for a vibrator, some lube, and a Saucy Santa outfit to go with it.

Jacqueline Gold, the CEO of Ann Summers, virtually invented the concept of the "naughty" Tupperware party in the 1970s—and with it, revolutionized the sex toy business in Britain. At these women-only parties, women could not only buy lingerie and vibrators in the privacy of their own homes, but talk about how to use them. They did, and do, in record numbers.

You wouldn't be the first American tourist to do a double-take—but clearly this playful attitude to what the British call "sex aids" is something well-worth bringing across the pond. So we turned to a Brit, Sarah Hedley, author of *Sex by the Numbers,* for some advice about how to get over feeling self-conscious and overwhelmed by the selection, so you can bring home a little of this British magic for her satisfaction.

Feel threatened? Women love toys—which, for you, may be part of the problem. She sees it as a way to keep warm at night when you're away, or a device designed to spark up your love life. You can't help but see it as an interloper—the tall, dark, handsome kind. "My wife has brought this up a couple of times, but I can't get into it," says Witold, who works for an airline in Poland. "She says, 'We use lube and lingerie—what's the difference?' But I draw the line at batteries."

You're not alone, Witold. "Many men still do have a deep-seated fear that they'll be replaced," says Robin Milhausen, PhD, associate professor at Canada's University of Guelph and the host of *Sex, Toys, and Chocolate*, a no-holds-barred Canadian TV show about sex. "But in my experience, women don't see it that way. Sex toys can do a lot of things, but they're really no substitute for a man! A sex toy is never going to ask you how your day was or give you a backrub."

> *Embrace a lady's love of toys—they can improve your shared sex life.*

Embrace a lady's love of toys—they can improve your shared sex life. "Women who masturbate know their bodies, and they're often able to reach orgasm with a partner more easily than those who don't," says Diana Wiley, PhD, a Los Angeles–based sexologist. And nothing makes a man a better lover than his dedication to a woman's pleasure, by whatever means necessary. What the heck, maybe she'll let you watch.

If she's not sure: What if you're rarin' to incorporate one of these bad boys, but your partner isn't quite so sure? Don't just whip it out during sex, says Ann Semans of Good Vibrations, the (forgive the pun) seminal sex-positive sex toy store in San Francisco. Talk about the possibilities first, maybe peruse a catalog or an Internet site together, then purchase it jointly.

You might want to start by giving each other back and body massages if it's a vibrator. "Approach it as an experiment," says Cathy Winks, co-author of *The Good Vibrations Guide to Sex,* "a new avenue of pleasure that you're trying together."

Another approach: Give her a gift-pack of different kinds of lubricants, some massage oil, and some body paints for use on her own time. (Good Vibrations has a Friday Nite Delight kit with a bath ball, orange-mango body oil, massage lotion, raspberry–chocolate truffle body butter, and a Magic Touch minibullet vibrator; $35, www.goodvibes.com.) Let her play with them, and tell her to bring her new toys along whenever she's ready. Or start slow—some lube and a blindfold, perhaps, and ask if there's anything else she'd like you to have in your bag of tricks next time.

If you can both get over whatever embarrassment you might feel and indulge your curiosity (and you have to admit that you're curious), you're opening the door to a very exciting world. Not long ago, we would have been ashamed to keep batteries in the bedroom. Now, you see more and more AA value packs on the bedside table. "Once they get used to the idea, guys love vibrators," says Sue Johanson, Canada's foremost sexual educator and counselor and the host of the TV show *Talk Sex with Sue Johanson.* "If she takes it and rubs it up the shaft of his penis very gently—around the shaft, over and around the head and testicles—that's very stimulating." Lube helps.

And it's good for spicing up long-term relationships that have fallen into a little bit of a you-do-this-I-do-that rut. "If you're going to be with someone for 20 years, you need variety in your sex life," says Gina Ogden, PhD, a sex therapist in Cambridge, Massachusetts. "It's the same reason you can't serve oatmeal at every meal: Without variety, your system will close down." Sex toys can add a little three-alarm chili to your lovemaking menu.

Going Shopping

For a first-timer, picking the proper sex accessory can be intimidating, even risky. There is a simply staggering array of sex toys available, and in some ways, the sheer volume of the choices can make the selection process difficult. Some products come with the same cheap battery packs you find on cereal-box toys; others are as complicated as sailors' knots and powerful enough to rattle your molars.

So here's the *Men's Health* Guide to Simplifying Sex Toys, an intimately researched look at some of the latest additions to the accessorized sex world.

The basics: There are three basic types of sex toys for her: the kind meant for her clit, the kind meant for either her vagina or anus (though you should never use a single toy in both areas, due to the risks of infection), and the kind meant for both. Within those, there are two different functionalities: the kind that vibrates, and the kind that doesn't. And you can use any or all of them on yourself. Additionally, there are a couple of toys just for you, like prostate massagers and cock rings.

See, wasn't that easy?

What to get: Your girlfriend may already have a toy that she likes to use. A recent survey showed that 20 percent of women masturbate once a week and 60 percent of those women use sexual devices to do so.

If she doesn't, you may want to invite her to join you in a trip to a store like the two Babelands in New York City, Grand Opening in Boston, or Good Vibrations in San Francisco. All of these are a far cry from the sticky, sordid men's-only sex shops of the past. Customers are waited on by good-humored, knowledgeable staff who want you to be happy with what you get. Asking questions and touching the merchandise is not just permitted but expected.

Just going to one of these stores can be an erotic experience in itself. You'll encounter toys and practices you may not have known about—and it certainly gives you an excuse to talk about putting some previously hidden fantasies into practice. "On a trip to New York, I took my husband to a woman-friendly sex store in Soho, and he loved it," says Marta, a professor in Guatemala. "I think the idea of our sexuality on exhibit like that was a turn-on for him."

If a public excursion isn't your cup of tea, you'll be happy to know that all of these stores have online and mail-order catalogs as well. Pretty much everything your perverted little heart desires is out there and can be on your doorstep in a discreet brown-paper wrapper within days. Some couples like the waiting game: "We never have a problem with delayed

THE THINGS WE DO FOR LOVE

Men in the Philippines and Borneo make a small cut or piercing in the skin of their penises, through which a rod can be inserted before intercourse, says Don Voorhees in his highly entertaining book of sex trivia, *Quickies*. This rod, about 2 inches long, made of gold or ivory, and featuring a small knob at the top, is said to greatly stimulate the female partner. Southeast Asians also insert small gold or silver balls, called tickling stones, just below the skin of the penis for their partner's pleasure. Burmese men sometimes insert small bells—Burmese bells—which make a faint sound when they walk.

gratification—we always have great sex the night we pick it out and order it," says Laura, a British postal worker.

Here's a rundown of the specific types of merchandise you'll have to choose from.

Vibrators

For a beginner, there's no better sex toy than the classic vibrator. More than just a lonely woman's pleasure tool, the vibrator has grown up over the years, and bringing one of these into the bedroom brings that elusive simultaneous orgasm ever closer. "If a woman uses a vibrator that sits on her clitoris, she can climax while he's inside her," says Candida Royalle, a producer of femme-friendly adult films and a veteran adult-film star.

Royalle recommends the Natural Contours Superbe ($24.95 at www. natural-contours.com), which, though designed for mind-blowing sex, looks as sweet and innocent as they come (ahem). Dr. Milhausen suggests the Ultraviolet ($9.95 at www.mypleasure.com). And if your partner has ever made you sit and watch *Sex and the City* with her, you may have heard of the Rabbit ($88, www.babeland.com), a true multitasker featuring a twirling shaft loaded with "pearls" that roll and tumble at her sensitive opening, while the bunny's ears tickle her clit. Tell her to lie back and wait: The bunny cometh.

Okay—so once the three of you are in the bedroom, then what? The opportunities are limitless: You can use it at the beginning, to warm her

RAW MATERIALS

Sex toys are made out of a bewildering spectrum of materials. We asked British expert Sarah Hedley, author of *Sex by the Numbers*, to walk us through what it all means.

Rubber (AKA Jelly)

These toys are soft and inexpensive. But they have a strong rubber smell, and some of them have been found to contain health-damaging phthalates, toxic chemical softeners used in PVC to make it soft and flexible. Greenpeace Netherlands asked an independent research organization to test eight different sex toys, including dildos and vibrators, for phthalates. Worryingly, seven out of eight contained them—in fairly dangerous concentrations. Before you buy, make sure that the toy you're interested in doesn't contain them.

Lube: Use water or silicone (not oil-based) lube.

Cleaning: Rubber toys are porous, which means that using a condom with them is the only way to keep them completely germ-free. They can be cleaned with soap and water.

Silicone

A little more expensive than rubber, these toys aren't porous, so they're easy to clean and can actually go through the dishwasher, provided they don't have a battery pack attached. The good thing about silicone is that it warms up quickly and retains heat. If you have a latex allergy, make absolutely sure that the toy is latex-free; sometimes the two materials are combined.

Lube: You should use water-based (not oil or silicone) lube.

Cleaning: Most silicone toys can be cleaned with soap and water. They can be disinfected by running them through the dishwasher (top shelf only, please!) or boiling them for a minute or two.

Hard Stuff

Toys are also available in hard plastic, glass, acrylic, or metal. You should check to make sure that glass is shatterproof.

Lube: Any kind.

Cleaning: Glass and metal toys can be boiled or run through the dishwasher (no battery packs!). With the others, you'll want to check cleaning and disinfection suggestions when you purchase.

up; during, to supplement the good work you're doing; or after you've run the bases and need a pinch hitter. Try these moves.

Experiment with positions. She can lie on top of it. It can lie on top of her. It can lie between you—you'll get all the vestigial vibrations, and the direct clitoral stimulation strongly increases the likelihood that you'll finish together.

Travel. Don't restrict it to her clit and vagina—the whole pubic area is very sensitive to vibrations. Lay it between her butt cheeks. Run it over her pubic mound. If she likes nipple stimulation—or you do—that can be a very satisfactory use for one of these. You can press it (or have her press it) against your perineum, scrotum, the base of your penis, your anus, your nipples, your armpits. (Just remember that, to avoid spreading germs that can cause infection, you must wash the toy immediately after anal contact, before using it in any other fashion.)

She may also enjoy the feeling of having a vibrator inside her while she's getting clitoral stimulation. But remember, if she can't come from having sex with you, she's not any more likely to come when she's having sex with a vibrator. Try using it inside of her while you find other ways to stimulate her clit.

Create a barrier. It's nice to get a model with varying speeds, but even the least intense can be too much for some people (and at some times, like just after an orgasm). When a more indirect sensation is indicated, create a barrier by using a piece of clothing, a rolled-up sheet, or your hand. "My favorite way to masturbate right now is with my vibrator on top of a pair of tight cotton panties. Yum!" says Emma, a British publicist.

Are you there? Numbing does happen—and it happens faster with a vibrator. No harm, no foul—give her a few minutes to recover, switch to another form of stimulation (a tongue can feel very pleasurably "real" after a good buzzing), or give her a break.

Dildos

The difference between a vibrator and a dildo is that the latter doesn't move (although some are hollow so that you can insert a smallish vibrator inside and get even more bang). The word *dildo* is probably derived from the Italian word *diletto*, which means "to delight," and delight they do. These come in a wide variety of colors, lengths, materials, and thicknesses.

Penis Rings

These toys fasten around the base of your penis, or your penis and balls. There are literally hundreds of variations on this theme; it's a good idea to find one that's adjustable and washable, since lube is a nice add-on. They can be made of pretty much any material under the sun—including leather, metal, and cloth—and they often come with an attachment—sometimes even a vibrating one—"for her pleasure."

Mike Perring, MD, the medical director of Optimal Health of Harley Street in London, recommends the use of a cock ring if it gets harder to sustain an erection in middle age. A ring doesn't restrict the blood going in, but it does prevent it from going out, which can be a help. Even if maintaining an erection isn't an issue, you may find that your erection feels harder, looks bigger, or lasts longer—a feeling that can be very pleasurable all on its own.

Goodvibes.com offers the disposable Screaming O Vibrating Ring for $8, or an adjustable leather cock ring for $25. No cock ring should be worn for more than 30 minutes—serious damage may result. Obviously, take it off—no matter how long it's been on—if it hurts or feels too tight.

Ben Wa Balls

Usually metal, these balls (which originated in China but also feature prominently in antique Japanese erotic art) can be worn inside her all day for an erotic charge. As an added bonus, these exercise her PC muscles, making her more orgasmic—and better able to grab you. Golden Ben Wa Balls are available for $12.95 at www.mypleasure.com.

Duotone Balls

Weighted pairs of balls within balls on a cord that she (or you) can insert into her vagina. These move as she moves, to her great delight. It's great to take this trick on the road—British expert Sarah Hedley recommends an evening of dancing—but if you stay home, it might be fun to let one of the balls hang down while the two of you make dinner together, so that the ball inside is subject to all that delicious tension and movement. Try the Smartballs, $25, from www.goodvibes.com.

Butt Plugs

Either one of you can wear this during sex or before. They come in a variety of sizes and colors; have fun picking one out. It's important to look for one that has a base that flares out—things can, and do, get sucked up there, necessitating a visit to the emergency room. That's just the truth, folks.

Prostate Massagers

The Aneros Prostate Massager MGX ($48 at www.aneros.com) was originally designed as a medical instrument but got so much off-label usage that it's now marketed as a toy. It's anatomically designed to work with your natural contractions to give a prostate massage you'll never forget. It's a little bit pricey, and it's probably not your best choice for a quickie—lots of time (not to mention lube) required. But it's so hugely popular that it's got a Yahoo group dedicated to it, and the Internet testimonials describe near-religious experiences. Best of all, it's designed to be hands-free—just insert, lie back, and enjoy the ride.

Anal Beads

A string of beads (or a stick with bumps, sometimes graduated) that you can insert into the rectum. For toe-curling results, remove when you're about to have an orgasm. Try Beauty Beads for $25 at www.goodvibes.com.

It Ain't Over 'Til It's Over

In the Kama Sutra, there is a reminder that it is impolite to sleep too soon after making love. "At the end of the congress, the lovers with modesty, and not looking at each other, should go separately to the washing-room. After this, sitting in their own places, they should eat some betel leaves, and the citizen should apply with his own hand to the body of the woman some pure sandalwood ointment, or ointment of some other kind. He should then embrace her with his left arm, and with agreeable words should cause her to drink from a cup held in his own hand, or he may give her water to drink. They can then eat sweetmeats, or anything else, according to their likings."

But falling asleep feels so delicious!

There's a biological reason for this, explains Marianne Legato, MD, New York–based author of *Why Men Never Remember and Women Never Forget.* "Oxytocin is a hormone that promotes bonding—it's so powerful that researchers actually call it 'the cuddle hormone.'" Now, both men and women release floods of oxytocin into their bloodstreams after orgasm. But once it encounters the other hormones there, the paths diverge dramatically, and with opposite results. The estrogen in a woman's blood magnifies and intensifies the effects of the oxytocin; her blood pressure drops, and she feels dreamy and relaxed—and an intense desire to continue bonding through cuddling, stroking, and talking.

By contrast, the testosterone in your bloodstream (further elevated by the sexual activity, incidentally) neutralizes the oxytocin—and with it, the impulse to cuddle. In a University of North Carolina study of oxytocin and blood pressure, men showed no increase in oxytocin production after stroking, probably because of the testosterone block.

Dr. Legato suggests a compromise, if she's in full-on cuddle mode and you're finding it hard to even remember your name: "Hang out in bed for 10 minutes before falling asleep. Bring your snack back to bed, or stroke her hair while you're watching television together."

The Taoists, of course, would say that we're so tired after we come because we've spent our *chi*. "People always ask when I knew my wife was the one. The true answer? I woke up, 2 hours after the best sex of my life, and I was still inside her," says Angelo, an Italian restaurant supplier. "We had fallen asleep together—in a pile, basically—without a word."

As Angelo's story proves, the most important thing is that you're together. Whatever you do, it helps to make sure you're in sync.

CHAPTER 11

TRY THE BEST POSITIONS IN THE WORLD
Go Exploring with Our Global Positioning System

Communism dampened sex in Hungary. Or so the theory goes. Until the country's liberation in 1989, "men didn't have access to magazines like *Playboy* or *Hustler*, full versions of the Kama Sutra, or even porn Web sites," says Agnes Beregszászi, a sex columnist in that country. "Now that these are available, Hungarian men are all of a sudden being exposed to many new ideas, and they are overly excited to try new things in bed."

And so it is that our international survey revealed that Hungarian men try the most number of positions during sex. Of course, there's a pretty good chance that, left to their own devices, hungry Hungarians would eventually have figured out most of these configurations on their own! Certainly, a willingness to try new positions, to experiment with what feels good—and with what feels really, *really* good—is the hallmark of a good lover.

What follows in this chapter

QUICKIE STATS

Number of positions in the average man's sexual arsenal:

1. Hungary		8.2
2. Argentina		5.7
3. Spain		4.6
4. Brazil		3.9
5. Greece		3.8
United States		**2.7**
World average		**3.3**

should not, by any stretch of the imagination, be considered a comprehensive overview of the options available to you. In fact, we hope you'll consider this a challenge. Every couple is different. Some positions are just better for some people, depending on your body types, preferences, and whether or not you like to watch what's going on.

In most of the ancient pillow books and illustrated sex manuals, the positions are sequenced, so that one naturally gives way to another, and another, and another. From these simple combinations, the permutations and combinations are virtually limitless, bounded only by your physical abilities and what brings you pleasure. We hope that you'll start in one of the positions we've suggested and then take her around the world! Dedicate yourself to finding a way to add on, to modify, and to generally freak it up so that it's the best possible fit for the two of you tonight.

Talking Her Into It

At *Men's Health*, we often answer some version of the following question: "I want to experiment with different positions in bed. How can I convince my wife/girlfriend/playmate to go along for the ride?"

Here are some suggestions.

Read all about it. An illustrated Kama Sutra is really a beautiful thing to behold—and looking through it together can be both educational and arousing. Make a sexy present of it—beautifully gift-wrapped and left under her pillow, or the last Christmas stocking stuffer after the kids have gone to bed. As you go through it together, you can ask her if she sees anything she'd like to try.

It's worth noting that a lot of erotic art exists not so much as an educational tool ("Insert Tab A into Slot B") but to whet the appetite, so to speak. Even if you stick to your top three and never make it into Downward Facing Sparrow in the Wilderness of the Moon Grotto, you'll benefit from the inspiration.

If you'd prefer an updated version, try *Anne Hooper's Kama Sutra*, which uses tasteful photographs.

Segue. Lots of the positions you'll find in this chapter are easy to transition into from more traditional positions, like missionary or spooning. Move a [insert appropriate part here] slightly, and see what reaction you're getting after a few thrusts. If she's into it, you're going to know it; if she gets quiet or seems uncomfortable, you may want to rewind.

Be careful—she doesn't want to be flipped around like a rag doll. And if you sense that she's close to coming, stay put! "Unlike men, women can lose an orgasm almost in the midst of having one," says Ian Kerner, PhD, a sex therapist and the author of *She Comes First*.

If you encounter resistance, find out why. "Women tend to be much more anxious about their route to orgasm," says Christine Webber, a British psychotherapist and sex columnist for Netdoctor UK. "She might be avoiding a position because she knows it won't be easy for her to come."

Webber recommends that you talk about trying it in spite of this, by saying something like "We may find it difficult to come this way, but maybe we could see whether we like it for a little while anyway?" Promise that if it doesn't deliver the right pressure to the right points, you'll finish off elsewhere.

Blindfold yourself. Many women who are insecure about their bodies stick to the missionary position because you can't see their bodies that way. We know—in the heat of passion, seeing her is a boon, not a drawback. But she can't hear it, in the way that you can't hear the thing about putting the toilet seat down.

Some of the positions in this chapter really will test the strength of her gym membership. If keeping the lights low and the compliments coming isn't good enough and there's something you really want to try, tell her you'll wear a blindfold. If you really can't see her because your eyes are covered, she'll do a lot more with you, to you, and for you.

Be sensitive. Be aware that there's a psychological aspect to many of the positions. Being on top, for instance, can make her feel much more powerful, while doggy style can make her feel degraded and dehumanized. (And if you're not already confused, what if we tell you that's not always a bad thing?)

Make it clear to her that you understand that what happens between you in the bedroom is play—a no-fault zone, if you will—and that it's not going to come back to haunt her. As long as there's

QUICKIE STATS

What's your favorite position for sex?

	He Said	She Said
Missionary	21%	36%
Doggy style	40	26
Cowgirl	33	30
Spooning	4	6

respect and good communication, it can all be part of the game, says Julianne Balmain, San Francisco–based coauthor of *The Kama Sutra Deck: 50 Ways to Love Your Lover.* "The bedroom should be a place where we can walk away from 'real life,'" she says. "Sometimes, the things we want aren't politically correct. A woman wants a partner who understands that liking to be spanked and to have your hair pulled doesn't translate to how she wants to be treated in the rest of the relationship."

And keep to your promise: "One of my boyfriends and I used to talk dirty to one another—about what kind of a nympho slut I was, and how I wanted to go with all his friends, and all that stuff. It got both of us turned on—I loved it. Then one night, we were having a fight, and he made a very ugly comment about me, based on something I'd said when we were doing our role play," says Christophe, a magazine editor in Paris. "I broke up with him the next day and never looked back. For me, someone who would use something we had done in bed together against me during a fight wasn't someone I wanted to be with at all."

> *Make it clear to her that what happens between you in the bedroom is play—a no-fault zone.*

Make her come. Great sex is the ultimate carrot, right? Most women need direct clitoral stimulation to have an orgasm, and there are a couple of ways to make that happen during intercourse. You can do it using the base of your penis and your pelvic bone. You can do it with your hands or a vibrator. She can do it with her hands or a vibrator. It doesn't matter how it happens, as long as it happens.

And perhaps the best way to get her to go outside her comfort zone is to indicate that you're willing to go there as well. If there's something you'd like to try, why don't you swap? Tell her that if she indulges your whim to try the position on page 217, you'll finally agree to have a go with the toy on page 196.

A Note to the Literal-Minded

Throughout this chapter, we refer to the surface you're propped up against as "a bed." In practice, there might be or there might not be a mattress, headboard, etc., involved in your personal proceedings. Sex in a bed is nice— but there are other places to get it on (see Chapter 15 if you need some suggestions.) So please be clear: Our use of the word *bed* is merely a shortcut for our convenience—not a suggestion. Feel free to substitute "refrigerator shelf," "bondage table," "chandelier"—whatever works for you.

Old Asian Dogs Know Plenty of Tricks

There are a number of unbeatable sources for new sexual positions from rich, ancient cultures, many hundreds of years old.

The first, the Kama Sutra, you're probably at least anecdotally familiar with—after all, it's pretty much synonymous with a catalog of sex positions. Not to mention the fact that we've mentioned it umpteen times in this very book. In his book *Sexual Reflexology,* Mantak Chia references *The Classic of the Arcane Maid,* an ancient Taoist text in which "The elemental maid discloses the Art of the Bedchamber to the Yellow Emperor." In it are outlined The Four Attainments, The Nine Essences, The Five Desires, The Five Symptoms, The Ten Movements—and yes, The Nine Postures. Throughout this chapter, we've included some of the Arcane Maid's names for these positions, which are quite beautiful—if improbable!

Another major source is *The Perfumed Garden of Sensual Delight,* originally written in Arabic by Muhammad ibn Muhammad al-Nafzawi— wait for it—*sometime in the 15th century.* It was translated into French, and then into English in the 19th century.

The Perfumed Garden contains, among other things, a list of thirty-odd very amusing names for the penis ("the rummager" and "the creeper" were our favorites), a list of names that you can call the genitals of animals, which will certainly come in handy, treatments for sexual dysfunctions, and homemade remedies to increase penis size, not a single one of which we endorse.

Some of the advice in *The Perfumed Garden* falls into the "dubious" category; for instance, we are not sure that you can cause a lion to flee simply by exposing your genitals to him, and we certainly would not recommend it as your first line of defense. However, *The Perfumed Garden* does contain an illustrated guide to at least 11 essential sexual positions— the classics.

The first is, of course, the missionary position. And according to the results of a survey we conducted on menshealth.com, this is still the go-to move for 42 percent of men worldwide. So let's start there.

The Missionary Position

AKA: Venus observa, Soaring Phoenix

How to do it: Your partner is lying on her back; you're between her legs.

Why you like it: It's comfortable and there's lots of friction.

Many women report that the upside-down orgasm is unparalleled.

What she likes about it: Though this is a difficult position for her to come in—one of the hardest, in fact—she still likes it because it feels intimate.

You can kiss one another, you can look one another in the eyes.

Spicing It Up!

One position, a million variations. Okay, maybe not a million—but a lot. What she does with her legs—and what you do with your body—*really* influences how it feels, for both of you.

To wit:

■ When she has her knees up and her legs spread, you'll be able to make deep, slow strokes that generate less friction.

■ On the other hand, when she clasps her feet together behind your back, you'll really feel like she's holding on to you. (Ancient Taoist texts refer to this position as Sheltering the Reclining Pine.)

■ If she raises one leg, the resulting tilt in her pelvis will put her g-spot in the line of fire.

■ If she's flexible, push her thighs back, parallel to the bed, so that her knees are near her ears. *The Perfumed Garden* calls this the second position and recommends it for the uh, poorly endowed. Even if you're not, you'll certainly enjoy how deep this allows you to get, and it's the best view you're going to get of her backside without turning her around. But you're really going spelunking in this position, so she'll want you to be careful about depth and position of entry if you're packing serious heat.

■ Pull her thighs and buttocks up so that they're resting on your lap. This isn't super-comfortable for her back, but it works beautifully for the bits that matter.

■ For more stimulation, have her lower her knees so that she's lying flat on the bed. Need even more friction? You'll get it if she closes her legs and you put your knees outside of hers.

■ For a very intimate, and surprisingly hot variation, stop moving—almost. Use just the tiniest movements to maintain an erection. In Taoist sexuality, this is called Morning Prayer, and the goal is complete physical and mental connection and reaching a sexually meditative state. It's worth checking out.

■ A technique called CAT (it stands for coital alignment technique) allows you to stimulate her clit with your pubic bone and the very base of your penis. In the missionary position, lie down so that your chest is in full contact with hers. You're going to feel like you're riding slightly higher up on her body than you usually would in this position. Using small movements, rock back and forth. She can wrap her legs around yours to give her the leverage to push back. This is the eleventh position of *The Perfumed Garden*, called Touching Soles because trying to touch the soles of your feet with hers will put her pelvis in the right position. Many women unable to come in the standard missionary position give the CAT two thumbs up: "This is the only way I can come just from intercourse," says Mary, an Australian nurse. "Without exaggeration, it changed my life!"

■ If she's amenable, healthy, and flexible, you may want to consider moving her head and upper back so that they're off the bed. She can put her hands on the floor (similar to The Wheel Pose in yoga) for support. Many women report that the upside-down orgasm is unparalleled.

PILLOW PARTY

One of the easiest ways to revolutionize the missionary position is right in plain sight on every bed in America: the pillow.

What are you waiting for? Pull it out from under her head, and stick it under her lower back, so that her pelvis is tilted up toward you. You can stand or kneel between her legs. If she likes, she can open her knees wide and cross her ankles behind your legs (this is sometimes called the butterfly position).

If you like the way this works, you might want to check out some props. Liberator Shapes (www.liberator.com) are velvet cushions in a variety of shapes—a wedge, a ramp, a cube, and a half-moon, among others—that you can incorporate. The wedge in particular is designed to give you an "orgasm-optimum" 26-degree pelvic tilt, maximizing contact between your body and her clitoris.

■ She lies so that her rear end is almost at the edge of the bed; you stand on the floor with her feet up around your shoulders. Having your feet on the floor lends a lot of power to your thrusting, and feels very dominant as well. (This position is known as Seagulls Flying.)

■ Most sexual positions can be vastly improved by the addition of large quantities of warmed oil. But this really works some wonders for the missionary position. Massage oil is best, but any vegetable oil in the pantry will do. (Be careful to avoid your genital area if you're using condoms—oil and latex don't mix.)

The Shoulder Holder

AKA: Wild Horses Leaping

How to do it: You're on top; her legs are up in the air, pushing against your torso, her feet up around your ears.

Why she likes it: If she slides her feet down so that they're planted on your chest, she can really control how you hit her g-spot.

Why you like it: This position narrows the vagina, so she feels tighter. Or you feel bigger, whichever. This is also a good position in which to get two perfectly full, round handfuls of ass.

Try this: Rock side-to-side or in an up-and-down motion. If she's very flexible, you can make this position very intimate by lowering yourself so you're face to face.

If she does yoga, she can push herself into the position known as shoulder stand, with her hands supporting her midback, and the majority of her body weight on her shoulder blades and the back of her neck. She shouldn't move her neck from side to side in this position, though, so don't jar her too much—and be careful, because this position allows for some deep thrusting indeed.

Doing the DOG

AKA: Dragons Twisting

How to do it: Not to be confused, of course, with doggy style, which is something else entirely; this DOG stands for "dual-orgasm position." In the missionary position, she has one leg up, one leg flat on the bed. You direct your thrusts toward the inner thigh of her raised leg. This is

PREGNANCY POSITIONS

Many couples really enjoy sex during pregnancy. And while we most often hear about women whose sex drive is diminished during this time, the hormonal swings can well go in the other direction, making her considerably more interested than usual. "The only thing on Earth that could convince me to have another kid is pregnancy sex," says Mark, a writer in South Africa.

The change in her body can be refreshing, especially in a long-term relationship. "It felt like being unfaithful! She is ordinarily very slender; now suddenly there were these big beautiful breasts and hips," says Alejandro from Madrid. "And she smelled and tasted different to me as well. I tell her we should have another baby so I can visit my 'mistress.'"

If she's in the last months of pregnancy:

■ Have her lie on her back while you lie on your side next to her. If you're right-handed, lie on your left side. She raises her right leg, and you pass your right leg between her legs and enter her from the side.

■ Or have her lie on her back with her feet almost at the bottom of the bed. That way you can stand and enter her without putting weight on her belly.

■ Another option, of course, is for her to be on top. This way, she controls the depth of penetration and the speed at which events proceed.

It's a good idea to talk about sex at your prenatal visits with her doctor; if you have questions, it's better to ask. And please note that if your partner is at risk for premature labor, you should avoid intercourse—and, in fact, any sexual arousal at all, including nipple play, which can prompt the release of oxytocin, a hormone that triggers contractions.

---

a nice change from the shoulder holder, and a good choice if she's less flexible.

The Spider

How to do it: Sit down on the bed or floor with your legs out in front of you. Lean back about 15 degrees, supporting yourself with your arms. Ask her to sit facing you and help her lower herself onto your penis while she leans back and supports her body with her arms behind her. Her knees should be bent and near your shoulders. Alternately, from the missionary position, sit back and pull her toward you while you both lift your knees.

What you like about it: "This is one of the few positions where the union of sexual organs is visible for both partners," says Mahinder Watsa, MD, a sex therapist in India. "That translates into an increase in sexual excitement."

What she likes about it: "Physically, it allows her to feel a deeper, more intense, more intimate stimulation than missionary, with less friction," says Candida Royalle, a producer of femme-friendly adult films and a veteran adult-film star.

The X

How to do it: Lie down on the bed or floor with your legs out in front of you. She straddles you with one of her thighs under you and the other atop you, and then she leans back until your body is between her legs. Hold one another's hands for support and to enable movement.

What you like about it: There isn't a lot of movement, so it slows you down. And there's nothing better if you're a leg or foot man.

What she likes about it: Your thigh is in prime position for some delicious clitoral grinding goodness.

Her on Top

You on Bottom

AKA: Fish Linking Scales

How to do it: Lie down on your back, with your legs together. Your partner is straddling you, with her knees on the bed.

What you like about it: The view. And having less control than you usually do can be very relaxing.

JOCKEY FOR POSITION

You're on top. She wants to be. But you get only so many revolutions before someone's on the floor. Try lying across the width of your bed, instead of lengthwise. You can flip over—and over and over and over—without falling off. Well, not as soon as you'd fall off if you were lying the other way, anyway.

What she likes about it: She can move in circles instead of up and down, or with a side-to-side vibration that some couples find very sexy indeed. She can lean forward even more and grind her clit against your pubic bone (you may feel some tenderness the next day—otherwise known as the sexiest bruise on Earth).

What to watch out for: In these positions, there's a lot to watch, and not much to watch out for. Except this: When she gets very excited in the woman-on-top positions—as she is likely to do!—she can get a little careless, and if she comes down wrong on your erection, it can not only ruin your good time, but cause serious problems later (see "The Ultimate Ouch" on page 60 for more details). So, if she's totally lost in the throes of ecstasy, you may want to keep your wits about you, just to make sure that nobody gets hurt.

Easy Rider

How to do it: Lie down on your back, with your partner straddling you on her knees. She arches her back so that she's leaning backward at a 45-degree angle, supporting the weight of her body on the palms of her hands. You raise your hips, thrusting shallowly and stimulating the upper walls of her vagina.

What you like about it: Because you share control of speed and depth, you have more control over when you come than if it's all in her, uh, hands. Plus, the view is fantastic. As are her fingers on your balls.

What she likes about it: You have lots of access to her clitoris, and she has quite a bit of control over the depth and speed of the thrusting. "That significantly improves her chances of reaching orgasm," says Judith Seifer, PhD, professor of sexual health at the Institute for the Advanced Study of Human Sexuality in San Francisco.

Cowgirl

Yee-haw!

How to do it: She straddles you with her feet flat on the bed, effectively squatting on your penis. You rest your elbows on the bed, and use your hands to support her hips, rising to meet each thrust. (This is sometimes referred to as Cowgirl's Helper. But you can call it Cowboy if it makes you feel better.)

The cowgirl position affords you a triple-X view of all the goodies.

What you like about it: This affords you a triple-X view of all the goodies. And the position she's in means that her ass will be bouncing up and down on your balls, if you like that sort of thing.

What she likes about it: Lots and lots of control. But it does take some pretty strong legs for her to maintain this for any period of time, so make sure you're doing your part.

Reverse Cowgirl

AKA: Wild Ducks Flying Backward

How to do it: She squats on top, feet flat on the bed. But instead of facing you, she faces your feet.

What you like about it: The view.

What she likes about it: The g-spot stimulation.

Straight-Leg Reverse Cowgirl

AKA: The Italian Chandelier. We have no idea why it might be called this, and we were too embarrassed to ask a real Italian person. There's also a rumor circulating on the Internet that it burns 972 calories for the woman on top. Let's make a deal—we tell you how to do it, and for the rest, you're on your own, okay?

How to do it: You lie on your back facing up, and she's on top of you facing up, legs straight, with her weight resting on her arms.

What you like about it: The weirdness?

What she likes about it: Besides the fact that it's a killer triceps workout?

Lazy Cowgirl

How to do it: She's in reverse cowgirl position, but instead of sitting up, she lies down. Because she can't move much, in this position, you do most of the work with your hips.

What you like about it: You've got lots of access to the front of her body. And, unlike reverse cowgirl, you control how fast and hard the action goes.

What she likes about it: You've got lots of access to the front of her body.

The Amazon

How to do it: Getting into this position requires some doing, but it's very fun once you're there. Lie on your back and bring your knees to your chest. Your partner will effectively sit on your thighs, facing you, while she lowers herself on to your erection, with one foot on each side of your abdomen. Then, you'll wrap your legs around her waist. Holding hands can help her to stay balanced, or she can reach around with one hand to touch your balls.

What you like about it: It's nice to let someone else drive every once in a while, isn't it?

What she likes about it: "This is a great position for women who don't have strong-enough quads to be on top for a long time," says Laura Muller, a sex advisor in Brazil and author of *500 Questions on Sex*. "It lets the woman control penetration and also leaves one hand free to caress her clitoris."

The Trapeze

How to do it: You sit with your legs open and she sits on top of you. You take hold of her wrists as she relaxes her body and leans backward until she falls back completely. "It's important that the woman be fully relaxed, and succumbs totally to her lover, as he pulls her to him, provoking the necessary friction for the sexual act," says Mabel Iam, an Argentinian psychotherapist, television host, and author of *Sex and the Perfect Lover*.

What you like about it: It's very sexy to have this much control.

What she likes about it: It's very relaxing to relinquish this much control.

The Face-Off

AKA: Humming Ape Embracing the Tree

How to do it: You sit on a chair, she faces you on your lap.

What you like about it: The fact that her legs are supported means that she can bounce around on top of you. Do this one in front of a mirror and you'll have a very erotic view of her back and butt.

What she likes about it: She's on top. But her legs are

Do the face-off in front of a mirror and you'll have a very erotic view of her back and butt.

supported, so that she can go for a long time, unlike other positions which require her to have and use a lot of leg strength. It's also a good way for her to deliver a nonverbal lesson about what kind of rhythm she likes. Also, your hands are free.

The Man Chair

How to do it: You sit up with your legs straight, arms behind you for support. She sits on top of you, and then puts her legs on top of your shoulders, leaning back on her arms for support.

What you like about it: The feeling of her butt and thighs against your torso, and being able to watch.

What she likes about it: The g-spot stimulation.

You Behind Her

Doggy Style

How to do it: She's on her hands and knees. You kneel behind her and enter.

What you like about it: "It's the most arousing position for men, because it's the most primal," says Linda Banner, PhD, a sex therapist in San Jose, California, and the author of *Advanced Sexual Techniques*. Angle your penis upward for more friction.

What she likes about it: The angle allows for deeper penetration, which ups your chances of stimulating her g-spot, especially if you angle your penis down a little. Plus, you're hands-free for a reach-around. She can direct the angle of entry by lowering and raising her chest off the bed, and she can move her hips—whether from side to side, or by backing into you.

What to watch out for: Both parties like it when you really grab her hips and go to it. But be careful—you can get very deep, and at the wrong angle, you can hit the mouth of her cervix.

Doggy style can make her nervous for the same reason it makes you so hot—it's primal.

"Like getting kicked in the balls," Allie, a bartender in Edinburgh, says succinctly. Doggy style is also not recommended for women with a history of back pain.

This position can be complicated emotionally, as well. It can make her nervous for the same reason it makes you so hot: It's primal. There's no eye contact. There's no smooching. There's nothing even approximating a cuddle about it. "I have to feel pretty comfortable with someone to be into doggy style," says Allie. "It can feel a little degrading. Of course, that's exactly what I like about it when I'm with someone I do trust!"

The Downward Dog

AKA: Stepping Tigers

How to do it: As with doggy style, she faces away from you, with you entering from behind. But instead of being on her hands, so that her back is like a table, she's facedown, leaning on her elbows, with her hips and rear end raised in the air.

What you like about it: This position creates a snug fit, "making you feel larger," says Rebecca Rosenblat, a Toronto sex therapist and the author of *Seducing Your Man.*

What she likes about it: Since you're thrusting up just slightly, the bottom of your penis massages her vaginal wall right where her g-spot is located. Bonus: "This position lengthens her vaginal wall," says Pedro Otero, a sexologist in Spain, "which in turn tightens her around your penis and makes you feel bigger to her."

If she's slightly off the mattress, her nipples are going to rub back and forth on the bed with every thrust.

Try this: Move your hips from side to side as well as pushing into her.

Belly Flop

AKA: Cleaving Cicadas

How to do it: She lies down on her front. You enter from behind. You can either extend your arms to keep your weight off her, or you can (at least partially) rest your chest on her back. A reach-around is always a nice touch as well—especially if she likes to have her legs straight when she comes.

What you like about it: If her legs are together, it's very tight.

What she likes about it: This is a very intimate version of a from-behind position.

Try this: With her facedown and you on top, have her cross her legs, and position yours outside of hers. Her vagina will feel tighter, and the added friction means more pleasure for you.

Side by Side

Side by Side and Face to Face

How to do it: You both lie on one side, facing one another. She has one leg over your hip. Initial penetration can be difficult; it may be easier to start out with one of you on top and roll off to the side. In this position, neither one of you is expending a lot of energy, which makes it great for lazy nights.

What you like about it: The intimacy. And her breasts rubbing up against you. But you can't penetrate very deeply, and movement can be difficult, so you may need to shift to a different position in order to come.

What she likes about it: This position is very intimate. Not only are you facing each other, allowing for kissing and eye contact, but the length of your bodies are touching. "My favorite for cold Russian nights!" says Anzhela, a randy Russkie lab technician.

Spoons

AKA: Mandarin Ducks Joining

How to do it: You both lie on your sides, with you behind her, propped up on your elbow. She raises her top knee and puts her top leg behind your butt, while you penetrate from behind.

What you like about it: It's lazy, and it gives you great access to the whole front of her body. This is the ideal position for a late-night interlude.

> The spoons position is basically a cuddle with penetration, and you have great access to her clit.

What she likes about it: Not only does this position involve little effort on her part, but the angle of penetration stimulates her g-spot and enables you to play gently with her nipples and, of course, her clitoris. "Because your chest will be hugging her back, you can coordinate your breathing, your rhythm, and thus be lulled into a very gentle and intimate togetherness," says Beregszászi. In other words, it's basically a cuddle with penetration, and you have great access to her clit. Good for late pregnancy.

The Pretzel

How to do it: She lies on one side (for the sake of argument, let's say her right side). You kneel between her legs, straddling her right leg, and curling her left leg around your right side. She won't have a lot of mobility, but you can use your hands on her hips to adjust the position.

What you like about it: It's the same ultra-deep penetration of doggy-style sex.

What she likes about it: There's no loss of intimacy, as there can be with doggy style. And it doesn't hurt her back, as being rammed from behind sometimes does.

Standing

Standing Rear Entry

How to do it: She bends over with legs spread or with one leg up on a stair-case. You're behind her, holding her hips.

What you like about it You're in a natural position to cup her breasts.

What she likes about it: It's very animalistic, which can be a turn-on for her.

Try this: We like this one right in front of the bathroom mirror; she can lean on the sink for support, and you can see—well, everything. Or try it in the shower, especially if you have one of those detachable shower-heads, which will provide a welcome change from (or addition to) your magic fingers.

The Wheelbarrow

How to do it: Carefully. Ultimately, you'll be standing, holding her thighs, which are in the air, while her hands rest on the ground. To get there, start with her on all fours near the end of the bed. You penetrate from behind, she maneuvers her hands off the bed, and you walk together—like the wheelbarrow race you remember from Field Day at camp.

What you like about it: The weirdness.

HANDY-DANDY SEX TIP

In positions where it's beneficial for her to be tipped forward, suggest stilettos. It's not just hot, but practical. At *Men's Health*, we're nothing if not practical.

ONE LESS THING TO WORRY ABOUT

You've heard about couples becoming clamped at the crotch; in 1980, the *British Medical Journal* even published a London doctor's 1947 recollection of penis captivus in which a couple was brought into the ER on one stretcher. But this intriguing phenomenon has never really been proved to occur. If your partner's vaginal muscles begin to spasm violently during intercourse (a condition called vaginismus), it'll cause her pain and you to feel mild tightness, but there's little chance it'll lead to a love lock.

What she likes about it: The weightlessness. And by all accounts, the orgasm achieved when the head is lower than the body is something to be written home about.

What to watch out for: Don't. Drop. Her.

▮

There you have it—and there are a million more, if the two of you are willing to get creative. Have fun!

PART III

THE WORLD'S MOST ADVANCED TECHNIQUES

CHAPTER 12

HAVE THE MOST SEX IN THE WORLD
Have Fun Much More Frequently

While Korean men are nearly double the world average for weekly sex, according to our global sex survey, there's an important caveat to this finding: 42 percent of Korean men we surveyed admitted to paying for sex. In addition, Korean women were the least sexually satisfied group, according to a 2006 international survey done by the drug company Eli Lilly. So we're going to award the default winners: the Greeks.

Want to steal their mythical qualities? Here's what the Greeks know that you could stand to learn.

Get outdoors. "Greece has abundant sunlight, with more than 310 sunny days per year," says Fedon Alexander Lindberg, MD, specialist in internal medicine and author of *The Greek Doctor's Diet*. "Sunlight plays an important role in regulating testosterone release in the brain, so it makes sense that this is impacting Greek men's sex lives." This probably holds up

QUICKIE STATS

Number of times per week the average man has sex:

1. Korea	4.5
2. Greece	4.2
3. Romania	4.0
4. Philippines	3.9
5. Russia	3.8
United States	**2.9**
World average	**2.8**

Stateside, too: Statistics show that the lowest birth rates in America are in November, December, and January—meaning that the dark and dreary months of February, March, and April are the least productive in the sack.

So get outside and soak up some rays; it's good advice, no matter where you live. "I often recommend that my couples go to a baseball game," says Howard Markman, PhD, founder of Love Your Relationship couples retreats and a psychologist at the University of Denver. "You sit close together, you're out in the sun, and it gives you time to talk as friends."

Eat well. The Mediterranean diet isn't just a recipe for a lean body—it's the secret to a rich love life as well!

A diet rich in legumes, cabbage, broccoli, cauliflower, nuts, seeds, whole grains, and omega-3 fatty acids, which is traditional to Greece, is essential to stimulating testosterone release, says Dr. Lindberg. And, as you'll learn in Chapter 14, what's good for your heart—as a Mediterranean diet surely is—is good for your penis.

Atherosclerosis, or the narrowing and hardening of the arteries, is the leading cause of impotence. Keeping your heart and arteries healthy is the best guarantee that you'll stick around to have lots of sex—and be able to do it when you want to. What's more, many staples of the Mediterranean diet, such as pine nuts and honey, are notorious aphrodisiacs.

Exercise. Not for nothing did the Greeks invent the marathon. The fitness culture that we take for granted today—and the cult of the perfect body that it spawns—has its roots in the gymnasia of ancient Athens. "It's a very athletic culture! Both men and women take a lot of pride in staying in shape," says Gianni, an Athenean Web site designer.

> *"Quit looking for sexy and look for fun instead—and you'll end up having more sex."*

Have fun. The Greek culture is also notorious for its passionate yet laid-back style. "It's part of our history! Think of the myths: Our gods were always sleeping around and eating and fighting and making up and feasting," Gianni says. "Ultimately, fun is the best aphrodisiac," says Paul Joannides, author of *The Guide to Getting It On!* "Quit looking for sexy and look for fun instead—and you'll end up having more sex."

So take those tips and use them. But first:

Three Incredibly Responsible Reasons to Have Lots of Sex

What haven't you done in the name of good health? You've burned out your knees on the treadmill, passed on a second helping of bratwurst, choked down wheatgrass shots. As it turns out, the panacea, the all-in-one health elixir promised on late-night television, was right in front of us the whole time. "Sex activates the human body the way it should be activated," says Valerie Gibson, sex and relationships columnist for the *Toronto Sun*. "It's good for your skin, your organs, your brain. It's a vital part of the human experience."

And it's a lot more fun than wheatgrass, we promise.

Here are all the ways that getting lots and lots of sex will enhance your life. Aside from the fact that you'll be getting lots and lots of sex!

1. Sex is a champion stress-buster. "Stress kills brain cells responsible for learning and memory, wrecks the immune system, causes weight gain, elevates blood pressure, and can ruin sleep and sex," according to *Men's Health* "Head Check" columnist Daniel Amen, MD. A recent Swedish study found that chronic stress increases a man's risk of developing cardiovascular disease and having a fatal stroke. And an Australian study found that men who had stressful jobs were more likely than others to suffer from anxiety and poor health.

So there's a pretty good argument for doing whatever you can to ease the pressure. And sex is one of the all-time very best stress-busters around. British researchers found that sex slashed anxiety and quelled blood-pressure spikes for people performing public speaking and taking math tests. Maybe that's why the Greeks are so laid back. . . .

How does it work? An orgasm releases beta-endorphins, the body's natural opiate. It's like heroin without the constipation and rehab. And this is true whether you're having sex or taking the matter into your own hands, so to speak.

But having sex is arguably more fun than dancing solo, and scientists in Scotland are happy to provide you with one more argument for tangoing together: A study in the journal *Biological Psychology* found that orgasms during intercourse are four times more satisfying than those from masturbation. How did researchers determine this, other than asking, "On a scale of one to four, was it good for you?" They drew post-orgasm blood samples from participants in order to measure levels of pro-lactin, the hormone that infuses us with contentment. Levels were considerably higher after intercourse than after masturbation. "People who had penile-vaginal intercourse did twice as well as people who only mas-turbated or had no sex at all," says Stuart Brody, PhD, the study's author. The complete physiological experience of intercourse—and possibly an emotional component as well—may explain the difference, says Dr. Brody. The surge of prolactin may also be evolution's way of "differentiating a potentially reproductive activity from one that is not," he says.

You and your honey don't have to go as far as making the double-backed beast to get some benefits. A cuddle works too. Research shows that 10 minutes of hand-holding and a 20-second hug from your spouse can significantly lessen the damaging effects of stress. But you don't have to tell her that.

2. Sex is heart healthy! Helping you better withstand the ravages of stress isn't the only benefit of sex. It's actually biologically good for you, especially for your heart.

Researchers at the University of Bristol in England found that men can cut their risk of dying of cardiovascular disease in *half* by having sex three or four times a week. Sex is just as good an exercise as walking for reducing the risk of stroke, according to a university spokesman.

> *Men can cut their risk of dying of cardiovascular disease in half by having sex three or four times a week.*

But don't cancel your gym membership just yet. Sex might be as good for your heart as the treadmill, but it won't work the same wonders on your waistline: You don't burn a lot of calories doing it—only about 27 during a 15-minute session.

A lack of sex, on the other hand, has been scientifically shown to com-promise health—even to the point of shortening life! One study found that 45-to-59-year-old men having sex twice a week had a 50 percent lower death rate than those having sex once a month or less. Another study found that college students having sex at least once a week had enhanced immune systems compared with those who weren't as active.

So get off the couch and start moving toward the bedroom.

3. Sex exercises your manly bits. Many men notice that their erections become less powerful and frequent later in life. Of course, there's always

Viagra, but prevention is the best medicine—especially when it's this much fun.

You see, sex provides your privates with lots of nourishing blood and oxygen—precisely what they need to stay healthy. A regularly worked-out penis is the best way to assure optimum sperm production, prostate health, and strong, healthy erections.

This was backed up by a study at the University of California, Berkeley, where psychologist Marc Breedlove, PhD, found that the brain cells that control erection and ejaculation were actually smaller in male rats who enjoyed 4-week-long nonstop sex binges, as compared with their celibate compatriots. In this case, at least, smaller is better. "Smaller nerve cells may be better able to maintain sustained, long-term activity," says Dr. Breedlove. "My guess is that the neurons of the mating animals were adapting to cope with more sexual activity in the future." In other words, the more the rats got, the more primed they were for more. And Dr. Breedlove believes that human brains work much the same way.

Next up: the miraculous heart-healing properties of prime rib, plus details on how 7 consecutive hours of Grand Theft Auto can make you a genius. All right, maybe not. But the next time she nags you about your cholesterol count, you have a counterargument. After all, if she really cares about your health. . . .

Foolproof Ways to Have More Sex

Now that you know how good it is for you, you're probably rarin' to go. Want to have more sex? Here are some ways to make the magic happen—as often as you'd like it to.

Cuddle. It might seem counterintuitive, but a great way to make sure you get laid is to not ask to get laid at all. A survey of 3,300 people for the Berman Center in Chicago found a strong correlation between relationship intimacy and the frequency of nonsexual kissing and cuddling. "If you start kissing and cuddling without the expectation of sex, she's going to want it even more—because she'll feel closer to you, and that's what turns her on," says therapist Laura Berman, PhD. Cuddling, says Dr. Berman, may trigger the release of oxytocin, "the chemical of attachment," which

WHAT IS SEX?

One good way to get more sex is to redefine it. Almost every single one of the experts we spoke to complained about a definition of sex as penis in vagina, to the exclusion of everything else. And, as you'll see throughout this book, both the Indians and the Chinese have traditions, thousands of years old, that steer couples away from this rigid, genital-meets-genital definition and toward a more holistic view.

"In ordinary lovemaking, the feelings, attention, and energy are focused mainly in one area: the genitals. The sensations in our genitals are delightful; however, when we're focused 'down there,' there is a goal and when that goal is realized, this particular sexual episode is over," say Stephen and Lokita Carter, experts in the ancient Indian tradition of Tantra and the authors of *Tantric Massage for Lovers*. "Instead, you can consciously decide to distribute your energy throughout the whole body, thus increasing the body's capacity for more energy and more pleasure."

As a start, it might be a good idea to take your eye off your—and even her—orgasm as the end-all and be-all, and see whether you're not getting more sex once you expand the definition.

---

leads to a feeling of closeness. With women, intimacy leads to sexuality. "A lot of women come into the clinic complaining of low libido," she says. "They tell us they've lost the intimacy in their relationship. They want to cuddle with their husband, but the second they do, he thinks it's an invitation for sex. Then the woman has to reject him because she's not in the mood, and the whole process begins again."

One solution is to address her need for intimacy without tying it to sex. Give her lots of affection—hugs, cuddles, a massage—and make no demands in return. If she feels that the two of you can touch one another without it automatically turning into sex, she'll be more likely to engage in it. Of course, physical intimacy and closeness through touch usually does give way to sexual feelings. Just be patient; it might not happen right away.

Touch yourself. "The more often people masturbate, the more often they have sex—it's a surprising correlation," says Helen Fisher, PhD, research professor in the anthropology department at Rutgers University in New Jersey and the author of *Why We Love*. "It's probably because sexual arousal elevates testosterone and dopamine, and that can lead to more sex."

Don't stop just because you're in a relationship. A woman who's cool with your self-pleasure—and who also masturbates—is likely to be a better lover because she knows what pleases her most, says sex therapist Gloria Brame, PhD, the author of *Come Hither*. Try it together!

Exercise. A University of California study shows that men who exercise 3 days a week have three times more sex—and better sex—than those who don't. If you're a couch potato, don't despair—just get your jockstrap and get moving. Sedentary men who began an exercise program reported making love 30 percent more often and masturbating 50 percent more often during a 9-month period.

Exercise not only makes the body more fit for sex but also stimulates the mind by making you feel sexier. "I think working out is an aphrodisiac," says Marina from Brazil. "It gets all those endorphins pumping, and then you feel good, and when you feel good, you don't mind dressing a

WORKING OUT TOGETHER

In keeping with our Greek friends' advice both to exercise and to get outside—not to mention the evidence that both of these things will increase her libido as well as your own—we asked our experts for some advice on outdoor activity. The consensus seems to be that it's a good idea to start something new: There's likely to be tension and bad feelings if you try to recruit one partner into an activity that the other is already good at. Instead, take up something that's new for both of you. "Learning something together is a bonding experience," says Howard Markman, PhD, founder of Love Your Relationship couples retreats.

Here are some of our favorites:

Rock climbing: You've got scenery, a good workout, and teamwork. Plus the thrill of danger, a natural lubricant. The only challenge might be finding a place comfortable enough to get busy; your best strategy might be to wait for the post-rappelling shower.

Kayaking: Rent a double, learn to paddle in sync, and laugh when you inevitably flip over. Enjoy the motion of the ocean and the feel of the sun on your skin. When it all gets too much, you can find a cove of your own and lick the salt off one another. See Chapter 15 for up-to-date information on beach sex from the Australians, who specialize in it.

Mountain biking: "You don't have to be at the same skill level to enjoy it," Dr. Markman says. It's speedier than running or hiking, but just as easy. Plus, she'll wear bike shorts.

little sexy. It works for Brazilian men too—it's very hot when you can tell that someone feels good about themselves."

Marina's right: The gym is an equal opportunity aphrodisiac. One study by the University of British Columbia found that 20 minutes of exercise spurred greater sexual response in the women participants compared with no exercise at all.

"Research has shown that the closeness, sweating, and improved self-image all help increase her sexual desire, and ultimately facilitate orgasm," says Maria Urso, an exercise physiologist at the University of Massachusetts in Amherst. Which is, of course, the happy ending we're all looking for.

Move in together. Single guys have sex an average of once a week, while their married counterparts get it twice a week. The big winner is the single guy who lives with his girlfriend, at an average of three times weekly.

Turn off the television. A recent Italian study tells us that couples with no television in the bedroom had sex twice as often as those with screens to stare at. Violent films were most likely to kill the mood; respondents weren't asked specifically about Triumph the Insult Dog.

Intend to have more sex! Annie Payne, a feng shui consultant and the author of *The Dance of Balance—Feng Shui for Body, Mind, and Spirit*, says that one of the old feng shui ways to get more sex was to put a red sheet between the mattress and the box spring. How does it work? Well, not because there's something magical about having a red sheet between the mattress and the box spring, but because of the way you behave as a result of it. Putting the sheet there is an action that signals an intent to have more sex—which means that you'll also do all the other things you need to do to attract sex. Intention is a very powerful thing; harness it to work for you.

In the same vein, Payne recommends that single people have the makings of a whole evening's seduction waiting for them at all times—including protection, some chocolates, and something nice to drink in the fridge. Plan for it, she advises, like you would plan for a Superbowl party. You'd never show up to tailgate without all the accoutrements, would you?

Getting Her in the Mood

That handles your side of the equation. But it takes two to tango, and many men tell us that it's not a lack of interest on their part that's keeping

WHAT EVERY MAN WANTS

There are very few things in life that have the same impact the five thousandth time they happen as they did the first, and oral sex is right at the top of that short list.

There's nothing quite like it, is there? But there isn't a guy alive who's getting as much oral as he'd like, and most of us feel like we'd like quite a bit more. So here are some ways to encourage your lover to increase the frequency with which she blows your, uh, mind.

One good strategy is to find out if there's something she doesn't like, and fix it. Here are some of women's common complaints, and some strategies for doing an end-run around them.

Be courteous. It should go without saying, but nothing less than scrupulous cleanliness will do, and girls being girls, a shower a couple of hours ago might not count. If she claims she doesn't even like the taste of Irish Spring, experiment with flavored lubes—or a generous dollop of chocolate fudge sauce.

Overcome a gag order. Some women have a hypersensitive gag reflex that can make oral sex extremely uncomfortable for them. The cure for this vexing problem comes not from an MD but from a DMD. Dentists deal with the gag reflex too, and a recent study brings some pretty interesting news for men and the women who want to orally love them. In the study, the tooth-torturers gathered the most "orally sensitive" (read: "hurrallagggh!") patients and, using acupuncture or acupressure, stimulated their P-6 regions while simultaneously poking around in their mouths. In the majority of patients, the gag reflex diminished considerably.

Okay, you ask, where's the P-6 region? No place too exciting: To find it, put the first three fingers of your hand together and place them on the inside of her wrist. You press there while she pleasures you, and everybody ought to be happy. (Incidentally, this is the same general relaxation pressure point you used to cool yourself down in Chapter 2—see "Nervous?" on page 34.)

Don't be insulted by a spit take. "After 9 years of marriage, my wife told me she loved going down on me, but she hated swallowing; it made her feel sick," says Singh, a computer programmer in India. "I was mad for a minute, and then I thought, who cares? If she'll go down on me more if she doesn't have to [swallow], then forget about it." Singh has the right attitude.

Give and ye shall receive. The more you go down, the more she will too. See Chapter 9 for tips on making all her dreams come true.

them down. One out of every three couples struggles with problems associated with low sexual desire, according to Australian-British expert Tracey Cox. One study she cites found that 20 percent of married couples have sex fewer than 10 times a year. An estimated 20 million American men are stuck in no-sex or low-sex relationships. When we posted a call on the *Men's Health* Web site for first-person experiences, we got hundreds of responses, many of them heartbreaking. "My wife and I rarely have sex," says Nathan, a 38-year-old history teacher in Toronto. "She's committed to me and the kids, but she has no time for romance and little interest in sex. I've asked her why, but she's uneasy talking about it. So imagine my surprise when I came home from work on my birthday and the kids were spending the night with relatives. After a romantic dinner, she suggested we go to bed early. As I slipped beneath the sheets, she handed me a card that read: 'Your birthday gift is Channel 454, the Playboy Channel.' With that she rolled over and said, 'I'm tired. You can do whatever.'"

"Despite all the allusions to sex, there just isn't as much of it going on as people think," says Daniel Stein, MD, medical director of the Foundation for Intimacy in Tampa. "Studies show that 45 percent of married couples have sex one to three times per month. Thirty-three percent have sex zero to three times per year. And only 8 percent have sex four or more times per week."

A mismatched interest in sex happens to every couple at some point in the relationship, especially if you're together for a long time. (And it seems to get worse the longer you're together: Studies have shown that when it comes to how much sex is happening between two people, the length of the relationship is more important than their ages. In other words, a 40-year-old who has been married for 20 years is probably having less sex than a 60-year-old widower who met a 60-year-old divorcée a week ago.) These temporary desire discrepancies generally work themselves out. The thing to watch out for is a negative feedback

QUICKIE STATS

We asked 8,000 visitors to MensHealth.com and Cosmopolitan.com why they turned down sex. Here's what they said:

	He Said	She Said
I never turn it down	54%	29%
I'm not in the mood	19	26
I'm too stressed out	13	12
Not enough foreplay	4	16
No emotional bond	2	8
The sex isn't worth it	4	3
She/he wants too much	1	3

cycle: She doesn't want to have sex, you get angry and resentful, she's angry and resentful of you for making demands, and suddenly a period of difficulty turns into a real problem in your marriage.

Most couples need regular sex not only to remain intimate, but also to stay civil to one other. "A relationship is a living thing that needs nourishment to grow. And that nourishment is sex," Dr. Stein says. Valerie Gibson, sex and relationships columnist for the *Toronto Sun*, agrees: "Sex is the glue in a relationship," she says. "Without sex, the whole thing comes undone because you're no longer communicating in this vital and intimate way."

"My wife's lack of desire has created tension between us," says Aaron, a 32-year-old architect in Santa Fe. "If I press the issue and she still doesn't want to have sex, then she feels bad for saying no, and I feel bad for forcing the issue. So over time you quit touching as much because it might lead to that awkward moment. It wears on you. You miss the contact, question your manhood, and wonder if you're still attractive. You consider having an affair, but you know that's just a temporary fix that brings larger problems. So you learn to live with it and watch this wall being built, brick by brick, between you."

But, according to Dr. Stein, the worst thing you can do is nothing. Living like this will hurt you emotionally and physically. "Sex is just as health-promoting as vitamins, exercise, and a balanced diet," says Dr. Stein. Sex therapists Masters and Johnson found that if women don't have sex for long periods, it gets harder for them to orgasm. Similarly, men who go without for a long time can often develop arousal problems or performance anxiety.

You can't have the best sex in the world if you're not having any sex. Here's some advice from around the globe to get your love life back on track so that the two of you can put the advice in the rest of this book to good use.

Talk about it. "So often I hear that men want more sex, women want more intimacy," says Dr. Patricia Weerakoon, a popular Australian sexologist and the coordinator of the graduate program in sexual health at the University of Sydney. There are no easy answers, she says. "Somewhere along the line, these two people will have to come to a compromise, the solution that's best for them, and the only way to do that is to talk about it."

Is it really sex you want? British expert Phillip Hodson, author of *How Perfect Is Your Mate?*, notes that sometimes a high sex drive is really a high anxiety drive. "Unless there's frequent sex, the person feels that the relationship is failing or falling apart. Sometimes a person just needs reassurance that they're not going to be thrown in the trash heap." If it's reassurance you want, ask for it, and don't be stingy with giving it, either.

Check the calendar. "It can be very useful for a man to know when his wife's best time of the month is," says Christine Wheeler, a British psychotherapist and sex columnist for Netdoctor UK. Scientists have conclusive evidence that women tend to have more sex when they're most fertile. A new study in the journal *Human Reproduction* shows that frequency of intercourse goes up 26 percent during the 6 most fertile days of her cycle—the day of ovulation and the 5 days beforehand. Women in the study submitted daily urine samples and kept a sex diary, giving scientific proof to a long-suspected theory.

Compromise. "As humans, we want to get what we want to get," says British sex therapist Lorraine Landau. "But I often tell the couples I work with, 'You look at this person and you think: *I love you. What can I do that will make you happy? How can I give you pleasure?*' Sometimes the answer is there."

"Sometimes when I want to and she doesn't, my wife will give me a hand job," says Jarek, who owns a security company in Warsaw. "I get the orgasm I was looking for, she gets to cuddle and be close to me without feeling any pressure to have sex. Sometimes she gets turned on and it turns into sex; other times we just go to sleep afterward. It's been a nice compromise for us."

View it as a "couple problem." This isn't her fault, nor is it your fault—it's a mutual problem, and you're going to work together to figure it out, points out Barry W. McCarthy, PhD, a certified sex therapist and a professor at American University.

> "When I want to and she doesn't, my wife will give me a hand job. . . . It's been a nice compromise."

"Making this better has got to be something the two of you are doing together," says Landau.

One option might be to take the pressure off by letting the lower-desire partner be the only one who initiates. "We were in a bad pattern: I wanted sex, she'd say no, then she'd feel guilty and I'd feel rejected and frustrated," says Raul, a woodworker in Portugal. "And if she did want sex, she'd be afraid to say anything—let sleeping bears lie! She said she felt I was pressuring her all the time. So we made a deal: I'd stop asking for a while, and wait for her to ask. Of course, I was worried that she never would! But it worked out great, and nobody felt bad."

Look at the relationship. "When I encounter a no- or low-sex relationship in my private practice, 99 times out of 100, it's not a sex problem at all but a relationship problem," says Wheeler. "So my first tip to anybody wanting more sex is to look after the relationship. Do things you enjoy together, talk to one another, treat one another with respect and courtesy."

Cook for her. Unleash your inner Emeril and you'll nail the top two mood-boosters for women. "When you cook for somebody, it says, 'You're worth my time,' and that's the biggest turn-on of all," says Martha Hopkins, author of *Intercourses: An Aphrodisiac Cookbook*. See page 73 for more tips on making her a meal to remember.

Pick up your own damn socks. "Women in Brazil have more time for taking care of themselves. They have more time, to be honest, to think about sex, to feel sexy, to get ready for it. I don't understand how American women ever feel like making love," says Marina.

Numerous studies—not to mention the anecdotal evidence all around us—suggest that women are still in charge of the lion's share of domestic duties, despite the fact that many of them work outside the home. Furthermore, even in households where the split is a little more even, women tend to end up with more time-sensitive chores, like feeding the kids. These can't be blown off until the weekend, the way mowing the lawn can; they have to be attended to right away, even if she's feeling tapped out. By the end of a long day of work, childrearing, and household chores, making love can feel like yet another bullet on the list of things to do. Helping her to carry the burden will increase your chances that she'll be in the mood—or will at least make you as tired as she is, so you can empathize.

Be a better partner! In a University of New Orleans study, nearly 70 percent of men reported that when they initiate sex, they overestimate their partners' desire to get it on. Alex Caroline Robboy, the founder of havegoodsex.com, says that the best way to get her to want sex is to improve your sexual technique. "You want it to be amazing so that she's thinking about it, anticipating it the way she would a delicious dessert at a restaurant." If the sex isn't that good, Robboy points out, eventually you're going to lose out to a more enjoyable activity: "Given the choice between a leisurely bath which she knows she's going to love, or mediocre sex, what do you think she's going to choose?" Refer to Part II for more tips on developing the skills that will have her begging for more.

Eliminate possible physical and emotional causes of low desire. There may be a straightforward reason your partner is uninterested in sex. Here are some of the most common.

■ *And then there were three.* Becoming a mother can dramatically affect a woman's sexuality. Breastfeeding, for instance, produces a hormone called prolactin that can suppress sexual desire. And your partner may be feeling "touched out" from having an infant cling to her all day and therefore less interested in being touched by you, says Robboy. "I nursed for about 15 months," says Andrea from Argentina. "And although I'd always loved it when my husband paid attention to my nipples, after the baby came, it was 'Enough already!' Thankfully, a couple of months after I stopped breastfeeding, my nipples were sexual again."

There's not much you can do about a reduction in her sex drive due to hormones; often, simply knowing that it's temporary can help. The best plan, if you want to be sexual, is to switch into caretaker mode, Robboy says, taking care of her so that she can take care of the baby. In most relationships—even the most liberated ones—the woman shoulders the majority of the childcare burden. Babies keep erratic hours and create an enormous amount of work, so new mothers are often very tired. What can you do to help? You feed her so that she can feed the baby; you clean up so that she can have some downtime. You babysit so that she can get back to the gym and feel happier about her body. "I always encourage men to give their partners lots of time and space for rest, rejuvenation, beauty rituals—anything that makes her feel like an independent person. That's more likely to lead to great sex than any special finger manipulation he can learn," says Robin Milhausen, PhD, associate professor at Canada's University of Guelph and the host of *Sex, Toys, and Chocolate,* a no-holds-barred Canadian TV show about sex.

Sex may have to become more scheduled, arranged to suit a nap schedule rather than the dictates of passion. But you need to make the time to reconnect on an adult level and to rekindle feelings that may have been tamped down by the new arrival—and that falls to you if she doesn't have the energy to do it. (For help, flip back to Chapter 6 and read "Making the Time for Love" on page 94.)

Of course, women aren't the only ones who find new parenthood disruptive. You may feel overwhelmed by your new responsibilities, which can detract from sex drive. Or you may see your wife differently now that she's a mom. A counselor can help you work through these feelings together.

■ **"Do I look fat?"** Has she gained weight? If she's feeling self-conscious about her body, she's going to feel much less enthusiastic about having you touch it. And if she has gained weight, you may be feeling less enthusiastic about her as a result. The best thing to do is to clean up your own act, and take her along with you. If you feel that you can talk about it with her, suggest that the two of you try to take off 10 pounds together. If you think she'd be hurt by the suggestion, start introducing healthier options at home—bring home some sorbet along with the full-fat stuff she asked you to pick up—and tell her it's your new fave. Or ask her if she'd join you in a walk after dinner—if you hold hands, you won't even notice it's exercise!

WHEN YOU DON'T WANT MORE

You say you don't know what the big deal is—you just don't feel the urge that often? If you and your significant other are both okay with that, cool. But if one, or both, of you want you to want her more frequently, you might consider getting your hormone levels checked. "Androgen (also known as testosterone) appears to be directly responsible for sexual thoughts in both men and women," says Victoria Zdrok, PhD—AKA "Dr. Z," a dating coach, relationship advisor, and *Penthouse* columnist. "People with low testosterone have far fewer sexual fantasies."

Men who are born with underdeveloped testicles (the so-called hypogonadal men) underproduce testosterone and, as a result, suffer from lack of sexual thought or desire. When such males are injected with testosterone, they begin experiencing sexual thoughts and fantasies (frequently, before they experience erections).

If you think you might have low testosterone, talk to your doctor; a simple battery of blood tests will let you know whether your concerns are well-founded, and testosterone can be taken by injection or skin patch.

■ **The sex-killer: stress.** Whether it's a heavy-duty deadline at work, a teenager in trouble, or an elderly parent who is beginning to require more care, stress takes a heavy toll on people, and sex often suffers as a result. It's not always possible, but do try to prioritize the relationship as much as possible. One night away from the turbulence of your life can make a big difference to the two of you.

■ **Is there anything else?** Has she had surgery recently? Is she going through menopause? Are your testosterone levels decreasing because of age? Are either of you taking medications, such as certain antidepressants, which can decrease your interest in sex?

Get help. If an easy solution to a desire discrepancy isn't forthcoming, it's time to see a therapist. Consult the yellow pages for a certified sex therapist in your area, or visit the Web site of the American Association of Sexuality Educators, Counselors, and Therapists (www.aasect.org) for a directory.

If one of you is too self-conscious to meet with anyone in person, Michele Weiner-Davis, MSW, runs the Divorce Busting Center (www.divorcebusting.com), which offers phone consultations with trained relationship coaches.

■

Hopefully, these tips will help. But what we heard over and over from the experts and the real women we talked to was that a happy woman is a willing one. "The best aphrodisiac for me is the feeling that I'm the only woman in the world for my man," says Agata, a 26-year-old Brazilian who works in television. "I want him to make me feel like he thinks I'm special, the most attractive, sexy woman in the world."

CHAPTER 13

BE A WORLD-CLASS ENDURANCE ATHLETE
Increase Your Sexual Stamina

Mexican culture is overtly passionate—there's passion for women, passion for food, passion for life, passion for dancing—and sex is a natural extension of that culture. It's also a leisurely culture, as are many societies that grew up under the hot sun. This combination of passion and a leisurely approach to it transfers seamlessly into the bedroom, where, according to our survey, Mexican men have the most staying power.

"Women need a little more time, and the best lovers give it to us," says Elsy Reyes, sex and relationship expert for the Mexican edition of *Men's Health*. "The best trick is making the initial game last as long as possible—kisses, hugs, oral sex, and stimulation. Breathe properly, and focus on giving pleasure, not just on your own satisfaction."

Marathoners aren't made overnight, as we learn from the Dutch, who last almost as long as the Mexicans. "In Holland, sexuality is not repressed," explains Ascha Vissel, a Dutch psychologist and sex therapist. "Here, young people can relax and experiment, and

QUICKIE STATS

Length of sex, from foreplay to climax (in minutes):

1. Mexico	23.1
2. Netherlands	22.4
3. Spain	22.3
4. Brazil	21.8
5. France	21.7
United States	**17.7**
World average	**19.16**

don't have to have sex or masturbate in a hurry while being afraid of getting caught." The moral: While in-the-moment techniques might buy you 15 extra seconds, retraining your sexual system will help you hop off the express train for good.

In this chapter, our experts will tell you how going *lentamente* makes it *caliente*.

How Long *Should* It Take?

A study done by the late, great Dr. Alfred Kinsey found that most men (about three-quarters) ejaculate within 2 minutes of penetration. Other studies show that at least one-third of all men report dissatisfaction with how long they can last. That was certainly borne out by our survey, in which 21 percent of you said that the superpower you'd most want would be the ability to last as long as you wanted to in bed.

But here's the million-dollar question: Does it really matter?

Less, perhaps, than you'd think.

It's fairly clear that men have benefited from the female sexual liberation of the past 50 years. A woman who initiates sex, enjoys it, and takes pleasure in sharing her body is infinitely preferable to one who lies there crafting her shopping list and waiting for it to be over.

> "Women need a little more time, and the best lovers give it."

But there's also more pressure on both partners to perform, and one of the foremost standards against which men are judged is the stud who can go "all night."

Ira L. Reiss, PhD, former president of the International Academy of Sex Research and the author of *An End to Shame: Shaping Our Next Sexual Revolution*, has an interesting take on this whole stamina issue. Coming quickly is still a sign of virility in boyhood circles (or perhaps we should say circle-jerks), and women with the same hair trigger are praised as sexually responsive. If there is a real problem, the best strategy is to "treat it, not demean it," he states (and you'll find help in Chapter 14). But he advises against jumping to a diagnosis too soon, because "most dysfunctions are societal, not physical."

Or, as Mantak Chia and Doug Abrams point out in their book *The Multi-Orgasmic Man*, which is based on ancient Chinese techniques, "the question is not whether you can last for a certain number of minutes on the stopwatch, but whether you and your partner are satisfied with the duration of your lovemaking." In other words, it might be time to take the clock out of the bedroom. After all, the average penis is not the kind of athlete who performs his best under stress.

And you might be a little surprised by what you find when you talk to women about the issue. Since most women don't orgasm from intercourse alone, the male drive to go all night may be slightly misplaced. "I don't come from sex anyway!" says Liat, a retail store manager from Israel.

Women do, on average, need more stimulation than men do in order to achieve orgasm. So she does want the sex act to last more than 5 minutes, for sure. And she does want you to give her as many orgasms as she can physically tolerate and to drive her to previously unseen heights of ecstatic bliss. But that's not quite the same thing as being able to pound her for hours on end. In fact, from the female perspective, there's often *too much* time spent on intercourse—many women get sore after too long. "What is it with these guys that think you're going to whine to your friends if they don't go for a certain amount of time or whatever?" complains Sylvia from Germany. "It's like they turn it into another athletic event, another competition with their friends. It has nothing whatsoever to do with what I want."

Perhaps we've had the wrong focus this whole time. Perhaps the goal is to stretch out the *encounter*, and not necessarily the intercourse. Chapter 7, "Enjoy the Most Leisurely Sex in the World," gives you some insight into women's favorite ways to do that. And in this chapter, we'll gladly provide you with some tricks to last longer. Ideally, you'll use the latter to make sex more fulfilling and exciting—not another time trial.

Tricks to Last Longer

Since there's no medical standard for the length of time a man "should" have sex before ejaculating, premature ejaculation, or PE, can only be defined by you and your partner—ejaculation that happens before either of you want it to, the majority of the time. It looks like there is some biological basis for premature ejaculation, but in many cases, it's the result of anxiety and stress. Guilty feelings about sex, concerns about a health problem, or worry about losing your erection all may contribute. The good news is that it's very common, and highly responsive to treatment. "These are problems that can be easily corrected with sex re-education or sex

THE ART OF SELF-CULTIVATION

Practice, as they say, makes perfect. And what is masturbation if not practice for sex? Most of us have quite a bit of experience with the solo tango by now. As a result we've got it down to an art form—and a pretty speedy affair. "I can make myself come before I'm even completely hard," confesses Eric, a librarian in Indonesia.

The ancient Chinese referred to masturbation as "self-cultivation" and viewed it as a way to get in shape for the main event. So, the next time you find yourself in the mood for a little self-love, take your time. Get into it, and then back off to recover a little. See how close you can push yourself to the edge without going over. And see how long you can stretch it out. You'll notice a big difference in the quality of your orgasm. And, with a little practice, you'll see that you're able to use some of these same tricks when you've got company.

---

training," says Robert Santo-Paolo, a French psychologist and sexologist and the founder of the Web site sexotherapie.com. "It would be a real pity to have an unhappy finish to a relationship so beautifully begun." Here are some options:

Play a practice round beforehand. Teenagers everywhere know that masturbating a few hours before the main event takes the edge off. That's both a good and a bad thing, of course. You'll notice that it takes you quite a bit longer to get turned on with her, and to come once you're inside. But while you may last longer for the main event, you may enjoy it a little less as well. So Mahinder Watsa, MD, a sex therapist in India, suggests increasing your staying power by having more sex—and who can argue with that?

Try again. "I always come really fast the first time, so we usually do it twice—once for me, and once for her!" says Junior, an environmental engineer from the Philippines. If you're able to achieve another erection soon after you've ejaculated, doing it again might be the best way to solve the problem. You're guaranteed to last longer the second time around.

Relax. You can increase your stamina by reducing your muscle tension, says Marc Goldstein, MD, professor of reproductive medicine and urology at Cornell University Medical College. One way to do that is to have her get on top, so you're not supporting her muscle tension as well as your own.

The most important thing you can do, however, is to breathe. "The problem with most men is that they don't know how to breathe and organize their energy," says Reyes—and 5,000 years of Tantric practice support her position. Breathing deeply and slowly does two things: (1) It calms the nervous system, which is helpful when you're trying to pull back from the brink. And (2) it circulates the sexual energy concentrated in your genitals throughout the rest of your body. Not only does this help to delay orgasm, but it makes it much more powerful when it finally happens.

Increase slowly. Your best strategy for building your sexual stamina? The same thing that works on the treadmill: Go a little longer every single time, until you've built up to where you want to be.

Close your eyes. Men are strongly influenced by the visual. That's why we like porn so much more than women do. The right visual—a bouncing breast, the down on the inside of her thigh—is all too often the straw that breaks the camel's hump. So insulate yourself from the possibility for a minute or two by closing your eyes.

Take your balls out of play. As you've probably noticed, the testicles are filled with lots and lots of nerve endings—a bad thing when you're playing ice hockey, but a wonderful thing when you're body checking her. Positions that stimulate them (like the missionary or rear-entry positions, where they brush—or bang—up against her body) may give you a little more stimulation than you can handle. Switch to a position that takes the testicles away from the action, like her on top and leaning forward.

Don't think about it. Easier said than done, we know. And yet, it makes sense. "There's a Hungarian proverb that says 'Do not paint the devil on the wall, for it will appear,'" says Agnes Beregszászi, a sex columnist in Hungary. Translation: The area of the brain responsible for triggering orgasm is engaged whether you're trying to *have* one or *halt* one. So stop thinking about it. How? Focus on what's going on with her instead.

"Good sex is like driving to a faraway city," says Beregszászi. "You know your destination, orgasm, but you need to concentrate on the road ahead of you—turn left here, turn right there. If you focus on what is happening now—her silky thighs on your hips, say—you can diffuse your pleasure throughout your whole body." So instead of worrying about how long you're lasting, concentrate on gauging your partner's response to each move—did she "oooh" or "ehh"?—until you find her sweet spot.

Slip-slide away. "A really slippery lubricant could decrease the amount of friction you feel and allow you to thrust longer before you reach

DEPARTMENT OF FUN FACTS

There seems to be a mysterious correlation between how you shave and how long you last in the sack. In a recent survey, men who used shaving cream and a razor said they lasted an average of 5 minutes, while those who used an electric razor lasted 10 minutes more.

orgasm," says Gerald Weeks, PhD, a psychologist at the University of Nevada at Las Vegas.

Wear a raincoat. Along the same lines, if you're not using a condom, consider doing so. The main complaint about condoms is that they reduce sensitivity—something that can work to your advantage if you're prone to going off too soon.

And if even that doesn't work, consider using a rubber specifically designed to reduce your sensitivity. Condoms treated with numbing agents like benzocaine and lidocaine can help to slow you down. These can prolong erection time by 3 to 8 minutes, says Debbie Herbenick, PhD, the *Men's Health* "Bedroom Confidential" columnist. "That's usually enough of an extension for many men—and women—to feel good about." Research has revealed that men who used a topical cream of prilocaine and lidocaine (available by prescription) increased their stamina from an average of 2 minutes without the cream to about 8 with it.

The downside is obvious—if evoking the dentist's chair wasn't un-sexy enough, "numb" isn't usually a word one wants associated with one's privates. Less sensitivity means less sensation, and less sensation usually means less enjoyment. You'll have to review the spreadsheet yourself: The stamina benefits may not be worth the pleasure cost.

Choose your positions wisely. You can actually do quite a bit while you're having sex to prolong the activity—and she'll never be the wiser!

■ Certain positions will make her feel tighter—like doggy style, for instance. Others provide less friction for you, like her on top.

■ The tip of your penis is the most sensitive part. The more direct stimulation it receives, the more likely you are to come. So even something as simple as your angle of entry makes a significant difference.

■ Alternating between deep and shallow thrusts will help you to increase stimulation gradually. Added bonus: She'll love the tease. Shallow thrusts also concentrate the stimulation precisely where she needs it, since the majority of the nerve endings in her vagina are in the very first few inches.

Vary your positions. The longer you spend in one position, the less control you have over when you come. Mix it up, and you'll last longer than usual. In a study at the University of New Brunswick, researchers found that men who frequently changed sexual positions were better able to delay ejaculation than those who used other methods to try to stall. See Chapter 11 for a wealth of different configurations.

Slow it down. "When my boyfriend slows it down, I feel every bit of him," says Maria, a receptionist in Mexico. "It helps me focus on the sensation, and puts me over the top when he speeds up again."

"Men need encouragement in the counterintuitive act of penetration and lying still," says Mike Perring, MD, the medical director of Optimal Health of Harley Street in London. He suggests that you share your breathing pattern and connect emotionally with your partner, but have absolutely minimal movement. This isn't simply a recommendation for men struggling with premature ejaculation, either, but an exercise with a much wider usefulness. "Men are prone to get in there and thrust away," he says. Slowing down "allows them to explore what their sexuality is for themselves. Too often, we're ignorant about our own sensations—how does it feel to be touched there, or there, or there?" Ironically, developing hyperawareness is the road to greater control.

> *"When my boyfriend slows it down, I feel every bit of him."*

BASEBALL IS NOT THE ANSWER

It's tempting to think about something else—anything, anything!—to keep from exploding, but it may not be the best strategy. First of all, the quality of your orgasm may suffer—it's hard to finish the job with enthusiasm when you've just forced yourself to think about your neighbor with the hairy mole. In fact, for some guys, there's no coming back at all, and that's really no fun.

Plus, lots of women report that they'd be willing to shave a few minutes off the clock in return for you keeping your eye on the ball. "I'd rather that he come a little faster than think about his grandmother or Cricket Victoria, to be honest," says Meghan, an Australian chef. "It's better for me when he stays in the moment, even if it ends sooner."

Take a break. The best scenario for both parties may very well be where you take a break when you feel yourself approaching your point of no return (technically, "ejaculatory inevitability"). Treat this feeling as a cue to slow yourself down and bring her up to speed.

What you do depends on you. Sometimes it's enough to stay inside her but simply stop moving. Lie still and touch her clit with your fingers. Of course, if she's enjoying what you're doing, she may move around in a way that defeats your best-laid plans. If this happens, pull out and touch her. Or, sexier still, tell her that you'll stop moving your fingers unless she stops moving everything else.

Or pull out and do something else entirely. Many men think of oral sex as something they can do only before intercourse, but there's no rule that says your tongue can't revisit a favorite stomping ground. And if she protested when you pulled out, use one hand or your tongue to stimulate her clit while your fingers on the other hand sub in for your recovering penis.

Another alternative is for you both to please yourselves. This is a lovely

---

THE POWER OF THE QUICKIE

You know what? There's nothing wrong with a little wham, bam, thank you, ma'am. A quickie is "fast furious fun that promises orgasms in less time than it takes to make coffee," says British expert Emily Dubberley in her book *Sex for Busy People*.

"I love it when my husband turns around and comes back to bed on his way out the door to work. There's something incredibly hot about a quickie when he's wearing his suit," says Marina from Brazil. "He usually gets a pretty nice welcome-home present, too, after cranking me up and leaving me at slow simmer all day!"

"Good quickies are about delirious, delicious sex that's just as good (and sometimes better!) than the kind you'd have in your comfortable bed with time for fabulous foreplay," says Dubberley. A quickie every once in a while is a significant sign that your relationship is strong—and that your partner understands your sexual needs, says Ava Cadell, PhD, a Hungarian-born, British-raised expert who has traveled and taught widely throughout the world. If you're worried she thinks you're quick on the trigger, tell her it's just a preview—and make sure you follow through. If she's nice enough to understand how much you need the 1-minute variety, reciprocate with the 1-hour kind (or at least the 18-minutes-of-foreplay kind).

thing to do, for any reason. It gives you a chance to look at her, and to watch how she touches herself and gives herself pleasure. At the same time, it's a more controlled situation, so that you can touch yourself only at the rate you know you can tolerate, while her experienced fingers play catchup.

Chances are, you won't need a lot of time to settle down—a minute or two is usually enough to pull you back from the edge. So when you're miles ahead of her, give your penis a break. Don't worry about losing your erection—her mounting excitement will bring it back even stronger than before.

Wait it out. It'll get easier to hold out as you age.

Talk to your doctor. If PE has suddenly begun to be a frequent problem for you, you'll want to mention it to your doctor. Inflammation of the prostate should be ruled out, says Hungarian urologist Ferenc Fekete, explaining that a prescription for an SSRI-type antidepressant may help.

You may also want to look for a sex therapist who can help you to understand what's behind the problem. One study showed that more than 70 percent of men were able to last longer in bed after discussing the problem with a sex counselor. He or she will teach you how to "retrain" yourself with practical exercises like the following:

■ *The Semans Stop-Start Method:* This technique was developed by Beavis-James Semans, a well-known urologist at Duke University in the 1950s. It's best to try this technique for the first time while you're masturbating. Start by stimulating yourself to the brink of orgasm, then pause and let your arousal diminish. Repeat this cycle three or four times until you begin to feel in control of your response.

■ *Kegels:* Strengthening your PC muscle with Kegel exercises will greatly improve your success rate with the stop-start method. The PC is the muscle you use to stop urine flow. Contract it now to familiarize yourself with the feeling—what you just did was a Kegel. Do 20, 50, 100, or more daily—at your desk or in your car. Since it's the same muscle that contracts for ejaculation, strengthening it will give you more control during sex.

■ *Peaking exercises:* "Label your arousal level on a 1-to-10 scale, where 1 is no arousal and 10 is ejaculation," says sex therapist Barbara Keesling, PhD, author of *Sexual Healing*. "Have your partner [or yourself] stimulate you to a 3; then let the peak go down. Next, go to a 4, then back off, and so on. Relax and focus on the sensation, flexing your PC muscle to keep from ejaculating. When you can withstand about 20 minutes of manual and oral stimulation, you're ready for intercourse." Next, try it during intercourse. Whenever things heat up, just slow down or stop thrusting as necessary. With enough practice, you'll be lasting so long you'll be able to put away the stopwatch.

Get hip to hypnotherapy. Hypnosis isn't tarot-card voodoo; it's simply an altered state of consciousness that both increases your concentration and makes you more susceptible to suggestion. It's gained a great deal of credibility as a behavior modification technique over the past 30 years; you probably know someone who used it to ditch his beer belly or pack of Camels. And a lot of men have gotten very good results from hypnotherapy when dealing with PE. To find a reputable hynotherapist in your area, contact the American Society of Clinical Hypnosis (www.asch.net), the Society for Clinical and Experimental Hypnosis (www.sceh.us), or the National Board for Certified Clinical Hynotherapists (www.natboard.com).

The Other Length You Worry About

We know you're probably concerned not only with lasting long enough but with, well, *being* long enough. We're talking about the age-old question of whether or not size matters, and if it does, how much?

Here's something to think about: We polled men in 38 countries, asking them how satisfied they were with their penis size. In every single country—*every single one*—the majority of respondents said that they were "somewhat satisfied," as opposed to "very satisfied." Some insecurities, apparently, know no borders.

All this self-doubt is largely (no pun intended) unfounded—or at least as it pertains to a man's ability to keep his lady happy. The average vagina is 3 to 5 inches long, and—we'll say it again—only the first third—that's 1 inch or so—has a large concentration of nerve endings. You do have at least an inch, right? "The average penis is perfectly suited to the average vagina," says British expert Phillip Hodson, author of *How Perfect Is Your Mate?* "It might not

QUICKIE STATS

Average penis length and diameter (flaccid) = 3.5 x 1.25 inches

Average penis length and diameter (erect) = 5.1 x 1.6 inches

Average percent increase in volume, flaccid to erect = 300

Longest medically recorded erection = 12 inches

be perfectly suited to appear in pornography, but that's a different story entirely."

Of course, consolation on this topic is nothing new. Of the many debts we owe to Dr. Alfred Kinsey, one stands out. He was the first expert to publicly say that penis size doesn't matter—in 1953. So sometimes women are right when they say we don't listen.

And, when you talk to the experts who really count—those women, in other words—you hear something very similar. "Every guy I've ever, um, known has confessed that he didn't think his penis size was anything to write home about," says the *Men's Health* Girl Next Door, Nicole Beland. "But they were all perfectly well hung." Women *don't* say that size doesn't matter—of course it does, along with your ability to entertain a toddler and watch football at the same time, your foot-massaging skills, and your air-percussion version of Duke Ellington's "Malletoba Spank."

But without fail, they also say something else: "It's not how big it is, but what you do with it." Here's the translation: Pretty much anything— skills in the bedroom and outside of it—easily trumps size in a woman's mind. See it from her perspective. Guy #1 has an armadillo in his pants, and zero oral or social skills. Guy #2 has a perfectly respectable member, can tie a cherry stem in a knot without using his hands, and offered to dance with her aged and toothless Aunt Millie at her cousin's wedding without prompting. Ask the average woman to choose, and she doesn't even have to think about it (unlike the way you might have to think before choosing between your beloved and a pair of triple-Ds). Guy #2 is getting lucky tonight—let's just hope he can banish all thoughts of Aunt Millie before the games begin.

In fact, it's not uncommon to hear women complain about a penis that's too large. Now, this raises some questions, given that the feminine space in question is designed to accommodate an entire 6-to-20-pound human being. But since the question of whether or not one's member can be too big is academic for most of us, let's return to the question at hand: If she doesn't care—or can be bought off with the sexy tongue-lashing you perfected by reading Chapter 9— then what's all the fuss about?

Answer: men. Other men. A South African study indicates

"It's not how big it is, but what you do with it."

that men's fears and anxieties about penis size have their roots not in the reactions of the women they'd been with but in the reactions of *other men.* This may be why researchers have found that the average man thinks he's below average. When Peter Lee conducted penis research at the University of Pittsburgh, he found that "men were good at appraising their overall physique," he says, "but when it came to relative penis size, as a group they tended to underestimate." Twenty-six percent of respondents to Lee's study gauged their own penis size as "below average," but a mere 5 percent ticked the "above average" box.

Why? "It's difficult to accurately assess penis size," says Lee. The damn thing is always growing bigger and smaller, and your point of view can be misleading. "If you're in a changing room with other men, theirs may look bigger because you're seeing them in profile. You look down at your own." In every sense of the phrase.

If she doesn't care, why should you? On the other hand, we're all neurotic about something. So if, even after all this reassurance, you're genuinely concerned about the size of your penis, here's what you can do to make it look bigger when it counts.

Lose weight. You know extra weight is bad for your heart, but it also shortens your penis—you lose a half-inch for every 15 pounds you gain. Here's why: The fat pad that protects your pubic area creeps over the shaft's base as you get fatter, obscuring perfectly good penis. A better diet and more exercise means more where it counts, too.

Trim your pubes. Yes, it works. And it's sexy to do together. Only if she's down there with a pair of scissors, your friend might go into a defensive crouch, defeating the purpose of the experiment.

Pump it up. If you've got a big night coming up, don't masturbate for at least 2 or 3 days beforehand; this will cause your erection to be at its largest and strongest, says Lou Paget, a certified sex educator in Los Angeles and the author of *365 Days of Sensational Sex.* When the fateful moment arrives, squeeze a little as you slide off your shorts. By flexing the muscles of your lower abdomen, you'll cause your penis to lift an inch or two. You'll also force blood into the head, making it momentarily swell even more than usual.

You've got to ac-cen-tu-ate the positive. Make the most of what you have by using powerful, deep thrusts at a slow-to-medium pace. "It can be wonderfully intense. Pistonlike porno thrusting feels horrible. It can leave a girl dry, sore, and bored," says Girl Next Door Beland. To vary the stimulation, add side-to-side movement, or up-and-down pelvic pressure against her clitoris when you're all the way inside.

For best results, avoid the following: Cold weather, chilly baths or showers, exhaustion, nonsexual excitement, and illness. All have been shown to shrink the average penis by as much as 2 inches.

Oh yes, and penis enlargement scams. We get the same spam you do, and yes, we've also wondered at least once if there's anything behind the promise of MaKe Your PEniS HuGe!

Some men—more than 15,000 in the United States, a very rough estimate since there are no official numbers available—*do* opt for surgical procedures to lengthen and widen the penis. This involves severing the ligament that holds the penis to the pelvic bone; once this is done, the penis hangs a bit lower and looks larger. Other girth-enhancing surgeries involve liposuction: sucking the fat out of some other part of the body (usually the abdomen) and injecting it into the shaft of the penis.

This is, to put it frankly, a terrible idea. The procedure isn't taught in medical schools, it's not regulated, and it's not safe. When things do go awry—as they often do—men are often too embarrassed to tell anyone.

GOING FROM BAD TO WORSE

In Uganda, weights are tied to the end of boys' penises at puberty, and the weight is gradually increased, says Don Voorhees in his highly entertaining book of sex trivia, *Quickies*. "A teenager may eventually end up with a 20-pound stone disc swinging from the end of his member!" Apparently, it's very effective—a boy's penis can be stretched to up to 18 inches.

However, as Voorhees points out, these extended penises may be long, but they're thin, making it difficult to do even simple things like sitting down. It may not have been a formal poll, but we weren't bowled over by the reaction we got from women when we asked them how they'd feel if their partners brought them a penis they could tie into a pretty bow.

Of course, that's not your only option. According to British expert Graham Masterson in his book *Up All Night*, in 16th century Brazil, the Topinama Indians found a way to enlarge their erections to immense sizes by encouraging poisonous snakes to bite them. Apparently, it worked—terrible pain for 6 months, then monstrous penises. But, as Masterson points out: "Like the first man to eat an oyster, it makes you wonder who was mad enough to try it first."

For these reasons and more, the American Urological Association (AUA) and the American Society of Plastic and Reconstructive Surgeons (ASPRS) do not endorse the procedure. But that's not stopping doctors from operating, or men from seeking out these doctors.

A number of urologists do a brisk business in correcting these surgeries. Some, like Gary Rheinschild, MD, an Anaheim, California, urologist, claim that if penis enlargement "is done properly, the results are good. Unfortunately, most of the time, it's not done properly." According to Dr. Rheinschild, proper technique involves two things: performing the lengthening and widening techniques at least 6 months apart to ensure that proper bloodflow is restored between procedures, and steering clear of the fat injections.

Not only is the procedure often performed improperly, but it's also performed on men who simply don't need it. A study in the *Journal of Urology* concluded that lengthening procedures should be advised only for men whose penises are 1.56 inches when flaccid, and 2.9 inches erect.

"I have men who come back time and time again wanting this surgery, and each time I reassure them that they fall well within the normal range, and in many cases above the normal range," says Laurence Levine, MD, director of the male sexual health and fertility program at Rush Presbyterian–St. Luke's Medical Center in Chicago. "I routinely recommend they see a sex therapist instead." He also points out that the surgery, even when properly performed, may not achieve the desired results. "In many cases, men see less than an inch added after the surgery, or even a decrease in length."

And the potential cost of that small gain may extend well beyond the doctor's fee. Keith Schulner is a Camarillo, California, attorney whose firm is handling 58 penis-enlargement lawsuits against one surgeon. Schulner says his clients have experienced everything from scarring and lack of sensation to curved penises and foul-smelling discharge. "After one man's surgery, his penis came out through the middle of his scrotum rather than over it," says Schulner.

"This surgery is something I've really come out against," says Ronald Iverson, MD, a plastic surgeon in the San Francisco area and president of the ASPRS. "There are no peer-reviewed articles that show that it's an effective and lasting procedure. Even in the best hands, it may not be a procedure that can be done safely and effectively," he says. "If you're considering a penis enlargement for purely cosmetic reasons, you'd better think twice. In fact, let me be blunt: Don't do it."

Come Again?

Moving on to a less cringe-worthy topic than botched weenie jobs: According to our survey results, more than a quarter of men worldwide would like to go beyond just lasting longer and looking bigger—they wish they could experience multiple orgasms. Frankly, we were surprised the number was so low—as far as we're concerned, the more the merrier!

Multiple orgasms are those that happen without a loss of sexual arousal. In other words, you stay hard in between. "Impossible," you're thinking—"when I'm done, I'm *done*." It's true that men do have what's called a *refractory period* after ejaculation, a time when it's impossible to become erect or to ejaculate again. Coming, in other words, is akin to firing a gun. You can't do it again until you've put another bullet in the chamber, and reloading takes a little time.

But that doesn't mean that you can't have orgasm after orgasm. The Chinese figured this out about 3,000 years ago, although it took until about the middle of the 20th century for the news to reach the United States. The catch? You just don't come—except for the last time.

You heard right: It turns out that orgasm and ejaculation are actually *different events*. If you

> *"Around 80 percent of men can have multiple orgasms after 3 months of training."*

think back to the period of time before puberty kicked in, when you were trying unsuccessfully to masturbate, you did a lot of this orgasm-without-ejaculation stuff. With some practice, you can learn to do it on purpose. "Around 80 percent of men can do this after 3 months of training," says Barnaby Barratt, PhD, a psychologist and sexologist in Santa Barbara, California, and the author of *Sexual Health and Erotic Freedom*.

Mastering these techniques gives most men longer, harder erections, and a much greater degree of sexual control than they've ever had in their lives. That, of course, is great for the women in their lives, and their relationships as a whole. If stamina is a concern for you—or your partner—this is the best party trick you'll ever learn.

Two very ancient traditions—Tantra, in India, and Taoism, in China—incorporate this practice, using many of the same techniques. We spoke to experts in both traditions and culled everything you need to know to make it happen. It might take a while—weeks, maybe even months. But trust us, training for this particular event is much more fun and rewarding than running a 6-minute mile. (Please note: If you have serious health problems or high blood pressure, talk to a knowledgeable practitioner—a Universal Tao educator, for instance, at www.universal-tao.com—before doing these exercises.)

Benefits of Multiple Orgasm

In Taoist sexuality, one of the primary goals of sex was to achieve health—in fact, doctors would often prescribe sex in various positions. In this tradition, the goal of orgasm without ejaculation is to conserve vital energy. Ejaculation represented a tremendous expenditure of energy—no accident, then, that men crash so hard after sex. Orgasms, on the other hand, allowed sexual energy to recirculate through the body beneficially. So, orgasms without ejaculation—preferably a couple of them!—is the best-case scenario.

Now that's not to say that people who practice this technique never ejaculate. They just pick their times. "I conserve now when I feel depleted, tired, or on the verge of getting sick, and I'll ejaculate less as I get older," says Zhou, a reporter in China.

Everyone's agreed on the most important thing: The orgasms are mind-blowing. Non-ejaculatory orgasms are sometimes called Valley Orgasms. "Full-body" is one of the things you hear over and over. "Day-long results" is another. "It's the best, cleanest high you can imagine," says Andreas, an artist from Bern, Germany. "You can go on having sex forever, and then you feel like you're jacked up all day."

Proponents even claim that these techniques can prevent prostate problems and impotence in later life. Not to mention lasting long enough that she can get off over and over again too—but more on that in a bit.

A little training is all you need to put this into practice. Cue "Eye of the Tiger". . . .

Gentlemen, Meet Your Pelvic Floor

The pelvic floor muscle is more sassily known as the pubococcygeal muscle, but let's call it the PC muscle for short, which is what most urologists do. Exercising it is the key to getting control of the ejaculatory process—not to mention better erections.

How do you find this love muscle? Take a whiz—and then stop. The muscle that enables you to stop the flow of urine midstream is your PC muscle. You can think of this pee test as the proving ground for your multiple orgasm ability: If it's hard to stop peeing, your muscle is weak, and you've got some work to do.

The good news is that you can see real gains in just a couple of days. You'll also be relieved to know that exercising your PC muscle is easy, and can be done anywhere—while you're driving, in line for the bank, talking to your co-workers. In fact, it's kind of a sexy feeling. The first time you try it, though, do it at home, and while naked, so that you can see and feel what's going on, says Carla Tara, a Tantric educator who was raised in Italy and who teaches in New York, California, and Hawaii.

> "You can go on having sex forever, and then you feel like you're jacked up all day."

Take the floor: Inhale deeply, pulling your belly back toward your spine and your balls up into your body. You may see your balls and penis move up and down with each squeeze; that movement will increase as your PC muscles strengthen. Keep your abs and glutes out of it—no gyrating butt cheeks, or clenched abs, says Dr. Herbenick. If you're not sure if you've got the right spot, press your fingertips against your perineum (the area between your testicles and anus). That's your pelvic floor; you should feel the muscles in there contract as you squeeze.

The rapid pump: Start this exercise by taking a breath deep into your abdomen; imagine that you're sending the breath down to your genitals, says Carla Tara. Hold your breath down there while you squeeze and release the PC muscles quickly 10 times. Exhale, and rest for a few seconds.

Repeat this exercise as often as you can. Tara has her clients do it up to 20 times a day, first in several short sessions and eventually in one long session. As your PC muscles get stronger, you'll be able to raise the number of squeeze-and-release movements from 10 to increasingly higher numbers.

The hold-and-squeeze: Begin this exercise by taking a deep breath, as you did with the first. Now squeeze your PC muscle—without releasing the pressure—for about 5 seconds. Exhale, and relax the muscle for a few seconds. (If you find the full 5 impossible to hold, start with 3.) Tara recommends at least 60 repetitions of this exercise every day, at first in several short sessions. When you're accustomed to the routine, you can do 60 repetitions in one long session.

As your PC muscle gets stronger, you can increase the length of time for each inhale-and-squeeze repetition to 6 seconds, then for progressively longer periods. You'll find that you can sustain the squeeze for up to 10 seconds and more as your muscle control improves.

Taoists call these exercises Sexual Kung Fu, which sounds incredibly cool (*kung fu* means "practice"). They also add an interesting twist: "As you contract your PC muscle, contract the muscles around the eyes and mouth as well," says Doug Abrams. According to traditional Chinese medicine, the circular muscles of the body—including those around the eyes, mouth, perineum, and anus—are connected. Try it, and you'll see that it increases your PC strength immediately.

Stopping the Train

What are you going to do with this pumped-up PC muscle? You're going to use it to stop your ejaculation. Here's how it works—and since we strongly suggest that you try this by yourself the first couple of times, that's how we'll walk you through it.

You'll have all the beautiful feelings you associate with orgasm—without ejaculating.

Build yourself up to the brink of orgasm, then, uh, stop. By brink, we mean the minute right before the point of no return. When you're there, squeeze your PC muscle, just like you've been doing in the bank line, but for a count of 10. Take a little break, and then get started again with the sexual stimulation.

Do this three times. In this case, as tempting as it may be to rush to the finish, slower is better. The last time, as you reach the point of no return, stop all stimulation and *squeeze*. Don't let yourself come (it's okay if you don't manage this the first time, or the 40th; it'll get easier as your PC muscle gets stronger and you get more comfortable with the timing). Instead, breathe deeply from the very base of your stomach, and relax all the muscles in your back, rear end, and pelvis.

It's difficult to describe, but many have called the next step as "relaxing into orgasm." You'll have all the beautiful feelings you associate with orgasm—racing pulse, waves of euphoria, and relaxation—without ejaculating.

After you're done, you'll need a minute or two to recover. Breathe

DON'T GO RETRO

A common technique for suppressing ejaculation is to press on the perineum (the landing strip between your balls and your anus) just as you're about to come. We don't recommend this, as it can lead to what's called "retroejaculation," which is a fancy way of saying ejaculating into your bladder. Besides just sounding gross, this move can cause nerve damage.

deeply and evenly. You should still feel really turned on, and many people report feeling a strong surge of energy at this point. Use it to continue—until you have another orgasm.

Taking It into the Bedroom

Once you've done this by yourself a couple of times, you'll want to bring your new trick into the bedroom. (Talk about a fantastic Valentine's Day present!) Some things that might help:

■ It may be easiest for you to focus on your PC muscle if you're in a position where all of your muscles are more relaxed—with her on top, for instance.

■ It's going to be harder not to ejaculate. "As you feel yourself approaching the point of ejaculatory inevitability," says Carla Tara, "change your pelvic movement from the fast and strong thrust to a slower and more relaxed one, perhaps directing the thrust away from your partner's body and softening the penetration."

■ If after a few ejaculate-free orgasms, you decide to ejaculate as well, Tara recommends that you do that by taking the longest, deepest breath and then exhaling slowly, vocalizing your excitement while you're ejaculating. "Tantric masters can prolong their ejaculations to last for nine consecutive deep breaths," says Tara. "In the end, even if you decide to ejaculate, you'll have absorbed most of the energetic content of your ejaculate."

The Worst-Case Scenarios Are Not So Bad

If you do ejaculate, even when you don't intend to, don't give yourself a hard time about it. It doesn't necessarily mean that you won't be able to go again. It may be tough to eliminate your refractory period altogether, but it's not that difficult to shorten it. Ask your partner for a relaxing massage. Relieving tension in your thrusting muscles improves bloodflow, helping encourage a rejuvenated erection.

And if the idea of sex without orgasm—without end—is that attractive to you, make it happen: Stop before you come, focus on her pleasure, and go to bed "hungry," so to speak. It may not be the most comfortable feeling in the world. One of the functions of the orgasm—besides pleasure, of course—is to help expel blood that is congested in genital tissue during sexual arousal. But even without an orgasm, the congested blood will eventually dissipate on its own and return to the un-aroused state. It can take anywhere from several minutes to several hours, but it's not harmful, and most men find the squeezed sensation of blue balls to be quite sexy. You'll certainly spend the rest of the night in a heightened state, and your partner will find you very enthusiastic the next time you meet.

Making Multiples Happen for Her

The first thing to keep in mind about serving her a second helping of ecstasy is that just because a woman can get off again doesn't necessarily mean that she wants to. "If a woman's partner prolongs that sequence of orgasms, she may ultimately find the experience not only unsatisfying, but unpleasant," says Marianne Legato, MD, New York–based author of *Why Men Never Remember and Women Never Forget*. "It's like eating more chocolate cake than you wanted—the first slice was terrific, and maybe even the first bite of the second, but by the fourth or fifth, it's really not what you want to be doing anymore."

Even if she is interested in another serving, a genitals-only approach to multiple orgasm won't work for most women, says Taoist sex expert Rachel Carlton Abrams, who co-wrote the *Multi-Orgasmic Couple* with Mantak Chia and her husband Doug Abrams. In order to build her up to an appropriate level of arousal, you have to multitask. What does that mean? First of all, you need her mind on board. Get her fully engaged mentally—whether that means using dirty talk or looking deeply into her eyes. You want her imagination and emotions

"The hotter I am, the easier it is for me to come again."

working with you, not against you. "The hotter I am, the easier it is for me to come again," says Natalia from Rio.

Carlton Abrams also stresses the importance of hitting multiple pleasure zones. Does she melt when you kiss her neck or lick her ear? Then do that—with one hand on her oh-so-sensitive nipples and the other between her legs. Only you (and she) know where her particular power points are, but this is a time to use them. For instance, for many women, stimulation of her g-spot as well as her clitoris is a factor in her being able to come more than once—and in the kind of orgasm she achieves when it happens.

Remember that what she wants where—rough pressure on her nipples, a feather-light touch on her clit—can depend on her level of arousal, the time of the month, and a hundred other factors, so ask her for feedback.

Don't forget to tease her: When going for your own multiple, you're encouraged to build up and back off, build up and back off. Guess what? It works for her as well. Stay sensitive, though—you don't want her getting bored or frustrated before the main event.

She will also benefit from doing the same PC muscle exercises that you've been doing. (Women, particularly if they've had children, tend to be more familiar with these moves than men are.) Encourage her to "grab" at your penis—it's a wonderful sensation for you that also greatly increases her orgasmic facility.

Once she's had her first orgasm, a window of opportunity presents itself. It's a little tricky—her clit will be very sensitive after she has come. But wait too long—more than about 30 seconds—and she'll move into a refractory period similar to yours. So your challenge is to maintain her arousal between orgasms while backing off enough so that you're not overstimulating her. Your best strategy is to switch to indirect touch: Focus on her breasts, thighs, lips (either set), or neck until she recharges. Apply lube and touch her clitoris indirectly. Encourage her to breathe deeply. And let her give you guidance. "My wife loves to have her first orgasm from oral sex, and her second while I am inside her, using my hands," says Aurelio, an advertising executive in Brazil.

■

So there's your introduction to a very complex system of energy management. Have fun trying again and again to get it right.

CHAPTER 14

BE THE WORLD'S MOST VIRILE MAN
Find the Most Effective Performance Enhancers

Nothing makes a man quite so uncomfortable as the idea of his equipment not working as well as it should. So we're going to do this as painlessly as we know how. Listen up.

The bad news is that our survey revealed that American guys lead the world in popping performance-enhancing pills. The good news: This chapter shows you how to avoid those prescription copays and uncomfortable transactions with the pharmacist by utilizing natural remedies and aphrodisiacs from around the world. Get ready to learn about the foods, supplements, and exercises that will help ensure optimum potency and function.

I Have Seen the Enemy, and His Name Is ED

There are two basic categories of male sexual dysfunction: ejaculation dysfunction, which usually refers to spontaneous or premature ejaculation, and erectile dysfunction (often abbreviated ED), the inability to achieve or maintain an erection long enough to have mutually satisfying intercourse. Not to jinx you or anything, but most men have at some point

Percentage of men who've taken a performance-enhancing pill:

1.	**United States**	**21.0 percent**
2.	South Africa	14.9 percent
3.	United Kingdom	14.7 percent
4.	Netherlands	12.8 percent
5.	Philippines	12.5 percent
	World average	**11.0 percent**

in their lives experienced one or both of these. Which means that if you haven't needed the information in this chapter yet, you probably will. And if you have, you're in good company.

That said, there are a couple of ways to look at the vagaries of the penis. You can take them in stride, as a normal part of doing business, or you can cripple yourself with performance anxiety—which is pretty much a surefire way to make sure it turns into a real problem, not just the occasional fluke occasioned by stress, sleep deprivation, or other temporal causes.

We really can't caution you strongly enough against the second approach. "The men who are writing to me with their concerns about failed erections are getting younger and younger," says Valerie Gibson, sex and relationships columnist for the *Toronto Sun*, "and I can't help but think that it's a function of their tremendous performance anxiety." And we're not going to take your porn away from you, but it's possible that always being just two clicks away from a 10-incher jack-hammering away on command hasn't helped.

> *There is no need for any man to think that he is doomed to spend the rest of his life in celibate misery.*

"It's hard on men because everything 'hangs out,' so to speak," says Mike Perring, MD, the medical director of Optimal Health of Harley Street in London. "If you can't get or maintain a good erection, it's on display for the world (or at least you and your partner) to see."

But don't despair. The one thing we have learned, from interviewing both regular guys and experts, is that there are a lot of safe treatments available to you. "Providing he is prepared to seek help, there is no longer any need for any man who is worried about his virility to think that he is doomed to spend the rest of his life in celibate misery," says British expert Graham Masterson, former editor of *Penthouse* and *Penthouse Forum* and author of *Up All Night*. So let's take a look at the disorders, how and why they happen, and what you can do about it.

Spontaneous Ejaculation

Sometimes men report coming without any sexual stimulation at all. Sounds like a good thing, no? Actually, no—it can happen during a very stressful situation, at the gym, or completely out of the blue. "I came a couple of times at the gym when I was lifting heavy weights. I wasn't even hard! It was incredibly embarrassing, and freaked me out big-time," confesses Lachan, an Irish sales rep for a software company.

When you contract your pelvic muscles—as when lifting a heavy weight—they exert pressure on the prostate and seminal vesicles and can squeeze out some seminal fluid. And experts believe that spontaneous ejaculations under stressful conditions, such as during a stressful meeting, may be the body's way of trying to get you to relax. Spontaneous ejaculation is also sometimes a side effect of antidepressants. While it isn't as

---

TAKING GOOD CARE

Your wife or girlfriend examines her breasts once monthly. Why aren't you doing the same for the family jewels?

Although relatively rare, testicular cancer has a 97 percent cure rate when discovered early. So you should be on the lookout for it. When your balls are loose (chillin'-on-a-fine-summer's-day-type loose), gently roll each testicle between your fingers. It should be smooth and oval-shaped, feeling kind of like a hard-boiled egg without the shell. Compress it gently, searching for any hard areas or lumps that don't feel like the surrounding tissue. (The bump you'll find behind each testicle is simply the epididymis, the tube that carries sperm; no cause for alarm.) If you detect anything unusual, see your doctor.

And take yourself in for a yearly inspection. Once your equipment reaches age 40, have your prostate checked annually. This gland surrounds the urethra like a doughnut and, if allowed to enlarge, can reduce your urine stream to a dribble. Prostate cancer is also a concern. Both of these problems can be avoided if detected early.

A complete yearly inspection should include three things: (1) a digital rectal exam (yeah, sorry—digital as in "finger," not "pixel"); (2) a blood test for prostate-specific antigen (PSA), an early warning sign of trouble; and (3) an ultrasound to create a visible image of the tissue.

Fun? Not particularly. But the alternative is even less so, so close the book and make an appointment. Or leave this page open and the woman in your life will do it for you.

---

common as some other sexual side effects (such as delayed orgasm), it certainly has been documented as an effect that some men do experience.

The first line of defense? "Ejaculate more often," says Laurence Levine, MD, director of the male sexual health and fertility program at Rush Presbyterian–St. Luke's Medical Center in Chicago. If that doesn't work and you're concerned, talk to your doctor or a sex therapist. But know that spontaneous ejaculation doesn't mean you're necessarily prone to premature ejaculation.

Erectile Dysfunction

Erectile dysfunction is defined as the inability to get or to sustain an erection. It is also "the principal cause of sexual unhappiness, bar none," says Masterson.

As you know, the best defense is a good offense, and there's a considerable amount that you can do—right now—to reduce the risk of ED. Before we begin, let's review the basics. Your penis is equipped with twin hydraulic chambers called the corpora cavernosa. During sexual stimulation, these fill with blood until the penis grows firm and erect. After stimulation ends or there's ejaculation, blood leaves these chambers and the penis softens again. Blood goes in, blood stays in, blood goes out: An erection is all about bloodflow.

So it turns out that everything your doctor has been telling you for years—drop 10 pounds, watch your cholesterol, start a workout regimen—is good not just for your heart but for the Bald Avenger. It's probably no mere coincidence that Americans lead the international pack in the use of performance-enhancing drugs, given that we're world beaters in rates of obesity and related diseases as well.

There's an easy correlation between health and sex, summed up thusly: *If it's good for your heart, it's good for your penis.* Here's the list of do's and don'ts to prevent systems failure from becoming a problem.

Lose weight. If you're overweight—even a little—losing weight is the single best preventive act you can take to make sure you've got strong wood all the days of your life. Why?

■ *Weight loss will help you prevent atherosclerosis.* In a great medical irony, being hard in the arteries can leave you soft in the shorts; atherosclerosis, or hardening of the arteries, is one of the leading causes of erectile dysfunction. "ED stands not only for erectile dysfunction but also for 'early diagnosis,' because you can use ED to predict a heart attack, potentially by years—arterial damage from cardiovascular disease affects the small arteries in the penis first," says Christopher Steidle, MD, clinical associate professor of urology at the Indiana University Medical Center at Fort Wayne. Every one-point gain in total cholesterol correlates to an almost 1.5 times greater risk of erection problems. If that thought doesn't have you choosing the egg white omelette over the Lumberjack special, what will?

■ *Weight loss will lower your estrogen levels.* "We know that heavier men convert testosterone to estrogen, and that a lower level of testosterone and a higher level of estrogen are not good for erectile function," says Larry Lipshultz, MD, a *Men's Health* advisor and chief of male reproductive medicine and surgery at Baylor College of Medicine. Fortunately, even moderate weight loss can rid you of excess estrogen and put your sex life back on track. A study published in the *Journal of the American Medical Association* found that one-third of clinically obese men—body mass index (BMI) of 30 or higher—with erectile dysfunction showed improvement after losing 10 percent of their body weight. To calculate your BMI, multiply your weight in pounds by 703, and divide the result by your height in inches squared. If your BMI comes in close to or over 25, you may be carrying just enough lard to drag down your erections. In a 2003 Harvard study of more than 30,000 men, guys with BMIs over 28 had more than a 30 percent higher risk of ED than did men whose BMIs were less than 23.

■ *Losing weight will help you avoid diabetes.* Besides the monastery, the quickest route to a lifetime of celibacy is to develop diabetes. In fact, more than 50 percent of all men with diabetes are impotent. The disease hits the penis with a double whammy. It speeds arterial disease and slows the transmission of stimuli along nerves throughout your body. A numb penis is not a happy penis. Staying trim is the best way to avoid diabetes. If it's too late for that, be vigilant in checking your blood sugar (talk to your doctor about the best methods). Men who are sloppy about controlling their levels have 70 percent more erection problems than those who stay on top of it, according to a recent Italian study.

Treat high blood pressure. "High blood pressure is an important cause of arteriosclerosis—and arteriosclerosis blocking the arteries to the penis may be the most common cause of erectile dysfunction," says Thomas Lee,

MD, professor of medicine at Harvard Medical School. But make sure to ask your doc for an anti-hypertension med that won't leave you limp.

Exercise. After studying more than 31,000 men, researchers at the Harvard School of Public Health reported that those who were physically active had a 30 percent lower risk for erectile dysfunction than men with little or no physical activity. If the opportunity to lose that spare tire isn't enough to drive you to the gym, perhaps the thought of losing your erection is. . . .

And in another study, researchers found that men who walked just 2 miles a day had half the rate of erection problems of more sedentary men. (Twenty minutes of jogging or 30 minutes of weight training will work, too.)

Researchers reported that men who were physically active had a 30 percent lower risk for ED.

"Guys tend to think of their arteries as simple pipes that can become clogged, but there's a lot more going on than that," says Dr. Levine. "The linings of those blood vessels are very biologically active areas where chemicals are being made and released into the bloodstream." The more you exercise, the healthier, cleaner, and more flexible those linings become.

Don't smoke. If you still light up, you've probably accepted your increased risk of heart disease, stroke, lung cancer, and bladder cancer. But if the stinking clothes, yellow fingers, and chunks of lung hacked into your palm haven't convinced you to stop smoking, what about coming up soft in bed?

Consider the evidence:

■ A study from the New England Research Institutes in Watertown, Massachusetts, shows that around 30 percent of smokers experience impotence. The good news? Quitting now may lower your flop risk to where it was in your pre-smoking days.

■ A study published in the *Journal of Urology* found that smoking causes arterial damage that doubles a man's risk of total erectile dysfunction. But, "if men quit in their fifties or earlier, we can usually reverse the damage," says Andre Guay, MD, director of the Lahey Clinic for Sexual Function in Massachusetts. When Dr. Guay measured nighttime erections in 10 impotent smokers (average age 49), he noted a 40 percent improvement after just 1 smoke-free day. Swap the cancer sticks for fish sticks:

Researchers at the Royal College of Surgeons in Ireland discovered that taurine, an amino acid found in fish, helps heal smoke-damaged arteries.

■ In a study conducted at the University of Kentucky, researchers found that when asked to rate their sex lives on a scale of one to 10, men who smoked averaged about a five—a far cry from nonsmokers, who rated theirs at nine.

■ There's some evidence that smoking affects erection size. In one study, researchers found that smokers' penises are significantly smaller than nonsmokers'. "In addition to damaging blood vessels, smoking may cause damage to penile tissue itself, making it less elastic and preventing it from stretching," says Irwin Goldstein, MD, a urologist at the Boston University Medical Center. We have yet to hear a better reason to quit.

Don't freak out. Everyone knows that stress is a psychological cold shower. But untamed tension also works in a more insidious way—by releasing epinephrine, a type of adrenaline that goes straight to your arteries and slowly wreaks havoc there. "Stress in the long term can contribute to hardening of the arteries," says J. Stephen Jones, MD, author of *Overcoming Impotence: A Leading Urologist Tells You Everything You Need to Know.*

The fix: Force yourself to concentrate on each of your five senses for a few minutes every day—the feel of the steering wheel in your hands, the sound of the engine revving to redline, the sight of the hot brunette in the next car. . . . "Obsessing on stressful thoughts will increase your epinephrine," says Jay Winner, MD, author of *Stress Management Made Simple.* "On the other hand, if you focus on current sensations, it decreases the epinephrine and ultimately improves your ability to have an erection." Or do the relaxation exercise featured on page 272 a couple of times a week.

Strap your boys in. You wear a helmet when you ride your motorcycle;

ANOTHER REASON LEISURE SUITS WENT OUT OF STYLE

Wearing polyester underwear may contribute to impotence because of the static electricity generated by man-made materials. Loose, 100 percent cotton shorts are recommended instead. Time to get rid of that tiger-striped boulder holder.

---

you wear a seatbelt every time you get behind the wheel of a car. So what are you thinking when you take to the court for your weekly pickup game wearing only briefs?

A recent study in the *Clinical Journal of Sports Medicine* found that 47 percent of high-school and college male athletes involved in contact sports do not wear any kind of genital protection. The upshot? These Darwin Award winners are less likely to breed and pass on their genes.

It's highly recommended that you wear an athletic supporter for activities that involve running, jumping, and sudden movement. This device tucks the testicles close to the undercarriage to protect them from jarring. For complete security, wear a cup.

If you do take a ball—or a knee—to the groin, lie down, apply an ice-packed cloth, and take some deep breaths. If there's swelling and the pain doesn't subside within a few minutes, continue the icing and get to a hospital. A severe groin injury can cause sterility.

Talk to your doctor about your medications. "A lot of prescription drugs may be associated with sexual dysfunction," says R. Taylor Segraves, MD, PhD, coauthor of *Sexual Pharmacology*. Open your medicine cabinet, write down the names of the prescription drugs you pop, and go to www.MensHealth.com/drug for a full list of erection offenders.

You're going to be surprised at how long the list is, and the popularity of many of the drugs on it. For instance, one possible culprit is the cholesterol-lowering drug simvastatin, brand name Zocor. If you're taking one of the drugs on the list (or anything else you suspect might be causing a problem), talk to your doctor. Often, a similar pill, sans side effects, is on the market.

Get a vasectomy. If you're finished producing offspring (or you're 100 percent sure you don't want any in the first place), consider investing in permanent renovations at the sperm factory. "The risk of a contraceptive failure can be a big source of anxiety for some men, especially those who've had a birth-control disaster—or a scare—in the past," says Karen Donahey, PhD, director of the sex- and marital-therapy program at Northwestern University. That anxiety can, in turn, lead to erection problems—and cause the same vicious circle that makes performance anxiety such a mood killer.

Do your Kegels. Go figure—one of the best ways to treat erectile dysfunction is to pretend that you suffer from premature ejaculation. British researchers discovered that the traditional treatment for a hair trigger—

strengthening the pelvic floor muscle—is also a remedy for men who can't point their pistols. In the study of 55 impotent men, 40 percent of those who practiced pelvic floor exercises, AKA Kegels, every day for 6 months regained normal sexual function. Apparently, the same muscle contraction that's used to stop peeing midstream can also prevent blood from escaping during an erection. Researchers at the University of Milan in Italy also found that stronger pelvic muscles lead to stronger erections.

Contract and relax your pelvic muscles anytime you're sitting or lying down. Work up to doing 18 contractions daily, holding each one for 10 seconds. Or, every time you get an e-mail at work, do six quick flexes. Hold the last one for 5 seconds.

Get lots of sleep. We know—you hate to give up on one minute of postcoital pillow talk, but ultimately you're going comatose for her benefit. Your penis needs as much shut-eye as it can get. Every night while you sleep, you have between three and five hour-long erections. You probably noticed this phenomenon the last time you had to pee at 4:00 a.m. Those erections are not there just to make life interesting for your bedmate. They work to recharge your penis—keeping it well nourished with oxygenated blood. "Theoretically, the more nocturnal erections you have, the more flexible your erectile tissue will become. And that may help keep erections strong as the years wear on," says Marc Goldstein, MD, professor of reproductive medicine and urology at Cornell University Medical College.

But don't snore. Snoring can sabotage a night of sex, and not just because it's difficult to engage in foreplay from the couch. "All of your tissue needs oxygen to be healthy, and the penile tissue is especially sensitive," says Dr. Jones. "When you snore, you're depriving your tissue of that oxygen."

NONE FOR THE ROAD

Operating your penis while under the influence of alcohol can severely impair its performance. If this has been an issue for you in the past, try alternating an alcoholic drink with a glass of water if you suspect that the evening will end up in naked revelry. (And order wine, not champagne; bubbles speed absorption of alcohol, depressing your testosterone levels and decreasing penile bloodflow.)

Roughly half of men who snore also have problems with erections, according to Mansoor Madani, DMD, a sleep apnea expert at the Bala Institute of Oral Surgery in Bala Cynwyd, Pennsylvania. When you snore, tissues in your throat vibrate and can block your windpipe, temporarily stopping your breathing. This can impair bloodflow to other vital areas, says Dr. Madani.

That said, don't waste your money on over-the-counter snore stoppers; research by the US Air Force shows that these products aren't effective. Instead, try placing bricks under the bedposts at the head of the bed. "Snoring has a lot to do with gravity," says Phillip Westerbrook, MD, founder of the sleep-disorders center at the Mayo Clinic. "If you elevate the torso without bending the neck, it changes the effect of gravity on the soft tissues of the throat."

If that doesn't work, snoring can usually be cured by outpatient laser surgeries that take 15 minutes and reduce snoring by more than 70 percent. Now if they could only do something about night drool.

Don't do drugs. Another reason to just say no. Cocaine may enhance sexual pleasure and delay ejaculation, but prolonged use will compromise function, while heroin and other morphine-type drugs neutralize sexual interest and ability right off the bat. This is your penis. This is your penis on drugs. . . .

Don't sleep around. It's common for men who start having affairs to stop having erections—so common, in fact, that doctors who treat erectile dysfunction often ask their patients if they're getting any action on the side. Unless your wife knows about, approves of, and participates in your new sex life—in which case, we'd like to meet her—you're bound to feel at least a little guilty about it when you're with her. Guilt can turn to anxiety, and that can kill an erection.

IT REALLY DOES HAPPEN TO EVERYBODY

And it really is a bigger deal to you than it is to her. So shake your sulk and salvage the evening by focusing your energy entirely on her. Let your fingers and tongue do the walking. This will waylay her silent worry that it's her, not you. And her expressions of gratitude might just be the magic you need. At the very least, you guarantee that she'll be talking about what you did, not what you didn't do, over Cosmopolitans tomorrow.

Turn on the lights. Men need visual stimulation to become really excited. In fact, in a *Men's Health* survey, that annoying female preference for making love in the dark was the number-one complaint men had about women in bed. If that 500-watt deer lamp you hung in the bedroom makes your partner self-conscious, then compromise with some soft candlelight or perhaps a black light, which makes skin look tan and sexy.

Okay, so we've reviewed your preventive options. Following most of them is good advice anyway. But what if you're regularly experiencing difficulties getting or maintaining an erection? It's still not time to panic. In fact, as Dr. Perring says reassuringly, "There's quite a lot that we can do for people." Here are some strategies.

Get help. In the same way that your penis is a barometer of your general physical health, it can also be a pretty accurate indicator of your mental state. Depression, anxiety, relationship problems, and stress are all leading causes of erectile dysfunction. While medications and some of the other solutions to follow can help you to perform no matter what, it would be foolish to ignore such a clear warning sign that you're in a troubled state of mind. Your doctor can refer you to someone to talk to, or you can contact the American Association of Sexuality Educators, Counselors, and Therapists (AASECT) at www.aasect.org.

Relax. The ability to truly let go is a skill that's increasingly hard to master in our fast-paced culture. Think about how you reacted the last time you were stuck in traffic, missed your train, or ended up on the losing side of an argument with a colleague or your spouse. Work worries, financial anxiety, relationship troubles, exhaustion—these can all mess with the working order. "For me, especially as I have gotten older, tension is a boner-killer," says Liam, an Irish lawyer. "If I am stressed about work, annoyed at my wife, worried about the children, I have difficulty getting cooperation from my penis. The best remedy for me is relaxation—a vacation, a massage, just to breathe."

Depression, anxiety, relationship problems, and stress are all leading causes of erectile dysfunction.

Easier said than done, perhaps, but we've said it before, and we'll say it again: Just about every man experiences the occasional problem. Worrying about it will just make the whole situation worse the next time—and can lead to a serious psychological problem: Tension and pleasure don't mix.

Relaxation is so important that sex surrogates trained to work with men with sexual dysfunction often open with a relaxation exercise. Select a place where you won't be disturbed, lie on your back, and close your eyes. Starting from the tip of your toes and working up, tense and relax every muscle group you encounter. When you're done, stay there, listening to your breath, for about 15 minutes. It's like a vacation, honestly.

Enter softly. In their book *The Multi-Orgasmic Man*, Mantak Chia and Douglas Abrams describe a Taoist sex practice used as a treatment for impotence. The solution? Have sex anyway. It's called "soft entry."

Making sure that your partner is well-lubricated, create a ring with your thumb and forefinger around the base of your penis, pushing the blood into the tip. Keeping your fingers where they are, insert your penis into your partner's vagina and begin to move. Squeeze your buttocks and perineum in order to move blood into your penis. In most cases, your penis will become engorged, and you can remove the finger ring.

Get pricked. Sometimes it *is* all in your head. If you think that you, well, think too much, see an acupuncturist. The results of a study published in the *International Journal of Impotence Research* suggest that acupuncture can help treat psychologically induced erectile dysfunction. (Relax—the prick points are all in your back.)

"In psychogenic erectile dysfunction, the patient has trouble with the balance of his sympathetic and parasympathetic nervous systems," says Paul Engelhardt, MD, the study author. "Traditional Chinese medicine tries to restore that balance." Sure, it sounds like using feng shui for your underwear drawer, but it works—64 percent of the men who underwent 6 weeks of acupuncture regained sexual function and needed no further treatment.

Score some herb. "The use of herbs to treat afflictions, sexual and otherwise, is as old as mankind," says Cynthia Mervis Watson, MD, author of *Love Potions: A Guide to Aphrodisiacs and Sexual Pleasures*. Most herbal aphrodisiacs work on both brain and bloodflow—the placebo effect is very powerful, and many of these substances do increase circulation, always a good thing for the penis. Some of them are also effective because they contain sterols, chemicals similar to the steroids found in professional baseball: They give you a hormonal jump on the competition—without all the shame and 'roid rage.

SIZING UP HERBAL REMEDIES

There's a lot of garbage out there. Follow these anti-B.S. guidelines when sizing up an herbal remedy.

"Studies show . . ." Well, studies can show a whole lot of things. If those studies aren't large, placebo-controlled, double-blind studies, then they're not actually worth the paper they're printed on. (These catch-phrases mean that neither the researchers nor the participants knew who was getting the real stuff and who was getting the sugar pills.) Ask the company if it doesn't say on the packaging.

"It changed my life!" Those testimonials can be very compelling, but they're hardly scientific. In fact, the people who are so effusively kvelling about the product may even believe what they're saying—but that doesn't necessarily make it true. "The placebo effect is responsible for about 30 percent of improved symptoms in studies," says Donald D. Hensrud, MD, of the Mayo Clinic. The power of suggestion is especially strong with herbs, since most promise subjective benefits, such as increased energy. "It worked for me" endorsements are worthless, except to the person who was paid to make them.

"This ancient remedy, used in [insert faraway land here] for thousands of years . . ." Many of these remedies *have* been used for thousands of years. So that might be true—but it doesn't mean that the stuff works, or that it won't kill you in the process. Our forefathers thought asbestos was a good idea too.

Clear it with your doctor. If you're interested in herbal remedies, it's worth finding a doctor who's knowledgeable about them. Before you pop a pill, call and ask whether there's any danger in taking the herbal remedy; remind the doctor of the other drugs you take, both prescription and over-the-counter. Then double-check with the pharmacist. It's not that much trouble when the alternative may be liver failure.

Look for the words "Guaranteed Potency Herb." Not every herb on this list will be standardized, but many of them are, and it's worth it to buy them, says Cynthia Mervis Watson, MD, author of *Love Potions: A Guide to Aphrodisiacs and Sexual Pleasures*, so you know what—and how much—you're getting. Also choose organic whenever possible, and buy from reputable companies. She recommends those from Herb Pharm, Eclectic Institute, Gaia Herbs, and Zand Herbal Formulas.

Here's an overview of the best from around the world.

■ **Ashwaganda.** The 3,000-year-old tradition of Indian medicine, Ayurveda, prescribes the dried root of the ashwaganda plant for many ailments. The herb is so versatile, it's used in remedies for everything from rheumatism to treating sexual dysfunction. It contains plant sterols and has been known to increase muscle mass. Administered to both men and women who suffer from low libido, it is said to rebuild lost sexual vitality and reinvigorate sexual function. The sex-enhancing powers of ashwaganda are thought to be dependent on the herb's unquestionable ability to fight stress. In the United States, it can be found in powdered and extract form.

■ **Catuaba.** The bark from the Catuaba tree of the Amazon forest is used by Brazilian herbalists as an aphrodisiac, a nerve tonic, and a stimulant to flagging libido. To the Topi Indians found in the region, "when an older man has a child, it's said to be Catuaba's child," says Dr. Watson. There is little scientific research as to how or why the bark from the Catuaba tree works to improve sexual function, but in 1992, Japanese researchers found that, aside from its sex-enhancing ability, Catuaba extract seemed to protect mice from E. coli and staph infections and prevented the HIV virus from entering cells. You'll often find it mixed with ginseng or muira puama.

■ **Damiana.** It's said to heighten sexual desire and improve sexual performance—that's why it's been used in folk medicine for centuries. Like most herbs considered to be aphrodisiacs, damiana increases bloodflow by widening blood vessels, an action that would relieve male impotence by varying degrees. Dr. Watson notes that it is also reputed to induce erotic dreams when drunk at bedtime. She recommends steeping an ounce of dried damiana leaves in 1 pint of vodka for 5 days, straining the results, and soaking the leaves in ¾ pint of spring water for another 5 days. Strain this, and heat the water just enough to dissolve ½ cup of honey (or more, to taste). Cool, then add this mixture to the vodka. The potion will keep for a few months; Dr. Watson says that drinking a small glass every night before bed will reap "delicious results" in about 5 days.

■ **Deer antler.** The Chinese have used this for centuries—and with good reason. It's nutritionally rich, loaded with minerals, fatty acids, and amino acids. It's used as a rejuvenating tonic—and one of the things it rejuvenates is your sex drive. Dr. Watson recommends choosing deer antler from New Zealand, and says that 500 milligrams daily should be enough. If you're worried about hurting Rudolph, don't be. These antlers regenerate after they've been clipped, and they're taken from well-treated herds that are raised to provide them.

■ *Ginseng.* How much would you be willing to spend for a ginseng root that looks a lot like, hmm . . . another kind of "root"? In Asia, ginseng roots resembling the human penis sell for as much as $500 a pound, and the older the root, the more valuable. One collector paid $180,000 for an aged, anatomically correct root! Ginseng increases testosterone levels, lifting libido and suppressing the production of prolactin, a hormone that can cause impotence. (The rare red Korean *Panax ginseng* type is the only one that has been shown to help guys defy gravity.) In a recent study of men with erectile dysfunction, researchers found that 60 percent of those who took 900 milligrams of red Korean ginseng three times daily had improved erections, compared with only 20 percent of the placebo poppers. You can find red Korean ginseng in most health food stores. To increase your chances of getting authentic ginseng, find a product that includes 100 to 125 milligrams of ginseng extract standardized to contain 4 to 7 percent ginsenosides (the key component of ginseng). If this is on the label, the odds are better that you've found a reputable manufacturer.

■ *Horny goat weed.* An herb that actually includes "horny" in its name? Horny goat weed gets the blood flowing to the genitals and boosts sexual energy. It's said to work for both sexes, which explains the herb's Chinese name: yin-yang, representing both female and male energy. (It is also known as epimedium.) This leafy plant has been used for over 2,000 years to improve the fatigued libido with testosterone-like plant alkaloids. Legend claims that horny goat weed got its English name when a surprised goat herder noticed the amorous tendencies of his herd after the animals feasted on the plant.

■ *Maca.* Also called "Peruvian ginseng," though it's not related to that other herb, maca is regularly used in Peru for its many health benefits. And it tastes great! The annual Maca Festival hosted in Churin, Peru, is home to cookies, cakes, and chips all made from the aphrodisiac. Maca's reputation for enhancing strength, libido, and fertility is growing as more people discover that the plant really does add a bit of combustion to their sex lives. It's common knowledge that the more maca you consume, the more benefit you'll get from the substance. And no harm will come of it—toxicity studies conducted in the United States found that maca had no adverse effects, although Dr. Watson warns people with hormone-sensitive cancers (such as prostate or breast cancer) away from it.

■ *Muira puama.* Yet another aphrodisiac with roots in South America. Although this hasn't undergone rigorous testing, Dr. Watson reports that men in a study done by the Institute of Sexology in Paris did experience improvement in sexual function. She recommends boiling 2 tablespoons of the powdered wood for 15 minutes in a pint of water; drink 1 fluid ounce before making love. If you don't mind the alcohol, you can also infuse 1 ounce of muira puama in 2 cups of vodka for 2 weeks, shaking daily. Take 1 ounce before hopping into the sack.

■ *Yohimbe.* The African Bantu people have traditionally used yohimbe as a hallucinogen in marriage rituals that include 15-day orgies. So it's up for whatever you're going to throw at it. Research has shown that the active ingredient, yohimbine, helps relax the smooth-muscle cells of the corpora cavernosa, allowing more blood to flood these love chambers. A recent review in the *Journal of Urology* of seven clinical trials including 419 impotent men found that a prescription version of the herb was more effective in producing erections than a placebo was. (A prescription version of the drug, called Yocon, is available.) Yohimbe can either raise or lower blood pressure depending on the person taking it, so it should be avoided by people with heart or liver disease, and by anyone taking MAO inhibitors. Some other cautions: It should not be taken with a variety of foods, including cheese, liver, red wine, chocolate, beer, nuts, aged or smoked meats, sauerkraut, and yeast. Yohimbe interferes with how the body interacts with tyramine, a substance found in all of these foods. Dr. Watson also warns that some users experience hallucinogenic sensory effects, as well as nausea, irritability, sweating, and palpitations. Because of these, she recommends it as an ingredient in an aphrodisiac preparation, not something for daily use.

Medical Interventions

If you and your doctor decide that the severity of your sexual dysfunction warrants more drastic measures, here are some solutions you can try.

Testosterone: Testosterone is the potent male hormone, manufactured chiefly in the testicles, that fuels sexual thoughts and fantasies. If you have low desire, you may have low circulating levels of what's called "free testosterone." Deficiencies are a main contributor to erectile problems and flagging desire. Studies show that your testosterone levels can drop by 1.2 percent each year of your life, with a more dramatic step-down after age 50. Your doctor can easily determine your level by doing a series of blood tests.

Testosterone is available by prescription, but there are other, more

BE CAREFUL WHAT YOU WISH FOR!

Priapism is a persistent, painful erection that lasts for several hours and isn't relieved by ejaculation. There's a one in 40,000 chance that it'll happen to you. Usually caused by a blockage in the penis, or by needlessly taking a drug like Viagra, priapism isn't something to mess around with. Rush to an emergency room if it happens, as the condition can cause tissue damage and impotence. And be careful with rubber bands. That's all we're saying.

enjoyable ways you can pump it up—just thinking about sex, for instance. You can also increase it by having more sex, eating meat, and playing General Maximus in *Gladiator*. And although stress does release cortisol, an erection offender, a stressful job (or even a dangerous one) involving some level of competition, as in law or sales, can actually improve testosterone levels. "Real competition can drive up testosterone, which boosts libido," says Helen Fisher, PhD, research professor in the anthropology department at Rutgers University in New Jersey and author of *Why We Love*. "Being amped up by a high-powered, high-stress job is more likely to make you more sexually active" than idling in a cushy, low-key career.

If work doesn't fire you up, seek a testosterone jolt in a recreational sports league. Men who get game increase testosterone levels by 15 percent, according to a Pennsylvania State University study. Even better, make her your steady doubles partner. The same study showed that women increased their libido-regulating testosterone by 49 percent during competition.

What about the risks of taking a prescription? "There's no evidence that testosterone causes cancer, although there is some evidence that it makes existing cancer worse, and the real problem with that is that it may activate a latent cancer that might never have caused a problem at all," says Dr. Perring. If you are going to go on a long-term course of testosterone, your treatment needs to be supervised by a doctor, and you'll need follow-up tests.

Viagra et al: There are a variety of medications available to stimulate bloodflow to the penis, including Viagra, Levitra, and Cialis. Viagra was a runaway success pretty much instantly, for obvious reasons: This category of drugs gave sex lives back to men who thought they'd never get wood again. "It's like a second chance at life," says Manuel, a Costa Rican lawyer.

These aids have been a particular boon to people of a certain age. "The chemical aids are worth about 10 years," says Dr. Perring. "In other words, with Viagra or Cialis, a 70-year-old man can do approximately what a 60-year-old can do without it."

"There's no question that these medical interventions have changed the face of midlife sexuality," says Gibson of the *Toronto Sun*. "There is life after 45, 55, 65—and there is sex!"

And who knows what miracles might happen once you prime the pump a few times? "What a lot of men find is that once they start these medications, they may not need them for every episode of sexual activity—they may need them only now and then," Dr. Steidle says.

Similarly, if you suffer from performance anxiety, a drug-fueled romp or two may be just what the urologist ordered to restore confidence. And while all three erection medications have the power to prevent you from psyching yourself out in the sack, Cialis's ability to work for up to 36 hours may provide an advantage, says Julian Slowinski, PsyD, assistant professor of psychiatry at the University of Pennsylvania School of Medicine. "This gives a man and his partner a lot of time over the weekend to be more spontaneous."

Doctors are wary about patients purchasing these meds on the Internet, so open up at your next office visit if you feel you could use a little boost. "I'm not a salesperson for the chemical aids, but in my practice, I certainly don't restrict my use of Viagra to people with no function at all," says Dr. Perring. "It helps lots of men get a better erection, and with a better erection you have more sensation, and with more sen-

---

ANOTHER DIAMOND SHE'LL WANT TO HOLD ON TO

In Novo Santo Antonio, Brazil, the town's mayor is handing out free Viagra to men of a certain age. Project *Pinto Alegre*, or "Happy Penis," was designed to cheer up the town's elderly inhabitants.

It worked—but perhaps not as intended: Immediately, the incidence of extramarital affairs skyrocketed. Apparently, once armed and dangerous, the senior men of Novo Santo Antonio went a-courting. The mayor has changed course, distributing the pills instead to the geezers' wives, for dispensing at the women's discretion.

---

sation you have a better orgasm. In short, it allows people to perform better and enjoy it more."

Word to the wiseguy: A number of sex therapists told us about desperate calls made from bathrooms: "It's not working, doc!" But pills aren't on-off switches—you do need to be stimulated for them to work. Jump in bed with your lady or look at some pictures to prime the pump, and we think you'll be happy with the results.

Injectables: Certain drugs can be injected directly into the penis, either with a syringe or with a plunger that inserts a small pellet of medication into the tip of the penis. These drugs produce long-lasting erections within moments. When you stop wincing, talk to your doctor about the options.

Implants: If the problem persists, you may also want to ask the doc about penile prostheses or implants that can be surgically placed inside the penis to make it firm enough for intercourse. There are two different types:

■ *A nonhydraulic implant* consists of a pair of flexible silicone rods that can be bent up or down by hand. It's the simplest design, but the penis remains semi-rigid at all times.

■ *A hydraulic implant* includes a pair of hollow rods, a reservoir of saline solution, and a pump, all concealed within the body. For an erection, you simply squeeze your scrotum to inflate the penis.

Vacuum constriction device: When the penis is inserted into this cylinder and the attached pump engages, a vacuum is formed that causes blood to flow into the penile shaft. A rubber ring is then slipped onto the base of the penis to trap the blood in the shaft.

Sex Surrogates

Surrogates have a 90 percent success rate in treating sexual dysfunctions, according to Ted McIlvenna, PhD, president of the Institute for Advanced Study of Human Sexuality in San Francisco. Although surrogates treat a variety of sexual problems, Dr. McIlvenna says they are most adept at curing three things: erection difficulties, lack of desire, and poor body image. Surrogate therapy works best when the problem is psychological rather than physical.

If you have tried traditional therapy and think a surrogate might be the

YOU'RE NOT THE ONLY ONE: FEMALE SEXUAL DYSFUNCTION

Jennifer Berman is an MD specializing in female urology; her sister Laura Berman, PhD, works as a sex therapist. Together, they run the Berman Center in Chicago and the Network for Excellence in Women's Sexual Health at UCLA, where they specialize in the study and treatment of female sexual dysfunction. The Bermans estimate that 43 percent of American women suffer from some type of sexual problem. "Our main mission is to get the word out about female sexual dysfunction," says Laura. "Women shouldn't be embarrassed about seeking help."

Unfortunately, doctors tend to dismiss women's sexual complaints as psychological or emotional. But many common sexual complaints—such as low libido or inability to reach orgasm—have physical causes. Complaints of genital pain are dismissed as hysterical, or the result of a long-ago (and perhaps suppressed) negative sexual experience, says Marianne Legato, MD, New York–based author of *Why Men Never Remember and Women Never Forget.* Dr. Legato believes that a complaint of this type always merits further investigation. There are a number of physical causes for genital pain, and they're not uncommon.

"All this research into female sexual dysfunction will help solve problems in male sexuality," says Dr. Jennifer Berman. Let's say your girlfriend or wife has an undiagnosed condition that's causing her to lose interest in sex or be unresponsive—you don't think that's going to affect your sex life? Best-case scenario, you're whining for something she doesn't want to give you. Worst-case scenario, her constant rejection of you is going to worm itself into your head—and that can lead to low libido, premature ejaculation, and erectile dysfunction. So if your lady is complaining, make sure she sees a doctor who will take her complaints seriously.

next step, ask your therapist for a referral or contact the International Professional Surrogates Association at www.surrogatetherapy.org. Experts advise that you choose a surrogate who works only in conjunction with a certified therapist. For a list of therapists who work with surrogates, contact the Bay Area Surrogate Association, PO Box 60971, Palo Alto, CA 94306.

CHAPTER 15

HAVE SEX ANYWHERE IN THE WORLD
Find Your Bliss in Exotic Locales

Whether they're wrestling crocodiles or giant cans of Foster's Lager, Australians have a reputation for adventure that's recognized around the world. And evidently that reputation extends to sex. Our survey found that Australian men have had sex in the most different locations.

Why are those lucky guys Down Under having the most fun sex in (and out of) bed—and how can we get some of that?

One theory is genetic. Adding to their daring nature is the fact that a large percentage of Australians originally came from a gene pool of criminals who were brought over from overcrowded English jails in the late 1700s. "These are men who have elevated levels of testosterone and dopamine in their brains," says Helen Fisher, PhD, research professor in the anthropology department at Rutgers University in New Jersey and author of *Why We Love*. "Testosterone is associated with sexuality, and dopamine is associated with risk-taking, novelty-seeking, and energy. It might be likely that such kinds of men would try a wider variety of locations for sex."

"Australians built their identity on what they call *larrikin* spirit," says Dr. Patricia Weerakoon, a popular Australian sexologist and the coordinator of the graduate program in sexual health at the University of Sydney. "*Larrikinism* is an Australian folk tradition of anti-authoritarianism and irreverence and a disregard for the norms of propriety." The culture, as she

Percentage of men worldwide who have had sex in the following places:

In a bed	84.1 percent
In the car (parked)	57.1 percent
In the kitchen	51.6 percent
In the woods	40.6 percent
On the beach	35.5 percent
In a swimming pool	31.6 percent
In the office	22.9 percent
In the car (while driving)	20.5 percent
In the bathroom of a club/restaurant	19.8 percent
On the washing machine	16.7 percent
In an elevator	9.3 percent
On the roof of a building	9.1 percent
On a hammock	7.0 percent
At the gym	7.0 percent
In public transportation	6.4 percent
In the hospital	5.5 percent
In an airplane	3.9 percent
In a taxicab	3.1 percent
At the airport	2.8 percent

sees it, is pro-pleasure and pro-sex—as evidenced by the fact that she is a frequent guest lecturer on the subject of healthy sex at Rotary Clubs and church groups. "It's really okay here to talk about fun and novelty. Cultures have said it throughout the ages, but Australian society has really made a place for people to have fun and push the boundaries of what's acceptable."

Clint Paddison, CEO of BlinkDating.com in Australia, has a different explanation. "It's very much an outdoors culture here, mostly because the weather's so good. For instance, almost every restaurant here has outside seating. It's one of the reasons we excel at sporting events like running and swimming and surfing—we're outside doing them all the time. So it doesn't seem like a huge leap for an Australian to take sex outdoors."

Jan Hall, PhD, an Australian psychologist who specializes in relationship and sexual issues and the author of *Sex-Life Solutions*, agrees with him: "Australian men *and* women are down-to-earth and love the outdoors, so it's only natural that sex in locations out of the house would be a turn-on."

Regardless of what the true explanation is, this much we know: hodophilia—that's sex in different places to you—is hot. "If it's possible, sometimes only just barely possible, to have sex in an unusual outdoor setting, someone has more than likely had sex there," says Buck Tilton, author of *Sex in the Outdoors: A Humorous Approach to Recreation*. What is it about sex in anyplace other than bed that gets the engine revving? Gabrielle Morrissey, PhD, an Australian sex expert and the author of *Urge: Hot Secrets for Great Sex*, explains: "When we add a new or different stimulation, our minds can process that stimulation into arousal."

This is especially true for what experts call agoraphilia—and we call getting it on in public. Spiking the risk sensors boosts bloodflow and brain activity, increasing your awareness of sensations. "It makes our senses ultra-sensitive," says Dr. Hall. "Trying to make sure we are not seen or heard makes it more of a turn-on." And the sex we have is better as a result: "The romantic thrill of possibly being caught increases all the processes that the body experiences when we approach orgasm. So those sensations are heightened," says Dr. Morrissey.

There may be a nostalgia factor as well. Remember high school, when you'd make out anywhere you could? Then, the kinkiest place you could imagine doing it was in a bed. But the coat-check rooms and secluded spots behind the dunes are still out there, waiting for you. And perhaps they can help you reclaim some of the youthful fervor that came from the certainty that someone was going to come around the corner any minute. . . .

It's worth noting that sex in many of these places may not be conducive to the world's best orgasm—for either one of you. Don't let that stop you. The memories (and bragging rights?) will pay tremendous dividends later when you're having regular Wednesday-night sex. And remember that you can always start in one place and go somewhere else.

In this chapter, we'll review the hottest of these off-road love spots and give you the advice you need to help ensure that your private interlude in a public space is as incredible as your fantasy of it was.

#1: A Bed

No surprises here: 84 percent of our respondents said they'd had sex in a bed. Our only other question: Since just 4 percent of the guys who answered are still virgins, where are the other 12 percent of you doing it?

Those adventurous Australians didn't have much to say on this topic, probably because they're too busy getting it on in other, more unconventional places. They chose to reserve comment for more exotic locales like the woods (page 288), the beach (page 290), and the hospital (page 301.) But here are some comments from the rest of the world.

What's great about it: What's not to like? It's comfy and properly proportioned, and you can crash right afterward. Add a bedside table full of condoms, lube, and whatever toys you like to incorporate, and you might even say it was the perfect venue. "It's comfortable," says Antzhela from Greece. Angela, 35, from Amsterdam, agrees: "It's comfortable, and ours alone."

Best positions: A good place to try anything and everything, as appropriate for the nastiest doggy-style as for the most loving face-to-face missionary position. Got a great headboard? That'll be perfect for tying her wrists above her head. (And if you don't have one, what were you thinking?)

Don't limit yourself to the flat surface, either. One (or both of you) partly off the bed—you standing while she sits at the edge, you leaning while she sits at the edge, her standing and leaning on her elbows (see Chapter 11 for lots more ideas)—can bring a whole new dimension to this tried-and-true.

What to watch out for: Acute, soul-killing, sex-life-extinguishing boredom. But don't worry—as long as you give some of the other locations in this chapter a test-drive, you can have your cake and eat it too.

#2: A Parked Car

What the average car lacks in amenities, it makes up for in convenience, apparently—because 57 percent of you owned up to some automotive love.

As turn-ons go, this one seems to be a generational thing. The 2006 global sex study done by the condom company Durex, for instance, found that just over one-third (34 percent) of 16-to-20-year-olds favored the car, compared with 69 percent of 45-to-55-year-olds. We're not statisticians, but this does seem to suggest that it's more fun when it's not your only option (as it is for many horny teenagers).

What's great about it: It's portable! You've got tunes, reclining seats, cup-holders—and nothing says illicit quite like steaming up the windows during a parking lot quickie.

Best positions: Hit the backseat horizontally, with her on the bottom. Or sit in the center of the backseat, as if you were in a cab, and let her straddle you, facing toward the front of the car and using the bucket seats for leverage.

IN THE TUSCAN PARKING LOT

If you and your sweetie are fans of car sex, you might want to plan a trip to Vinci, birthplace of the great Leonardo, in the Tuscany area of Italy. A large percentage of young Italians live at home, leaving them without privacy or a safe alternative. In response, Vinci's mayor authorized Italy's first "Love Park," complete with soft lighting, condom machines, and 172 parking spaces in which to get your groove on.

What to watch out for: The Son of Sam—or Italy's version, the still-at-large Monster of Florence. Uh, just kidding. Mostly what you need to watch out for is the cops. Although if a police officer in Coeur d'Alene, Idaho, suspects you're getting busy, he has to honk his horn twice and give you a few minutes before approaching. Isn't that civilized?

When in London, it is specifically illegal to have sex on a parked motorcycle. So keep your eye out for the bobbies.

#3: The Kitchen

Everyone's got one, and a lot of you—51 percent—are using it for a lot more than blending protein smoothies.

What's great about it: A whole host of delicious sex enhancers are within reach (see "Playing with Your Food" on page 286 for ideas about what to use and how to use them). Let's face it, whipped cream wouldn't be such a terrible Hollywood cliché if it weren't so incredibly fun—both the application and the cleanup get high points.

Best positions: Stand up while she sits on the edge of the kitchen counter, sink, or table. "The solid surface will make even slow, small thrusts intense," says Isadora Alman, a California sexologist who writes a syndicated column called *Ask Isadora*.

Or give yourself over to the slippery-when-wet pleasures of linoleum, and keep the fridge door open for easy access to the Jell-O. We think you're going to like the way that tiny light bulb makes her look.

What to watch out for: We're assuming that you're not subject to regular inspection by the health department. Even so, bear in mind that usual kitchen hazards are amplified when you're (a) naked and (b) distracted.

PLAYING WITH YOUR FOOD

You can't go wrong with the tried-and-trues: There's a reason that chocolate syrup and whipped cream get all the kinky play in movies. But your refrigerator contains any number of delicious treats that are even more delectable when served up on the warm, silky skin of your beloved.

Play with different textures. Honey, molasses, and jam are sticky; brown sugar has a very pleasant grittiness. Avocados are creamy; heavy cream is rich and thick.

Feed her. "The best foods for sex are fruits that you can rub onto the body, such as soft mango or papaya," says Ava Cadell, PhD, a Hungarian-born, British-raised expert who has traveled and taught widely throughout the world. "Then devour both her and the fruit." Even the most determined carnivore will discover that fruit tastes good when it's mashed in the heat of passion and has to be licked off someone else's skin. "An overripe date is a very good thing to smash and then lick off a man," says Liat, a retail store manager from Israel.

But you're not restricted to sweet stuff. Experiment with a salty olive in her belly button, a sour slice of grapefruit sucked from between her lips. "I once ate an entire pound of thinly sliced smoked salmon from between my girlfriend's legs," says Adam from Poland. "It was a perfect pairing." "The avocado is very common in Mexico, and my boyfriend likes the ripe ones very much!" says Paula, a Mexican hotel administrator. "I know one thing from playing with them: It is very good for the hair and skin."

Dine in style. *Nyotaimori*, the act of eating sushi off a naked woman's body, goes back to the ancient Japanese courts; a version has become popular at parties in the United States as well. Traditional rules include: no speaking to the "platter," no touching of her body, no lewd or inappropriate gestures, and mandatory use of chopsticks. See how many of these rules you can break—and make sure to take your turn as the platter as well. (Bathing with fragrance-free soap is advised prior to the event—and remember, all the food safety rules about preparing, serving, and eating raw fish still apply, no matter how toothsome she looks!)

Body shots. "Stuck without air conditioning in the country, I rolled a cold can of Coke all over my girlfriend's body and then poured the contents all over her and licked it off," says Alistair from South Africa.

Watch out for hot elements and sharp knives—it's all fun and games until someone backs into the corkscrew.

Sweet stuff is delicious for sex play, but you should avoid getting any of it inside of her. Foods with high sugar content—including chocolate,

"Sweet and salty; I've never enjoyed a Coke like that since."

Pour dessert wine into her navel and lick it out. Or make it tequila, complete with a salt trail all the way up to her mouth, where your lime is waiting. *Arriba!*

Take a mouthful of champagne, and let the bubbles do their good work on her clit. Or do as the Russians do: Take a swig of cold vodka and then lick her nipples. The alcohol will sting in a very gentle, very erotic way.

And when having that private sushi bar, try *wakamesake*, the Japanese practice of drinking sake poured down her body from the "cup" formed by her lap.

Some like it cold. A judiciously placed ice cube can be a wonderful thing. "Cold is sensed by more nerve endings than mere touch can reach, so you're expanding her range of response," says British expert Phillip Hodson. If the intensity is too much when directly applied to her skin, tease her by holding an ice cube in your hand above her body; as it melts, target the droplets at her most sensitive spots. "I once had an orgasm this way," says Marina, a Czech writer. "My lover dripped, dripped, dripped, dripped cold water from ice on my nipples, my abdomen, my pussy, into my mouth. It was sensational."

Ice cream can be another sweet addition to your play. Feed it to her from the carton with your fingers. Paint some on her body—or anywhere you'd like to be licked. Make a banana split, complete with whipped cream, sprinkles, and a cherry on top, using her as the sundae boat. Or use yourself as the banana. No spoons allowed. "We have these frozen ice pops, juice frozen into long thin sticks. We always keep a few in the freezer; my girl always laughs now when we see a kid eating one on the street," says Nico, a construction worker from the Dominican Republic.

Or try this: "I was too busy coming to care at the time, but I found out later that he'd put a single, frozen pea into his mouth when he was down on me," says Mariebelle in France. "The pressure of the cold pea contrasted with his warm mouth—I will never forget it."

Once you've gotten her cold, use your mouth to warm her up again. Take a mouthful of tea or coffee and then lick her clit. She won't believe you're hotter than she is!

---

honey, and fruits—can change the pH of the vagina and lead to an infection, which means a sex time-out for you!

And be careful with those frozen foods—very cold stuff can numb sensitive areas, even to the point of pain.

#4: The Woods

An endless, star-filled sky, the fresh air, the sounds of nature—there's nothing like a little bit of wild nookie to bring out the chest-beating, red-meat-eating beast within every man.

It's time-honored as well. Erotic paintings and poetry from China often depicted sex in a beautiful garden, amidst rocks and flowers with very suggestive shapes. The seasons were often used as a metaphor for the progression of the sexual act, with acts of foreplay depicted in spring, for instance.

There's something about being outside that returns us to our most primal and animalistic selves—and that's a great recipe for great sex. "My husband and I go camping at least twice a year. We find a remote location, wear clothes only when we feel like it, and get back to our animal roots!" says Dominique, a clothing store owner in Brazil.

What's great about it: It's like summer camp, but without the sexual frustration. Having sex outside was central to the Celtic rituals of Ireland, which held that nakedness and sex al fresco allowed you to tap into and channel the elemental energies of the earth. And it is true, from a novelty standpoint, you can't beat the outdoors—especially if you're urban. "Everything's different: The smells are different, the sounds, the way light looks, the way sound carries—it's a totally novel experience," says Japanese-German sex educator Midori, author of *Wild Side Sex*.

And if exhibitionism's your bag, this is a good way to indulge—no matter how far out in the bush you think you are. "We were in the most remote location in the countryside you can possibly imagine; I thought there wasn't anyone for miles. And what do you know, we're going at it, and we hear this couple out for a hike and having the most horrible fight," says Antonia, a travel writer in Britain. "We couldn't keep the giggles in; they were embarrassed and even more furious once they realized what we'd been up to."

Bear in mind, sound carries well at night, especially along water, and when there's nothing else out there making noise except for a few crickets. "We go camping with friends a lot and have found that it's best to either disappear while everyone is gathered around the campfire after dinner, or wait until very late when everyone is sleeping at night," says Friedrich, a sales rep from Mainz, Germany. "The time when everyone is settling in for sleep is the worst—I have heard many couples that way!"

Of course, you don't have to confine your primal urges to the tent. Like any good Boy Scout, we hope you'll come prepared. On a hike, it's worth carrying the extra weight of blankets and a pad like the Big Agnes Air Core pad (www.rei.com). It's cushy but durable and doubles as a raft for skinny-dipping. Just get off the trail, find a sheltered spot, and let it happen.

Speaking of skinny-dipping: "On a trip to the Hawaiian islands last year, my husband and I found this beautiful little waterfall and had incredible sex under, in, and around it," says Mac, a doctor from Perth, Australia. "It was like the world's strongest and nicest detachable shower head!"

Want an added dash of excitement? "Plan outdoor sex to coincide with a rare event," says Dr. Hall. "It's such a bigger turn-on to do it on the beach under a full moon or in a park during an eclipse." Bear in mind that if your girl is game, the weather doesn't have to be perfect, either. As long as you're mindful of lightning warnings, a torrential summer rain or the early morning mist can be a very cinematic backdrop. (Rain is also a very good cover-up for whatever noises you're making in your tent.)

Best positions: Dr. Morrissey says an outdoor session should include plenty of manual arousal before the clothes come off, to minimize the length of exposure. (It's not a practical choice for hiking, but for other public sex locales we highly recommend that she wear a skirt.) Once the clothes are off, let her take control. "What a man needs to do is have her on top so he can relax his muscles and delay orgasm," Dr. Morrissey says.

What to watch out for: Hygiene may be compromised after a lot of time outdoors. "If you've worked up a real sweat hiking out to a remote location, it's probably not a great time to suggest oral," says Paddison. But many people find that the slight funkiness—sweat, bug spray, and real dirt—is part of the allure.

An outdoor session should include plenty of manual arousal before the clothes come off.

In fact, there's quite a bit to worry about. The big danger: that you're not the only beast out there. Let's face it, if you're getting busy in the wild, you'll be not only less likely to notice the appearance of a bear but also in a particularly bad position for either fight or flight. (There's some question about whether the smells and sounds of human lovemaking attract bears. Unless you want to be making the beast with three backs—one of them belonging to a 900-pounder—it's probably best to hold off if you're in bear country.) Don't forget to treat used condoms as you would trash or food or anything else that might attract a wild animal (double-bagged and hung); it's certainly not a good idea to sleep with one in the tent with you.

As you may remember from Scouts, a poison ivy rash is nothing to joke about—and that time, it was just around your ankles. Finally, if any clothes remain, may we suggest hunter's orange, just to be on the safe side?

#5: The Beach

Beach sex is so great that there's a girl-drink named after it. What's the secret? Beaches connote *both* sex and romance, says Canadian sex educator Ellen Kate Friedrichs, of sexedvice.com. Not to mention that if you're on the beach, you're probably on vacation. The weather is good, the sun is hot, and the clothing is skimpy. That's probably why this was such a prevalent fantasy in our survey.

What's great about it: What isn't? Whether it's a sun-stunned late afternooner or a slightly chilly, post-clambake romp just out of range of the campfire, there's much to appreciate about beach sex. Expectations of beach sex tend to run high—turn that to your advantage by mentioning the possibility to your sweetie early in the trip.

Once again, preparation is key. A blanket or an extra-large beach towel is the bare minimum, of course; if you're going to be frolicking for a while, heavy-duty sunscreen is also a good idea.

If you want to step it up a notch, the mini-cabana is beach sex in high style; it will not only protect you from sunburn but afford you some privacy as well. No tent? "Wait until long after sunset, then get away from the ambient light of the boardwalk or pier," suggests Lorelei Sharkey, author of *Rec Sex* and one half of the *New York* magazine sex-advice duo Em and Lo. Steer clear of the dunes; "you won't be able to hear an interloper until he or she is on top of you."

If it's the sunlight that turns you on, find somewhere secluded and take a picnic basket as camouflage. Or go in the water—from shore, it'll just look like you're kissing. "Being outside and the lack of gravity really turned me on," says Sarah, an Australian student. Later, you can raise a cerveza in honor of whoever invented the side-tie bikini.

Best positions: On shore, start in the missionary position, and roll, à la *Here to Eternity*. In the water, you can stand, with her leg (or legs) around your waist. Pack a waterproof Babelight—a keychain, vibrator, and flashlight all in one (www.babeland.com). You can clip it to your shorts, get her off, and find your way back to the clambake in style.

What to watch out for: If you do go submarining, make sure to pack some silicone-based lube in your board shorts—water in general (and salt water in particular) will make you both very sore. Also beware of sand—if water makes a poor lubricant, sand makes a truly terrible one. And try not to traumatize those little kids playing paddleball.

#6: The Office

Ah, the office. What is it about fluorescent lights, industrial carpeting, and the smell of toner that makes the heart beat just a little bit faster after hours? A lot of you—about one-quarter of you—know.

What's great about it: Let us count the ways. It's exhibitionist: The thrill of discovery that always accompanies semipublic sex is greatly enhanced by the idea that the discoverer might be your boss—or that hot chick from PR. It's naughty: You can be pretty sure that Louise in accounts payable would not be happy to see your girlfriend's bare ass on her desk. It's discordant: If there were ever a less sexy place than the modern corporate office, we'd like to know what it is—and yet that unsexiness has a certain sexiness all its own, no?

Probably the best thing about office sex is the gift that keeps on giving: It permanently imprints the most humdrum of everyday locations with the memory of illicit sex. Trust us, that fax machine will never look the same to you again.

Best positions: Get ergonomic on her. "When I got together with my boyfriend, we'd been working together and sustaining this very high level of sexual tension for months. When it finally happened, we had sex everywhere we'd ever thought about it," says Beatriz, a lawyer in Venezuela. "We had sex on my desk. We had sex on his desk. We had sex under his desk. We had sex in my boss's chair. He bent me over the photocopier and we copied my tits. We left fingerprints (and other prints) on the glass in

(continued on page 294)

NOT-SO-EXOTIC DESTINATIONS FOR GETAWAY SEX

There's nothing like the thrill of the exotic, but let's face it—it's not always possible to go somewhere truly illicit and glamorous. When that's the case, make love in all the rooms of the house, says Mabel Iam, Argentinian author of *Sex and the Perfect Lover*—and when she tells us to do something, we do it. And once you've done that, try these....

You've done the kitchen; now try the closet. Sex in the closet might sound more like a punchline than a sex tip, but don't knock it till you've tried it. Any unusual setting gets the blood racing, but the closet is an unexplored bonanza. Why? Noises are muffled, and you're surrounded by the textures of different fabrics—a wool coat, a nylon windbreaker, a silk scarf. As an added bonus, you might catch a whiff of the perfume she wears when she gets dressed up; scent stays in clothes much longer than it stays on the skin. Also, the close quarters add a very titillating sense of restraint.

Bonus points: Sneak in while your in-laws are making Thanksgiving dinner.

Up the down staircase. Like the home gym, stairs are sort of like sex furniture that comes with your house. They're particularly good for couples with the kind of height differential that usually makes standing-up sex impossible.

Best positions: Sit on the stairs, facing the railing, with one leg braced a step or two down and the other leg slightly bent. She lowers herself on to you, also facing the rail and holding it for support. For her, it's reverse cowgirl without the charley horse.

Another alternative: She stands with her back to the railing, one leg up on it. You stand in front of her, on whichever step makes sense, and enter her from the front.

And another: She bends over, holding the railing, while you take her from behind. Or she gets on all fours, hands a few steps higher than her knees, and you a few more below.

The couch. All the comforts of the bed, with slightly different (but still familiar) scenery. You can choose your pleasures here—including a supercharged missionary position, afforded by pushing your feet against the arms.

Or ask her to straddle the arm of the couch, facedown, as you enter her from behind. This allows her hot spots to grind on the cushy arm of the sofa, so she gets multiple stimulation with minimal effort. And you can keep one eye on the game.

Give her a tune-up. If the walls of your teenage bedroom were plastered with posters of hot chicks spread-eagled on hot rods, you'll want to take this one out for a spin. Wait until the kids are asleep, and then sneak into the—wait for it—*garage*, says Mary Taylor, a former exotic dancer in

Toronto and the author of *Bedroom Games*. "It's really a sexy way to break the bedroom habit," she says. "First of all, you're leaving the house without really leaving the house, and women love it because it's such a masculine place." Of course, you'd never be stupid enough to leave the car running with the garage door closed. Of course you wouldn't.

This is also a good way to have sex in someone else's house. Sneak out during halftime at cousin Bernard's Super Bowl party, or excuse yourself to get more cranberries from the spare fridge in the garage at Thanksgiving.

Take it outside. You don't necessarily have to go camping to experience the fun of sex under the stars. Prop her up on the porch balcony; have sex in the sunroom with complete darkness outside (and all the lights on inside, if you feel like showing off what you've got). Pitch a pup tent in your backyard and try the Sweetie Pie Sleeping Bag Doubler (functional-design.net) to turn a regular bag into one big fun-house for two. Or while the kids are away at camp, commandeer their treehouse for a quickie by flashlight.

Stroll in the park. Sit down on a bench, unzip, and have her join you on your lap, facing you. For best results, we suggest the cover of night. Sex in public places—often in parks—called "dogging" in Britain, is a serious pastime for lots of people. Check online and you'll find Web sites devoted to the best places to dog or to watch fellow doggers, if that's your, er, cup of tea.

Go to the movies. Sex with a celebrity was one of the leading fantasies in our poll. Which makes having sex at the movies the closest thing that some of us are going to get to another leading fantasy: a threesome. Failing a completely empty theater and sleeping ushers, actual intercourse is only for the bold—or those who don't mind braving the inch-thick layer of old Coke and popcorn on the floor. For the rest of us, movie sex is manual sex—or oral, if you can lift the armrests between seats.

Feeling daring? Knock out the bottom of your popcorn tub for a little extra camouflage. Now all they have to do is make another George Clooney/Catherine Zeta-Jones flick, and everyone will be happy.

Make a deposit. To really add some spice to your sex life, make a quick stop at your bank. A safe-deposit-box room is quiet, the door is locked, and there's no camera. It's a great place to make a deposit and withdrawal.

Pull over. "The showers at truck stops are great places if you want to break up the monotony during a long road trip but don't want to stop at a motel," says Japanese-German sex educator Midori. "They're usually pretty clean and private, but it feels very kinky indeed."

the client foyer. It was like a sexy-secretary porno movie. We couldn't stop!"

What to watch out for: Being walked in on by your boss, for one. It might heighten the fantasy, but getting caught with your pants down (literally) is the type of thing that tends to haunt you at review time. Also, if the person with whom you're dallying is a co-worker, you're exposing yourself to some potentially unpleasant possibilities.

First of all, you're going to have to work together, whether you want to keep sleeping with one another or not. Second, work relationships are nearly impossible to keep under wraps, so operate under the assumption that everyone—including clients and people you liaise with at other firms—will know. Third, there's the very real possibility of a sexual harassment suit. (Flip back to Chapter 1 for some additional advice about these complications.)

And you'll want to make sure that your workplace—the main trading floor of an investment banking firm, for instance, or a casino—doesn't use closed circuit cameras.

#7: A Restaurant or Club Bathroom

Dinner and dancing—what better way to set the mood? At a restaurant, the wine is flowing, the candlelight is twinkling. At a club, the beats are pounding, sweaty bodies moving. You're hot, she's hot—why wait until you get home? No wonder 19 percent of you have ended up returning to the table with her panties in your pocket!

What's great about it: The mood has been set, the threat of discovery is imminent, and it's so *dirty*. "I couldn't believe it was me! It's something one of the *Sex and the City* girls would do with a male model, isn't it—not a nice young doctor couple like us," say Bettina and Russell, a pediatrician and cardiologist from Leeds, England.

Best positions: Standing up is probably your best bet, hygienically speaking. She can put one foot up on the toilet paper holder (gently, please, ladies) and use the top of the stall door for a little extra leverage. If the architecture agrees, you can keep the stall door open and watch yourselves in the mirror, and that's a pretty picture of debauchery and everything that's wrong with the Western world, isn't it?

If you prefer a subtler approach, lift her up completely so that her legs are around your waist, and only one pair of feet will be visible under the stall door. Nobody will ever know your little secret. Unless the rhythmic groaning and the shifting of the side wall give the game away. . . .

But the bathroom isn't the only option, particularly in a big club with lots of dark corners, VIP lounges, cloakrooms, and the like. (Stay out of the office, growls Doug, a restaurant manager in New York.) If things get too advanced on the dance floor, you can always repair to the comfort of the banquettes for some relief. "My girlfriend and I love to go out dancing. After we've gotten each other worked up on the dance floor, we go back to our table, have a drink, and go at it," says Felipe, a singer in Brazil. "If everybody is having a good time, who cares what we're doing?" Thank God for bottle service.

What to watch out for: (1) Bathroom attendants. As if it isn't enough that they have to sit in the crapper all night.

> *"After we've gotten each other worked up on the dance floor, we go back to our table, have a drink, and go at it."*

(2) Breakage. You see, sinks and urinals aren't actually designed to support the weight of two people doing the funky chicken. Take it from Sarah, a Canadian marketing manager: "The night before my sister's wedding, I snuck into the men's bathroom during the rehearsal dinner to get it on with my future brother-in-law's gorgeous cousin. I was sitting on the sink, with my foot up against the urinal opposite for leverage. At a climactic moment, I must have pushed too hard, because the urinal came crashing off the wall and broke into a thousand pieces. At the wedding the next day, nobody talked about anything else. My sister thought it was hysterical."

#8: The Washing Machine

Seventeen percent of you have gotten dirty while your clothes were getting clean.

What's great about it: Besides the fact that it's the biggest vibrator around?

There's something about laundry that's deeply intimate and personal. Plus, you know she's wearing that zebra underwear that someone gave her as a joke because there's nothing else left in the drawer. And let's face it, doing laundry is boring and sex a great time-killer—and a 32-minute wash cycle is about right! Not to mention that a front-loader is about the right height for most couples. There's also an exhibitionistic factor; many apartment dwellers share a laundry room with the rest of the building. And let us not forget the Doritos Girl.

Best positions: Sit her on the edge of the machine with her legs bent and hooked over your arms. If she's flexible, put her feet on your shoulders. As a bonus, give her a little attention with your tongue while she rocks away.

Alternately, sit on the machine yourself and have her straddle you. Stay still—at least at first; the vibrations will carry through your penis. You can adjust the cycles to suit the mood. Start slow and work up—for your information, the spin cycle is the fastest.

What to watch out for: We can't think of a single reason against making laundry a more enjoyable chore.

On the other hand, "washing machine" is a deprecating term used for a guy with only one (circular) move in the cunnilingus department. So that's something to watch out for.

#9: An Elevator

Almost 10 percent of you have gotten it up while it was going down.

What's great about it: The thrill of discovery escalates with every floor. Unless you stop in between floors, of course. A crowded one is also a great place to cop a surreptitious feel. And don't get us started on the glass ones. . . .

Best positions: Her standing, with one leg up. Pray for one of those horizontal handrails they sometimes have along the back wall—what else is that thing for, if not leverage? Or she can bend over, spread her legs, and bend her knees to allow you access. British expert Emily Dubberley also suggests that one of you try "going down while you're going down."

"I never would have, but we got stuck, and I got a little claustrophobic and weepy and he gave me a hug," says Trine in Denmark. "And suddenly we were all over each other on the floor of the thing. It took my mind right off what would happen when we ran out of oxygen. Great sex, and satisfied a fantasy I didn't even know I had!"

What to watch out for: Accidentally hitting the alarm button. And if you hit the red button that stops the car between floors, make sure you don't stay too long—it's all fun and games until the cops come through the ceiling panels to rescue you.

You also might want to check for cameras in the ceiling corners; most modern elevators have them as a security measure. Unless, of course, you're into that sort of thing. Or you own the building, and want the tape for later. . . .

#10: The Roof of a Building

We like to think of this as sex-in-the-woods, urban-style. And almost 10 percent of you have done it up there.

What's great about it: "You're surrounded by the noise of the city, but you're totally apart from it," says Tom, an Irishman who lost his virginity on a rooftop in Belfast. Not to mention the views, a New Yorker reminds us. Location, location, location, baby.

Tom's not alone in having had many of his formative sexual experiences up there. An informal poll showed that rooftops are the go-to spot for lots of car-free urban teenagers when parks are too unsafe. "We had it down to an art form; we used to leave a blanket and a hurricane candle above the fire hose at the top of the stairs. I'm sure the maintenance guys were getting a big kick out of it," says Alan, a hedge fund manager who grew up in New York.

"You're completely exposed. With all those lights on all around you, how could somebody *not* see?" says Laura, a nanny in London. "It's practically guaranteed that some random bloke, brushing his teeth before bed, is going to get an eyeful. But it's not like someone walking in on you—no matter what he sees, I'll never know! Nevertheless, I make an effort to put on a good show." Bless your heart, Laura.

The roof is an ideal place for delicacies and champagne. Pack a basket, and some padding.

Best positions: You're limited only by your imagination—and common safety concerns, of course.

What to watch out for: The view is romantic, but the site itself can be considerably less romantic. It's dirty up there! Before you spread your blanket, make sure there are no nails, chunks of concrete, or other debris on the ground.

And if someone calls the cops, you're going to have to deal with the smirk on the doorman's face forever.

#11: In a Hammock

Well, if you're having sex in a hammock, it's pretty much a given that you're on vacation—or that you live in the kind of place that other, less lucky people might visit on a vacation. Seven percent of you have made this dream come true. Good for you.

What's great about it: Midori sensibly points out that there are different kinds of hammocks—the inexpensive kind with the large weave that campers sometimes carry, and the heavy-duty canvas ones that you typically find at resorts. Both have benefits, she notes. It might be uncomfortable if a limb slips through the first kind—or it might be the kind of impromptu bondage you were looking for. As for the second, that's basically sex while floating.

Urban dwellers, and those who don't get on vacation as much as they'd like, should consider those chairs that suspend from the ceiling. They're sex furniture in camouflage! Midori recommends these especially for people with partial disabilities, temporary or otherwise—just make sure the attachment is structurally secure before you ask it to hold the weight of two of you.

And if you're really into it on vacation, bring some of the excitement home. Try the Love Swing, from www.mypleasure.com, to "add spinning, bouncing, and entire ranges of movement to your lovemaking." Or the Nicaraguan Nicamaka Marital Aid Hammocks at www.sex-hammocks.com.

Best positions: Hammocks generally work best when you stand and she sits. A number of other possibilities are open to you, though. For instance, you can sit facing each other in what Tantric practitioners call Yab-Yum and rock away. Or maybe you're on top, she's on her front, and you're using your toes and fingers in the weave of the hammock for leverage. And if the hammock is relatively low to the ground, perhaps one of you (probably whoever's on top) can keep one foot on the ground. Or she can have her hands on the ground, belly and chest resting sideways on the hammock while you stand behind.

What to watch out for: Falling out. Flipping over. Getting stuck. The hammock coming unstuck from whatever's supporting it, dumping the two of you on the ground. In general, be careful here.

#12: The Gym

If fantasies always came true, this statistic would probably be significantly higher than 7 percent—what guy hasn't made a boring treadmill session more pleasant with a reverie about the bodacious rump on the machine in front of him? (And she thought you were watching *Project Runway*!)

What's great about it: The gym can be a great place for a romantic interlude. First of all, exercise is a powerful aphrodisiac, as it kicks your central nervous system into high gear. Clothing is also skimpier than usual—especially if there's a yoga studio attached.

Best positions: It depends. If the gym is crowded, a quickie in a locker-room bathroom is going to be tricky enough to pull off. But if you are alone for whatever reason—or have

> *What guy hasn't made a boring treadmill session more pleasant with a reverie about the bodacious rump on the machine in front of him?*

a home gym—then you've got the run of the equipment, and that's when the fun really starts. "The whole place is filled with adjustable benches, chairs, incline planes, all covered with padded black vinyl. Not to mention the mirrors or the fit balls," says Carlos, a personal trainer from the Dominican Republic. "It's going to take me a lifetime to exhaust the possibilities."

"I worked as a lifeguard at a fitness center last summer, and my boyfriend used to come in and wait for me on nights when I had to close the pool. We had sex all over the equipment," says Zola, a graduate student in South Africa. "And those mirrors. . . ."

What to watch out for: It's really bad manners, if that's the sort of thing you care about. In fact, a group of janitors sued a large gym chain in the United States, claiming that they frequently had to witness and clean up after wanton sex-having members in steam rooms and saunas and showers. So please make sure to wipe the equipment clean after you're done!

#13: Public Transportation

Trains, planes, and automobiles, indeed—6 percent of you have had sex on some form of public transportation.

What's great about it: It's no accident that Hollywood filmmakers used the image of a train going into a tunnel to symbolize sex. Whether it's the motion of the vehicle, the anonymity and proximity to so many other people, or the opportunity delivered by a patch of forced idleness in our otherwise overscheduled lives, traveling often gives way to sexed-up thoughts and feelings. "I basically use my commute to think about having sex," says Jon, a French academic. "By the time I get home, I'm ready to fall on my girlfriend."

It's even better when you can share the love *en route*. "My college boyfriend and I had some of the hottest sex we ever had on the TGV [the French interurban train] back and forth from university," says Alix, a pastry chef in Paris. "I'd bring a blanket to throw over our laps and we'd drive each other nuts! It made it better that we couldn't have actual sex, but were forced to use our hands."

Strangers on a train, anyone? "When I was a student, a German girl stuck her leg across the sleeping car into my couchette. I invited her over, and we had a great (if quiet) time," remembers Pablo, a Spanish music teacher. "And I don't speak a word of German!"

What to watch out for: Besides arrest? Offending others. Midori sensibly notes that there's a difference between privacy in a somewhat public location and thrusting the nasty details of your sex life into someone else's face. For instance, silently fingering someone under a blanket in an empty train row while everyone else in the car is asleep is privacy in a somewhat public location—if no one's the wiser, then who cares? But subjecting a busful of unwitting commuters to your own personal porno film is another thing entirely. "Other people are not props in your sex life," says Midori. "It's an encroachment to make someone an unwilling witness to your sexual expression."

> *"Remote-controlled sex toys can make for a lot of fun if you have to be together without being together."*

But Midori would never leave you high and dry. Instead she suggests something a little more subtle and sophisticated: "The new remote-controlled sex toys can make for a lot of fun if you have to be together without *being* together." You can control the speed and intensity of what she feels in her pants, even from across the aisle.

Try the Butterfly Effect, a strap-on, multi-speed waterproof vibrator that tickles her clit, her g-spot, and her anus all at the same time. You hold the remote, so she never knows when it's coming. Alternatively, the Robin's Egg Wireless Vibrator, with seven functions (three speeds and four pulsing patterns), has a range of up to 30 feet. You can get both at www.goodvibes.com.

#14: The Hospital

Five percent of you have had sex in a hospital. After all, there *are* plenty of beds there—adjustable ones, even.

What's great about it: The inappropriateness, for one. You're supposed to be getting better, not getting lucky.

As Midori points out, it's easier if you work there. That's what we heard, too. "I'd never have sex with a patient. But I've had lots of fun with people visiting patients!" says Bree, a German nurse. And no matter where you're from, the naughty nurse figures largely in many men's and women's fantasy lives.

"I met my husband while we were both residents at the hospital. All the students were having tragic affairs; it was quite funny—it felt like you were always walking into a closet or an empty room and getting an eyeful," says Mac from Australia. "We had quite a bit of fun ourselves. He still works there, so for our 10th anniversary, I snuck in and texted him to meet in our old laundry supply closet. Delish!"

"I think it's an escape, too—a way of dealing with the stress of having to be in a hospital at all," says Jorge, a doctor in Spain. "Most people hate them with a passion, especially if they have to be there for a long time, like with a sick parent. Getting a little love is a nice relief."

"I gave my husband a blow job the day after I gave birth," says Nikki, a jewelry designer in Australia. "We fell on each other like animals— maybe it was our way of dealing with the stress of new parenthood!" Most new dads should not count on their wives being as frisky as Nikki.

Best positions: If you're in a room, put that bed to work for you! Missionary position takes on all kinds of new relevance when she's sitting up a little. If you're in a closet, stairway, or bathroom, the standing-up positions are what you're looking for.

What to watch out for: Interfering with recovery. If one (or the both of you) is there for legitimate reasons, do move carefully around those IV tubes. . . .

#15: An Airplane

Only 4 percent of you have reached new heights while airborne. "I'm astonished that only 4 percent have done it while flying!" says Liz, of Liz and Julie, British stewardesses extraordinaire and authors of *You F'Coffee Sir?!!* "They have all been on my flights, the dirty monkeys!"

That select 4 percent can count themselves part of the elite Mile High Club, retroactively "founded" by the inventor of the autopilot, who in 1916 crashed with his paramour into a Long Island pond and lived to tell the tale. And if that sounds like something we found on the Internet, well, you're not wrong.

What we do know for certain is this: Although only a small percentage of you have joined the club, it's not for lack of interest. This is a very popular fantasy. "This is a fantasy for many, many people, to bonk or be bonked in an aircraft toilet at 39,000 feet," say Liz and Julie. "But to those of us who spend an awful lot of our time at 39,000 feet as part of our working lives, you really do baffle us!"

What's great about it: "Not comfortable, but fun to brag about," reports Nadja from Croatia. What accounts for the appeal of having sex in mid-air? Perhaps it's the thrill of doing something naughty, illegal, and otherwise frowned upon while just a thin plastic wall (or an even thinner wool blanket) away from 500 unsuspecting travelers. Perhaps it's the lower atmospheric pressure and thin oxygen of the cabin, which makes an orgasm seem so sweet. Perhaps it's gaining membership to a relatively exclusive club. Whatever it is, the thrill definitely endures.

QUICKIE STATS

Percentage of men who fantasize about joining the Mile High Club:

1. Croatia	24.4 percent
2. Russia	21.5 percent
3. Ukraine	20.7 percent
4. Czech	20.0 percent
5. Australia	15.1 percent
Least (Indonesia)	1.0 percent

Best positions: For advice on

making this fantasy come true, we turned to James, a Brit who works for an international bank, and a self-proclaimed airplane expert. "I fly about 150,000 miles a year and find talking to women in airports to be considerably less boring than reading magazines or working on my laptop. So I've gotten quite good at shagging on planes." Here's his preferred method: Wait for the in-flight movie, or, on a late-night flight, for lights out in the cabin. When the time is right, get up and head to the bathroom; the girl you're meeting should join you a minute or two afterward. While you're waiting for her, squirt a generous amount of hand sanitizer on the bathroom seat, wipe it off with a towel, sit down, and, uh, get ready. Your traveling partner, when she arrives, can straddle your lap. "The safety bars are spectacular aids," James says. "I want them in my bedroom at home." (Liz and Julie caution that this is best on larger jets, where there's more room.)

"I've gotten quite good at shagging on planes."

Turbulence, James says, "can be scary—there was one time on a flight from Hong Kong when the girl I was with panicked. But if it's not serious, it can be quite fun, and add to the thrill." There's not a lot of time, he warns: "A queue forms quite rapidly outside the door, even in the middle of the night."

Afterward, she leaves the bathroom, and you follow a minute or two afterward. "It's only polite, in case there's some difficulty," says James. "I've heard that the best thing to do if you're caught by a steward is to say that you were feeling rough and your lady friend was helping, but it's never happened to me."

Liz and Julie have some other suggestions:

■ She bends over the toilet seat or, if she's adventurous, kneels on it, while you stand behind.

■ She perches on the edge of the basin, wrapping her legs around you as you stand. This may be uncomfortable for her, as the little tap will be jammed into her buttocks, which in turn will be crammed into the basin. Best for the slender.

■ She can sit on the toilet to perform fellatio; to return the favor, you sit and she stands one-legged with a knee hooked up on the little sink.

■ For the very daring, one of you kneels on the floor, while the other sits on the toilet seat, knees up and bottom shuffled forward. The two of you can even try for the feet-hooked-over-the-shoulders addition. "This is only

WHEN EVEN A LITTLE PDA IS TOO MUCH

If you're traveling abroad with your honey, you may want to keep your hands to yourself—in public, anyway. In some countries, public kissing and carrying on—even between married couples—is illegal. So it's important to remember that American ideas about freedom of expression are, well, American.

For instance, in Asia, it's very unusual to see couples even holding hands, let alone kissing. When a Beijing movie theater promoted a date movie by offering a 20 percent discount to couples who'd kiss and hug at the box office, not one couple took them up on the offer—20 percent off wasn't nearly enough to overcome the taboo against public displays of affection.

The Turkish government censors emoticons, so that you can't even send a wireless wink to your honey. The Indonesian edition of *Playboy* does not feature nudity, and in fact, the editor-in-chief was prosecuted for obscenity. The country is contemplating a law that would criminalize the exposure of "sensual body parts" like the hips or thighs.

The simple fact is that the better you fit in to the culture you're visiting, the better a time you're going to have. Not to mention the satisfaction you'll get from subverting the image of "the ugly American." Most guidebooks contain good information about social mores, such as standards of appropriate dress for women and the prevailing view on public handholding. Educate yourself and be mindful of the culture.

---

for those with a total disregard for hygiene," say Liz and Julie. "Aircraft toilet floors are practically toxic, and covered in ancient piss."

If chemical toilets aren't appealing, the other alternative is to wait for the lights to go down, throw one of those little blankets over the two of you, and let your fingers do the walking. If you're alone in your row and sure that nobody else is awake or will be bothered, why not? But do be considerate. How would you feel if the guy sitting in the seat attached to your tray table was doing the same?

So there you go—a guide to the *very* friendly skies, straight from the pros. Of course, those pros have galleys and bunk areas on the flight deck if they want to get up to something, which Liz and Julie tell us does happen.

What to watch out for: Federal interference charges, for one. It seems like every 6 months there's a news story about a flight forced to land due to a frisky couple who wouldn't quit groping each other. It's illegal to get busy in the bathrooms, too—not to mention vaguely unsanitary, which is what most flight attendants seem to fixate on.

#16: A Taxi

Taxicab confessions indeed. Three percent of you have quite a bit to talk about, apparently.

What's great about it: It's rolling foreplay, for those times when you can't keep your hands off each other. Give yourselves a challenge—can you get her to where she needs to go before you get to where you're going?

Best positions: Flip back to "A Parked Car" on page 284 to refresh your memory of the best backseat antics.

What to watch out for: Sudden stops—remember *The World According to Garp*?

Not to mention the human being driving the car. "I mind less than some other stuff, I can tell you," says Ronald, a London cabbie. "I'd rather her back there giving him one than sicking up all over the place because she's had too much to drink."

You can add some fun to the game by sitting up properly next to one another, hands in each other's laps, not letting your faces give anything away. And if that's not going to work, Midori once again steps in with thoughtful advice: "Tip *big*. I might even suggest you tip in advance. Even better, hire a private limo for the evening, and tell the company it's for a romantic evening. They've seen it all before, and the driver is better compensated."

#17: The Airport

If you have a long layover, what's to stop you from using the airport hotel as your own personal no-tell motel? Even for a short layover, there are plenty of other places in which to say bon voyage.

What's great about it: Parting is such sweet sorrow, and nothing makes sex more poignant.

Best positions: More and more airport bathrooms are single-stall to

DANGEROUS PLACES: WHERE *NOT* TO DO IT

We're all for experimentation, but there are some places and times that really are not suitable for a tryst. They are:

A swimming pool or hot tub. As sexy as the whole Jacuzzi setup might seem, it's actually not a great place to have sex—although 32 percent of you have done it anyway. "Chlorine and other chemicals in pools and hot tubs can enter a woman's vaginal skin through microscopic tears, causing up to 10 days of soreness and swelling," says Bruce Bekkar, MD, coauthor of *Your Guy's Guide to Gynecology*. That means a 10-day dry spell until she heals.

While driving. A surprising 21 percent of you have enjoyed some kind of sexual congress while driving. We hate to be killjoys—but what were you thinking? A 2005 study of drivers in Perth, Australia, by the Insurance Institute for Highway Safety found that motorists who use cell phones while driving are four times as likely to get into crashes serious enough to cause injury. We can only imagine what the numbers would look like for motorists having their own gear-shifts polished. Seriously—pull over.

accommodate families and people with disabilities, Midori notes. Be quick, so you don't inconvenience someone who really needs the facilities. She also points out that, for those of you with executive lounge privileges, the conference rooms are usually very private. Shhh! Fiona Patten of Australia's Eros Society says, "The shower in the Quantas Club is a convenient location."

What to watch out for: It says something about the new level of airport security that almost every single person we asked about this warned against sneaking off into some unauthorized zone. "I'm originally from Pakistan, so it goes without saying that I'm pretty much detained as soon as I get out of the cab," says Nawaz. "Sorry, honey, you're going to have to wait until we get home!"

CHAPTER 16

HAVE THE WILDEST SEX IN THE WORLD
Make Your Fantasies Come True

It's not for nothing that they say the brain is your most important sexual organ. Pretty much everything you want—between the sheets, and outside of them as well—starts as an idea in your head. "A sexual fantasy refers to any mental image that is erotic and arousing to that person. It can be an elaborate story, a reminiscence of a past encounter, or a dream of a future one," says Victoria Zdrok, PhD, AKA Dr. Z, a Russian-born dating coach, author, radio host, and *Penthouse* columnist. (Did we mention that she was a *Playboy* centerfold, too?)

According to Dr. Z, those who frequently fantasize masturbate more often, have sex more often, have more partners, and engage in a wider variety of erotic activities than infrequent fantasizers. So get your thinking cap on! In this chapter, we'll show you who in the world thinks about what most often (and who thinks about it least!) and how to put this tremendous pleasure power to work for you.

Bringing Fantasies into the Bedroom

As any sex therapist can tell you, there's tremendous variety in what "normal" people think about. One man's dreams of oversized rumps are another man's reverie about thigh-high rubber boots. This diversity makes us very anxious. Dr. Z says that according to research, about one in four people feel strong guilt about their fantasies, and the way most of us deal with this guilt is to repress it. In one study of college students, 22 percent of women and 8 percent of men said they usually try to suppress the feelings associated with fantasy. But research has shown that those who feel guilt about their fantasies have sex less often and enjoy it considerably less.

"People feel guilty when their fantasy and personal ideology are in conflict," says Dr. Z. "A strong and independent woman may feel guilty and ashamed about having fantasies of being dominated by an insensitive brute. People who have what they consider to be unusual or deviant fantasies may also feel guilt and shame about them—and may even fear that such fantasies will cause them to lose control or act out in socially unacceptable ways."

There's tremendous variety in what "normal" people think about.

But there's no need to feel uncomfortable. Sometimes, fantasies *are* a dress rehearsal for the real thing. Other times, they're the best place to act out things we'd never otherwise do; in fact, sometimes they're sexy precisely because they're not in the realm of reality.

Another, major source of anxiety comes from thinking about someone who's not your partner. Does doing so make you unfaithful? It doesn't, actually—a good thing, since most people's fantasies aren't about their current partners. "We consider such fantasies a form of symbolic betrayal or cognitive infidelity, and they make us question our integrity—how can we be in love with one person and thinking about another?" says Dr. Z. But thinking about someone else in your most private moment doesn't mean that you are disloyal or no longer find your current partner desirable. It's just a case of the mind doing what comes naturally. What's unnatural is trying to stop it.

In fact, an active fantasy life can be a real benefit to your relationship: You can use your fantasies to spark up your sex life when the fizzle has set in. And if you're more sexually curious than your partner is, an active fantasy life can help you to stay contented with a less-adventurous physical relationship.

Are all fantasies appropriate to share? Not necessarily, say many experts. Here's a litmus test for whether you should show her yours—or just keep your big mouth shut.

Is she going to freak out? "You know the person you're with, and you need to ask yourself if she's going to freak out," says Robin Milhausen, PhD, associate professor at Canada's University of Guelph and the host of *Sex, Toys, and Chocolate*, a no-holds-barred Canadian TV show about sex. "Before you introduce something, ask yourself: Is this something that she can handle, or will this push her past her comfort level?" For instance, you wouldn't want to introduce the idea of a strong dominance fantasy with a woman who's had a history of violent relationships.

Is she going to read too much into it? "Sometimes we attribute more importance to fantasies than we should," says Dr. Milhausen. "Just because something turns you on to think about doesn't necessarily mean that it's an expression of your deepest, darkest desires. A lot of women think about having sex with five guys at once, for instance. But they don't really want to; the reality would be terrifying."

"I have a fantasy about converting a lesbian—you know, 'My man-loving is so good, she'll never go back to women' type of a thing," says Witold, who works for an airline in Poland. "It's just a silly thing that I think about sometimes. I made the mistake of telling my girlfriend about it, and she went crazy! Suddenly, she was convinced that there was something wrong with me or that I was attracted to gay women; she couldn't let it go."

In such a case, it's better to keep quiet. After all, the goal of sharing your fantasies is to make your sex life more erotic and to help you realize your sexual potential. And you can't do that sleeping on the porch. With that in mind, we talked to some of the world's foremost experts about how to bring your partner along as you dip your toe into the world of adventurous sex.

"Tell Me What You're Thinking About"

Few men have trouble telling dirty jokes or bragging to a buddy about their Saturday-night conquests. But when it comes to talking openly, honestly, and explicitly about sex with a partner, inhibitions often choke the words.

"Inhibitions are leftovers from old messages transmitted to us as children that sex is disgusting, sinful, and harmful," says Ira L. Reiss, PhD, former president of the International Academy of Sex Research and the author of *An End to Shame: Shaping Our Next Sexual Revolution.* We hold on to those beliefs as adults, he says, and the result is often shame and the inability to fully enjoy sex.

The first thing to remember, according to Barbara Carrellas, sex educator and author of *Urban Tantra: Sacred Sex for the Twenty-First Century,* is this: "Asking for what you want is not a demand or an ultimatum. It's a sincere request which your partner may honor or politely decline."

In general, women love secrets and finding out new things about you. "There's no set way to do this—you're talking about a tremendous amount of variations here: how comfortable someone is talking about sex, how much trust and emotional intimacy exists in the partnership, how similar their goals and drives are," says David Seal, PhD, associate professor in the department of psychiatry and behavioral medicine at the Medical College of Wisconsin. "Essentially, what you're talking about is the degree of sexual compatibility that two people have, and the degree to which they're able to, or willing to, compromise to accommodate the other person."

These conversations can be difficult, Dr. Seal admits, but he also says that the couples who are able to navigate them successfully have the best relationships, not just sexually but emotionally.

There's a certain degree of inherent risk in a conversation of this sort, says Dr. Seal. A bad response, like it or not, is a possibility. And even if you're prepared, it can really be hurtful. Consider these two stories: "I shared something I had thought about since adolescence with my girlfriend, and she laughed," says Carlos, a doctor in Venezuela. "She didn't mean to, and she apologized, but for me, the relationship was dead after that."

"I had a fantasy of being taken by an intruder—surprised, tied up, taken by force—the whole thing. When I finally got the courage to tell my husband, I could tell he was a little put-off, but we tried it anyway, and the whole thing was just totally pathetic," says Jessica, a Brit who lives in Cairo. "I wish I'd kept my mouth shut—then at least I'd still have the fantasy."

So look before you leap. "Ask yourself, 'Is this something that can be taken back?' If you're about to initiate a conversation about something, you might want to ask yourself if it's going to be something she can easily recover from," says Dr. Milhausen.

Some good first steps:

Figure it out for yourself. It's a good idea to know what you want from a fantasy and to be able to articulate it clearly to yourself before you introduce it to your partner.

Let's say, for instance, that thinking about a threesome gets you incredibly hot and bothered. There are a lot of different variations on this common fantasy—what is it about it that makes *you* so turned on? Is it the idea of two women servicing you sexually? Is it the feeling of mastery you get from knowing that you can satisfy both of them? Is it the idea of watching two women enjoy one another? Would you actually want to participate, or just watch?

Most important, is this a fantasy you just like thinking about, or is it something you'd actually like to experience?

Wade, don't dive. "Sharing sexual fantasies with your partner requires good communication and a high degree of trust," says Dr. Z. You can say that again!

She proposes that you start by discussing the topic generally, and see how your partner responds. "One way a man can do it without risking revulsion or feeling too vulnerable is by renting a movie or DVD involving this fantasy and then discussing it together," says Dr. Z.

Almost every single expert we asked for advice on broaching the topic of a fantasy with a partner mentioned using a magazine article, a talk show, a sitcom, or some other "real world" prop as a trigger. A botched threesome is the comedic premise on the *Friends* rerun you're watching in bed together; you find out that two of your friends shared a very public tryst on the Staten Island Ferry; paparazzi capture a celebrity having her toes sucked by her boyfriend. (Dr. Z recommends the TV series *Nip/Tuck*, which features pretty much any off-road fantasy—sex with a transvestite!—you might have.) All of these can be launching pads for a discussion, opportunities for you to share a fantasy you've been thinking about.

"I've always really been into the idea of roleplay, so one night, I 'accidentally' left an article about it in one of my women's magazines open on the table," says Dorke, a documentary filmmaker in Germany. "When I *Tell her you had a wild dream about her, then make her pry it out of you.* came back, my husband was flipping through the article, and he asked me if I thought we could try something. I practically did a cartwheel."

Tell her you had a wild dream about her, then make her pry it out of you, suggests Ian Kerner, PhD, a sex therapist and the author of *She Comes First*. Nobody can blame you for a dream, after all—and if it's not something she's interested in pursuing, it's easy to let the subject drop.

Make her feel good about herself. "The sexier she feels and the better she thinks she is at sex, the more inclined she'll be to try new things," says Australian-British expert Tracey Cox, author of *Supersex*. "The secret to talking her into doing anything she's nervous about? Send a very clear message: I want you more than I want to do this. Followed closely by: You don't have to agree if you don't want to."

Take it outside. Dr. Seal suggests that such conversations are better held outside of the bedroom and the emotions and natural vulnerabilities of the arousal state. Dr. Milhausen agrees: "Talking about sex in the bedroom is a mistake—it's too proximal. It's always better to bring it up in a calm, cool, separate way."

In other words, it's probably best not to spring something new on her while you're hot and heavy between the sheets—unless your fantasy is hearing her yell, "What the hell are you trying to do?" Introduce the topic at a private but nonsexual time—over dinner, for instance, or while the two of you are quietly sitting on the couch. (A foot massage during this conversation is not going to hurt your cause, incidentally.)

If she's sexually adventurous, you can make a game out of this too. Go to dinner at a super-fancy restaurant and agree that "during the meal, you're allowed to talk only about sexual fantasies," suggests Patricia Love, MD, coauthor of *Hot Monogamy*. "There's something very erotic about being public and being surreptitious about your sexuality."

But the conversation is essential. "It's better to know what the boundaries are—even if you don't like them—than to try to go somewhere that someone doesn't want you to go," says Dr. Seal.

Keep the tone playful. Sex doesn't have to be serious! And you're going to freak her out if she thinks that what you're proposing is a deal-breaker. If there's something you want to try, talk to her about it in a light and playful way. Dr. Z recommends an adult game of Truth or Dare.

No matter what, keep your head held high. "Don't inject guilt or shame into the mix—those guys have no place in the bedroom at all!" says Japanese-German sex educator Midori, author of *Wild Side Sex*. "Instead of saying, 'You're probably going to think I'm a freak for even wanting this, but would you tie me up?' try this instead: 'Hey, I've been having these naughty thoughts—do you want to try something new tonight?'"

Get her turned on about it. If you pressure her, she's going to balk. Instead, harness her own desire, and use that power for good. Plant the seed of your fantasy—"I've been thinking about how incredibly sexy you'd look with sand all over you, and the way your skin would feel, all hot from the sun"—and let her libido do the work for you.

It worked with Marina from Brazil: "He made me see myself as a sexual adventuress—someone who would have sex in public because *I* wanted it. He'd push me a little further every time—feeling me up on a balcony at a party, going really far on a crowded train. We finally did it in a park, after what felt like months of foreplay. And it was my idea when we finally did!"

Plant the seed of your fantasy and let her libido do the work for you.

It ain't broke! Make it clear that you're suggesting an addition to, not a replacement for, your current sex life—that what you're proposing isn't an intervention but an enhancement of an already fantastic sex life.

She may not want to put on that Catholic schoolgirl uniform because she's afraid she's going to have to do it every time. And she may feel hurt by the suggestion that the regular sex you're having needs some spicing up—even if she agrees. So make it clear that she won't have to wear the Britney costume every time, and that you're really happy and content with the way things are between you right now.

"Don't imply that you want this because the sex has grown stale," says Mark Elliot, PhD, director of the Institute for Psychological and Sexual Health, in Columbus, Ohio. "When you phrase it as something fun you want to try, it's about having a good time, not fixing something that's broken."

Keep her in the picture. She doesn't want to feel like she's an interchangeable part of the fantasy—a prop like the clothes or the location. Make it clear that it's not the tartan skirt that turns you on, but the idea of *her* as a slutty parochial schoolgirl that makes you hot.

"When you introduce something out of the ordinary, be sure to make her the focal point," says Lorelei Sharkey, author of *Rec Sex* and one half of the *New York* magazine sex-advice duo Em and Lo. "This makes it more about your relationship with her than about your private fantasies."

If you sense that she's receptive, you can start talking about your fantasies when you're intimate—"I can't stop thinking about you tying me up," for instance—and see how she responds.

What's in it for her? "Have the conversation in a collaborative way," advises Christine Webber, a British psychotherapist and sex columnist for Netdoctor UK. She suggests language like: "We get along so well, I was wondering if there's anything that you have been thinking about or would like to try."

Midori also suggests that when you broach the subject, you make sure you're asking as many questions as you're answering. If you create a nonjudgmental space where she can share her fantasies too, she's more likely to turn a sympathetic ear to yours. And if you take it to the next step and put one of her fantasies into play, you're opening the door for one of yours to come true as well.

What do you do if what *she's* into isn't your bag? Midori says that's the time to smile, nod, and move on. "Thank you for being open with me; I love knowing what you think about. I'm not sure that dressing up like a pirate is necessarily my cup of tea, though I'd like to hear more about it. But first, is there anything else you've been thinking about?"

Wait. Unless you met her at a fetish party, the first date isn't the best time for you to whip out your, uh, bullwhip. In most cases, time, tact, and trust will get you where you need to go. Sixty-six percent of the women we talked to during a *Men's Health* poll said that they're most willing to experiment after some time in a relationship.

Create a safe zone. "We were having sex in a park, and a cop caught us and made us stop," says Jon, a French academic. "I actually thought it was pretty funny (I think the cop did too). But even though there were no real consequences, my girlfriend was furious and humiliated about it for weeks afterward."

Don't underestimate the power of social conditioning; even the most liberated woman has been taught that behaving in a sexually open and provocative manner will cheapen her value. "There's the whole 'slut' complex you have to get past," says Candida Royalle, a producer of femme-friendly adult films and a veteran adult-film star. "Make her feel like she won't be judged."

Write it down. If she's shy, suggest that you swap fantasies on paper, one naughty one (sex in public) and one nice one (a long foot-rub) each.

Dr. Z suggests trading disclosures: Each person can write down sexual wishes and put them into the "sexual wish" basket, taking turns drawing them every night. Writing things down can be easier than saying them—and it can be very sexy indeed to see your honey's deepest, darkest fantasies in writing!

If you both tend toward the exhibitionist, send her a dirty postcard with suggestions for the weekend. What you want will be just between you, her, and her postal carrier.

Find out why not. "If your partner is reluctant to engage in a fantasy with you, you need to find out why—not just that she doesn't want to, but why she doesn't want to," says Dr. Milhausen. For instance, if a woman has a troublesome body image, sex with all the lights on or in front of a mirror isn't just "not sexy" to her, it's the worst-case scenario—an absolute nightmare.

Sometimes those needs can be addressed so that both of you can get what you want. Maybe a gorgeous new black satin bustier would hold her tummy in enough that she wouldn't mind a round in front of the full-length mirror. Maybe light bondage would appeal to her more if you got her a pair of fuzzy pink cuffs and let her use them on you first.

Permission to laugh. Cox suggests that you reassure your partner that you're just as likely to be embarrassed by something, and that you're laughing with her, not at her. "It's often simply a matter of giving her—actually, make that both of you—permission not just to laugh, but really laugh if things go wrong. It's better to laugh than to be overserious."

The Next Steps

Okay, she's agreed to give it a shot. How do you go about incorporating your fantasy into your real-life sex life?

Normalize it. "The first step in getting your partner to try out a fantasy is to 'normalize' the experience. Show her that other people have this fantasy as well," says Dr. Z. She suggests reading books that compile people's fantasies, such as Nancy Friday's *My Secret Garden*, or checking out some Web sites and chat groups together. Watching mainstream films is another good way to normalize your partner's fantasies. (See "Let's Go to the Movies" on page 316 for some suggestions.)

LET'S GO TO THE MOVIES

Mainstream movies with not-so-mainstream scenes:

The Bitter Moon: mild S&M, voyeurism, and exhibitionism

Last Tango in Paris: anal play

Bound: lesbianism

9½ Weeks: sex and food; stripper fantasies

Body of Evidence: mild S&M

Emmanuelle: mile-high club, lesbianism

If you're ready to take the next step, Dr. Z recommends introducing couples-oriented X-rated films featuring the fantasies in question. (She recommends women-friendly films by Candida Royalle, dreamy films by Andrew Blake, or fast-paced music video–like films by Michael Ninn.)

Plan it. If you've both decided to make it happen, "it should be well planned out and discussed in advance," says Dr. Z. She also warns you that "fantasies often lose their erotic appeal after they are brought into practice, so if a fantasy is a particularly cherished one, it may be best left unfulfilled."

And it pays to move in increments. "I recommend that my patients introduce a new sexual concept no more than once a week, or every second time they have sex," says Alex Caroline Robboy, the founder of www.havegoodsex.com. Otherwise, you're going to overwhelm her.

Baby steps are always the best first move, says Dee McDonald, the founder of the Centre for Sexual Wellbeing in London and Sussex. "Even if the two of you are both into the full-on fantasy, it's still best to start slow, talking a lot about it and incorporating a little of what you'd like to try into your ordinary lovemaking."

Use a safe word. People who play seriously with bondage, sadomasochism, and domination use what's called a "safe word." A safe word is one that's completely out of context of the fantasy—the color green, for instance, or the word "Bayonne"—that either partner can use to stop the action. After all, if the game is that you're tying her up and taking her "by force" while she "begs" you to stop, how will you know when it really is too much?

This trick brings a welcome degree of freedom: When either of you hears that word, you snap out of character and stop whatever you're doing (and if she's in restraints, ask her if she wants to be released).

Some people even use a graded safe word—"gray," for instance—to indicate that they need a break, or need to check in with their partner about something; "black" to call a stop to the action altogether. And a word like "green"—for green light—can be used to indicate that you're still on board to a partner who's worried about how you're doing without breaking the fantasy.

MIDORI'S SANDWICH METHOD

Japanese-German sex educator Midori has spent the last 20 years teaching men all over the world how to make their sex lives more adventurous, and she's come up with a brilliant approach for incorporating something. She calls it The Sandwich Method. Listen, and learn.

"Imagine a sandwich. Now imagine that the Regular Good Sex you have with your partner is the bread, and whatever new activity you want to introduce is the filling. So let's say that your Regular Good Sex (RGS for short) usually follows this template: You make out a little, you play with her breasts, you give oral sex, you receive a little oral sex, and then you proceed to intercourse.

"Now let's say you want to introduce a light spanking into this routine, and your partner has agreed that this is something she's willing to try. So you go about doing everything the way you would normally, but before you go down on her, you tickle her ass a little, and then give her a couple of smacks."

Here's why The Sandwich Method is great: Let's say she's loving it. Then you're going to have a thick sandwich tonight, one with a little more filling before you get back to the bread. But let's say it flops—she's uncomfortable, or you don't like it as much as you thought you were going to—then you simply pick up where you left off, going right back to the RGS. You go down on her, she goes down on you, and you both proceed on to your happy ending like always. And because humans are programmed to remember the beginning and the ending of an experience better than the middle, your romantic opener and her great orgasm are going to be what she remembers best."

The beauty of this method is that it's the perfect way to introduce practically everything.

It's time now to look at who in the world thinks about what, and what their advice is for dipping your toe in—or, if you're up for it, taking the plunge.

Watching Porn with Your Partner

It's long been said that men are more aroused by visual stimuli than women are. But that's not what the research shows. A study at the Washington University School of Medicine in St. Louis measured brainwave activity of 264 women as they viewed erotic imagery. The conclusion: Women have responses as strong as those seen in men. And Australian researchers found that when men and women watched the same scenes from adult films, women got a bigger adrenaline rush.

So why don't more women like to watch porn? First of all, a lot of them do, but they may not like the same movies you do. The cheesy plots and absence of intimacy between the characters don't help. "I don't need hearts and flowers, but it's nice if they don't look like they hate each other," says Marina from Brazil.

It can also be intimidating. "A lot of women feel threatened by the way the women look—all gorgeous legs and blonde hair and giant breasts," says Valerie Gibson, sex and relationships columnist for the *Toronto Sun*. In fact, there's been a dramatic upsurge in female genital reconstruction because women want to look more like porn stars (or one of the celebrities that has recently been photographed disembarking from a limo sans panties). In the same way that his 9 inches can give you a bit of pause when you look down at your own more modest endowment, seeing all that perfect blonde silicone onscreen can make her wonder whether her lack of surgically enhanced bodaciousness leaves you cold. Reassure her prolifically on that count, and you'll be in good shape.

But Gibson raises another point to explain why porn doesn't do it for more women: "A lot of women feel that sex, as it is shown in most traditional pornography, is misrepresentative. It looks like what it

QUICKIE STATS

Percentage of men who watch porn every day:

1. Brazil	30.1 percent
2. Indonesia	28.4 percent
3. United Kingdom	24.5 percent
4. Philippines	23.3 percent
5. Portugal	22.7 percent
United States	**19.5 percent**
World average	**15.9 percent**

Have the Wildest Sex in the World

is—a performance." We heard this reflected in comments from many of the women we talked to. "I always think porn does men such a disservice," says Emma, a British publicist. "In a way, it really teaches them to 'do it' wrong, doesn't it? I mean, all these women who come just from sex, and all the pounding and the ridiculous way they all give oral sex, which would just be a disaster for a real woman."

Ease in gently. Naked News, a news program based in Toronto, has both male and female webcasts. Close your eyes and it sounds like a normal newscast; open them, and you'll see that all the newsreaders are strangely nekkid.

No, it's not porn—in fact, the news is really solid. But it is a way for you to hang out with your partner and watch people who aren't wearing any clothes. And to catch up on current events while you're at it. Log on at www.nakednews.com.

Educate yourself. The most popular educational video sold at Good Vibrations, a sex-positive sex toy store in San Francisco, is *Sex: A Lifelong Pleasure*. It's a five-part Dutch-made series designed for heterosexual couples. Other options include the Better Sex and Sinclair Library titles, or *How to Female Ejaculate*, which defines the g-spot and concludes with—are you ready for this?—five women having simultaneous orgasms.

Go ancient. Another option is to give her a pillow book. Much of erotic art throughout history was designed not only to educate (put her leg here) but to titillate. *Shunga* are Japanese erotic paintings of the 16th, 17th, and 18th centuries; many reprints are available, as well as reproductions of the Kama Sutra and other antique and ancient texts. Tasteful and yet super-explicit, this is a classy way to get her looking at naked pictures.

Although our advice is generally to involve her, going to the movie store to pick something out might very well be something she's too uncomfortable to do. Choose something online, or offer to pick something out yourself. Don't forget that you can handily use porn to incorporate one of the other fantasies in this chapter. If she won't actually go home with you and another girl, for instance, you can watch porn about a threesome and dream. . . .

Sarah Hedley, British expert and author of *Sex by Numbers*, suggests that you might want to give her oral sex during the movie. Always a bonus feature.

1. Ukraine	37.1 percent
2. Russia	32.5 percent
3. Portugal	25.0 percent
4. Hungary	23.1 percent
5. Netherlands	22.6 percent
6. Brazil	19.0 percent
Least (Slovenia)	9.4 percent
United States	**12.2 percent**

Having Sex in the Great Outdoors

Frankly, we were a little surprised that this was such a popular choice in places with such difficult climates. "Just in the summertime!" says Anna from Ukraine. "Unless there are many furs." It's also curious that such geographically proximate places had such strong reactions for and against. And are we the only people who saw *The Blair Witch Project*?

At any rate, for more information about making this dream come true, see page 288, which has lots of tips.

Outrageous Lingerie

Nearly 17 percent of men worldwide wish they had the magical ability to see through women's clothes. We can't actually give you x-ray vision, but here's the next best thing (and the seventh most popular fantasy out there): Get her to wear sexy lingerie.

Women love erotic underwear, and it can be a very indulgent present—and a hot one—even for a good girl. "My boyfriend bought me lacy lingerie that's unlike anything I've ever worn," says Brittany, a teacher from Canada. "It's not my style at all, but when I wear it, I feel like a different person in bed—sexy, crazy, empowered."

You wouldn't know it from the pajama party movies, but a lot of women don't have a lot of experience with lingerie. Many more find that wearing revealing clothes, even in the sanctity of the bedroom, calls

1. Czech Republic	26.3 percent
2. Portugal	26.2 percent
3. Indonesia	25.2 percent
4. Hungary	23.8 percent
5. Netherlands	21.7 percent
Least (Ukraine)	4.3 percent
United States	**16.3 percent**

up too many uncomfortable body image issues. But just because she hasn't worn lingerie before doesn't mean she'll never wear it, especially if you show a little patience. She might not be ready for a red Merry Widow-and-stocking set just yet—but perhaps she might be convinced to swap her flannel granny nightie for a pretty cotton tank-top and boxer set. When she wears it, go heavy on the compliments. Start slowly, and build from there.

Have fun shopping! Lingerie boutiques today cater as much to men as to women, and if you can relax and enjoy it, the experience itself can be a form of foreplay. It's a good idea to call ahead; some stores will actually allow you to make an appointment.

Give the salesperson as much information as you can about the woman you're buying for—what type of perfume she favors, her hair color and skin tone, the type of lingerie she's bought for herself in the past. Check her underwear drawer for her sizes, and if you can get away with it, sneak a bra and panty set out of her drawer and take it with you for comparison purposes. Sizes can vary pretty widely, and fit is important. In any case, save the receipt.

There are the obvious retailers, of course:

www.victoriassecret.com

www.fredericksofhollywood.com

www.agentprovocateur.com

WINE, CHEESE, AND ONE MORE REASON TO THANK THE FRENCH

High-heeled shoes didn't appear in the United States until the mid-1800s, says Don Voorhees, the author of *Quickies: Fascinating Facts about the Facts of Life.* They had been popular amongst the European aristocracy for a long time and were finally introduced to the States by a French prostitute who brought several pairs with her to a New Orleans brothel.

The French also invented the negligee. In fact, the word comes from the French word for negligent—as in, she was so busy lying around the house in her sexy underthings that she neglected to empty the dishwasher. Which is totally okay, by the way. Carry on.

For something a little more special, you might try one of the following:

■ **37=1 Atelier:** This New York store has reduced lingerie to the simplest geometry; they will make it to order. http://jeanyu.com/

■ **Eres Paris:** The legendary French line of lingerie from the country that invented it. www.eresparis.com

■ **La Perla:** Founded in 1954. Italian tailoring meets the sexiest underwear out there. www.laperla.com

■ **Myla:** This British company's unofficial motto is "Great sex is a private indulgence and the ultimate luxury." While you're there, check out their line of ultra-luxe sex toys, so beautiful you could display them on your coffee table, never mind the nightstand. www.myla.com/us/

Prepare yourself for sticker shock. You may be surprised to discover how much a few handkerchief-size pieces of silk can run you. Real lingerie—the good stuff—can be expensive, but beautiful pieces last for a long time, and the quality and workmanship are part of what make it such a good present. Don't get us wrong: There's definitely a place in her life for the cheap slutty stuff, and the rug burn you'll get from rubbing up against all that cheap lace can be titillating in its own right. But unless you've talked about it before, a polyester French maid's outfit with matching pasties isn't a great gift.

Presentation is everything. You're not going to get the reception you're looking for if you shove the box at her while she's unloading the dishwasher. Instead, tease her by dropping hints about a mystery present, and then wait until she gets into the shower to light some candles in the bedroom; leave the present on the bed.

Alternately, give it to her where she least expects it. Pass a silk thong under the table at a restaurant and ask her to go to the ladies' room and change into it.

Have Her Strip for You

Striptease and lap dance are the third most common fantasy worldwide, as well as third among American men.

Let her know how much it appeals to you, and maybe she'll give you a show, like Ati from Indonesia: "I don't know what got into me—okay, the better part of a bottle of champagne got into me—but I did this striptease for him on the way out of the bathroom."

Try a stripper/customer role-play. Put together a men's club–worthy playlist, request a lap dance, and keep your hands to yourself, just as you would in a real club. After you've bought a bottle in the Champagne Lounge, see if a little extra green won't get you some hands-on attention.

Props: ridiculously high stiletto heels, trashy lingerie, lots and lots and lots of dollar bills.

Hit the clubs. If your girl is game, take her to a peep-show and make out as the shutters go up and down. Another option is a straight-up strip club; many welcome couples. Do tip well; it's the cost of the fantasy, and it's only polite.

Turn the tables. Mary Taylor, a former exotic dancer in Toronto and the author of *Bedroom Games,* runs a company called Peel and Play that teaches women to strip. "Whenever I ask the women in my workshops how they'd feel if their partners took it all off, I get a terrific response." Her advice? You're both going to feel silly if you take this too seriously, so have fun with it—and definitely don't worry about a less-than-Chippendales body. Take it off slowly and throw clothes into the "audience" with attitude, until there's nothing left but a smile.

Edmond from Montreal took Taylor's advice: "My girlfriend gave me a pack of tiny briefs in my stocking at Christmas; I'm ordinarily a boxer man, and these were a size smaller than I usually wear! I gave her a good show, and left that banana hammock on for as long as I could. . . ."

QUICKIE STATS

Percentage of men who fantasize about watching their partner strip and then do a lap dance:

1.	Indonesia	34.3 percent
2.	Poland	31.0 percent
3.	South Africa	29.7 percent
4.	Philippines	28.2 percent
5.	United Kingdom	26.8 percent
	Least (Russia)	3.7 percent
	United States	**26.6 percent**

AN AEROBIC WORKOUT WE CAN GET BEHIND

Crunch gyms in Los Angeles and New York City offer a Cardio Striptease class that incorporates strippers' moves into a workout.

Dirty Talk

"Is there anything quite so sexy as the sound of your lover's voice, husky with desire, in your ear?" asks Anna from Ukraine. Words are one of the most powerful aphrodisiacs you have in your arsenal, and women are especially vulnerable to their power. While women can be visually stimulated as readily as men are, they can be even more powerfully aroused by fantasizing—and their preferred method is the spoken word.

"A woman has a more erotic mind than a man," says Robert Birch, PhD, of the American College of Sexologists. "Women are more into the theater, the romance, and the drama surrounding sex, rather than just the act." With that in mind . . .

Ask her to go first. The best way to know what your partner likes is to turn the tables and ask her to talk dirty to you. Pick up clues from what she does: Is there a fantasy she returns to over and over again? Certain words? A tone?

Wait 'til she's hot. It goes without saying, but extreme sexual arousal is an inhibition-buster. Wait to talk dirty—or to ask her to talk dirty—until you know she's completely in the throes of passion. Or if you want to torture her, do as Andreas, an artist from Bern, Germany, does: "I like to tease my girlfriend by stopping what I am doing when she is very excited and talking dirty to her instead. I tell her what I would be doing to her if I was touching her, and I don't resume until she is begging! This is very fun when she is tied up."

Use someone else's words. Start by reading erotica or porn out loud to one another. It can prime the pump, so to speak, for later action. This is a great go-to move, even later, when you're more comfortable. You don't have to breathe heavily or sound like you're doing phone sex—desire will naturally change your voice, and that's sexy enough. But do read slowly; even a normal pace can make the raunchiest book sound clinical.

Midori recommends that you try anthologies of erotic short stories—and there are many of them, available both from mainstream bookstores and sex stores. "That way, if one of you isn't into the story, you can just skip ahead to the next one."

Go back to school. As you're reading, mentally bookmark the phrases that you can imagine saying yourself in the heat of the moment. Rent porn and—maybe for the first time in your life—listen to what the actors are saying (ignore the music, if at all possible).

Bit by bit. Another good way to start is simply by listing body parts. Touch her somewhere, and ask what she likes to call it/them. Slowly, you'll build a collection that you can incorporate when the mood strikes.

Leave a message. Sometimes it's easier to talk dirty if you don't have to look at her. Leave her an XXX-rated voicemail, or call her some night you're apart and talk dirty into her ear over the phone.

Whisper. You're not on stage at the Royal Globe; they don't have to hear you in the cheap seats. Whispering is (a) sexy and (b) less embarrassing, for some reason. Let your lips brush her ear and neck while you're doing it, and she won't even notice when you lose your train of thought.

Leave something to the imagination. It's not an auction, either—you don't have to talk nonstop and include every detail. A pregnant pause, in fact, is sometimes just the space she needs to let her imagination run wild. Does she have to know it's because you lost your nerve?

Be comfortable. As with everything in the bedroom, it helps to feel

THE LITERATURE OF LOVE, INTERNATIONAL STYLE

Some international favorites:

Austria: Leopold von Sacher-Masoch's *Venus in Furs*

France: Anaïs Nin's *The Delta of Venus*, Colette's *Cheri*, Marguerite Duras' *The Lover*; Pauline Réage's *The Story of O*, Catherine Millet's *The Sexual Life of Catherine M.*

Greece: poems by Sappho

Italy: Ovid's *The Art of Love*

Japan: Junichiro Tanizaki's *The Key*

comfortable in your own skin. Just talk about what really turns *you* on. You may not have the gift of gab, but if you did think about grabbing her around the waist and taking her while she was getting the cauliflower out of the crisper, tell her. And be specific. Tell her how good her ass looked, and what you thought about doing to her. Or talk about what you're doing, seeing, or feeling—at that very moment.

"You're beautiful in this light."

"You're so wet."

"It feels so good inside you."

"I'm not going to last if you keep moving like that."

Flattery works. Pretty much any sentence that starts: "I love it when . . ." as in, "I love it when I can see myself pushing into you," or "I love it when you bend over and I can grab you" is going to work for her.

Give her a history lesson. Enumerate everything you liked about a five-alarm sexual experience in your recent past. This is also a good way to remind her of something she used to do that's fallen out of regular rotation—where is that hot pink garter belt, anyway?

Keep it simple, stupid. If you're nervous about how you'll sound (or how your partner will take it), try these tried and trues, courtesy of Lynne Stanton, the author of *Dirty Talk*:

"Do you like that?"

"I want you."

"Touch me here."

"I'm so horny."

"You turn me on."

"I love it when you do _____."

Give her orders. This may come as some surprise, but a lot of women like to be told what to do—in bed, anyway. Something as simple as using a commanding voice to tell her to open her legs has been known to get a very big response. And no matter how shy you are, you can tell her to open her legs.

Pretend to be someone else. One of our favorite someone elses, of course, is a lover from an exotic clime. Master a few key phrases, and you won't even have to know what you're saying. If it sounds exotic and erotic, and you say it in a sexy whisper right in the middle of very hot foreplay, who cares if the actual translation of your "dirty talk" is "May I use the payphone?"

Forget about being politically correct. The dirtier the better—this is

VOULEZ-VOUS COUCHEZ AVEC MOI, CE SOIR?

You might pretend to be a lover from an exotic clime—but how do lovers from exotic climes spice up their pillow talk?

Phone play is a big one—maybe not surprising, given how much the Euros love their phones. "I imagine that she's a lonely, horny housewife who has called a gigolo phone sex service, and I have to keep her on the line for as long as possible to run up the charges on her phone bill," says Liam, an Irish lawyer. "It really forces me to go into lots of detail, and for things to unfold very slowly—which she loves!"

"We both travel for work a lot. She likes to tell me about all the men who looked at her in the hotel bar," says Bram, a Dutch businessman.

"We use dirty talk to talk about crazy stuff we'd never do—we're very faithful to one another. But when I talk dirty to her, it's all about orgies, swingers clubs, sex parties, hardcore domination—stuff we'd never in a million years try," says Paolo from Verona, Italy.

"My wife and I pass different versions of a fantasy back and forth. She's a prostitute, I'm her pimp. She has to do what I tell her to do, go with whoever I tell her to go with. Please, you must understand—I am not this kind of person! This was her fantasy from the beginning," says an embarrassed Fernando from Tulum, Mexico.

---

the time to dust off words you never thought you'd say out loud. "My husband calls me names I would slap him silly for using outside the bedroom," says Charlene from Sydney.

One word of warning: Some words are really too loaded to use. It should go without saying, but it's sometimes hard to draw the line when you're in the swing of things, so here are some guidelines. Racial epithets and anything you know has been used against her in violence or hurt should be considered off-limits unless specifically discussed beforehand. Comments about her body, ditto. And, of course, it's probably best to be a little conservative with a new partner—while some women are very comfortable using words like "bitch" themselves, others have a visceral reaction to them that does not, uh, enhance the sexual experience.

Describe roleplay. Did she drag you to another costume drama movie where everyone is talking in accents? Fine—then use it as the backdrop for a lurid sexual fantasy, and on the way home, tell her exactly what you were thinking about during the movie.

Make your own movie for her by describing an erotic scene as slowly and in as much detail as you can. Lynne Stanton recommends that you set the stage for your partner as completely as you can, and get her in on it. Describe where you are, what you're wearing, who might see you, what you are dying to do.

Don't be surprised if you turn your partner on so much that she takes it to the next level, by adding details and perhaps even other people into the scene. Soon, through your words, you'll be far from your everyday bedroom and imagining yourselves in an airplane cockpit, a Paris bor-

---

NAUGHTY BERLITZ

It can be very effective to pepper garden-variety English dirty talk with sexy foreign words and phrases. "Learn a few key phrases in another language, particularly a romantic one like French, Spanish, or Italian," says Lynne Stanton, author of *Dirty Talk*. "Your words will sound terribly exotic, the foreign tongue will take you out of yourself, and everything will likely be less embarrassing for you to say, particularly if you're new to talking dirty. After all, many people find a whispered '*baisez-moi*' both sexier to hear, and sexier to say, than 'Do me,' *oui?*"

Sexier to say, sexier to hear—that's pretty much our mission. So here's our guide to the nastiest words in a variety of languages.

Tu es si caliente: "You're so hot." (Spanish)

Hagalo a mi: "Do it to me." (Spanish)

Dieu, je suis si exite: "God, I am so horny." (French)

Je veux te baiser: "I want to have sex with you." (French)

Suce-le: "Suck it." (French)

duro come una roccia: "hard as a rock" (Italian)

fighetta: a hot woman—literally, "adorable little vagina" (Italian)

una cosine veloce, una sveltina: a quickie (Italian)

Dreh' dich um: "Turn around." (German)

Issho-ni neyou?: "Shall we sleep together?" (Japanese)

Semai: "You are tight." (Japanese)

Kuchi no naka itte ii?: "Can I come in your mouth?" (Japanese)

Have the Wildest Sex in the World

dello, a '60s swingers party, or a covered wagon—whatever it is that gets you hot. Describe it, and come back to it. It'll be your little secret!

Tell her what you want. If you want to hear her beg, tell her you want her to beg you for it. If you want her to tell you how incredibly enormous you are, tell her to tell you.

Don't keep it in the bedroom. Dirty talk is a great way to take sex out of the bedroom, so that you're constantly communicating in an erotic way, ensuring that you're both on slow simmer all the time. Public is good: Whisper something filthy to her just as the lights go down at the Philharmonic, at your kid's school pageant, at the condo board meeting. But private is good too: over the phone when you're in a hotel room across the world, as you kiss her good-bye when you're leaving early and she's still in bed.

Having Sex Underwater

There's a natural association between water and sex—something about the weightlessness, the sensuality of being surrounded, not to mention all the obvious fluids.

Read all about it. Printed on waterproof paper, *Aquaerotica* (www.babeland.com) is a collection of literary erotica with a water theme.

Take it to the tub. Bath gel, 5 inches of hot water, silicone lube, and a candle. What more do you need? (Please note, the shower head is not designed to support the weight of an adult human. And remember, lube is slippery—in a good way and also in a "I've fallen and I can't get up" way.)

Rubber ducky, you're the one. Whatever will they think of next? Get your very own rubber ducky vibrating toy at www.babeland.com. Give this classic yellow duck a squeeze, and he'll make bathtime *lots* of fun indeed.

Naked scuba. This is the final frontier—complete immersion. Joining the "Mile-Below" club requires careful planning, given the equipment you'll need and the

QUICKIE STATS

Percentage of men who fantasize about having sex underwater:

1. Serbia		21.9 percent
2. Romania		16.3 percent
3. Germany		15.1 percent
4. Spain		14.8 percent
5. Mexico		14.3 percent
Least (Ukraine)		2.7 percent
United States		**3.1 percent**

What you're looking for in a lube—and trust us, you're looking for a lube, because water is a terrible lubricant—is 100 percent silicone. It won't wash away.

whole lack-of-air situation. You'll probably want something to hold on to so you can actually do it and not just float around. Most important, make sure to follow all safety procedures, just as you would for a regular dive. (You're going to want some extra hand signals, so she can tell the difference between the throes of passion and the throes of drowning.)

Sex with a Forbidden Lover

"Forbidden fruit is the sweetest, isn't it?" muses Teodora from Russia. Even if that succulent morsel is the nanny. Or your wife's sister. Or her best friend. Or your best friend's wife. Or your boss. Or your boss's daughter. Or maybe especially your boss's daughter.

If you're tired of the same old, same old, go ahead and cheat—just do it with your wife. Roleplay! (See Chapter 6 for some saucy ideas, and everything you need to implement them.) "Sexual play allows us to act out some of our most secret sexual fantasies without having to be too committed or serious about them," says British expert Graham Masterson, former editor of *Penthouse* and *Penthouse Forum* and author of the *Secrets of Sexual Play*.

QUICKIE STATS

Percentage of men who fantasize about a forbidden lover:

1. Russia — 25.45 percent
2. Italy — 25.05 percent
3. Singapore — 25.00 percent
4. A tie between Portugal and South Africa — 23.57 percent

Least (Indonesia) — 7.09 percent

United States — **19.37 percent**

Lots of couples turn to roleplaying in order to spice up a relationship. It can be a way to explore—or reverse—power dynamics without anyone feeling overly vulnerable and upset. It can be a way to get what you never had: You never got off the junior varsity bench, and she was president of the chess club—but who's to say that you're not the captain of the football team trying to get up underneath that hot cheerleader's letter sweater? It's a way to taste some of those forbidden delights—macking a stranger at a bar, or hitting on your hot dental hygienist—that you've promised to forgo.

A Threesome

This was the top sexual fantasy for nearly half of *Men's Health* readers.

"Two women together is my ultimate fantasy."—Eric, a librarian in Indonesia

"I've always loved watching two girls together. I know that my wife messed around with girls at uni; this would give me a chance to get in on some of that action."—William, a journalist in London

"It's like I'm a sheik in my harem—all those hands and breasts and tongues—and all for me!"—Ian in Bali

"You know you're good in bed when you can wear out two women!"—Carlos in Venezuela

As should be clear from these quotes, the thought of a threesome does a lot of different things for a lot of different guys. Some men are attracted to the idea of so much stimulation—there's more stuff to watch, more stuff to touch and to do than in sex with just a single partner.

Some love the idea of watching two women together, or the idea of being the center of all that female attention. "If you're a slight voyeur, this is an opportunity to watch your partner having sex. If you're an exhibitionist, it's an opportunity to show off," says Dee McDonald of the Centre for Sexual Wellbeing.

For many people, the frisson lies simply in the knowledge that

QUICKIE STATS

Percentage of men who were most likely to fantasize about having a threesome:

1. Portugal		59.7 percent
2. Netherlands		53.3 percent
3. Australia		52.3 percent
4. Spain		47.9 percent
5. Germany		45.4 percent
Least (Ukraine)		1.9 percent
United States		**49.1 percent**

they've broken one of the big taboos: sex outside of a pair. "We grow up thinking two is normal, and anything that isn't two isn't normal," says McDonald.

"Men like to be 'sexually incorrect' in bed! This is part of their masculinity," says Mariagrazia Marini, PhD, a clinical psychologist in Lisbon.

Note: We're assuming, as most men will, that the threesome configuration is two girls and a guy. And a study in *Psychological Science* confirms that women are more game for a same-sex experience than most men are: Straight women with high sex drives are 27 times more likely to be attracted to both sexes than are straight men with high sex drives, according to a survey of more than 3,500 people.

"A lot of women have had sexual fantasies about other women, or have experimented," says Ascha Vissel, a Dutch psychologist and sex therapist. "But you have to be patient, helping them feel comfortable with the idea."

"Women tend to come in more shades of gray, while men are more polarized—more either/or—in their sexual orientation," says Richard Lippa, PhD, a psychologist at California State University at Fullerton. But, he warns, just because she finds women attractive doesn't mean she wants a threesome. In fact, some women fantasize about having sex with a woman because they imagine it will be slow, tender, touching, teasing, instead of oil-drilling guy-style.

That's not to say that the other configuration doesn't have much to recommend it. It can be great for a guy who likes the idea of seeing his partner with another man, or for a guy who's bi-curious. It's also a very nice, open-minded present for the woman who has everything but has always wondered if she's up for two guys at once. . . .

Of course, just because this is something you really—really, really—like to think about doesn't necessarily mean you actually want

QUICKIE STATS

Percentage of men who have had a threesome:

1. Brazil	19.00 percent
2. United Kingdom	17.55 percent
3. Australia	17.52 percent
4. United States	**17.00 percent**
5. Russia	14.89 percent
World average	**14.23 percent**

"Women in Brazil are open-minded and feel that a threesome is just another item on the list of sexual fantasies and experiences that they want to try," says Laura Muller, a sex advisor in Brazil. "A man in Brazil will ask for a threesome as a 'present' from his partner, either for his birthday or for an anniversary." And our statistics suggest that he gets it!

that dream to come true. Let's face it: You may not want to watch your partner have sex with someone else. You yourself may not want to have sex with someone else. But there are lots of ways to incorporate this fantasy into sex à deux without putting yourself—and others—into a situation that makes you uncomfortable.

Pretend. Heat things up by pretending someone else is in the room and asking what she'd like that person to do to her, says Ava Cadell, PhD, a Hungarian-born, British-raised expert who has traveled and taught widely throughout the world.

"We talk dirty a lot, and it's often about someone else—a woman or a man—watching us and masturbating while we put on a show for them," says Adam from Poland.

Watch it. Mainstream movies featuring threesomes aren't all that hard to come by, and they're a good place to start. *Wild Things*, for instance, portrays a hot threesome with Denise Richards and Neve Campbell. *Henry and June* has that period-piece flavor she likes. And once you move to the XXX aisle, your options are virtually limitless.

Outsource it. "I loved the idea of my wife being dominated by another woman, but we agreed that it would be too weird if I was actually there

> *"We talk dirty a lot, and it's often about someone else watching us put on a show for them."*

with another woman. So on our way home from a charity benefit, we answered an ad for a professional dominatrix," says Bram in Holland. "The woman was great—she really got into the roleplay. My wife told me about everything that happened in that dungeon—she even had a few light bruises to show me! And the sex between us was never better than afterward."

Invite some, uh, thing else. "Lifelike dolls like RealDoll can be employed by couples to live out threesome fantasies without involving a third person and all the subsequent emotions that might involve," says British expert Sarah Hedley. As she points out, it's a crying shame the playthings cost so much.

What if you really do want to try a real-life ménage à trois? "A threesome can be a whole new sexual experience, but only if *all* participants really want to share this experience," says Dr. Marini. "If one party is doing it just to please their partner, they could damage the psychological harmony and intimacy in the relationship."

"Of course it's tricky," says British expert Phillip Hodson, author of *How Perfect Is Your Mate?* "There's really no avoiding the message it sends, which is: You are not the be-all and end-all for me."

First, Hodson says, it's essential to establish the likelihood of her having any interest in the subject at all. "You have to ask yourself: Is this a starter? Because if you know it isn't, and you introduce it, you're really just sabotaging the relationship." He advises you to rack your brain for clues as to her interest. Does she often comment on how attractive other women are? Has she mentioned having "crushes" on other women? Was there perhaps a dalliance with a friend when she was at college?

And then you have to pick a good time to ask it. Is the right time to ask while you're planning the family budget, or after a terrible time stuck in traffic in the tunnel? Or perhaps after the most exciting sexual experience of the month? "Check," says Hodson. He suggests language like, "That was just fantastic—can I have my brain back. Do you know what flashed into my head right after I'd come? This tall, dark woman who was kissing both of us." If she gets excited again, you know you're on the right track.

So that's really the first rule—everybody has to be enthusiastically on board. If not, abort mission. No ifs, ands, or buts.

Next, before a stitch of clothing is shed, take the following precautions:

Lay the ground rules. Negotiate exactly what behaviors you and your partner are comfortable with beforehand. "Soft swinging" means kissing and touching—and sometimes oral sex—with a third person (or multiple others). Is she okay if you kiss the other person? Give her oral sex? If the third gives you oral sex? Will there be penetration?

"I love watching the sex, but I do struggle with jealousy when there's too much of what I think of as intimacy: cuddling or kissing," says Antonia, a travel writer in Britain. "So when we get together with someone, he does that with me instead."

In addition, it helps to know exactly what she's fantasizing about. We talk about "a threesome" like it's a single, unilateral fantasy, but actually there's a practically infinite number of permutations and combinations. Does she want to watch you have sex with someone else—or does she want you to watch her? Is she looking forward to getting her hands on another woman, or is that part of it less important to her? "Talk, talk, talk," says Dee McDonald. "There must be absolute honesty around absolutely everything to do with this situation."

You may get into a situation where it's more difficult to communicate with each other verbally (if you're at a club or party with loud music, for instance). Come up with a "safe gesture"—as opposed to a "safe word"— just in case you or your partner wants to cut and run.

Assemble the ingredients. "Most threesomes in Brazil happen by chance at a party or club," says Laura Muller, a sex advisor in Brazil and author of *500 Questions on Sex.* "If a woman is having so much fun that she feels like she'd do anything, then she just might." Look for all-bets-are-off occasions: vacations, spring breaks, and wild parties. "The more a woman feels like she's stepped outside of her normal life, like she's having a once-in-a-lifetime experience, the easier it will be for her to leave behind her normal boundaries," says Muller.

Find someone you and your partner can trust, but not someone either of you knows *"Most threesomes in Brazil happen by chance at a party or club."* well or is likely to run into at church. Younger women are more likely to be up for it. Researchers at the Australian National University found that women ages 20 to 24 were 1.5 times more likely to be open to same-sex experiences than women ages 40 to 44.

Let her make the move. If you have a willing partner already, let her approach other women—she's less likely to come off as aggressive. Courting a pair of friends? Steer the conversation toward fantasies.

The Main Event

"When men actually live out this fantasy," says Lou Paget, a certified sex educator in Los Angeles and the author of *365 Days of Sensational Sex,* "it's often nothing like they expected." *Toronto Sun* columnist Gibson adds that in her experience, men often discover that "it's a rather demanding ménage and somewhat difficult for them to fulfill everyone's expectations. As some wise person once said wryly, if men were supposed to have group sex, they would have been created with extra personal equipment." Here are some things to watch out for.

Follow the rules of the house. Specific clubs and parties will have their own rules, which must be rigidly adhered to or you'll get kicked out and blackballed. There are a couple of general rules to keep in mind, however. The first is that no means no. That's absolute and final. If you're saying no to someone else's advances, try to do it courteously and with a smile. But feel free to say it—and know that you don't have to offer any justification or reason. The reverse, of course, is also true: If you approach someone who would prefer not to, accept their decision graciously.

Another basic rule is that you can't just jump into the action; there's generally no touching without permission. Know that alcohol is prohibited at most events, and people under the influence are not welcome. Safe sex is a given.

Preempt jealousy. If you've ever watched three children playing, you know that three is a tricky number: It pretty much guarantees that someone will feel left out. "Sometimes men think that two women will mean lots of attention for him, and then when they get into the room, the two women are paying lots of attention to one another and he finds that he's sitting by himself," says Dee McDonald.

Take your time—as with all sex, it will be better if the parties involved are relaxed and feel some kind of bond with one another. "I like the rhythm of a threesome. You can always take a break and watch the other two. Relax and don't worry when the spotlight of attention is off you; it'll swing back again!" says Ian in Bali.

"Make sure you indicate throughout the activity where your sexual and emotional loyalties lie: with the most important person in the group for you—namely your partner rather than the third participant," says Gibson. This is something Jörg, a Swiss financial analyst, has learned over time: "It's my general policy to pay the lion's share of attention to my wife. I like to have sex with her first, and make sure she has the first orgasm. I let her direct the action, like a conductor—sometimes she wants me to spend a lot of time with the other person; other times she feels happier if I'm more attentive to her."

Keep one foot on the brake. "You have to be prepared to stop—at any time," says McDonald. You've just hit the best part, and she blows the whistle? Find your pants, partner. It's game over when she pulls the plug. Or you do. And you can, for any reason. There's a material difference between fantasizing about seeing your wife with someone else and actually seeing someone else touch her. You may not be good with it. And that's okay.

It's not over yet. "Afterwards, keep the conversation about the event light and easy in case anyone's struggling with their feelings," advises

Gibson. Be prepared for your partner's reaction, which could range from sheer disgust to "girls rule." And indicate to her that you're willing to talk about whatever she wants to talk about.

"The day after we had our threesome, we spent the whole day together, just a sickeningly normal day. We had brunch at our favorite spot, went to a movie, and then home for dinner together. We didn't talk about it that much, but the fact that he really seemed to enjoy going back to our real life reassured me," says Marina, a Czech writer.

The biggest rule of all, according to Gibson? "Never, ever try to see the other woman on her own, outside of the threesome, if you're married or attached. Not only is it unpleasantly sneaky, but it will inevitably be destructive."

Have fun! The position where you're lying on your back, and one woman is sitting on your face while the other straddles you is called The Feast of Ponies. Enjoy!

Spanking

Don't call it pain. Sex educator Midori calls these "sensations that are more intense than what you might be used to. Pain is knee surgery. This isn't pain."

What's the attraction? Endorphins, the natural drugs produced by the body in response to these sensations. Endorphins are chemically similar to some other time-honored crowd-pleasers—like heroin, for instance.

Experienced sadists and masochists look to take someone to the very edge of their physical boundaries, a subject for another book—Midori's *Wild Side Sex*, for instance. But the endorphin rush you get from even just a quick slap on the bottom can be very invigorating, not to mention erotic.

Start with a tickle and a light tap. If she laughs, laugh along with her. Consider a moan permission to continue. "How hard one should spank depends on the person," says Emma Taylor, coauthor of *Nerve's Guide to Sex Etiquette* and one half of the *New York* magazine

QUICKIE STATS

Percentage of men who fantasize about spanking:

1. Indonesia		10.7 percent
2. Netherlands		10.3 percent
3. Greece		8.6 percent
4. Ukraine		7.4 percent
5. Serbia		5.4 percent
Least (Croatia)		Zero percent
United States		**2.4 percent**

sex-advice duo Em and Lo. "Always err on the side of reserve, and gradually build up to rudeness."

Use both hands. The hand that's tapping her shouldn't be the only physical contact you have with her. If she's bent over, sandwich one of her legs between yours so that she can feel how happy you are. And aim is important: You're not hitting the tops of her buttocks, but rather what's known as the sweet spot—the lowermost inside quadrant. Think of your target as the area that would be covered by a not-very-substantial bikini bottom—and don't go outside the lines.

Suffer the vibrations. "Men can feel the aftershock of the smack in their g-spot (prostate)," says British expert Sarah Hedley, "and women can feel it in the forked legs of the clitoris, which extend down around the walls of the vagina towards the bottom." Spanking brings the blood to the surface, making the skin more sensitive. Hedley suggests following firm spanking with light fingernail strokes, for a truly erotic finale.

Do as the doms do. We turned to an expert—Fetish Goddess Eva, a Greek dominatrix—for further thoughts on erotic spanking. Enjoy. Or not—she'd probably prefer it that way. Here's what she says:

> "Erotic spanking is a secret pleasure, easily played by people who don't have a deep understanding of the BDSM ways. It is also a very good introduction to this lifestyle.
>
> "A spanking should be done over the knee, or with a cushion or other support underneath. The feeling of 'surrender' or 'submission' is important; many people need to give up control to feel sexual. You must create a safe environment, and gain your sub's trust first. Don't hesitate to warn her in advance what is coming; the anticipation of this 'punishment' will add to the sexual excitement. Tell her that if she does not obey your wishes, her punishment will be even harsher.

WHAT ARE YOU WAITING FOR?

According to a *Men's Health* poll of 2,000 *Cosmopolitan* readers:

89 percent of women who have never had kinky sex think it could improve their sex lives.

93 percent of women who tried kinky sex say it did.

"The best way to spank is with your palm, slightly cupped, fingers held close together. It makes a good sound and makes the skin red without causing a lot of pain. Use a firm but sensual stroke to spread the heat over her bottom. Don't hit the same spot twice. Alternate between spanking and using your fingers to caress and explore her body; this will help her to associate the spanking with pleasure and arousal. Take your time.

"You can also employ spanking during intercourse. Light spanking during intercourse can establish tempo, just as a rider creates a tempo for his horse, and it will certainly increase everyone's arousal. During intercourse, have your lover on top; wrap both your arms around her as you spank. Increase both your tempo and force while she is climaxing."

So there you have it. Remember, Eva expects to be obeyed.

Sex with a Stranger

This was a pretty prevalent fantasy. It's also the one that's most likely to come true. When we asked who men cheated with, a stranger came first on the list (13.02 percent).

What is it about a mysterious stranger? "The lack of baggage," says Vanessa from Seoul. "And the fact that you can do anything, be anything, say anything, ask for anything you want."

There is certainly something compelling about a pull so strong it transcends social convention. So much for dinner and dancing and first date chit-chat. Sex with a stranger is raw, unvarnished sexual attraction, a chemistry that's bigger than both of you and crosses all barriers.

Whew!

What if you're married? Here's where roleplay comes in again. Pretend you've never seen her before. Now try to get her into bed.

It's true that if you're not really given to theatrics, this can be kind of embarrassing. "It's okay if you both fall on the floor laughing," says Sue Johanson, Canada's foremost sexual educator and counselor and the host of the TV show *Talk Sex with Sue Johanson*. "If you can't laugh about sex, you shouldn't be having it."

Even if you're only halfway on board, the results can be quite

(continued on page 342)

TIE HER UP, TIE HER DOWN

When *Men's Health* polled more than 2,000 *Cosmopolitan* readers, we learned that more than 90 percent of women are willing to deviate from the norm—they're either "game to try" something kinky (70 percent) or downright "excited" at the prospect (21.5 percent), if only we'd ask. What did they consider kink? The women in our poll rated bondage as the form of nontraditional sex that most excites them—two out of three were interested!

Amanda, a 27-year-old advertising saleswoman here in the United States, is typical: "I'm a pretty confident, successful career woman. The feeling of being helpless and dominated was really novel and a massive turn-on."

Because bondage takes all control away from the person who is tied up, it can exquisitely heighten the anticipation of pleasure. "There is a sense of being erotically overwhelmed that comes along with being restrained, and many women find it quite passionate," says San Francisco-based sexologist Carol Queen, PhD. "Women are encouraged to understand themselves as objects of desire, and through bondage and restraint, there's an acting out of that."

"My boyfriend has very cleverly figured out that when I'm tied up, I can be 'forced' to do things that I'm embarrassed to do—that I'd never do otherwise," says Tatiana, a 36-year-old professor from Rio.

The more she's immobilized, the more power you have, so use the force for good.

Exercise restraints. Pinning her arms above her head is time-honored and can be done with one hand, leaving the other free to remind her what's so good about staying put. Another softcore option is to wrap her up gently in the sheet so that she can't move her arms. Leave lots uncovered—her head, shoulders, lower legs, etc., and kiss every inch of available skin. Or head to the kitchen for a roll of plastic wrap. Or arrange her on the bed the way you want her, and "forbid" her to move unless she's told to—with threats that you won't finish what you've started if she breaks the rules.

The next step might be to tie her wrists so loosely with something soft—a silk tie, a cashmere scarf—that she could easily escape if she wanted to. You get all the visual stimuli of her in chains, while she knows that there's an escape route if she wants one. "Keep it comfortable," says Japanese-German sex educator Midori. "If it's too tight, loosen it; if it's too loose and you can't get in the mood, tighten it up a little."

Up the ante. To intensify her feeling of powerlessness, tie her feet as well—spread-eagled, if you want access. And for an added frisson, add a blindfold. Keep a hand on her at all times or speak softly so that she knows where you are in the room. When you're comfortable with playing like this, surprises can become a very pleasurable part of the game!

Keep her comfy. You should always be able to slip at least two fingers between the restraint and her skin; otherwise, you're cutting off her blood-flow. Midori warns against going all Boy Scout. "I can't tell you how many times I've heard a story about a guy trying to replicate something elabo-rate from a nautical knot book while his girlfriend sits bored on the bed." There should be no knots underneath her, or anywhere she's bearing a significant amount of weight.

Even if she's very loosely tied, the clock is ticking—it can be very uncomfortable to stay in one position for a long time. Changing it up doesn't mean the party has to stop; if her arms were tied above her head, put them behind her back, or in front of her.

If a part of her body swells or turns a different color, untie her immedi-ately (you may know that there's a problem before she does—numbness can set in). Never tie a knot that you can't get her out of in a hurry (most serious players use slip knots, particularly around really sensitive areas, and usually have a pair of scissors close at hand as well in case of an emergency).

Fill a toy box. Your best option is premade bondage equipment, which is available in a variety of materials (and price levels). Midori recommends wrist restraints (often called "cuffs") made of leather or nylon and lined with some kind of soft fabric. Metal handcuffs are no fun on delicate wrists. And no, that yellow nylon rope you use to tie things to the top of your car is no good. The bungee cords aren't bad, though. . . . One of the best online retailers for a wide variety of BDSM toys and supplies is JT's Stockroom Catalog: www.stockroom.com.

Just be warned: "This type of stuff should be recreational," says Mark Elliott, PhD, director of the Institute for Psychological and Sexual Health in Columbus, Ohio. "If it starts to get to the point where you can't have sex unless you break out the handcuffs, women can start to feel objectified."

Percentage of men who fantasize about sex with a stranger:

1.	Korea	16.16 percent
2.	Singapore	15.43 percent
3.	Poland	15.41 percent
4.	Czech Republic	15.21 percent
5.	Russia	14.75 percent
	Least (Mexico)	5.00 percent
	United States	**11.52 percent**

titillating: "My girlfriend and I had talked about pretending to pick one another up as strangers, but we never really got around to planning anything. Then, a little late to meet her at our pub one night, I took the seat next to her, asked her name, and offered to buy her a drink as if I was just trying to chat her up," says Will, a teacher in Bristol, England. "She couldn't stop laughing and taking the piss, but even with her making jokes, we had the best sex of our lives that night."

If you're single: People go home with strangers all the time—we have the stats to prove it. (Your best bets are Australians and Brazilians, in case you were wondering.) Flip back to Chapter 3 for tips on how to make it happen.

Sex with an Older Woman

It's no secret that men experience their sexual peak in their teens, while women come into their own much later. Graophilia is gaining in popularity—probably because plastic surgery and well, okay, more plastic surgery has enabled this generation of porn stars to stay in the game much longer than their predecessors. The wave of hot over-40 celebrities—Michelle, Julianne, Kim, and Demi, to name just a few—hasn't hurt either.

Many men's first crush—and sometimes first sexual experience—took place with a Mrs. Robinson type, so the association is strong. "My first was an older woman—she was my brother's teacher, actually," confesses Luis, an accountant in Mexico. "I can still smell her perfume if I try."

"The attractions of an older woman—a cougar—are very obvious," says *Toronto Sun* columnist Valerie Gibson, author of *Cougar: A Guide for Older Women Dating Younger Men*. "In many cases, she's already had marriage, children, a mortgage. She's looking now for a little fun. And she brings a tremendous amount of independence to the relationship—she owns her own home, her own car, her own business, she takes her own trips. So you're getting someone very vital, very alive, someone who's very interested in sex and very experienced sexually, without a lot of the 'relationship' requirements that you might have with someone younger."

Older women know what they like and will tell you. And at menopause, "levels of estrogen recede, unmasking the power of testosterone," says Helen Fisher, PhD, research professor in the anthropology department at Rutgers University in New Jersey and author of *Why We Love*. "This allows women to be more assertive and demanding, and many of them become more interested in sex."

Sure, Ms. Pfeiffer, we'd love to see your golden globes!

Polish your apple for the teacher. Watch *The Graduate*, then ask her if she'd be interested in roleplaying a scenario where she "spoils" a tender young thing like yourself. A study at the University of Michigan found that female rats receive a boost of dopamine (a euphoria-inducing neurotransmitter) only when they control sex.

Don't be surprised if this act is well received by your partner—lots of women have a fantasy about being the more experienced partner, the one who takes control. Turn yourself over—she knows what to do with you. Don't forget your Superman Underoos and a comic book; she'll pack you a snack for the ride home.

Go cougar hunting. There are lots of places to meet unattached older women—cultural events such as plays, the ballet, and the opera are some of them. You can also check out one of the many online dating sites devoted to hooking younger guys up with women of a certain age, like www.urbancougar.com.

Sex with a Younger Woman

Men, it turns out, are interested in younger women. What would you do without *Men's Health* bringing you the latest in health research?

Percentage of men who fantasize
about sex with a woman half their age:

1. Croatia	16.3 percent
2. Philippines	12.3 percent
3. Czech Republic	11.7 percent
4. Malaysia	11.6 percent
5. Italy	11.1 percent
Least (China)	3.4 percent
United States	**13.5 percent**

This is probably evolutionary at its heart: We're looking for the young and healthy partners who are most likely to bear the fruit of our loins. That's the excuse you can give yourself, anyway.

Get out the tweed jacket and spectacles. Your lady friend can play this one of two ways: the wise-beyond-her-years Lolita who's scheming to lead you into sin, or the innocent, trembling young thing that you can't wait to despoil. Either way, you'll both enjoy detention. Other suggested props: ruler, tiny plaid skirt. Don't stand so close to me, indeed.

As long as she's at least the age of consent: Don Steele, author of *How to Date Young Women for Men Over 35*, tells us there are three keys to keeping younger women interested in you:

1. Have a quick first date. Suggest having lunch sometime. Lunch implies you're busy, which makes you look more youthful and interesting.

2. Limit your conversations. Don't bring up topics that show your age: children, ex-wives, or the wars you've fought in.

3. Don't bring her to your home for the first five dates. You don't want her to see anything that reminds her of your age—like photos of your kids or your *Best of Bread* album.

MAYBE WE'RE ON TO SOMETHING AFTER ALL

A 1994 study of 134,000 couples found that the greater the age gap between older husbands and younger wives, the lower the chance they'd split up.

Sex and Videotape (Lies Optional)

"She's so beautiful and sexy—I love to watch them over and over!" says Angelo, an Italian restaurant supplier, of the sex tapes he made with his wife.

"To see what we look like in the heat of passion fulfills our deepest curiosity about something primal in our lives," says veteran adult-film star Candida Royalle. You can try her line. No guarantee it'll work. Here's what will.

Start with some cheesecake poses, featuring her goofing around. Let her wear some clothes, or use a sheet to cover herself. In other words, let her decide when to show a little more.

"I can't handle real pictures, but we compromise," says Maria in Italy. "He has an old single-lens-reflex camera, and we play 'photo shoot' but with no film. I'm a lingerie model, he's the lecherous photographer." Polaroids are another low-tech way to scratch your itch without freaking her out.

Let her go shopping first. One guy told us the key to convincing his girlfriend to make a sex tape was "giving her control over the wardrobe. I handed her my AmEx card and told her to buy an outfit that made her feel sexy and comfortable, starting with the lingerie." That's an inspired move, and she gets to keep the clothes.

Offer to tape without hitting the "record" button. The camera's mere presence can be exciting. Flip the camera's LCD screen around for an occasional glimpse, or plug it into the TV so you're onscreen. That way you're on display but not being captured for posterity. The thrill of this audition could lead to recording later. "Once she sees herself onscreen, she might get over the fears," says Maggie Berman, cowriter of *How to Have a XXX Sex Life.*

Make a self-portrait. This could make a very sexy present for an open-minded partner. "My girlfriend didn't want us to tape ourselves. So I made a video on my cell phone of myself jerking off—something I know she really likes—and sent it to her when she was having drinks with friends," says Paolo from Italy. "She came home in a hurry."

Is this the Wiggles DVD? Whenever you commit something to tape, there's always the threat (some would say thrill) of exposure. And the recent rash of stolen celebrity sex tapes hasn't helped women's paranoia about "oops porn." (By the way, arguing that those were all publicity stunts—and that she's no Paris Hilton anyway—is unlikely to get you any closer to living out this fantasy.)

If you want to make this happen, you have to promise that whatever you produce will be a secret you'll carry to your grave, at which point your blind best friend will destroy it so that it is lost for all eternity. Or you can hand over the results to her as soon as you're done—or destroy it together.

Midori reminds you—unnecessarily, we hope—that photos taken in the bedroom should never, ever, ever, ever, EVER go on the Internet. You can't ever be sure that her boss or her father—or *your* father—doesn't frequent the same amateur porn site you're so fond of.

Work it. If you're a fan of amateur porn, you know that without benefit of great lighting and silicone, even a good-looking girl can look less-than-great onscreen. And women, as you've probably gathered by now, are often sensitive about things like that.

So turn down the dimmer, and put candles or a lamp on the floor to light your shoot—it's the most flattering. "Never use overhead lighting," says Candida Royalle. "It creates shadows, and besides, overhead lights are just plain ugly."

You'll be guaranteed a sequel if you take pictures she likes; if you know she's proud of her breasts and her smile, position the camera to show them in their best light.

Sex in Front of a Mirror

"Wall lights should gleam around the wall, reflected by a hundred mirrors, whilst both man and woman should contend against any reserve, or false shame, giving themselves up in complete nakedness to unrestrained voluptuousness," says the 1,000-year-old Ananga Ranga sex manual. Who are we to argue?

"Best birthday present ever: We've had a great dinner, we're having hot birthday sex, and when I'm about ready to come, my girlfriend rolls over and gets on top. I look up to see a mirror on her bedroom ceiling with 'Happy Birthday' written in lipstick. That was it!" says Ian, an Englishman living in Bali. Sex in a mirror is a very low-key, low-tech way to add a titillating dash of voyeurism and exhibitionism.

Start with a sneak peek. The next time you're near a mirror, pull her close and let her have the full view as you kiss her neck and caress her body, suggests Sonia Parreira Duque, a clinical psychologist in Lisbon, Portugal.

Be attracted to shiny objects. "I like to keep all the lights on and watch us in the big picture window going out to the field when it's pitch black outside," says Paolo in Italy. "There's nobody for miles, but I like to think that someone could be watching."

Move some furniture. There's probably a framed mirror somewhere in your house; surely it can migrate closer to the bed. "The first night we moved into our house, we leaned our full-length mirror on the dresser by the bed, and I noticed my husband checking it out when we were making love," says Katalin in Hungary. "I could tell it made him really hot, and—what do you know—even once the boxes got unpacked, that mirror never got hung on the back of the bedroom door. I eventually gave up and bought another one so I could finally see what I looked like before leaving the house."

Certainly, there are inexpensive mirrors designed to hang on the back of the door that can easily be propped up against the back wall of your closet when not "in use."

Sex in Public

"The weather's perfect for it," says Steve, an Australian money manager, about his countrymen's proclivity toward doing it outside.

But that doesn't explain why the oft-rained-out British have also raised exhibitionism to an art form. Crowds gather to watch couples (often hooked up through the Internet) having sex in cars. Famous athletes have confessed to doing it, songs have been written about it, and the government is taking the accompanying public health problem so seriously that many superstore parking lots and parks now sport safe-sex messages. Bring your brolly.

Dress for the occasion. Go commando when you leave the house, with her in a skirt or dress. Throughout the evening, give each other a few quick, private shows. Use any opportunity—helping her with a pool shot, pressing up against each other as a concert lets out—to get all up in her business for a moment.

Be covert. For a little bit more of a rush, try having sex somewhere you can see but not be seen—up against a window, for instance. Or, like Mary, an Australian nurse, somewhere so low-traffic that there's no chance you'll ever be discovered. "We have sex in the service stairwell of our building. It's never used—there's actually dust on the stairs—so there's no chance of discovery, but it still feels thrilling."

Turn back to Chapter 15 for much advice on sex with the potential for spectators.

Sex with a Starlet

"I don't so much have the hots for Angelina Jolie—okay, that's not true, I totally have the hots for Angelina Jolie. But I really want her as Lara Croft from that *Tomb Raider* movie," says Fernando from Tulum, Mexico. "And at the end of the day, my wife as Lara Croft isn't half bad."

"We have a joking list of people

we'd be allowed to have sex with if somehow, miraculously, they showed up offering it," says Agulto, a Filipino who lives in the UK. "I don't want to have sex with Becks [soccer star David Beckham], but I'm not 100 percent sure I'd mind watching him do my wife. . . ."

You don't need our help with this one: That's what *US Weekly* is for.

CONCLUSION

Have the Best Sex in the World

You might think it would be impossible to sum up the advice in this book in a single paragraph, but you should know by now that we don't back down from a challenge. It's true that in the preceding pages we've explored many sexual nuances and erotic subtleties—more, in fact, than you may even have suspected existed. But while it might be complicated in the execution, the guiding principle is simple: Your mission, should you choose to accept it, is to have a blast. Talk to the woman you're having sex with. Keep your eyes open. Get to know her and what she likes, and encourage her to do the same with you. Put your inhibitions in the bedside table and try some stuff you haven't tried before; if it works, you've got a new trick—if not, no harm, no foul. Most of all, enjoy yourself! Have fun with one another, both inside and outside the bedroom, wherever in the world you may be.

ACKNOWLEDGMENTS

This book was truly a collaboration. If people who study and write about sex have one thing in common, it would have to be their tremendous generosity. Without exception, our panel of international experts went above and beyond the call of duty to help. In particular, we'd like to thank: Daniel Amen, MD; Jina Bacarr; Juliette Balmain; Barnaby Barratt, PhD; Nicole Beland; Jennifer Berman, MD; Laura Berman, PhD; Steve Biddulph; Vanna Bonta; Gloria Brame, PhD; Marc Breedlove, PhD; Susie Bright; Patti Britton, PhD; Stuart Brody, PhD; Carolyn Bushong; Cherie Byrd; Ava Cadell, PhD; William Cane; Gilda Carle, PhD; Stephen and Lokita Carter; Stan Charnofsky, EdD; Lisa Clampitt; Al Cooper, PhD; Tracey Cox; Dr. Miguel Cuetos; Michael Cunningham, PhD; Lisa Daily; Yuri Datsyk; Joy Davidson; Andréa Demirjian; Dr. Daniel Denoel; Linda De Villers, PhD; Karen Donahey, PhD; Grace Dorey, PhD; Deborah Driggs; Emily Dubberley; Robin Dunbar; Birgit Ehrenberg; Allen Elkin; Mark Elliott; Enzo Emanuele, MD; Paul Engelhardt, MD; Dr. Ferenc Fekete; Helen Fisher, PhD; William Fitzgerald, PhD; David Fletcher, MD; Vicki Ford; Valerie Gibson; David Givens, PhD; William Glasser, MD; Irwin Goldstein, MD; Marc Goldstein, MD; Michelle Grahame; Andre Guay, MD; Jan Hall, PhD; Nikki Hayia; Sarah Hedley; Donald D. Hensrud, MD; Debby Herbenick, PhD; Charles Hill, PhD; Alan Hirsch, MD; Phillip Hodson; Martha Hopkins; Caroline Hurry; Mabel Iam; Ronald Iverson, MD; Judi James; Emmanuele A. Jannini, MD; Paul Joannides; Sue Johanson; Lisa Jones; John Kale; Barbara Keesling, PhD; Staci Keith; Ian Kerner, PhD; Ray Khandpur; Lorraine Landau; Richard La Ruina; Peter Lee; Thomas Lee, MD; Marianne Legato, MD; Amy Levine; Laurence Levine, MD; Logan Levkoff, PhD; Fedon Alexander Lindberg, MD; Larry Lipshultz, MD; Mansoor Madani, DMD; Mariagrazia Marini, PhD; Howard Markman, PhD; Graham Masterson;

Barry McCarthy; Dee McDonald; Ted McIlvenna, PhD; Midori; Robin Milhausen, PhD; Emily Nagoski, PhD; Steven L. Nock, PhD; Gina Ogden, PhD; Clint Paddison; Lou Paget; Patricia Pasick, PhD; Annie Payne; Julie Peasgood; Mike Perring, MD; Dennis Powers; Carol Queen, PhD; Heather T. Remoff, PhD, author of *Sexual Choice*; Barbara Kate Repa; Gary Rheinschild, MD; Kim Richter; Karen Risch; Laura Rivolta; Alex Caroline Robboy; Megan Roberts; Robert Santo-Paolo; Keith Schulner; R. Taylor Segraves, MD, PhD; Ann Semans; Lorelei Sharkey; Chiara Simonelli, PhD; Nancy Slotnick; Julian Slowinski, PsyD; Dr. Pam Spurr; Lynne Stanton; Christopher Steidle, MD; Daniel Stein, MD; Carla Tara; Emma Taylor; Mary Taylor; Patricia Taylor, PhD; Alex Todorov, PhD; Maria Urso; Don Voorhees; Stephanie Wadell; Mahinder Watsa, MD; Cynthia Mervis Watson, MD; Dr. Patricia Weerakoon; Michele Weiner-Davis; Phillip Westerbrook, MD; Christine Wheeler; Judith White; Diana Wiley, PhD; Jay Winner, MD; Megan Yost, PhD; Victoria Zdrok, PhD; and our favorite stewardesses, Liz and Julie.

Laura Tucker would like to thank her pit crew, Lily and Doug Crowell. Many thanks to Kathy LeSage for her calm stewardship and good humor along the way.

Most of all, we'd like to thank the men and women from around the world who shared their stories—the funny, the embarrassing, the heart-breaking, the inspirational, and the downright hot. They bared all so that you might benefit from their mistakes and successes, and this book would not have been possible without their candor.

Photography Credits

Singapore, Thailand: © Jake Versoza; Philippines, Mexico, Vietnam: © Adam Watson; Indonesia: © Dennie Ramon; Belgium: © Jacques Weyers; Malaysia: © Joan Bitagcol; Romania, Slovenia, Ukraine, United Kingdom: © Aleksander Stokelj; Monaco: © Darek Majewski/Forum; Portugal: © Jerson Bergamo; South Africa, Venezuela: © Mark Cameron; Bulgaria, Poland: © Tatiana Jachyra/Forum; Hungary: © Pete Leonard/Zefa/Corbis; Colombia: © Luiz Azevedo; Russia: © Mimmo Cattarinich/MC Photo International s.r.l; Brazil: © White Packert/Getty Images; China, Japan: © Guo Sansheng; Czech Republic: © Beauty Photo Studio/Age Fotostock; Spain, Turkey: © Mara Desipri/Effex; Germany: © Ondrea Barbe; Curaçao: © Don Simorangkir; Dominican Republic: © Mark Leibowitz; Netherlands: © Patricia Steur; Panama: © Superstock/Age Fotostock; Australia: © Gavin O'Neill; Argentina, France: © Jason Odell; Senegal: © Getty Images; Italy: © Traficstudio; Ecuador: © Franco Sorel/Folio ID; India: © Sheetal Menon, photographed by Atul Kasbeker. Courtesy of the United Breweries Group.

INDEX

Retroejaculation, <u>257</u>
Reverse Cowgirl sex position, 214
the Ring (birth control), <u>62–63</u>
Robin's Egg Wireless Vibrator, 301
Rock climbing with partner, <u>229</u>
Role-plays, sexual
  describing scenarios, 327–29
  Doctor/Nurse, <u>115</u>
  infidelity and, avoiding, <u>114–15</u>
  introducing to partner, 311
  Prison Guard/Inmate, <u>115</u>
  Prostitute/John, <u>114–15</u>
  stripper/customer, 323
  on telephone, <u>327</u>
Romance. *See also* Seduction
  aphrodisiacs, <u>78–81</u>
  dinner, 73–76, 107
  gifts
    to avoid, 83, <u>84</u>
    best, <u>82</u>, 85
    big, 84–85
    commitment signal and, <u>72</u>
    ideas, 77, 80–81
    for no reason, 81, 83
    saying "I love you," 85
    sexy, 83
    small, 72–73, 131
    of time, <u>72</u>
    tradition and, 77
  money spent on, 71–72, <u>71</u>, <u>72</u>
  serenading woman, 80
  star named after woman, 81
Roof of building, sex on, 297–98
Roommate, being best, 91–93, 96–97
Roses, 140
Rub-a-Dub Dice, <u>100</u>
Russia, seduction in, <u>27</u>

S

Sadomasochism, 316
Safe sex, 60–62. *See also*
  Contraception
Safe words for stopping sexual
  fantasy, 316–17
Sandalwood, 140
Sandwich Method, <u>317</u>
San Faustino celebration (Italy), <u>13</u>

Scallops
  Scallops Buenos Aires, 75
Scent
  aromatherapy, 137–40
  changing the way you smell, <u>111</u>
  essential oils, 138–39
  foreplay involving, 137–40
  pheromones and, 29
  of woman, 182
S-Check (special spray), <u>116</u>
Scheduled sex, <u>96–97</u>, 106
Schick Protector Safety Razor, <u>183</u>
School, meeting women at, 7
Screaming O Vibrating Ring, 199
Scuba diving naked, 329–30
Seduction. *See also* First encounter
    and impression; One-night
    stands; Romance
  in Australia, <u>24</u>
  in Brazil, <u>24</u>
  flirting, 51
  in France, <u>25–26</u>
  fun and, 23
  in Germany, <u>26</u>
  in India, <u>27</u>
  in Italy, <u>25</u>
  in Japan, <u>27</u>
  in Portugal, <u>24–25</u>
  in Russia, <u>27</u>
  sexual tension and, building,
    33–35
  in South Africa, <u>26–27</u>
  turn-offs, <u>32</u>
  in United Kingdom, <u>26</u>
Semans stop-start method of
    ejaculatory control, 247
Sensate focus, <u>109</u>
Serenading woman, 80
Sex. *See also* Locales for sex; Oral
    sex; Positions for sex
  age of men's first time having, <u>48</u>
  anal, <u>188–89</u>
  arguments and, effect on, 103
  atmosphere for, creating different,
    107
  banning, temporarily, <u>108</u>
  bathing before, <u>100</u>
  bondage, 316, <u>340–41</u>